Angel Sanctuary™

story and art by Kaori Yuki
vol.6

Angel Sanctuary

Vol. 6
Shōjo Edition

STORY AND ART BY KAORI YUKI

Translation/Alexis Kirsch
English Adaptation/Matt Segale
Touch-up & Lettering/James Hudnall
Cover, Graphics & Design/Izumi Evers
Editor/Pancha Diaz

Managing Editor/Annette Roman
Director of Production/Noboru Watanabe
Editorial Director/Alvin Lu
Sr. Director of Licensing & Acquisitions/Rika Inouye
Vice President of Sales & Marketing/Liza Coppola
Executive Vice President/Hyoe Narita
Publisher/Seiji Horibuchi

Printed in Canada.

Published by VIZ, LLC
P.O. Box 77010
San Francisco, CA 94107

10 9 8 7 6 5 4 3 2 1
First printing, January 2005

www.viz.com store.viz.com ANIMERICA
ANIME & MANGA MONTHLY

Angel Sanctuary

story and art by **Kaori Yuki**   vol.6

The Story Thus Far

High school boy Setsuna Mudo has gone to Hell. Literally. He's always been a troublemaker, but his worst sin was falling incestuously in love with his beautiful sister Sara. But it's not all his fault—his troubles are preordained because he is the reincarnation of the angel Lady Alexiel, who led the Evils of Hell in revolt against Heaven. Her punishment was to be reborn into tragic life after tragic life. This time, her life is as Setsuna.

Led through Hell by Kato, a drug dealer he killed back on Earth, Setsuna continues his hunt for Sara. When they become lost and separated in a thick fog, Setsuna stumbles on Yggdrasil, the World Tree. He's attacked by Kato, who has been possessed by a mask that is under the control of a girl who looks just like Sara. Setsuna helps Kato shatter the mask, but in the process Kato's spirit is also destroyed. Setsuna furiously unleashes Alexiel's power at the strange girl. The angel Uriel, who is also under the control of a mask, joins the fight, and Alexiel's power destroys his mask, releasing him.

Uriel invites Setsuna into Yggdrasil and tells him that Sara has gone on to Heaven. He also tells Setsuna that he can bring Kato's spirit back if he enters Kato's dark and troubled mind. Once there, Setsuna learns of Kato's tragic early life, but he gives his friend enough hope that they are both able to escape Kato's bleak world.

In Heaven, the angel Rosiel plots a dark and awful revenge on Dobiel for spying.

Contents

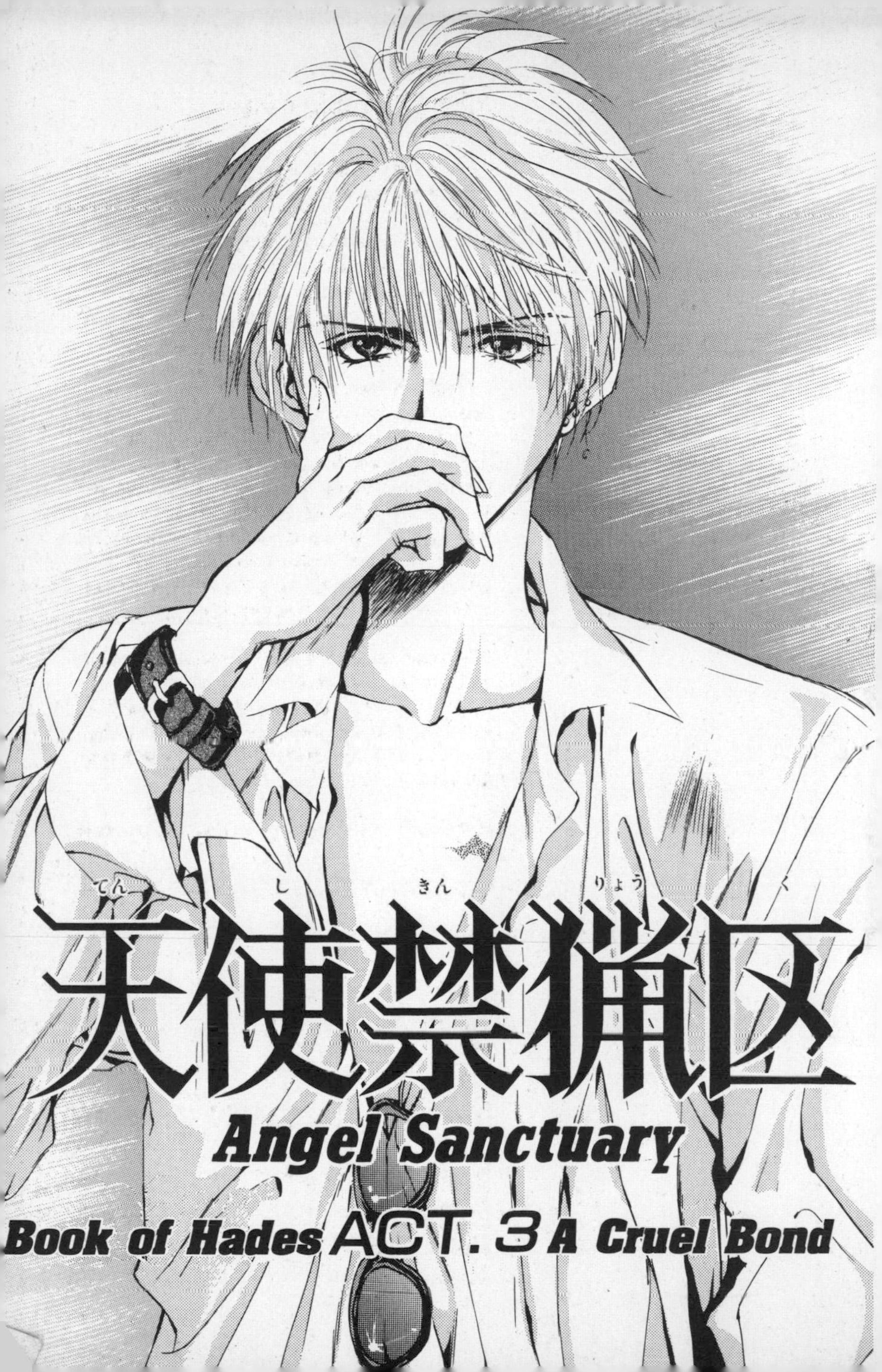
天使禁猟区
Angel Sanctuary
Book of Hades ACT. 3 A Cruel Bond

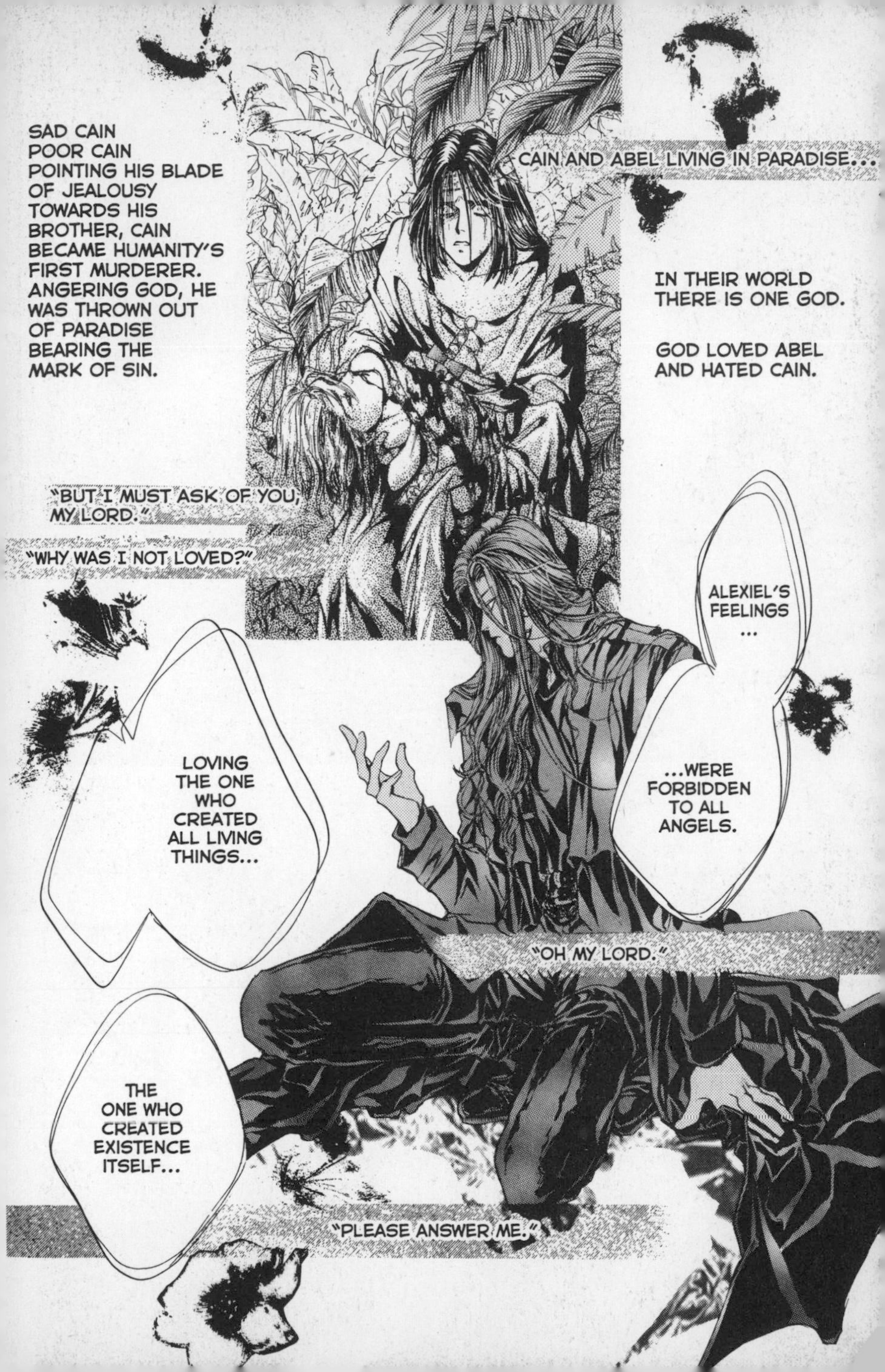
CAIN AND ABEL LIVING IN PARADISE...
IN THEIR WORLD THERE IS ONE GOD.
GOD LOVED ABEL AND HATED CAIN.
SAD CAIN POOR CAIN POINTING HIS BLADE OF JEALOUSY TOWARDS HIS BROTHER, CAIN BECAME HUMANITY'S FIRST MURDERER. ANGERING GOD, HE WAS THROWN OUT OF PARADISE BEARING THE MARK OF SIN.
"BUT I MUST ASK OF YOU, MY LORD."
"WHY WAS I NOT LOVED?"
ALEXIEL'S FEELINGS ...
...WERE FORBIDDEN TO ALL ANGELS.
LOVING THE ONE WHO CREATED ALL LIVING THINGS...
"OH MY LORD."
THE ONE WHO CREATED EXISTENCE ITSELF...
"PLEASE ANSWER ME."

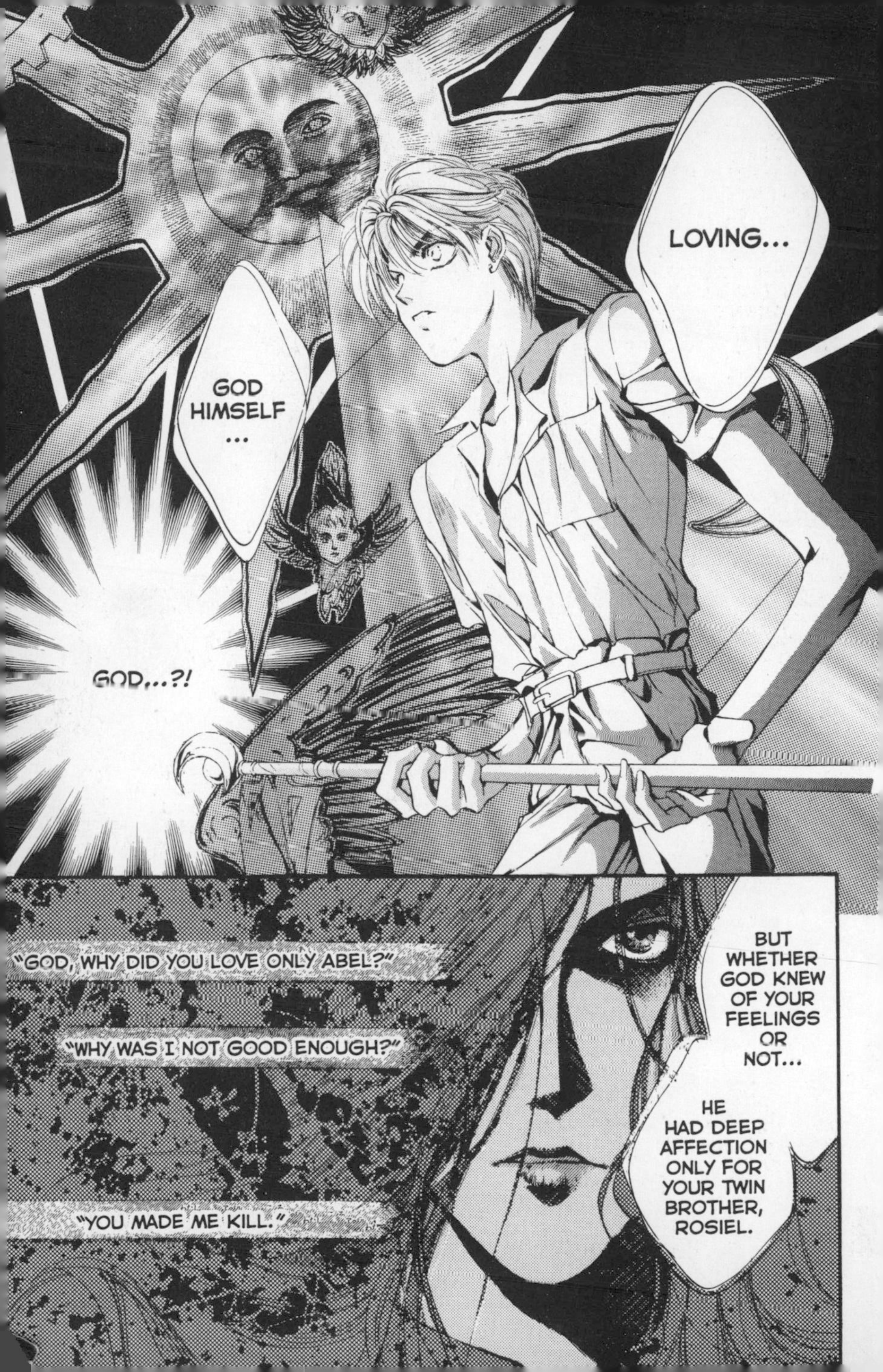
LOVING...
GOD HIMSELF ...
GOD...?!
BUT WHETHER GOD KNEW OF YOUR FEELINGS OR NOT...
HE HAD DEEP AFFECTION ONLY FOR YOUR TWIN BROTHER, ROSIEL.
"GOD, WHY DID YOU LOVE ONLY ABEL?"
"WHY WAS I NOT GOOD ENOUGH?"
"YOU MADE ME KILL."

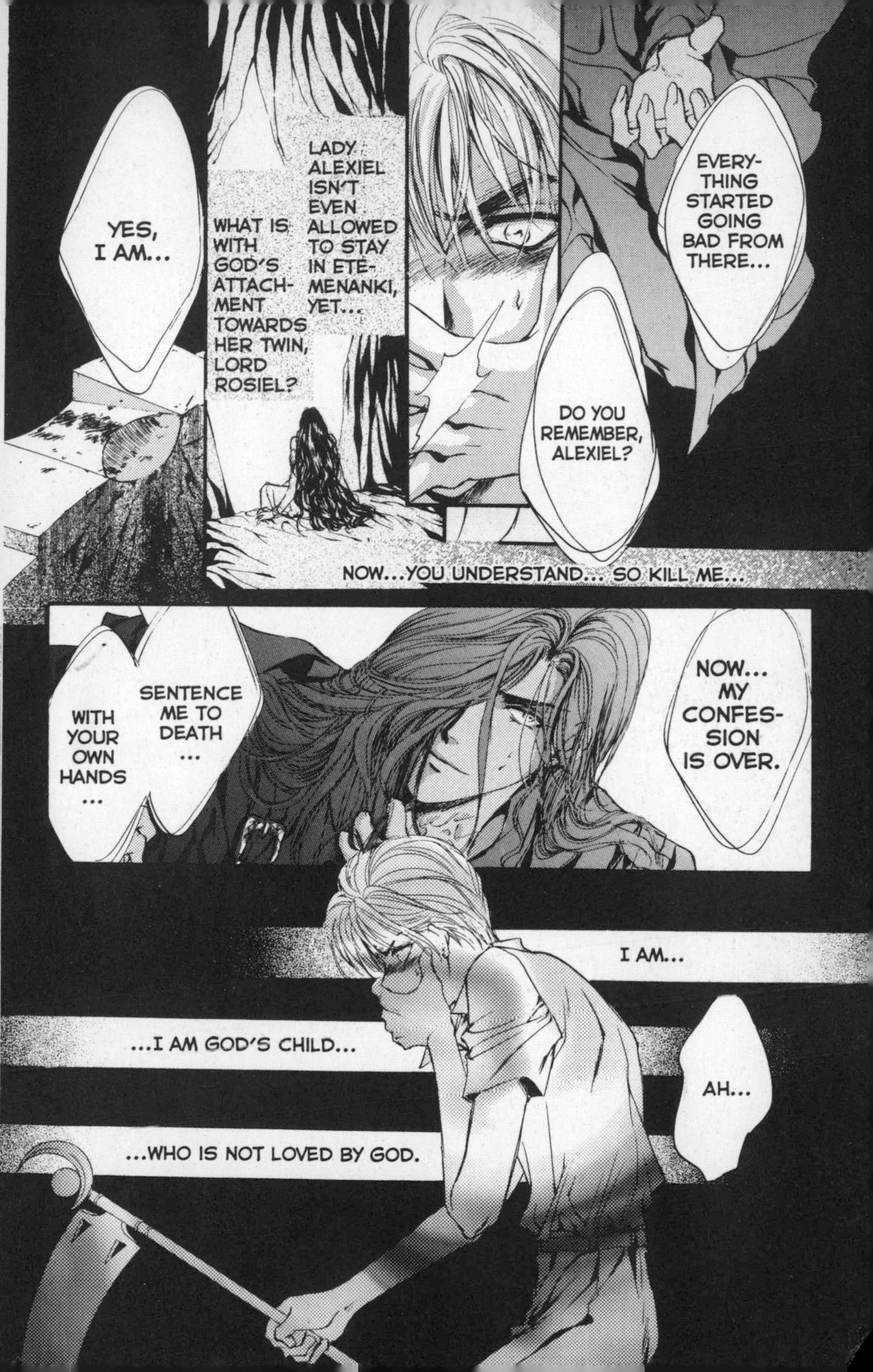
EVERY-THING STARTED GOING BAD FROM THERE...
DO YOU REMEMBER, ALEXIEL?
LADY ALEXIEL ISN'T EVEN ALLOWED TO STAY IN ETE-MENANKI, YET...
WHAT IS WITH GOD'S ATTACH-MENT TOWARDS HER TWIN, LORD ROSIEL?
YES, I AM...
NOW...YOU UNDERSTAND... SO KILL ME...
NOW... MY CONFES-SION IS OVER.
SENTENCE ME TO DEATH ...
WITH YOUR OWN HANDS ...
I AM...
AH...
...I AM GOD'S CHILD...
...WHO IS NOT LOVED BY GOD.

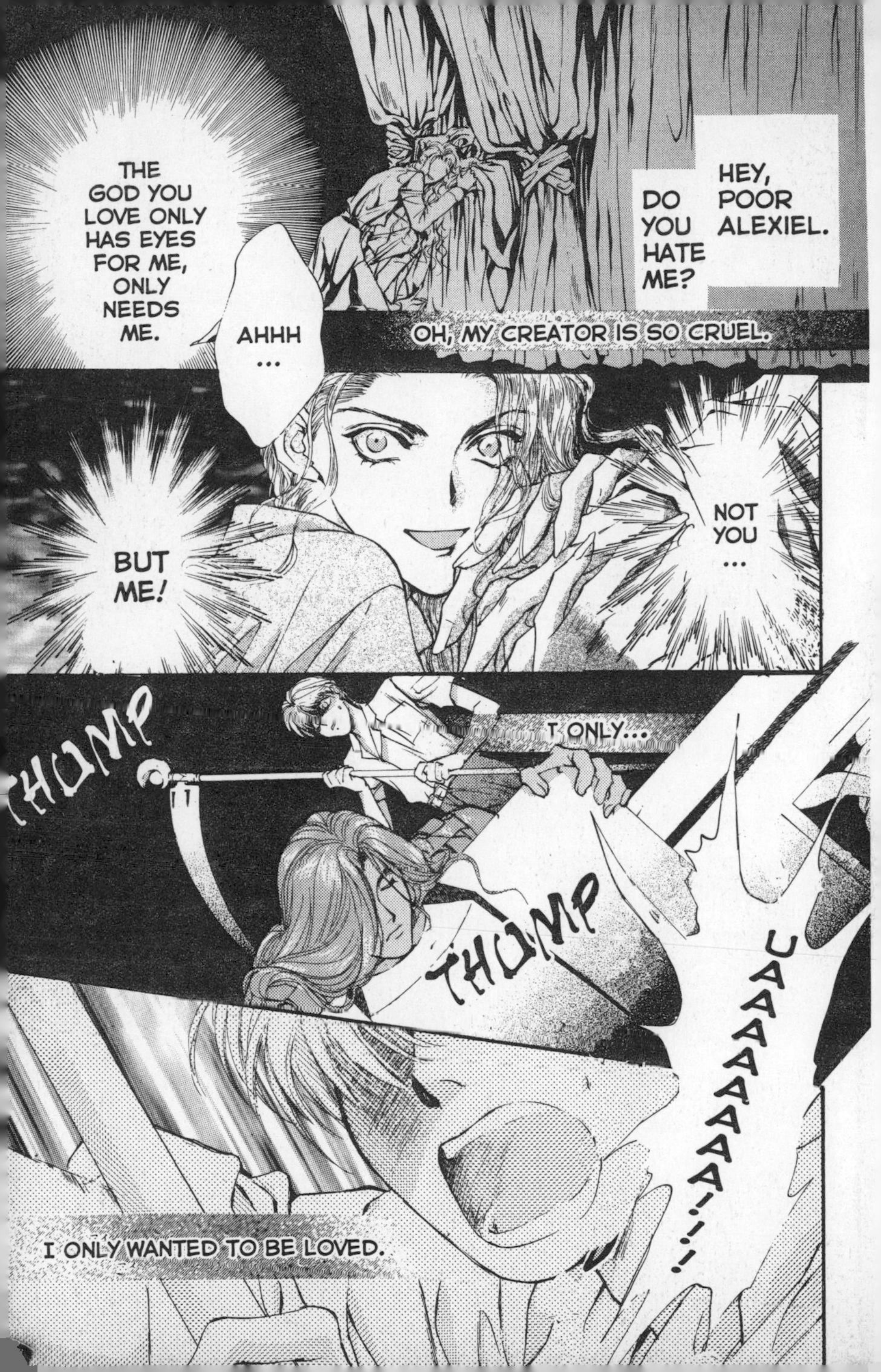
HEY, POOR ALEXIEL.
DO YOU HATE ME?
OH, MY CREATOR IS SO CRUEL.
THE GOD YOU LOVE ONLY HAS EYES FOR ME, ONLY NEEDS ME.
AHHH ...
NOT YOU ...
BUT ME!
I ONLY...
THUMP
THUMP
UAAAAAAAA!!!
I ONLY WANTED TO BE LOVED.

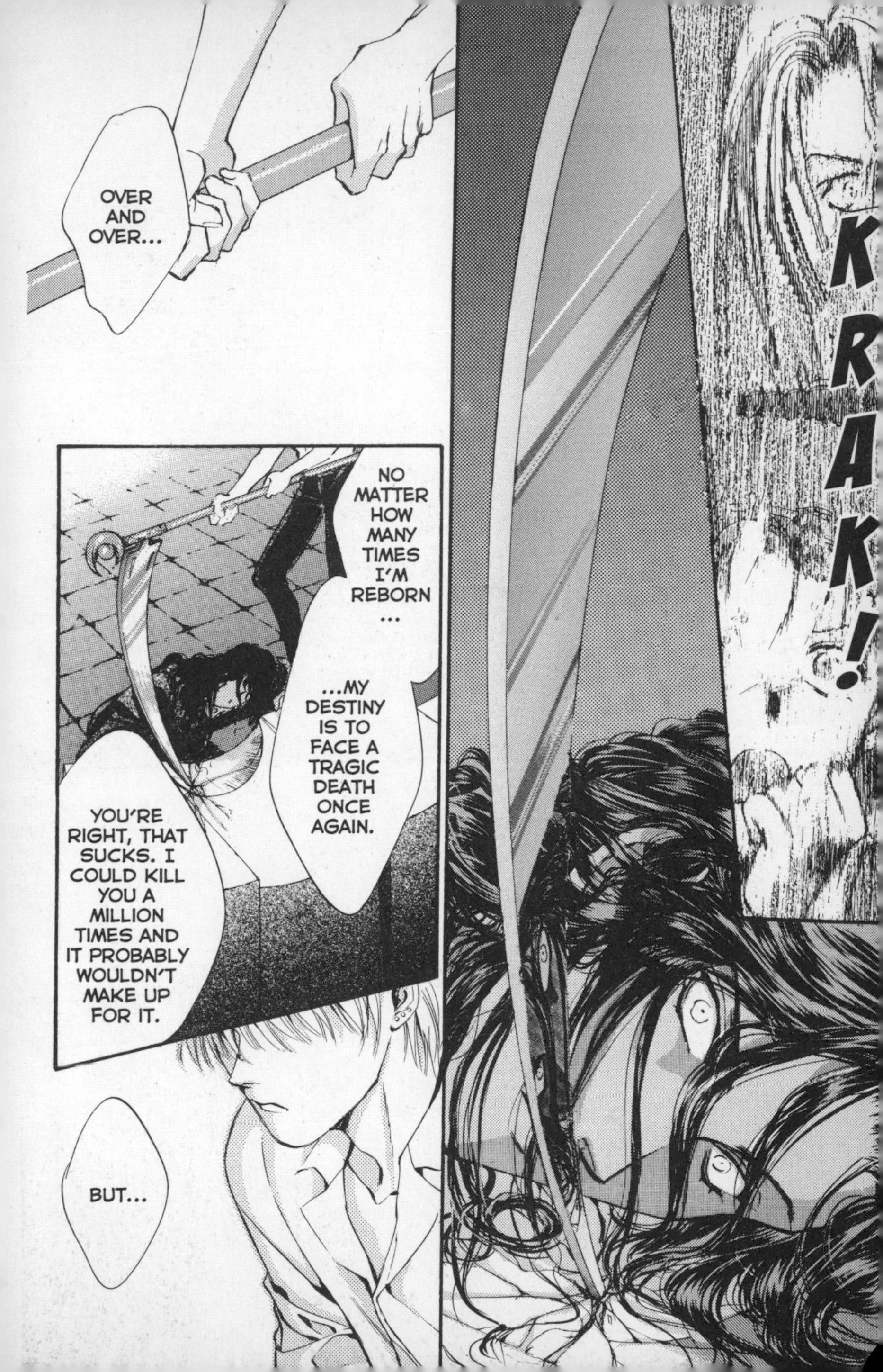
KRAK!
OVER AND OVER...
NO MATTER HOW MANY TIMES I'M REBORN...
...MY DESTINY IS TO FACE A TRAGIC DEATH ONCE AGAIN.
YOU'RE RIGHT, THAT SUCKS. I COULD KILL YOU A MILLION TIMES AND IT PROBABLY WOULDN'T MAKE UP FOR IT.
BUT...

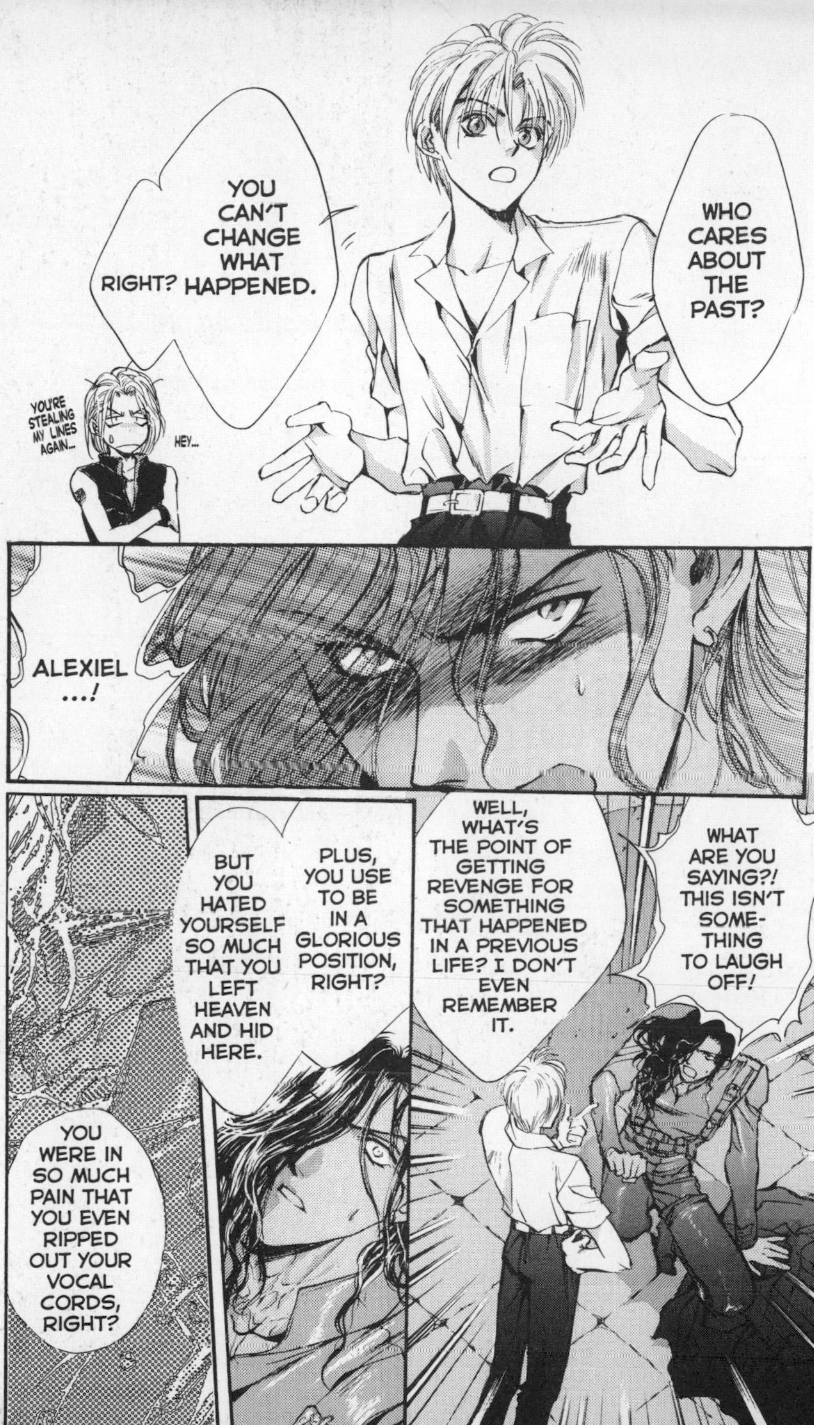
WHO CARES ABOUT THE PAST?
YOU CAN'T CHANGE WHAT HAPPENED.
RIGHT?
HEY...
YOU'RE STEALING MY LINES AGAIN...
ALEXIEL ...!
WHAT ARE YOU SAYING?! THIS ISN'T SOME-THING TO LAUGH OFF!
WELL, WHAT'S THE POINT OF GETTING REVENGE FOR SOMETHING THAT HAPPENED IN A PREVIOUS LIFE? I DON'T EVEN REMEMBER IT.
PLUS, YOU USE TO BE IN A GLORIOUS POSITION, RIGHT?
BUT YOU HATED YOURSELF SO MUCH THAT YOU LEFT HEAVEN AND HID HERE.
YOU WERE IN SO MUCH PAIN THAT YOU EVEN RIPPED OUT YOUR VOCAL CORDS, RIGHT?

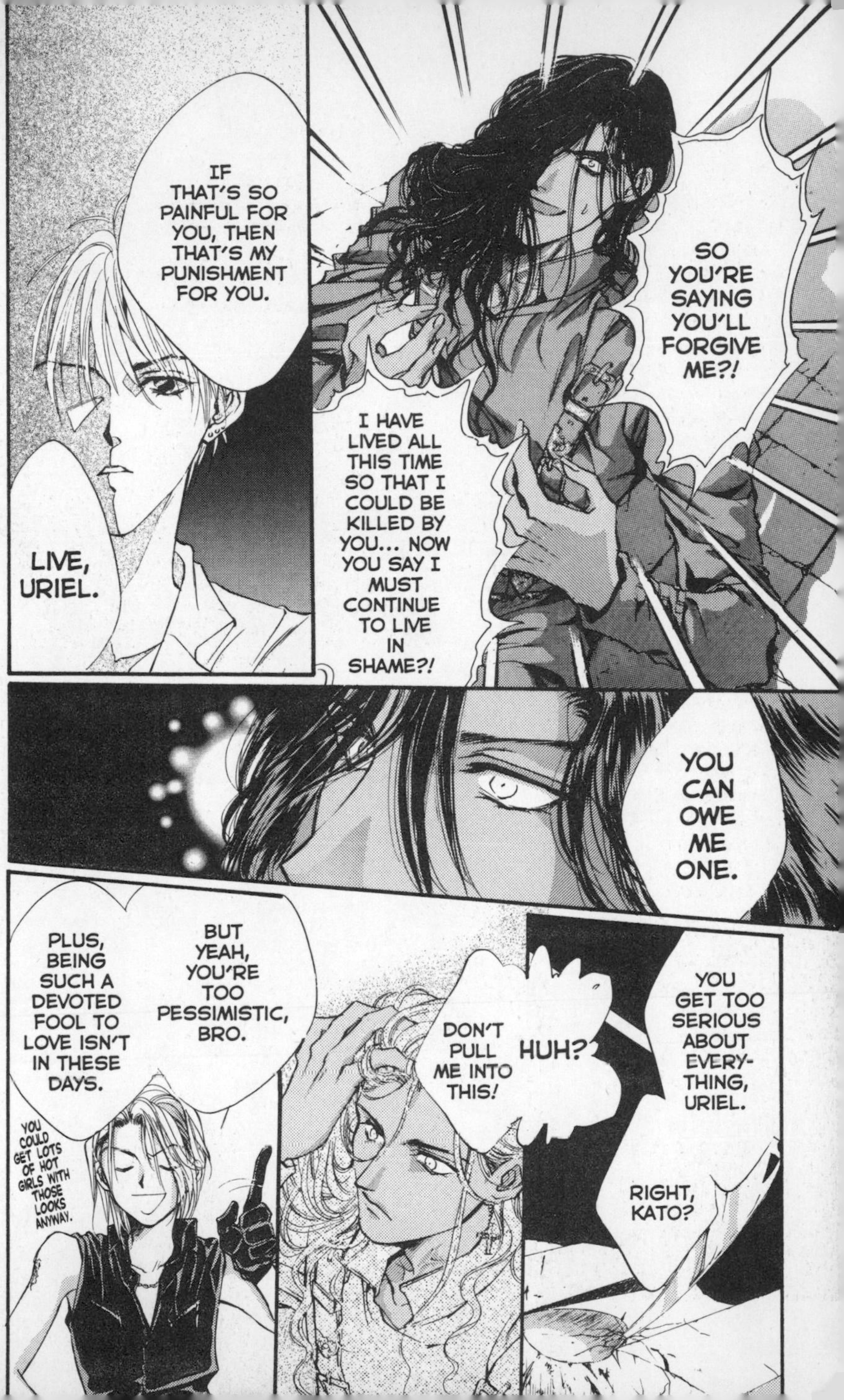
SO YOU'RE SAYING YOU'LL FORGIVE ME?!
I HAVE LIVED ALL THIS TIME SO THAT I COULD BE KILLED BY YOU... NOW YOU SAY I MUST CONTINUE TO LIVE IN SHAME?!
IF THAT'S SO PAINFUL FOR YOU, THEN THAT'S MY PUNISHMENT FOR YOU.
LIVE, URIEL.
YOU CAN OWE ME ONE.
YOU GET TOO SERIOUS ABOUT EVERY-THING, URIEL.
RIGHT, KATO?
HUH?
DON'T PULL ME INTO THIS!
BUT YEAH, YOU'RE TOO PESSIMISTIC, BRO.
PLUS, BEING SUCH A DEVOTED FOOL TO LOVE ISN'T IN THESE DAYS.
YOU COULD GET LOTS OF HOT GIRLS WITH THOSE LOOKS ANYWAY.

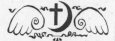

We meet again! This is Angel Sanctuary volume six. That's it...? Or, already?! I didn't think this Hades saga would take so many books. The characters just kind of started walking around on their own. Oh yeah, in the last book I asked "Are there any male readers?" and I received many letters saying "There are!" Thank you very much! I've always thought that my manga isn't so typically shōjo. Well sure, some characters have long eyelashes. I use to say that men wearing lipstick was horrible... Long hair too! Anyway, I like how Uriel is pathetic. And also how Kato is weak but acts strong. I really like pathetic men...

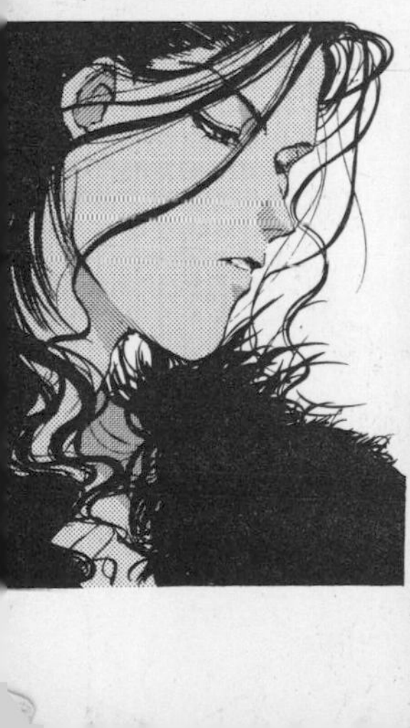

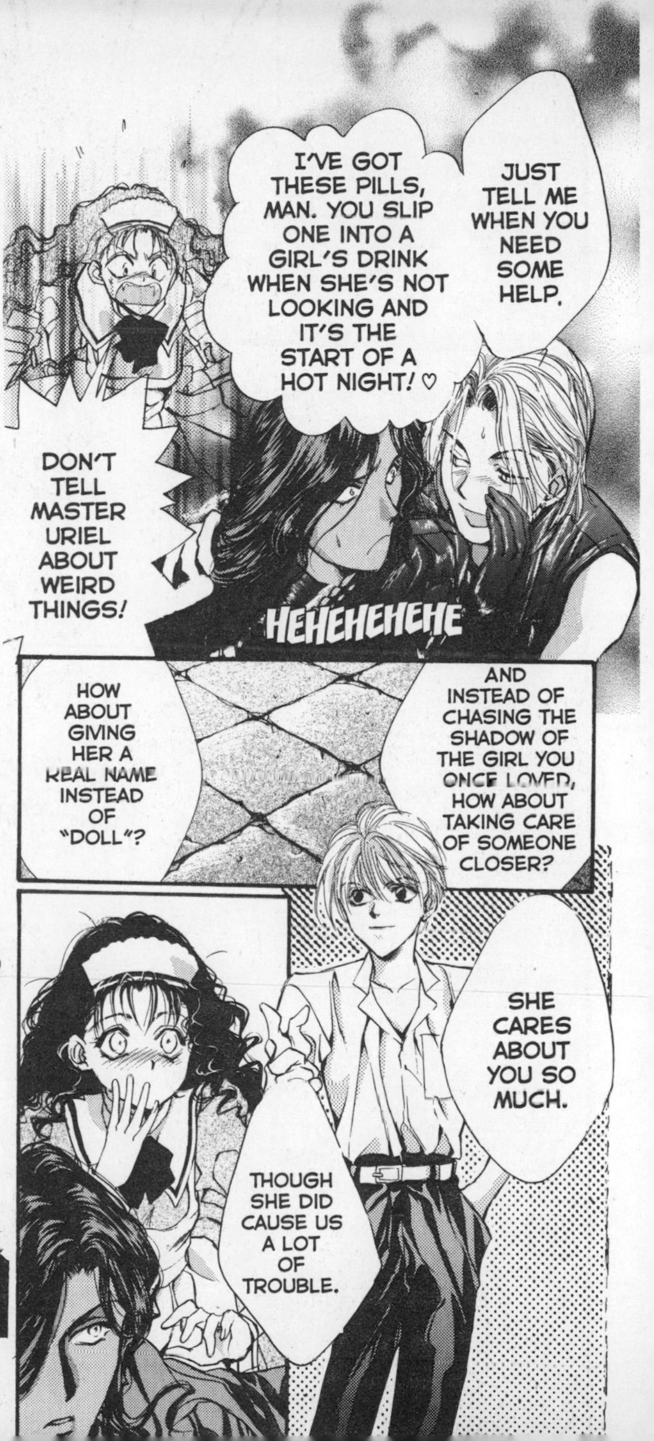
JUST TELL ME WHEN YOU NEED SOME HELP.
I'VE GOT THESE PILLS, MAN. YOU SLIP ONE INTO A GIRL'S DRINK WHEN SHE'S NOT LOOKING AND IT'S THE START OF A HOT NIGHT! ♡
HEHEHEHEHE
DON'T TELL MASTER URIEL ABOUT WEIRD THINGS!
AND INSTEAD OF CHASING THE SHADOW OF THE GIRL YOU ONCE LOVED, HOW ABOUT TAKING CARE OF SOMEONE CLOSER?
HOW ABOUT GIVING HER A REAL NAME INSTEAD OF "DOLL"?
SHE CARES ABOUT YOU SO MUCH.
THOUGH SHE DID CAUSE US A LOT OF TROUBLE.

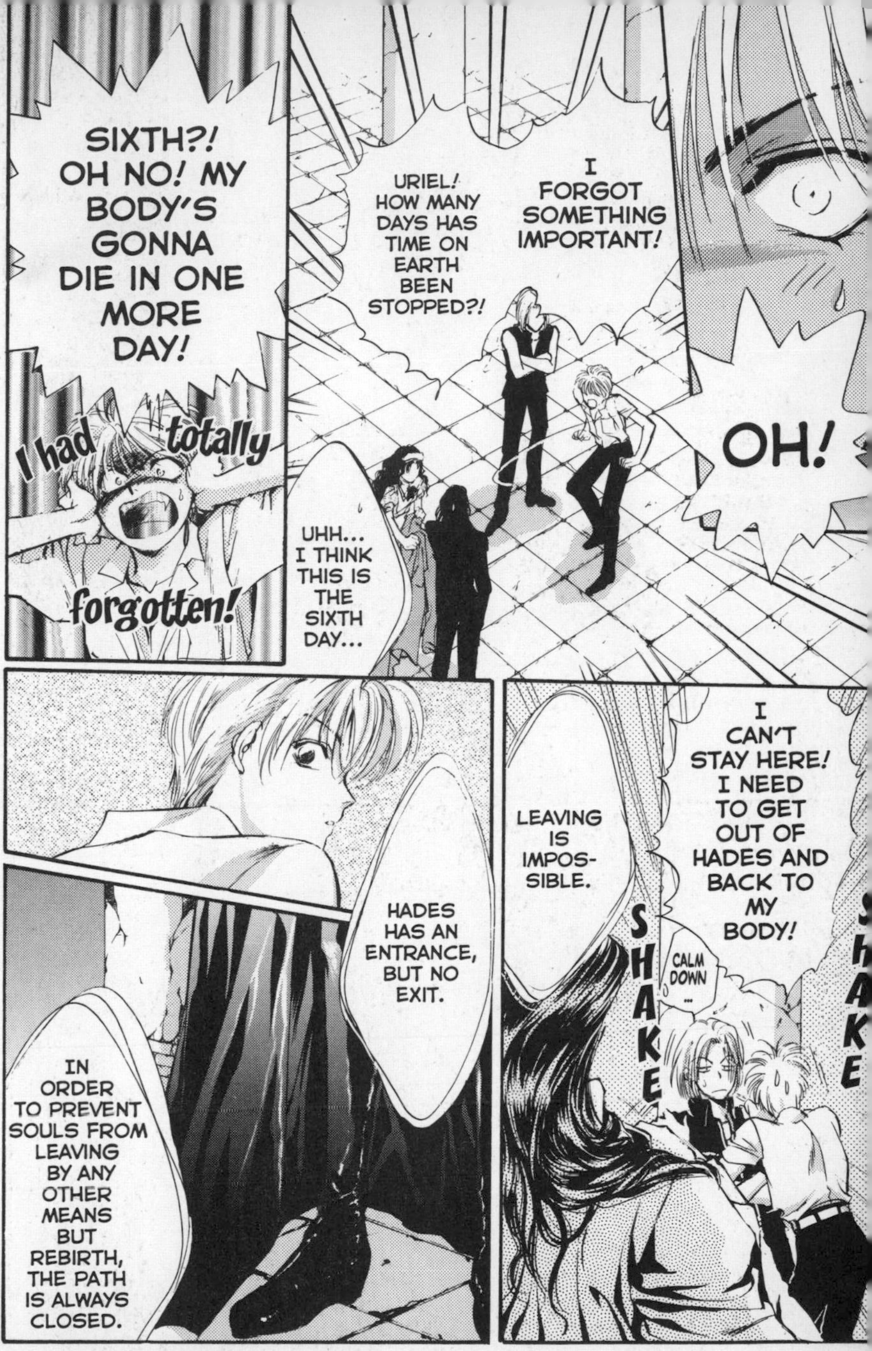
OH!
I FORGOT SOMETHING IMPORTANT!
URIEL! HOW MANY DAYS HAS TIME ON EARTH BEEN STOPPED?!
UHH... I THINK THIS IS THE SIXTH DAY...
SIXTH?! OH NO! MY BODY'S GONNA DIE IN ONE MORE DAY!
I had totally forgotten!
I CAN'T STAY HERE! I NEED TO GET OUT OF HADES AND BACK TO MY BODY!
SHAKE
SHAKE
CALM DOWN...
LEAVING IS IMPOSSIBLE.
HADES HAS AN ENTRANCE, BUT NO EXIT.
IN ORDER TO PREVENT SOULS FROM LEAVING BY ANY OTHER MEANS BUT REBIRTH, THE PATH IS ALWAYS CLOSED.

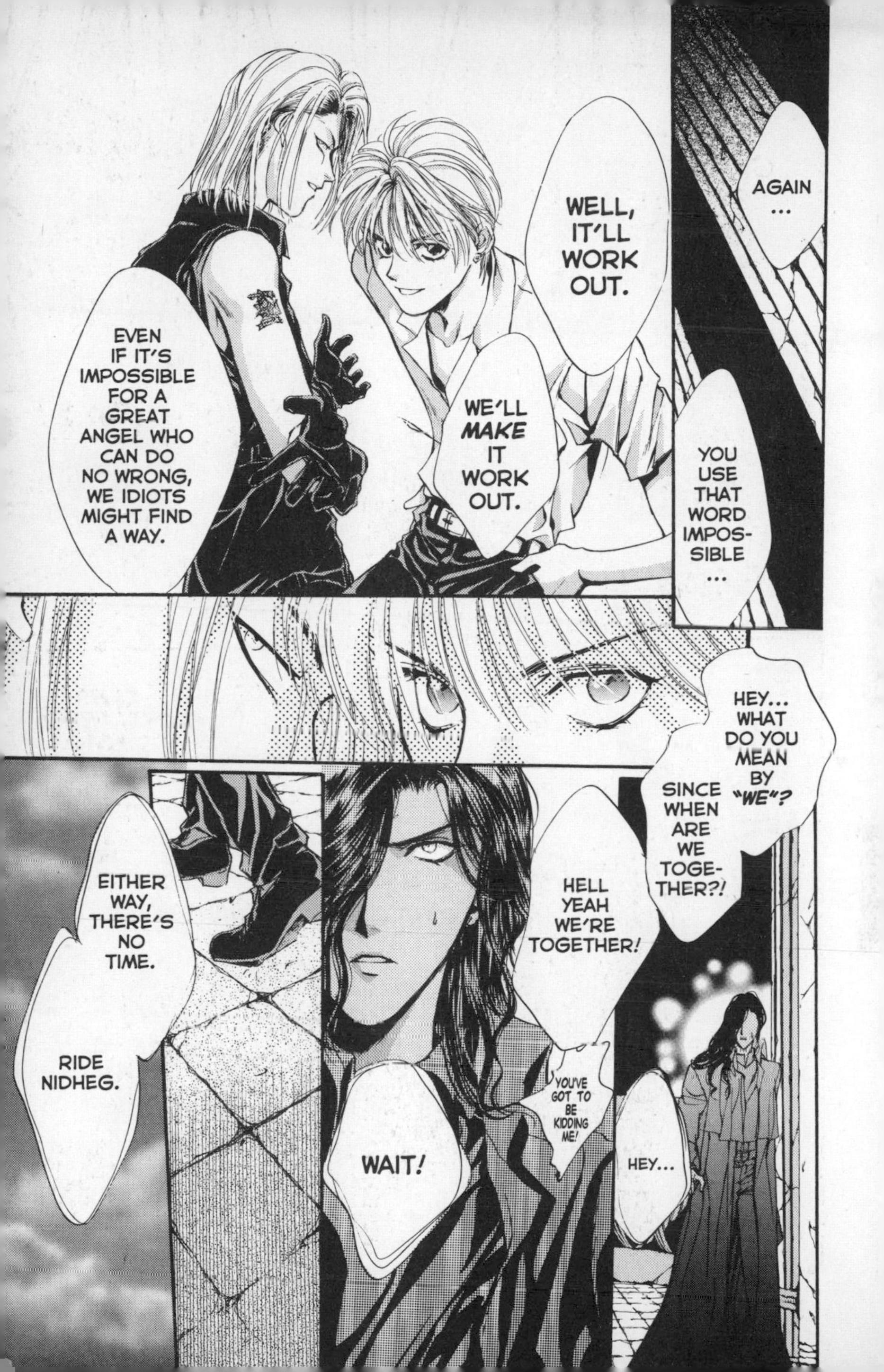
AGAIN...
YOU USE THAT WORD IMPOSSIBLE...
WELL, IT'LL WORK OUT.
WE'LL *MAKE* IT WORK OUT.
EVEN IF IT'S IMPOSSIBLE FOR A GREAT ANGEL WHO CAN DO NO WRONG, WE IDIOTS MIGHT FIND A WAY.
HEY... WHAT DO YOU MEAN BY *"WE"*?
HEY...
SINCE WHEN ARE WE TOGETHER?!
HELL YEAH WE'RE TOGETHER!
YOU'VE GOT TO BE KIDDING ME!
WAIT!
EITHER WAY, THERE'S NO TIME.
RIDE NIDHEG.

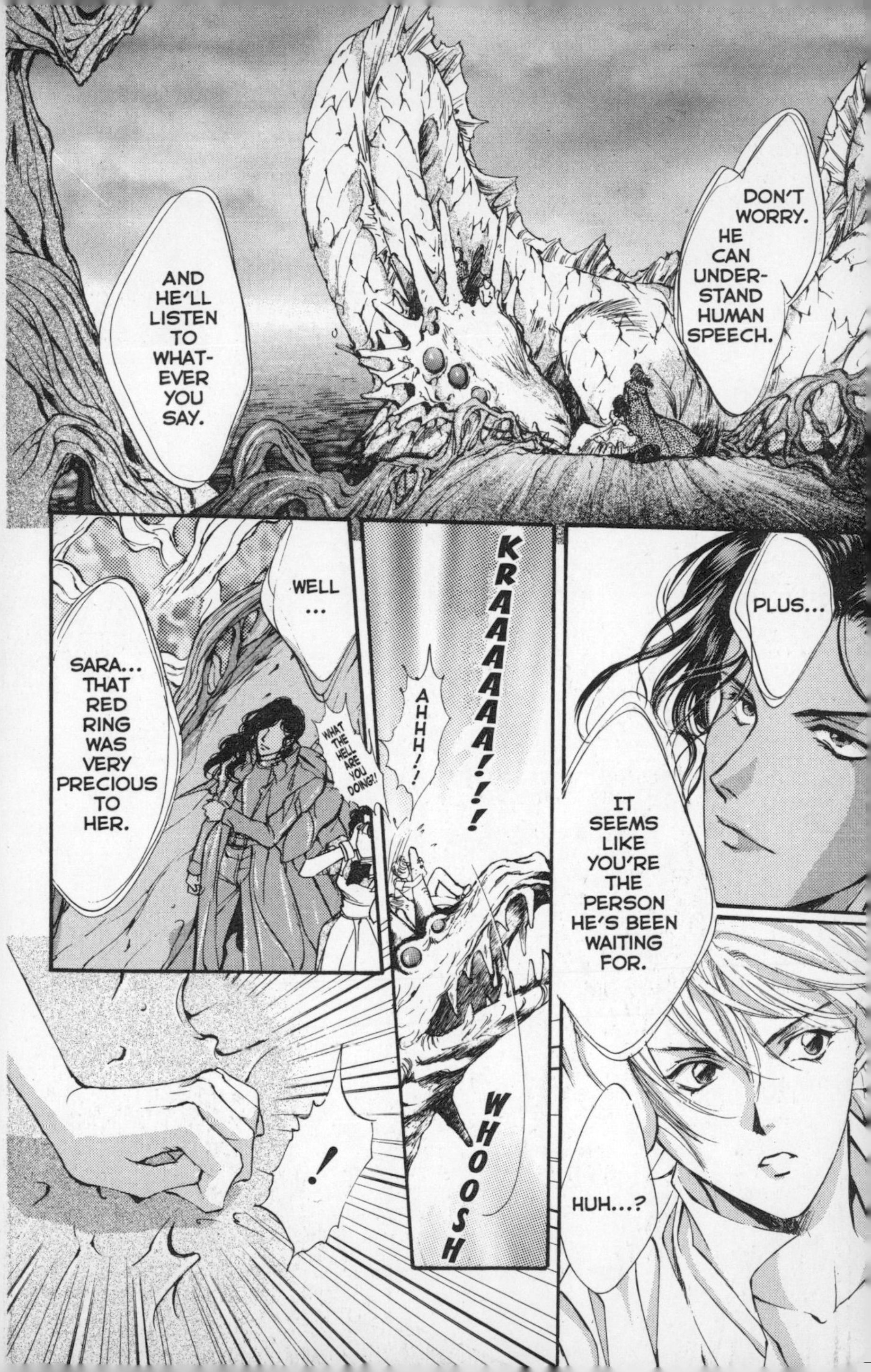

DON'T WORRY. HE CAN UNDER-STAND HUMAN SPEECH.
AND HE'LL LISTEN TO WHAT-EVER YOU SAY.
PLUS...
IT SEEMS LIKE YOU'RE THE PERSON HE'S BEEN WAITING FOR.
HUH...?
KRAAAAAAA!!!
AHHH!!
WHOOOSH
WELL ...
SARA... THAT RED RING WAS VERY PRECIOUS TO HER.
WHAT THE HELL ARE YOU DOING?!
!

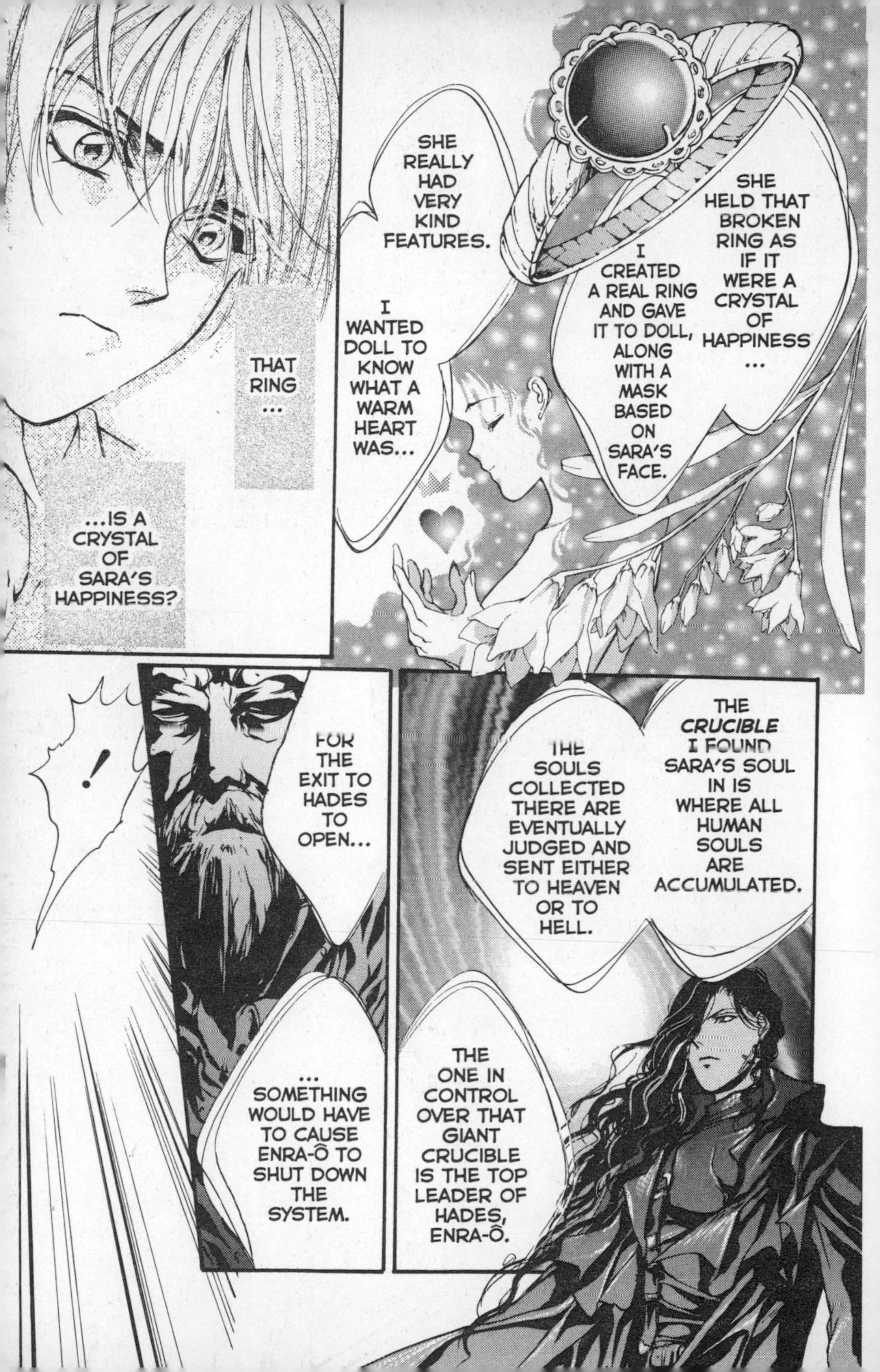
SHE HELD THAT BROKEN RING AS IF IT WERE A CRYSTAL OF HAPPINESS...
I CREATED A REAL RING AND GAVE IT TO DOLL, ALONG WITH A MASK BASED ON SARA'S FACE.
SHE REALLY HAD VERY KIND FEATURES.
I WANTED DOLL TO KNOW WHAT A WARM HEART WAS...
THAT RING...
...IS A CRYSTAL OF SARA'S HAPPINESS?
THE *CRUCIBLE* I FOUND SARA'S SOUL IN IS WHERE ALL HUMAN SOULS ARE ACCUMULATED.
THE SOULS COLLECTED THERE ARE EVENTUALLY JUDGED AND SENT EITHER TO HEAVEN OR TO HELL.
THE ONE IN CONTROL OVER THAT GIANT CRUCIBLE IS THE TOP LEADER OF HADES, ENRA-Ō.
FOR THE EXIT TO HADES TO OPEN...
...SOMETHING WOULD HAVE TO CAUSE ENRA-Ō TO SHUT DOWN THE SYSTEM.
!

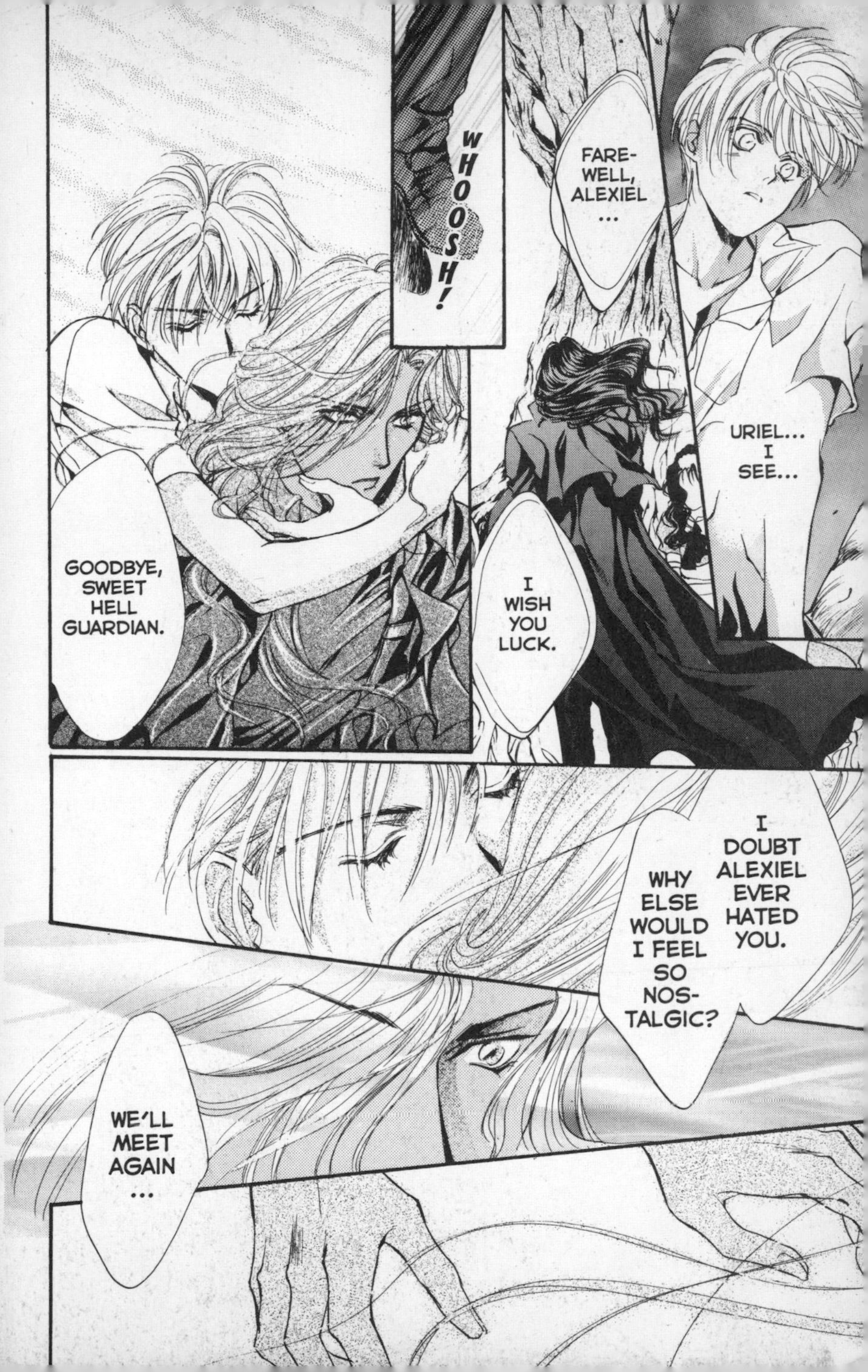
FARE-WELL, ALEXIEL...
URIEL... I SEE...
I WISH YOU LUCK.
WHOOOSH!
GOODBYE, SWEET HELL GUARDIAN.
I DOUBT ALEXIEL EVER HATED YOU.
WHY ELSE WOULD I FEEL SO NOS-TALGIC?
WE'LL MEET AGAIN...

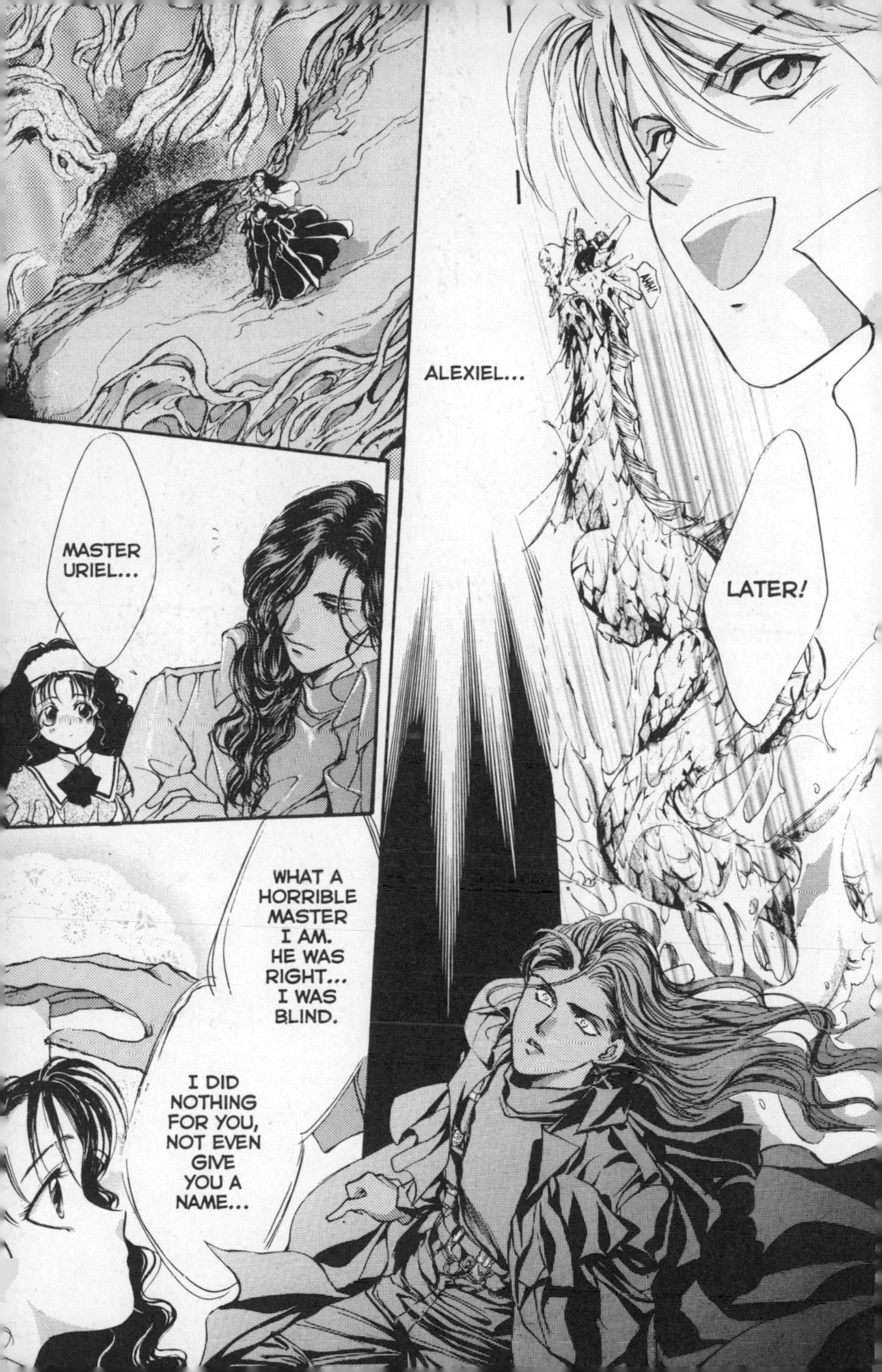
AHH!
ALEXIEL...
LATER!
MASTER URIEL...
WHAT A HORRIBLE MASTER I AM. HE WAS RIGHT... I WAS BLIND.
I DID NOTHING FOR YOU, NOT EVEN GIVE YOU A NAME...

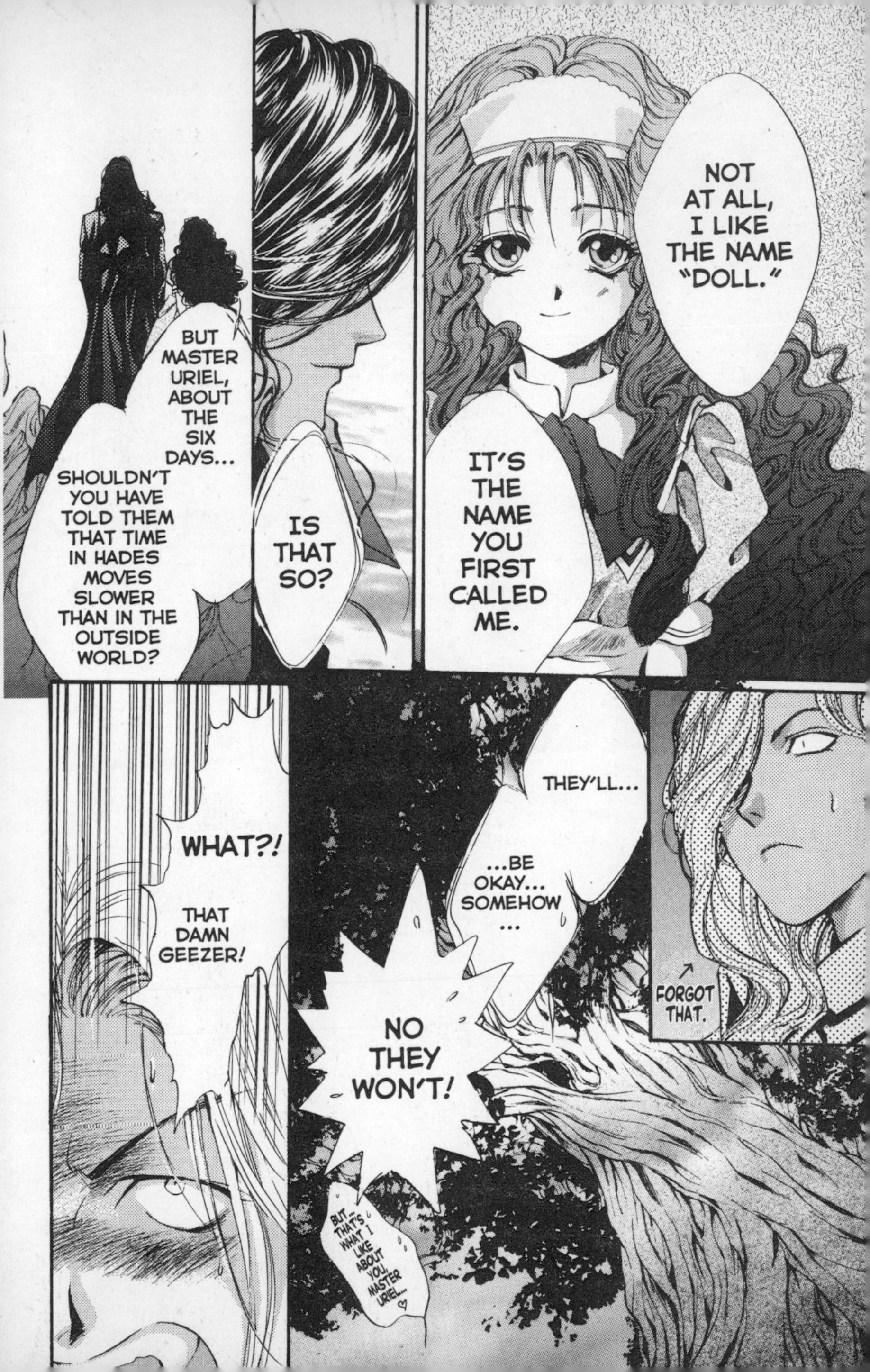
NOT AT ALL, I LIKE THE NAME "DOLL."
IT'S THE NAME YOU FIRST CALLED ME.
IS THAT SO?
BUT MASTER URIEL, ABOUT THE SIX DAYS...
SHOULDN'T YOU HAVE TOLD THEM THAT TIME IN HADES MOVES SLOWER THAN IN THE OUTSIDE WORLD?
FORGOT THAT.
THEY'LL...
...BE OKAY... SOMEHOW ...
NO THEY WON'T!
BUT... THAT'S WHAT I LIKE ABOUT YOU, MASTER URIEL... ♥
WHAT?!
THAT DAMN GEEZER!

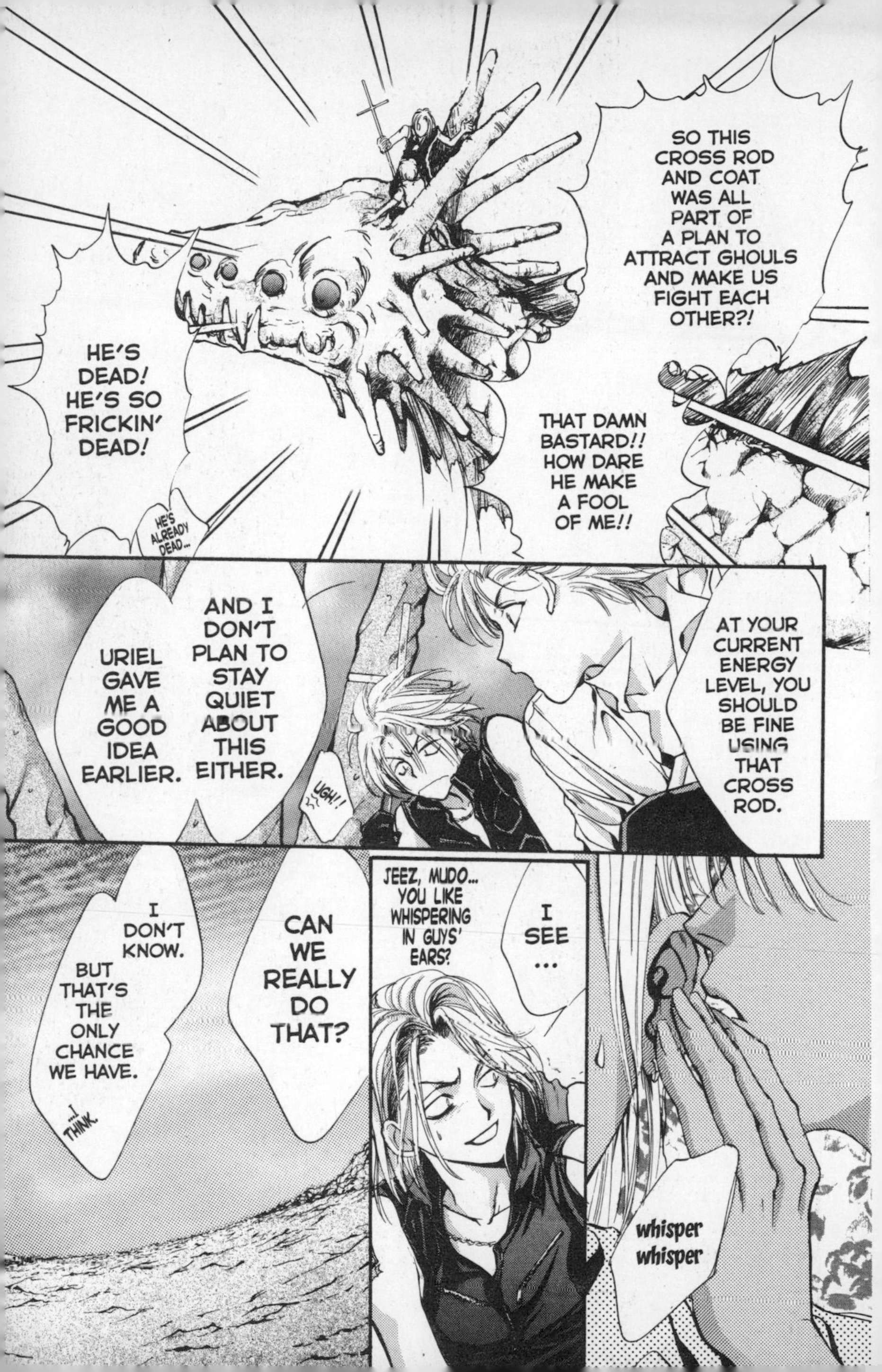
SO THIS CROSS ROD AND COAT WAS ALL PART OF A PLAN TO ATTRACT GHOULS AND MAKE US FIGHT EACH OTHER?!
THAT DAMN BASTARD!! HOW DARE HE MAKE A FOOL OF ME!!
HE'S DEAD! HE'S SO FRICKIN' DEAD!
HE'S ALREADY DEAD...
AT YOUR CURRENT ENERGY LEVEL, YOU SHOULD BE FINE USING THAT CROSS ROD.
UGH!!
AND I DON'T PLAN TO STAY QUIET ABOUT THIS EITHER.
URIEL GAVE ME A GOOD IDEA EARLIER.
whisper whisper
I SEE ...
JEEZ, MUDO... YOU LIKE WHISPERING IN GUYS' EARS?
CAN WE REALLY DO THAT?
I DON'T KNOW.
BUT THAT'S THE ONLY CHANCE WE HAVE.
...I THINK.

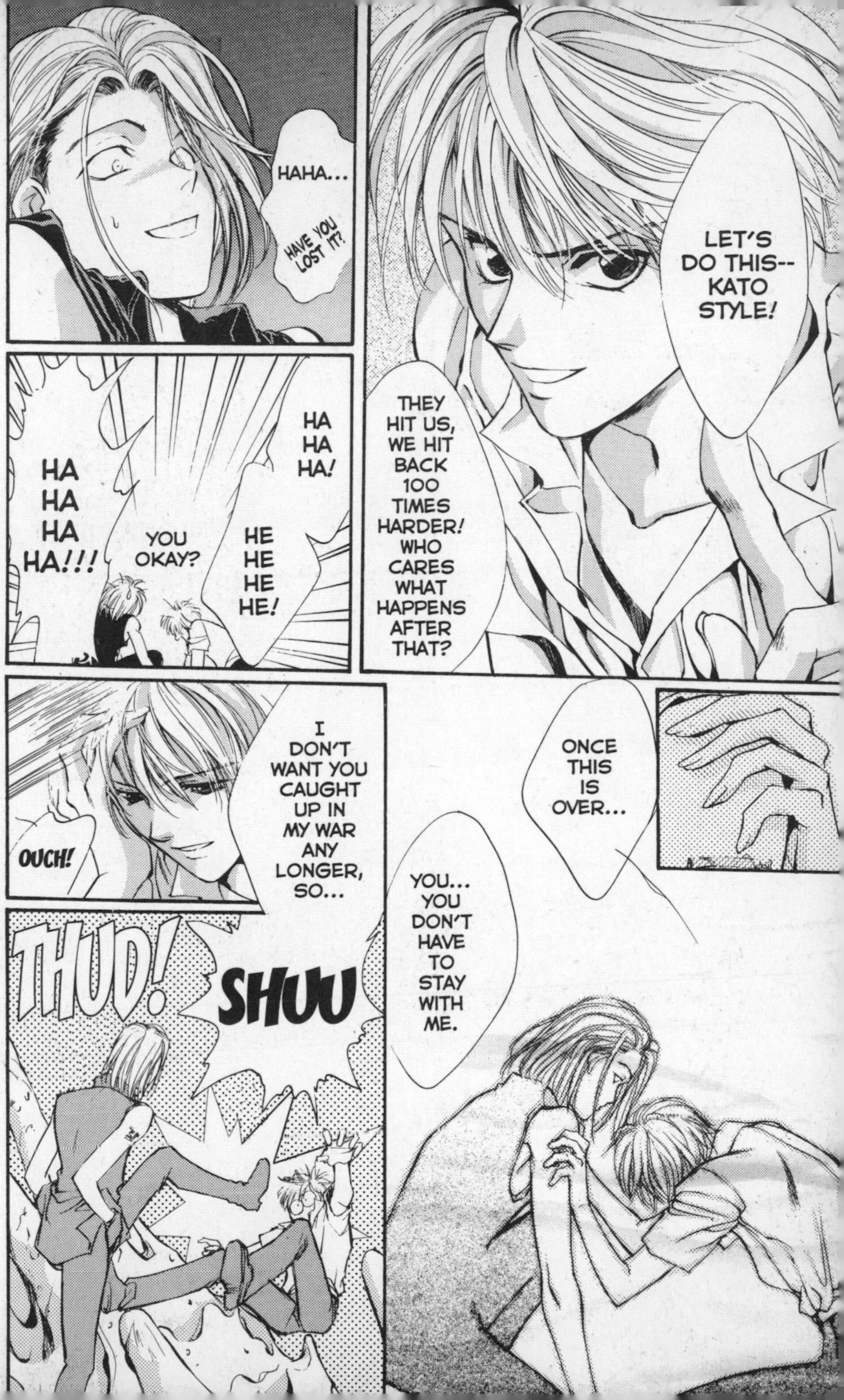
LET'S DO THIS-- KATO STYLE!
THEY HIT US, WE HIT BACK 100 TIMES HARDER! WHO CARES WHAT HAPPENS AFTER THAT?
HAHA...
HAVE YOU LOST IT?
HA HA HA!
HE HE HE HE!
YOU OKAY?
HA HA HA HA!!!
ONCE THIS IS OVER...
YOU... YOU DON'T HAVE TO STAY WITH ME.
I DON'T WANT YOU CAUGHT UP IN MY WAR ANY LONGER, SO...
OUCH!
SHUU
THUD!

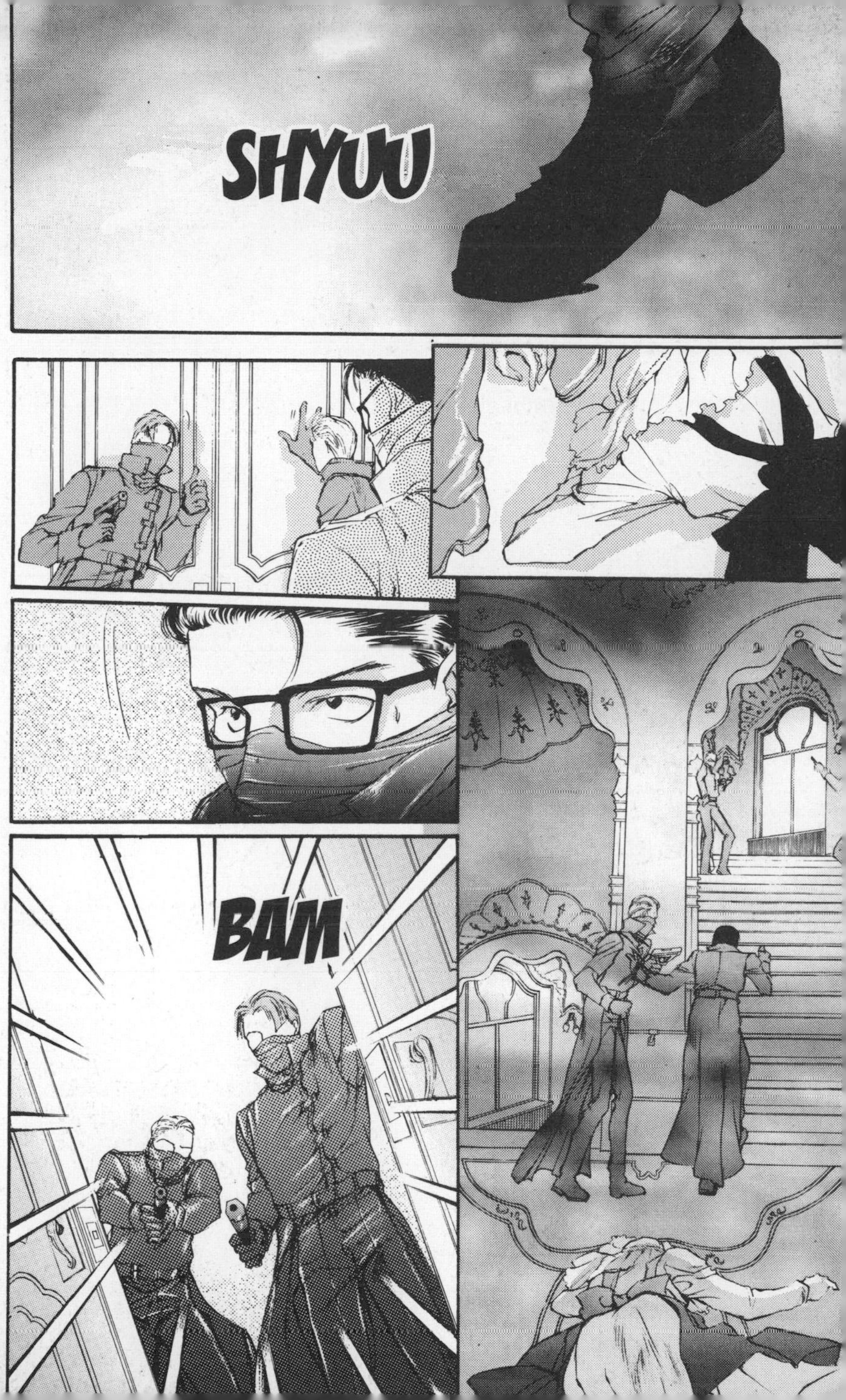
SHYUU
BAM

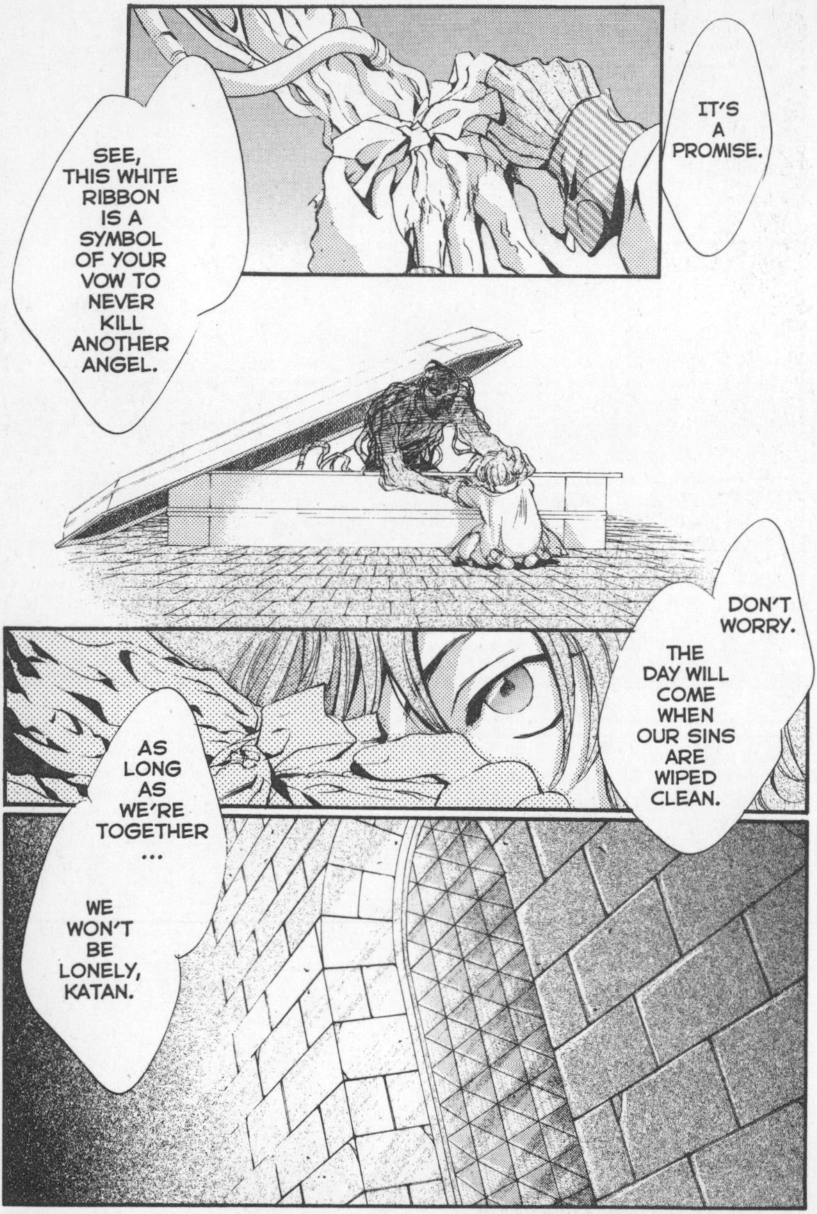
IT'S A PROMISE.
SEE, THIS WHITE RIBBON IS A SYMBOL OF YOUR VOW TO NEVER KILL ANOTHER ANGEL.
DON'T WORRY.
THE DAY WILL COME WHEN OUR SINS ARE WIPED CLEAN.
AS LONG AS WE'RE TOGETHER...
WE WON'T BE LONELY, KATAN.

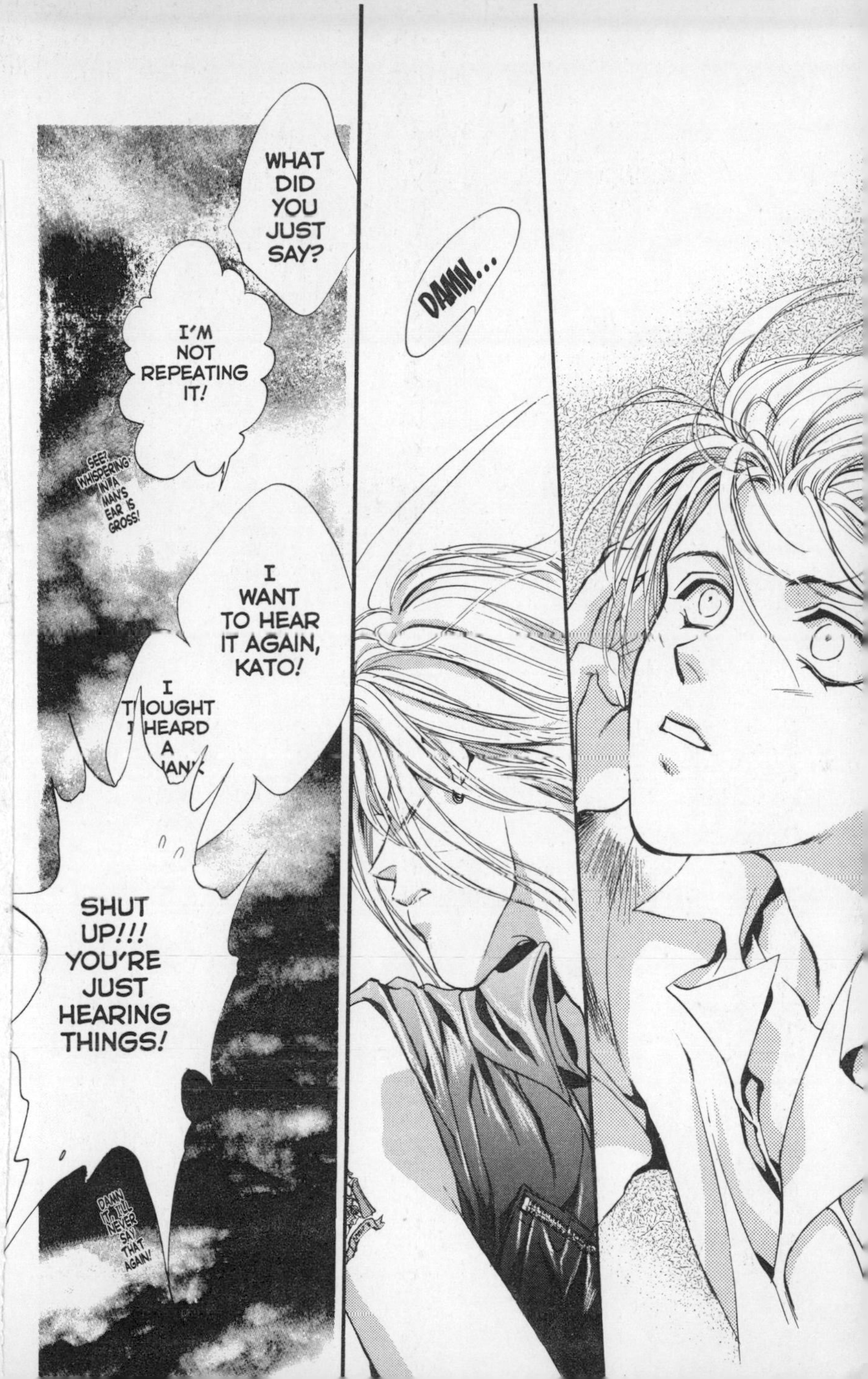
DAMN...
WHAT DID YOU JUST SAY?
I'M NOT REPEATING IT!
SEE? WHISPERING IN A MAN'S EAR IS GROSS!
I WANT TO HEAR IT AGAIN, KATO!
I THOUGHT I HEARD A
SHUT UP!!! YOU'RE JUST HEARING THINGS!
DAMN IT, I'LL NEVER SAY THAT AGAIN!

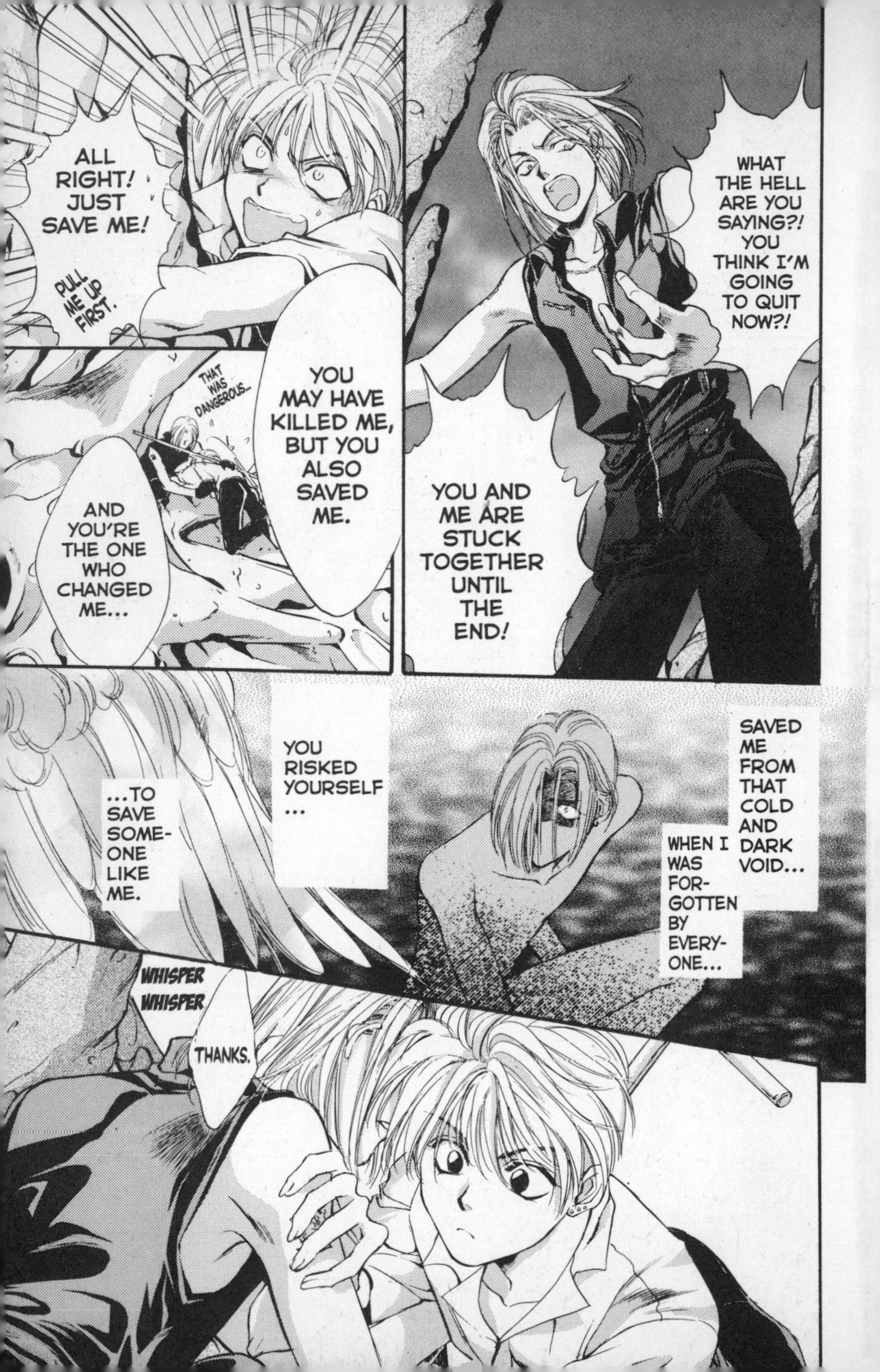
WHAT THE HELL ARE YOU SAYING?! YOU THINK I'M GOING TO QUIT NOW?!
YOU AND ME ARE STUCK TOGETHER UNTIL THE END!
ALL RIGHT! JUST SAVE ME!
PULL ME UP FIRST.
YOU MAY HAVE KILLED ME, BUT YOU ALSO SAVED ME.
THAT WAS DANGEROUS...
AND YOU'RE THE ONE WHO CHANGED ME...
SAVED ME FROM THAT COLD AND DARK VOID...
WHEN I WAS FOR-GOTTEN BY EVERY-ONE...
YOU RISKED YOURSELF ...
...TO SAVE SOME-ONE LIKE ME.
WHISPER WHISPER
THANKS.

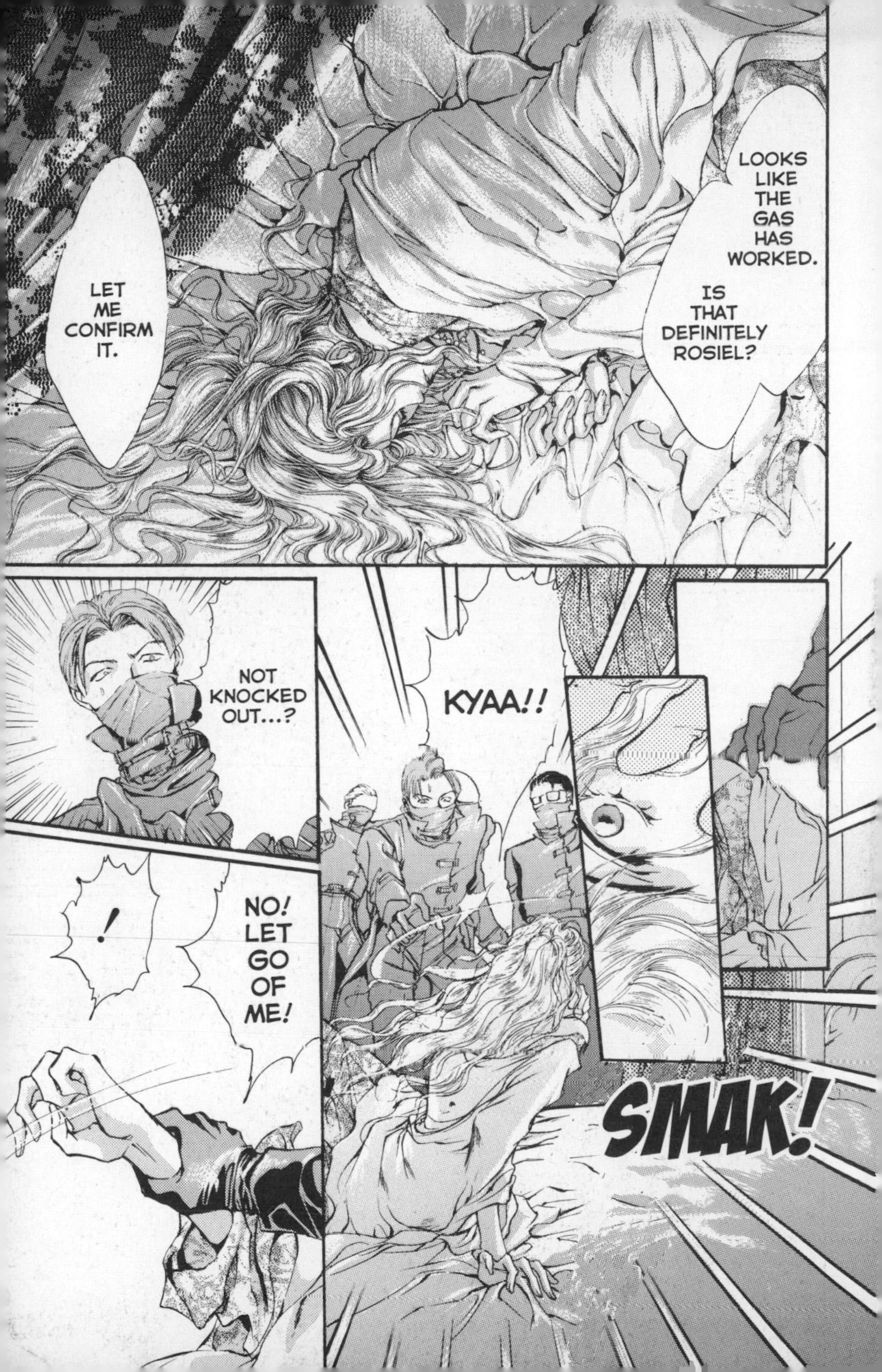
LOOKS LIKE THE GAS HAS WORKED.
IS THAT DEFINITELY ROSIEL?
LET ME CONFIRM IT.
KYAA!!
SMAK!
NOT KNOCKED OUT...?
NO! LET GO OF ME!
!

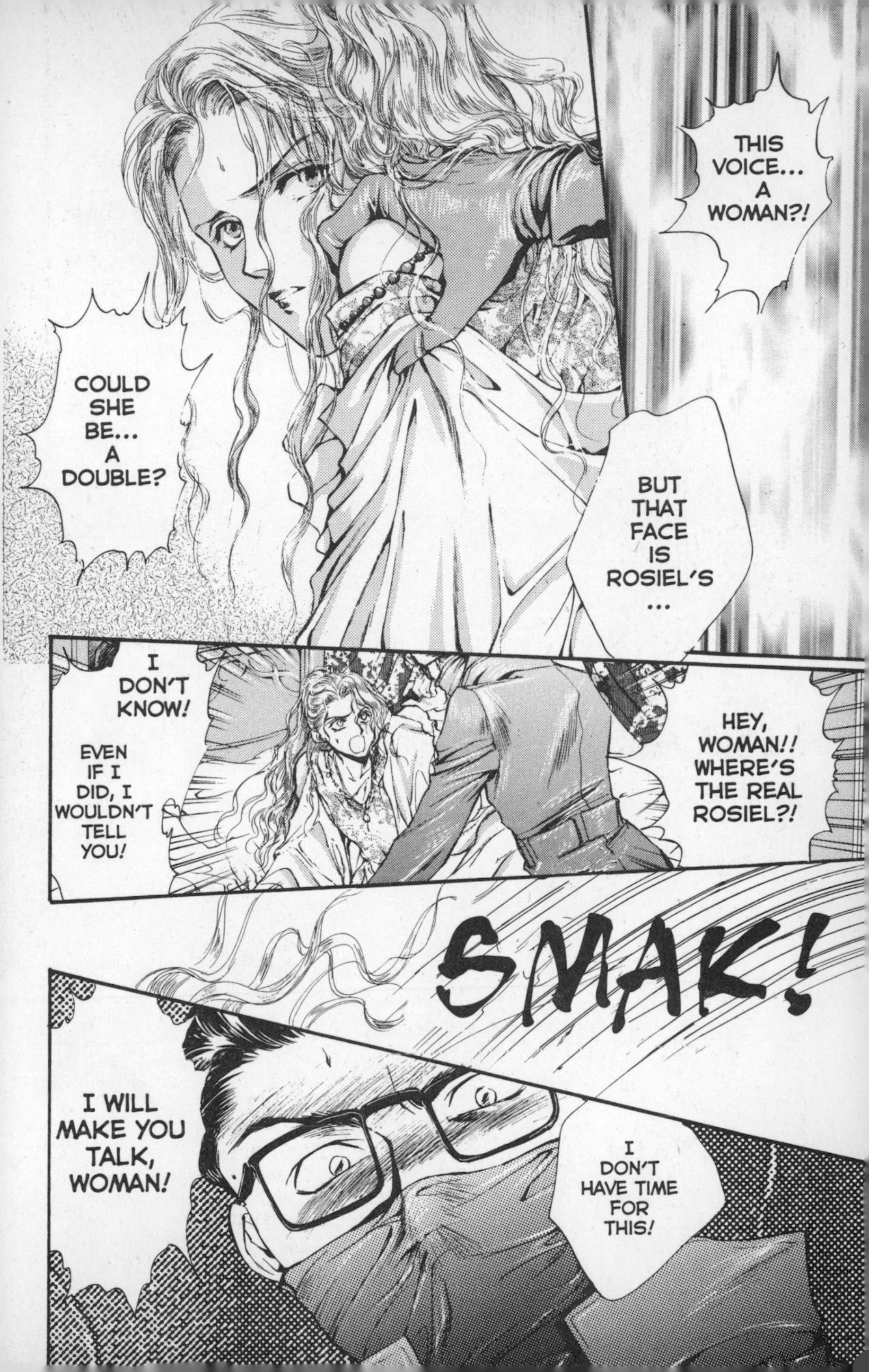
THIS VOICE... A WOMAN?!
BUT THAT FACE IS ROSIEL'S ...
COULD SHE BE... A DOUBLE?
HEY, WOMAN!! WHERE'S THE REAL ROSIEL?!
I DON'T KNOW!
EVEN IF I DID, I WOULDN'T TELL YOU!
SMAK!
I DON'T HAVE TIME FOR THIS!
I WILL MAKE YOU TALK, WOMAN!

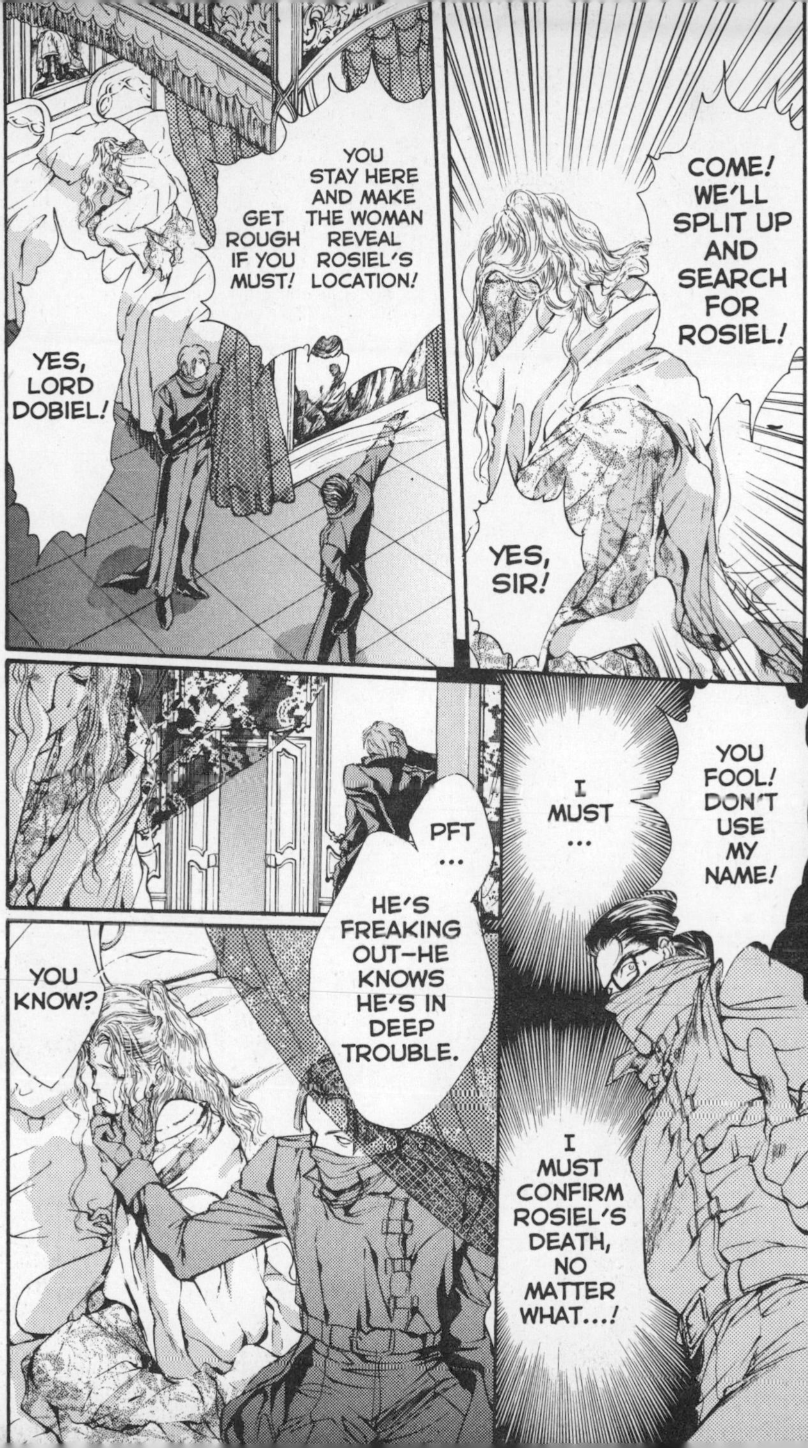
COME! WE'LL SPLIT UP AND SEARCH FOR ROSIEL!
YES, SIR!
YOU STAY HERE AND MAKE THE WOMAN REVEAL ROSIEL'S LOCATION!
GET ROUGH IF YOU MUST!
YES, LORD DOBIEL!
YOU FOOL! DON'T USE MY NAME!
I MUST ...
I MUST CONFIRM ROSIEL'S DEATH, NO MATTER WHAT...!
PFT ...
HE'S FREAKING OUT—HE KNOWS HE'S IN DEEP TROUBLE.
YOU KNOW?

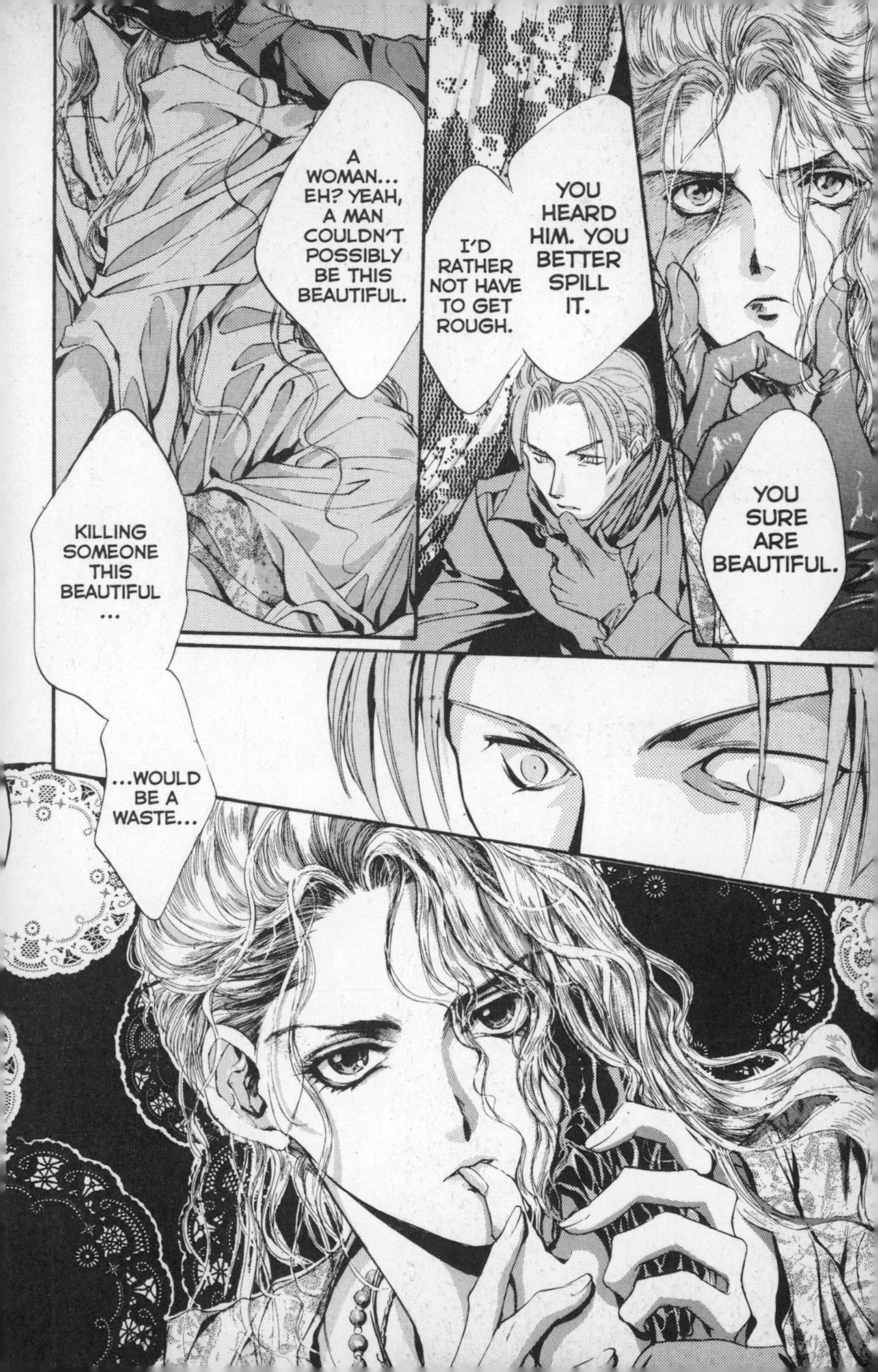
YOU SURE ARE BEAUTIFUL.
YOU HEARD HIM. YOU BETTER SPILL IT.
I'D RATHER NOT HAVE TO GET ROUGH.
A WOMAN... EH? YEAH, A MAN COULDN'T POSSIBLY BE THIS BEAUTIFUL.
KILLING SOMEONE THIS BEAUTIFUL ...
...WOULD BE A WASTE...

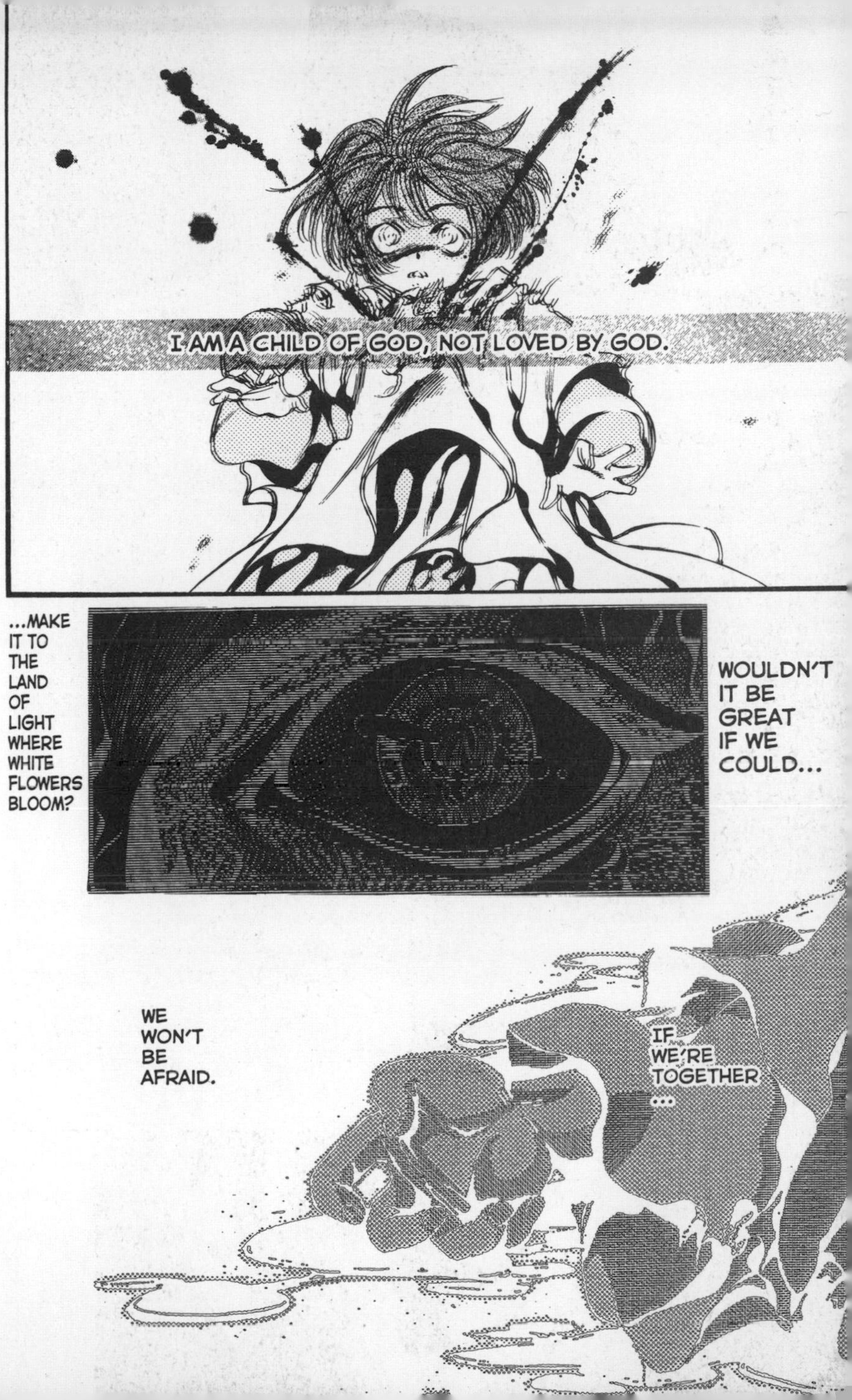
I AM A CHILD OF GOD, NOT LOVED BY GOD.
WOULDN'T IT BE GREAT IF WE COULD...
...MAKE IT TO THE LAND OF LIGHT WHERE WHITE FLOWERS BLOOM?
IF WE'RE TOGETHER...
WE WON'T BE AFRAID.

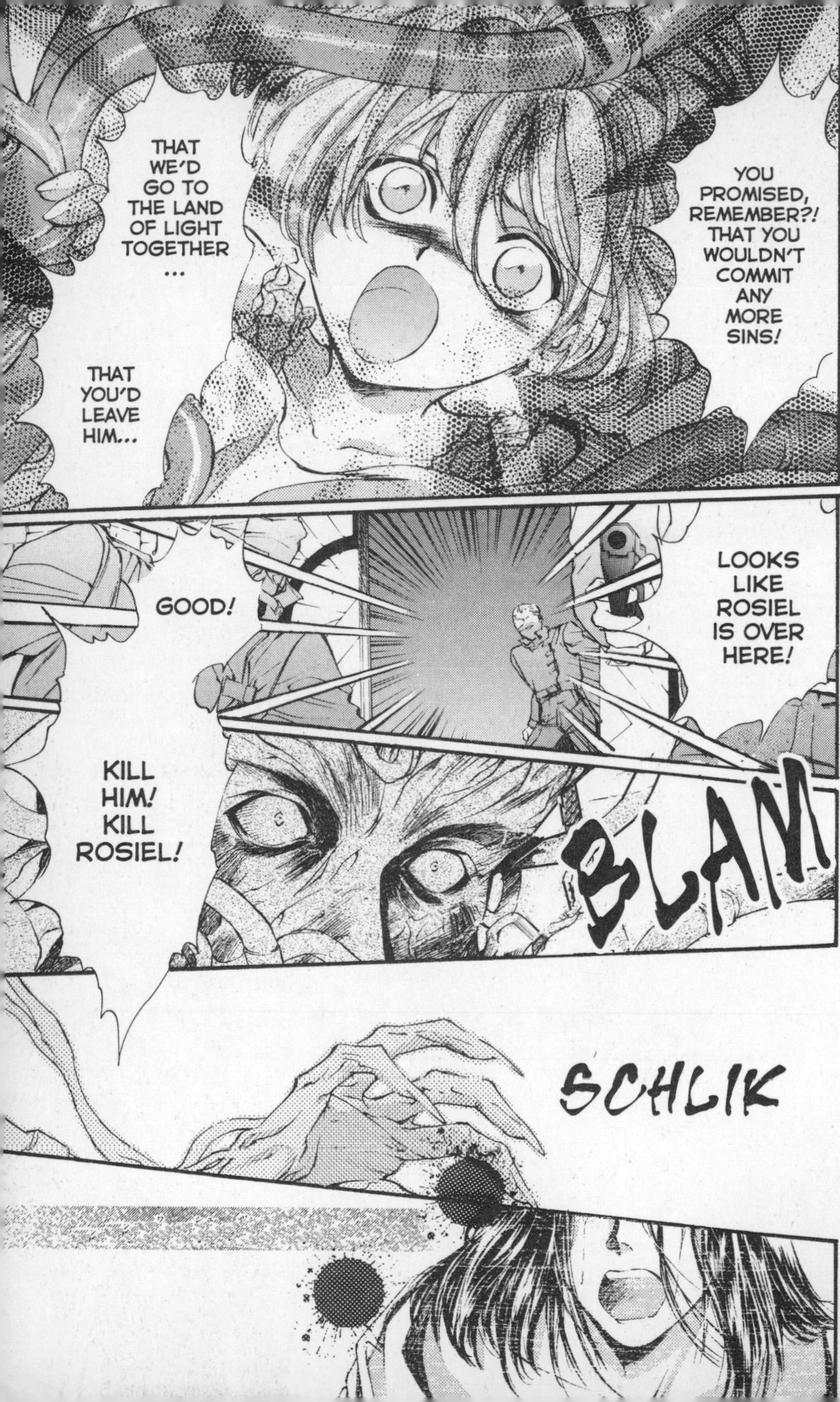
YOU PROMISED, REMEMBER?! THAT YOU WOULDN'T COMMIT ANY MORE SINS!
THAT WE'D GO TO THE LAND OF LIGHT TOGETHER ...
THAT YOU'D LEAVE HIM...
LOOKS LIKE ROSIEL IS OVER HERE!
GOOD!
KILL HIM! KILL ROSIEL!
BLAM
SCHLIK

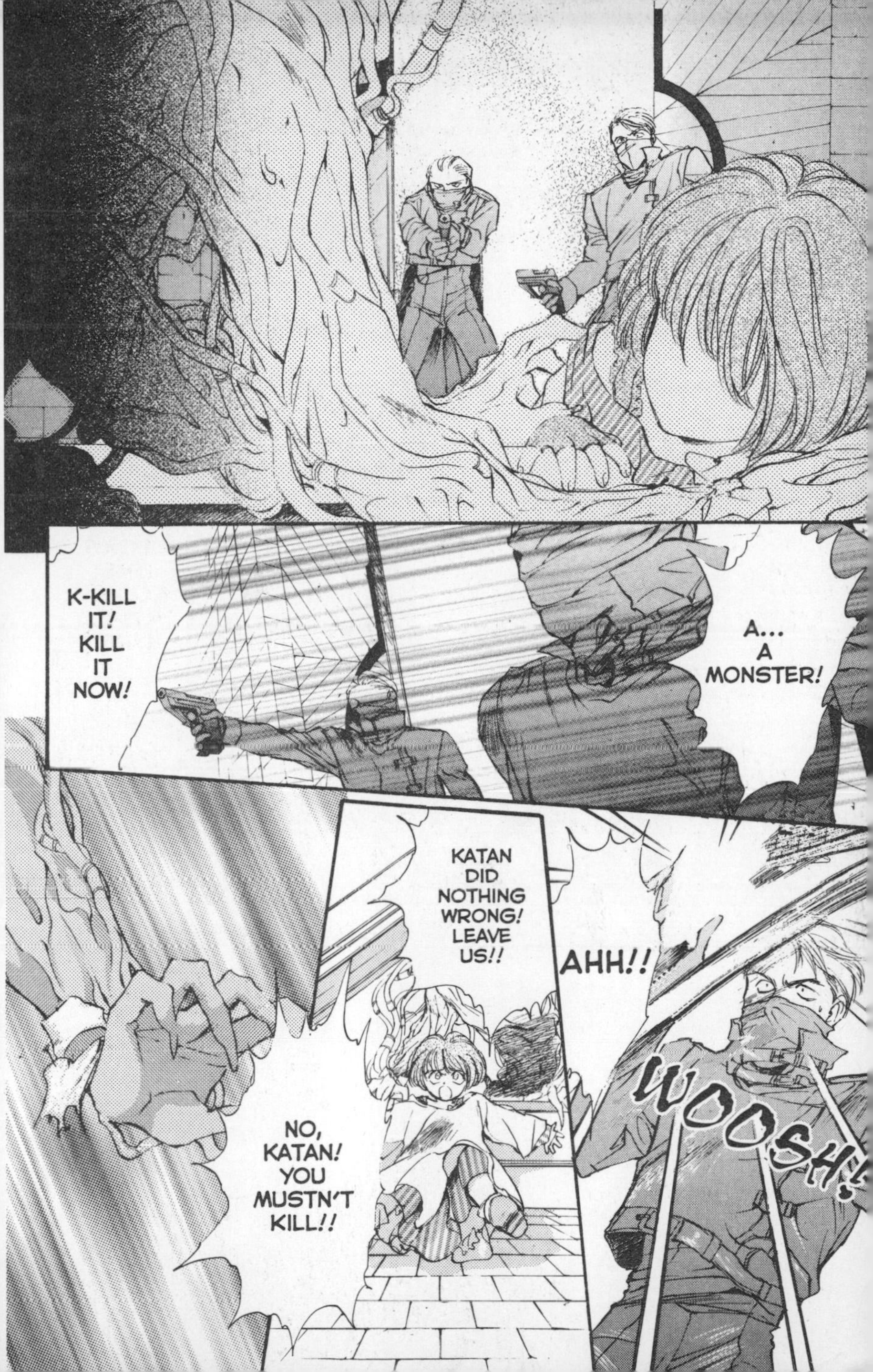
A... A MONSTER!
K-KILL IT! KILL IT NOW!
AHH!!
WOOSH!!
KATAN DID NOTHING WRONG! LEAVE US!!
NO, KATAN! YOU MUSTN'T KILL!!

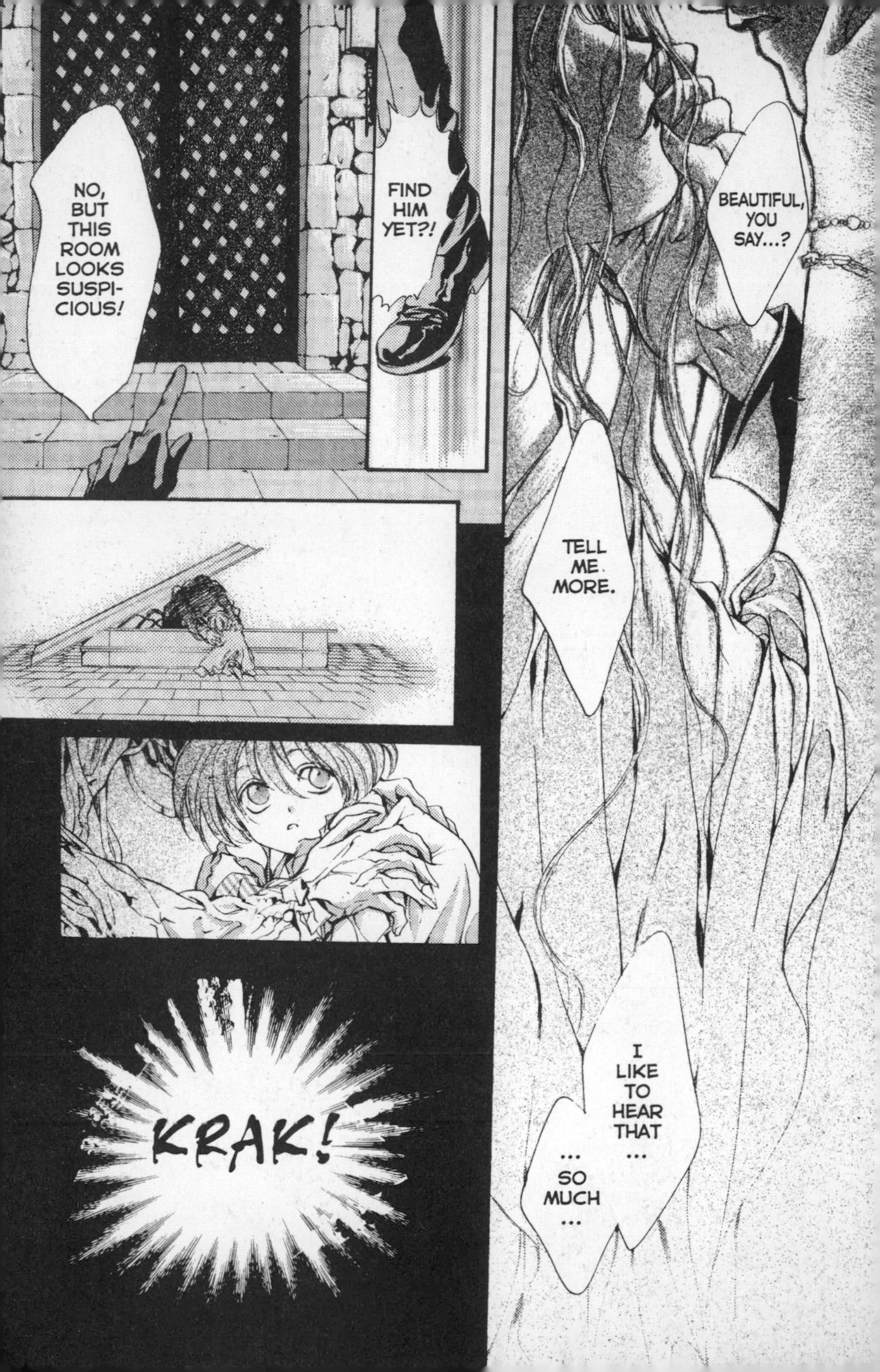
BEAUTIFUL, YOU SAY...?
TELL ME MORE.
I LIKE TO HEAR THAT ...
... SO MUCH ...
FIND HIM YET?!
NO, BUT THIS ROOM LOOKS SUSPICIOUS!
KRAK!

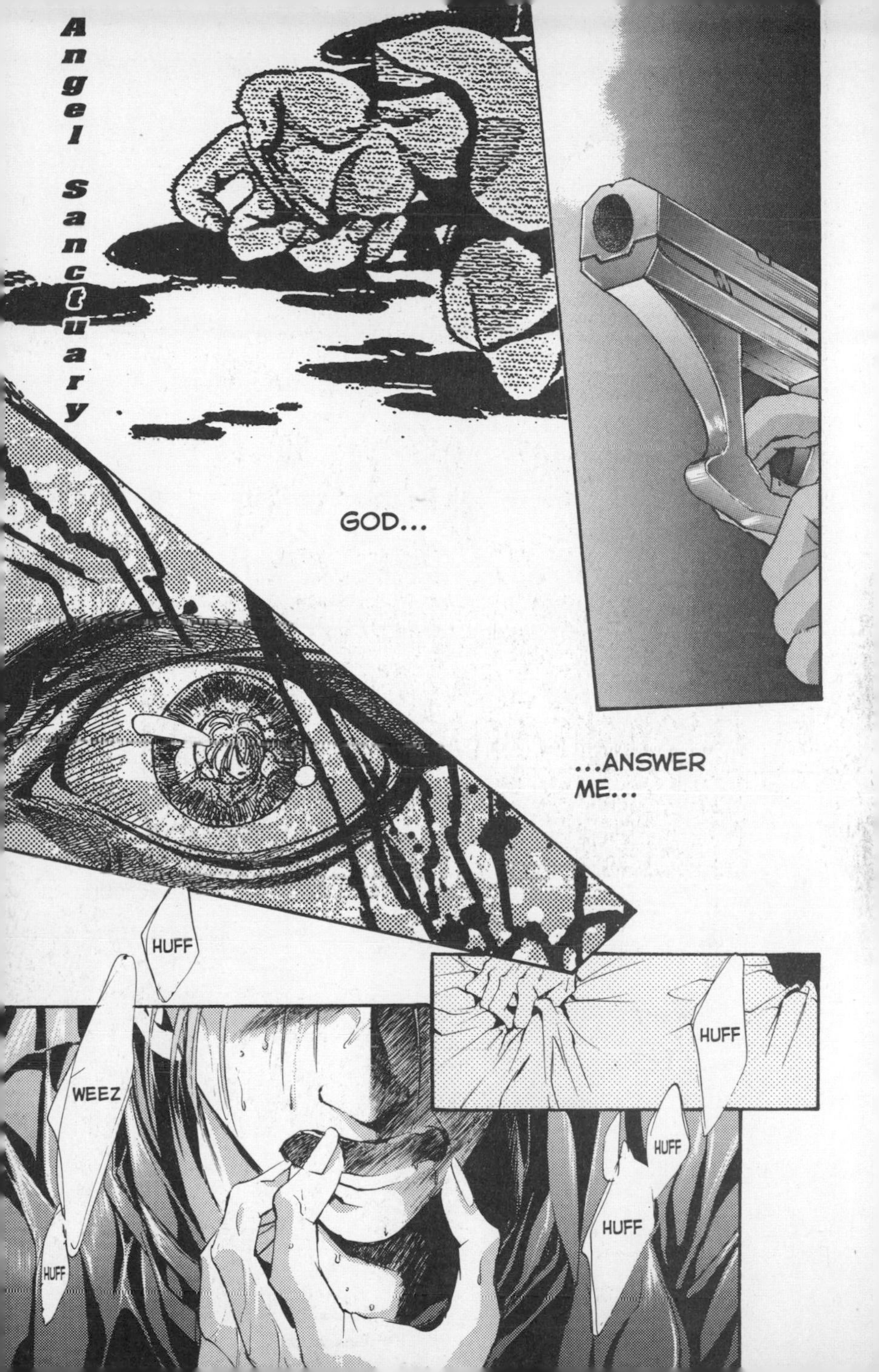
GOD...
...ANSWER ME...
HUFF
HUFF
HUFF
HUFF
WEEZ
HUFF

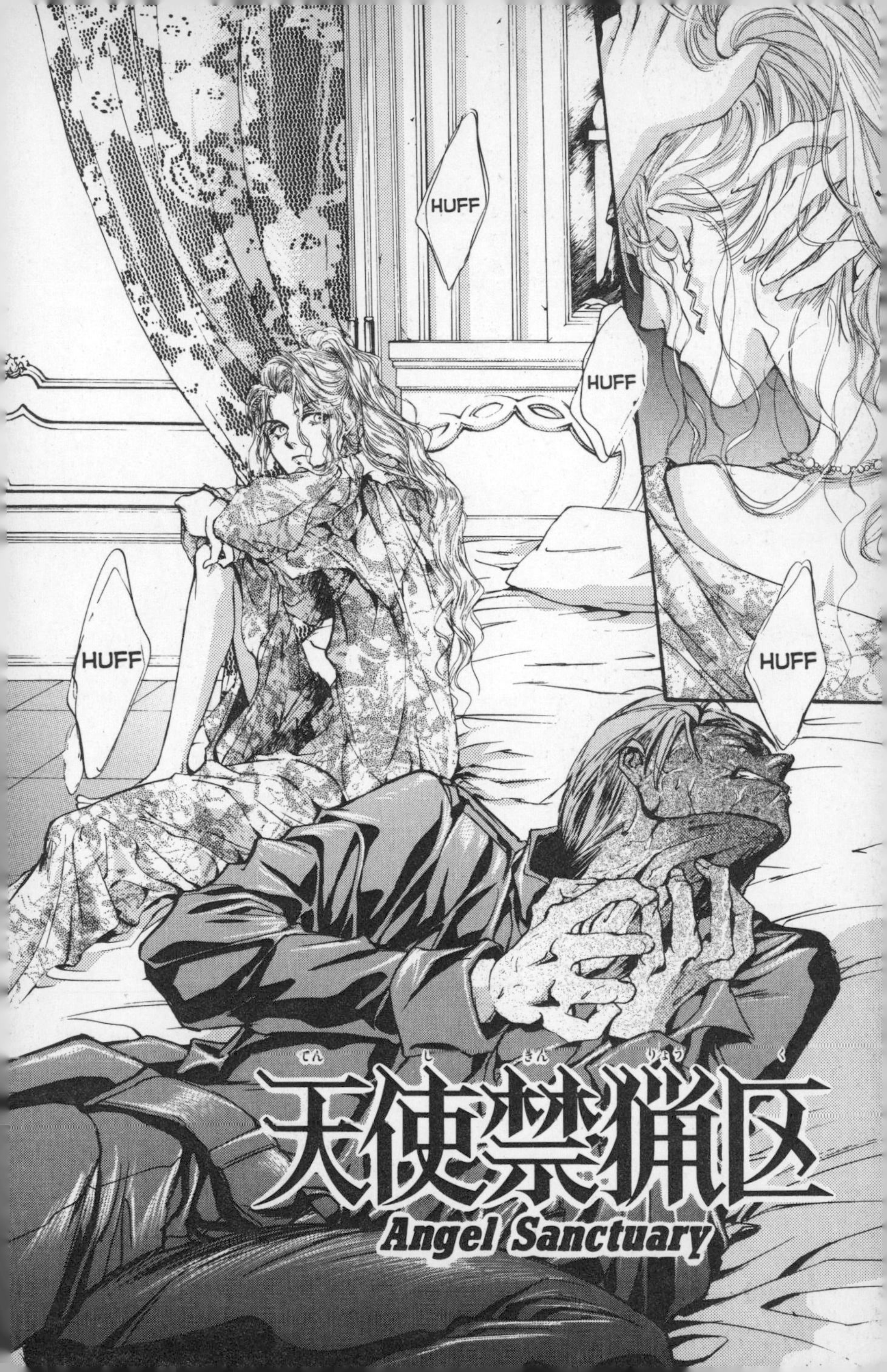
HUFF
HUFF
HUFF
HUFF
天使禁猟区
Angel Sanctuary

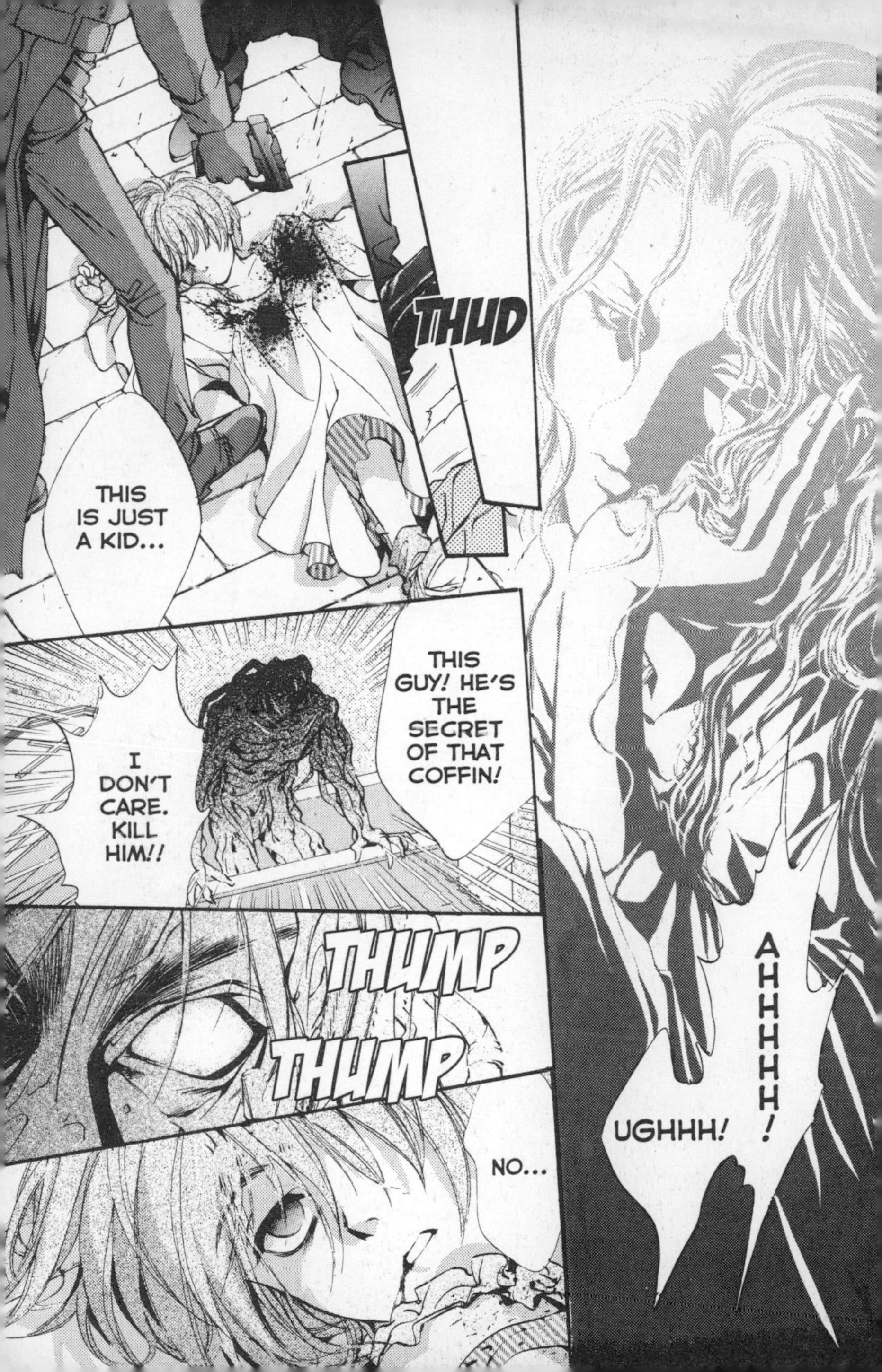
AHHHHH!
UGHHH!
THUD
THIS IS JUST A KID...
THIS GUY! HE'S THE SECRET OF THAT COFFIN!
I DON'T CARE. KILL HIM!!
THUMP
THUMP
NO...

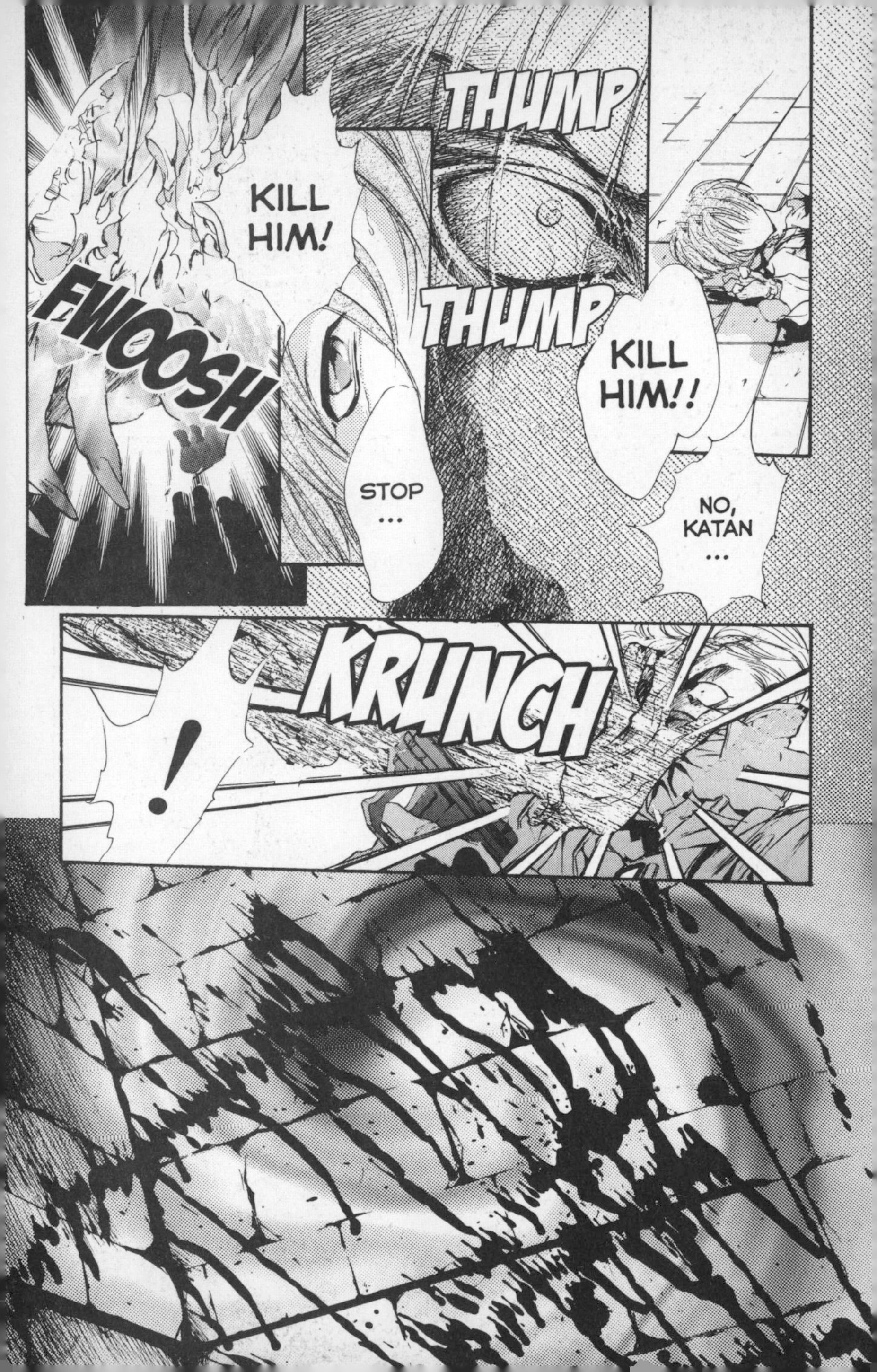
THUMP
THUMP
KILL HIM!!
NO, KATAN ...
KILL HIM!
STOP ...
FWOOSH
KRUNCH
!

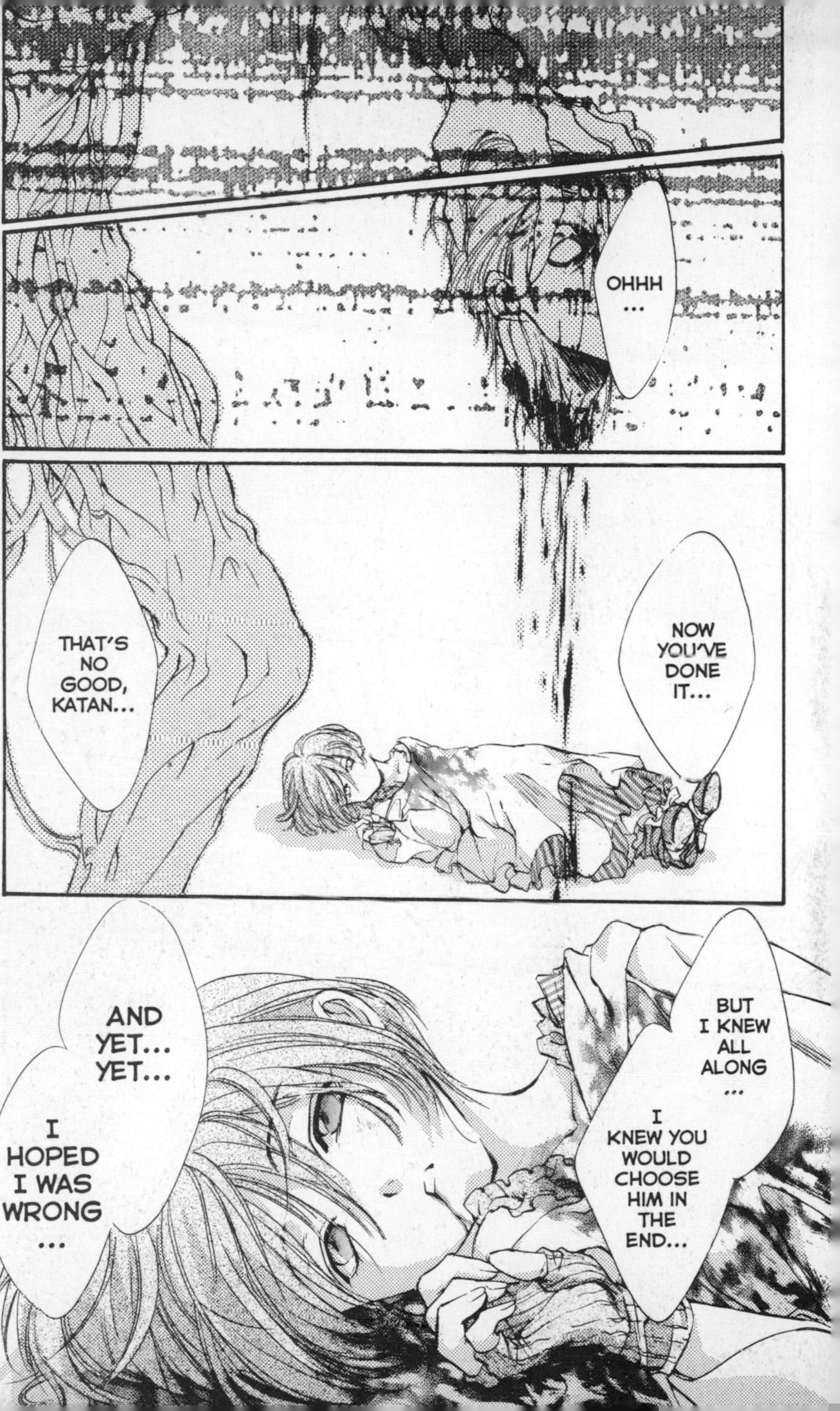
OHHH...
NOW YOU'VE DONE IT...
THAT'S NO GOOD, KATAN...
BUT I KNEW ALL ALONG...
I KNEW YOU WOULD CHOOSE HIM IN THE END...
AND YET... YET...
I HOPED I WAS WRONG...

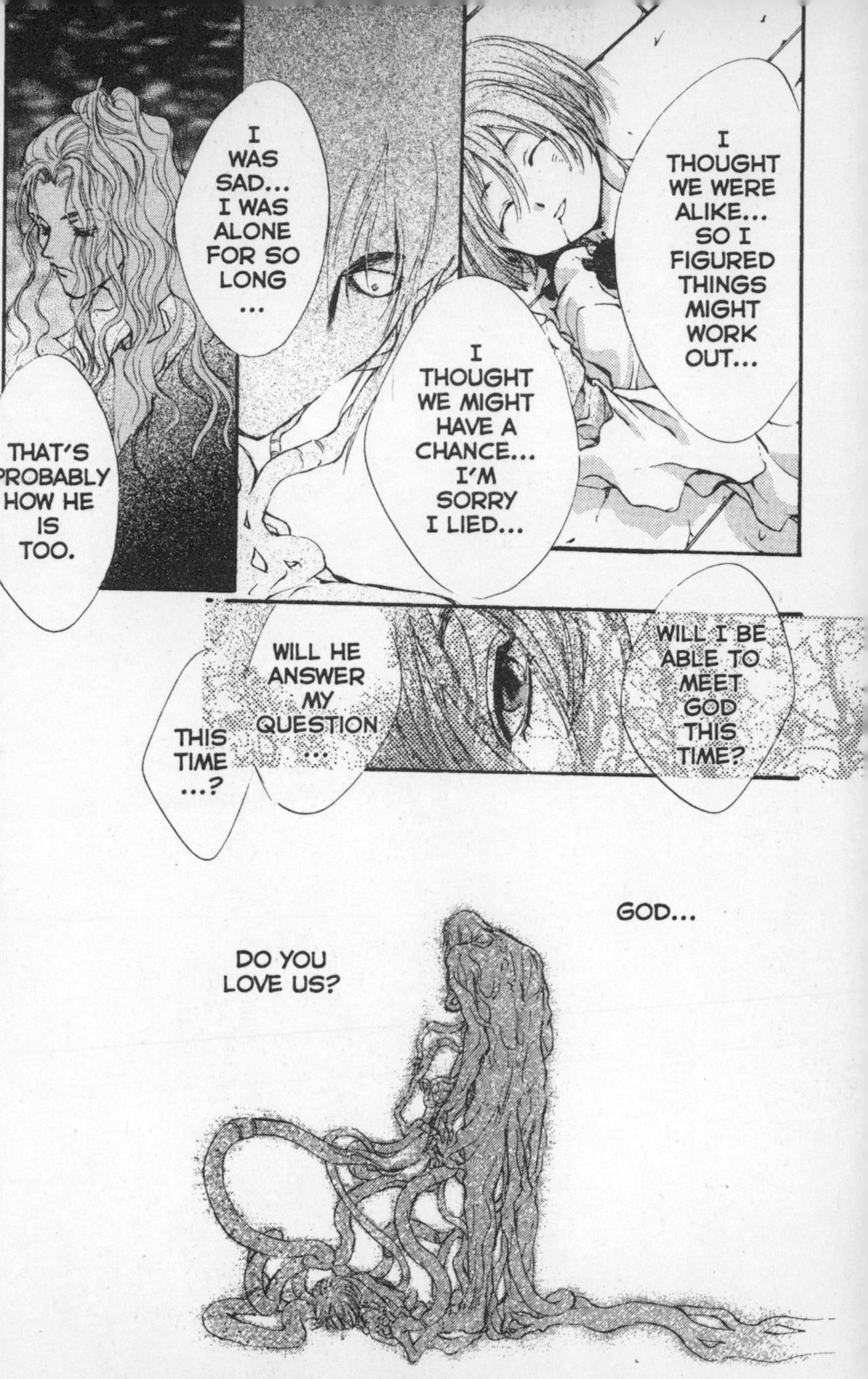
I THOUGHT WE WERE ALIKE... SO I FIGURED THINGS MIGHT WORK OUT...
I THOUGHT WE MIGHT HAVE A CHANCE... I'M SORRY I LIED...
I WAS SAD... I WAS ALONE FOR SO LONG...
THAT'S PROBABLY HOW HE IS TOO.
WILL I BE ABLE TO MEET GOD THIS TIME?
WILL HE ANSWER MY QUESTION...
THIS TIME...?
GOD...
DO YOU LOVE US?

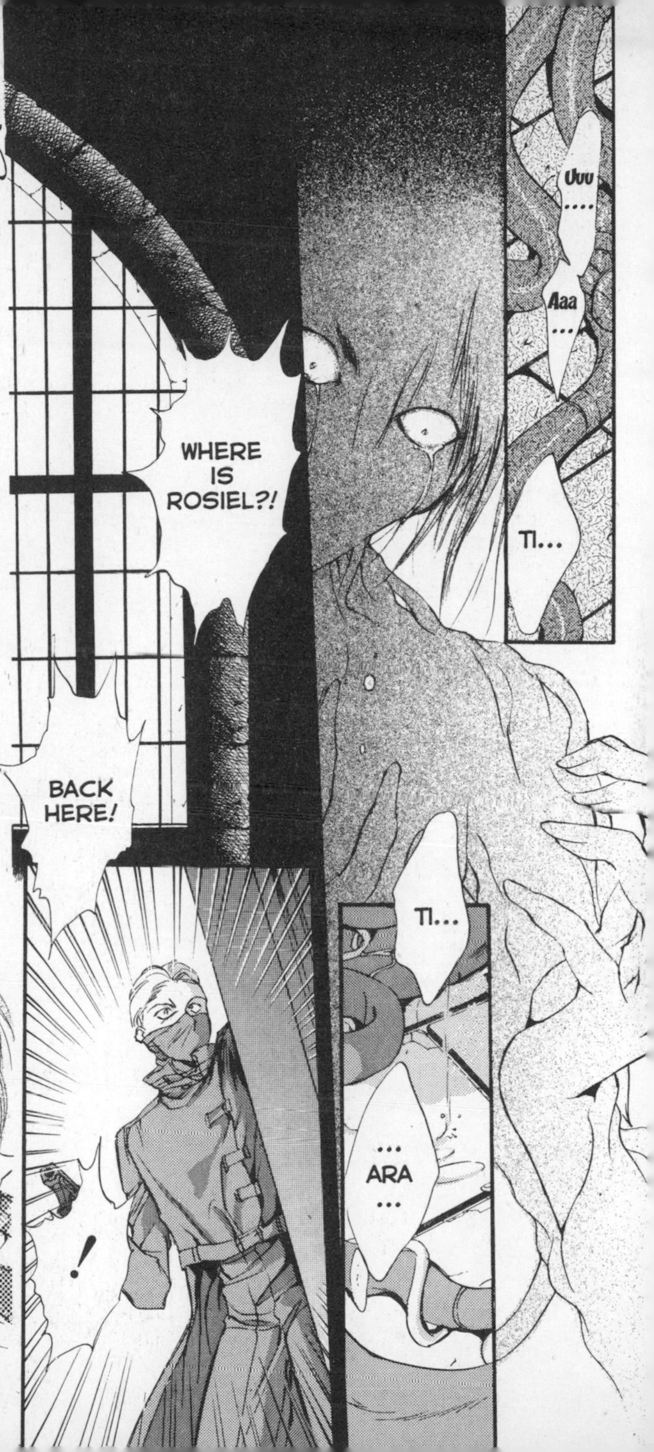
Uuu ....
Aaa ...
TI...
WHERE IS ROSIEL?!
TI...
... ARA ...
BACK HERE!
!

The "Angel-Eating lil' girl" Tiara. This has nothing to do with the album name of a certain band. There's a source for the name "Tieaiel" means "Angel of the Future." Yeah, for the previous chapter cover, the caption (when the chapter was published in magazine form) was very similar to lyrics from that certain band. I got so many letters about that, but it's actually my editor who writes those captions and not me. So I'm innocent! I swear! I had the same reaction as you guys "what the?" (And also for the "Sounds of Virtue" caption...) Anyway, Tiara-chan was introduced for the purpose of killing her later, so I felt pretty bad.

I did like her a lot but. .. well, it's her fate...

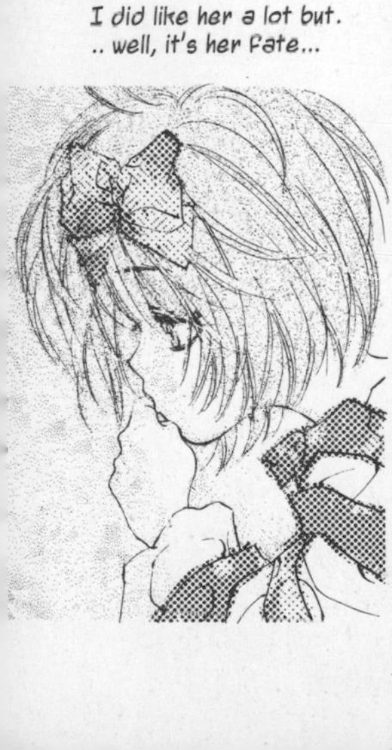

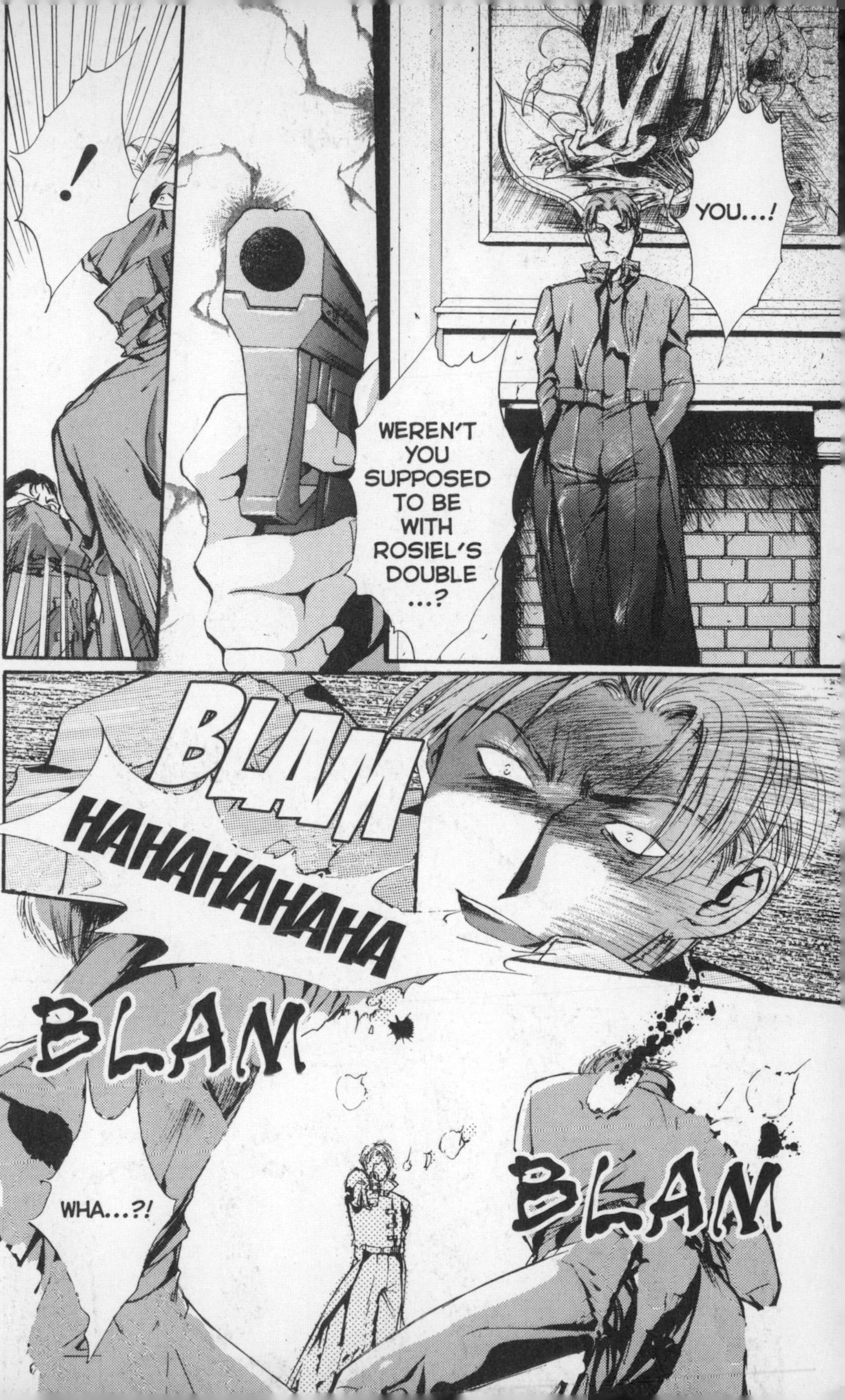
YOU...!
WEREN'T YOU SUPPOSED TO BE WITH ROSIEL'S DOUBLE ...?
!
BLAM
HAHAHAHAHAHA
BLAM
BLAM
WHA...?!

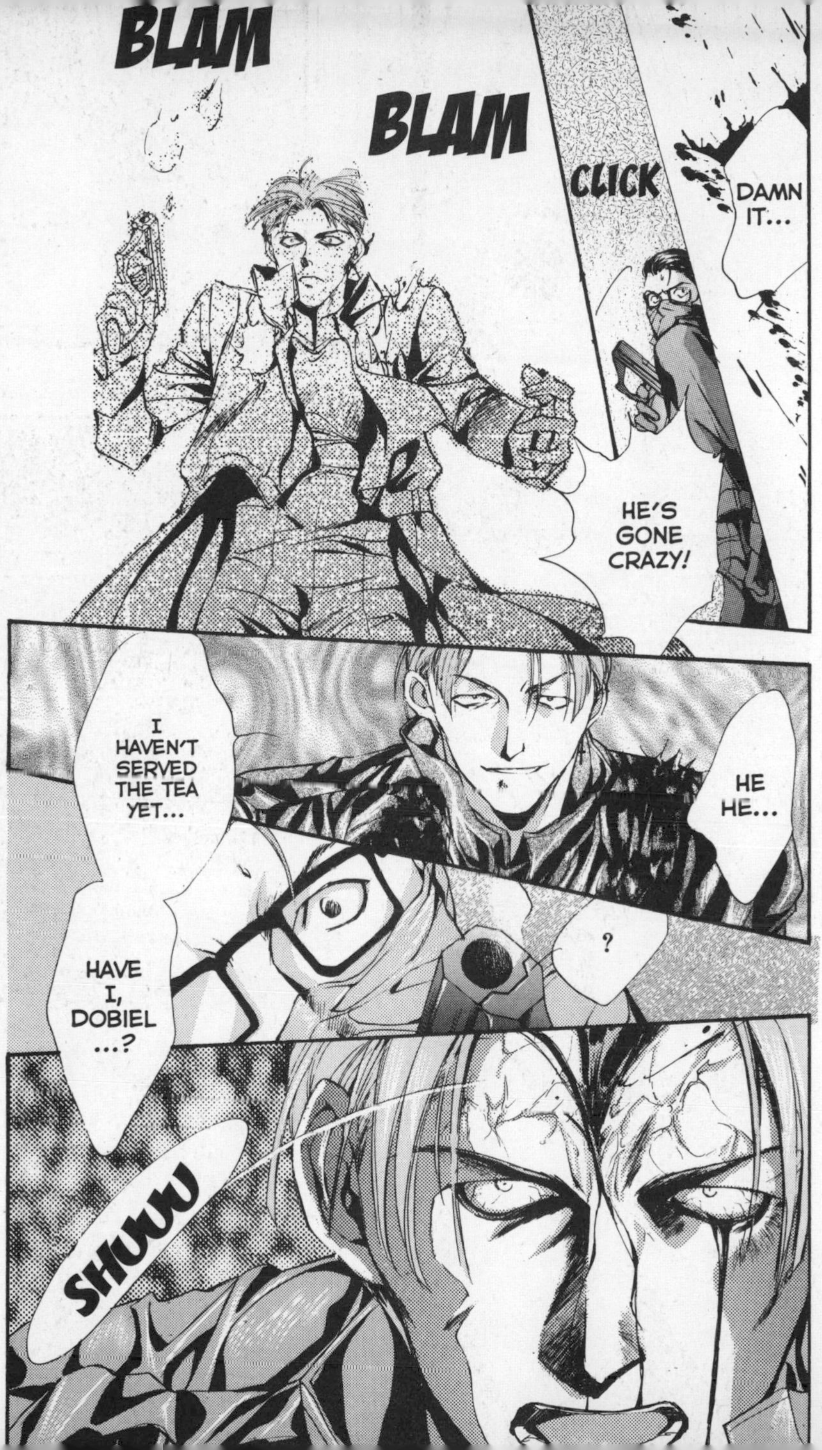
DAMN IT...
CLICK
BLAM
BLAM
HE'S GONE CRAZY!
HE HE...
I HAVEN'T SERVED THE TEA YET...
?
HAVE I, DOBIEL ...?
SHUUU

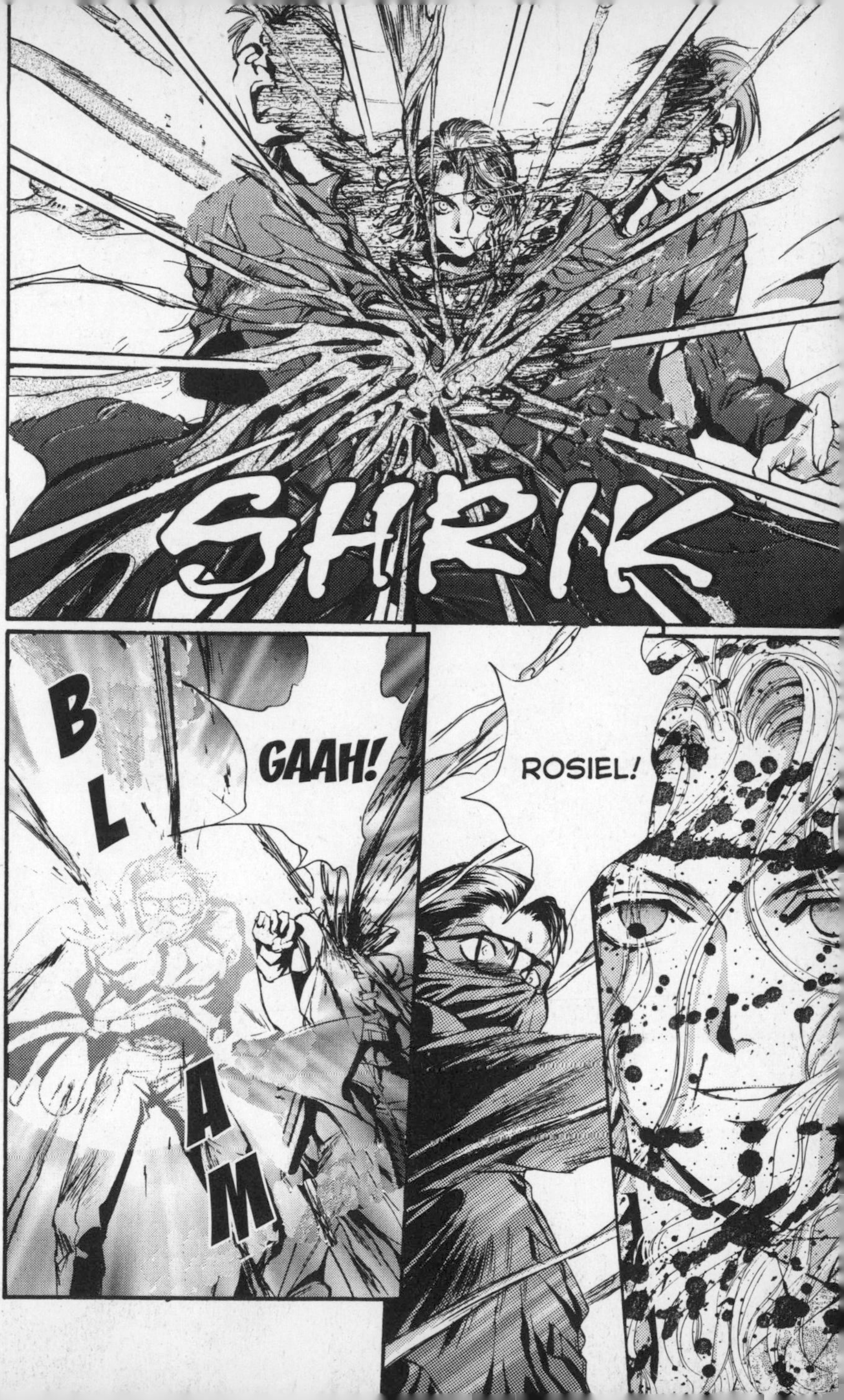
SHRIK
ROSIEL!
GAAH!
BLAM

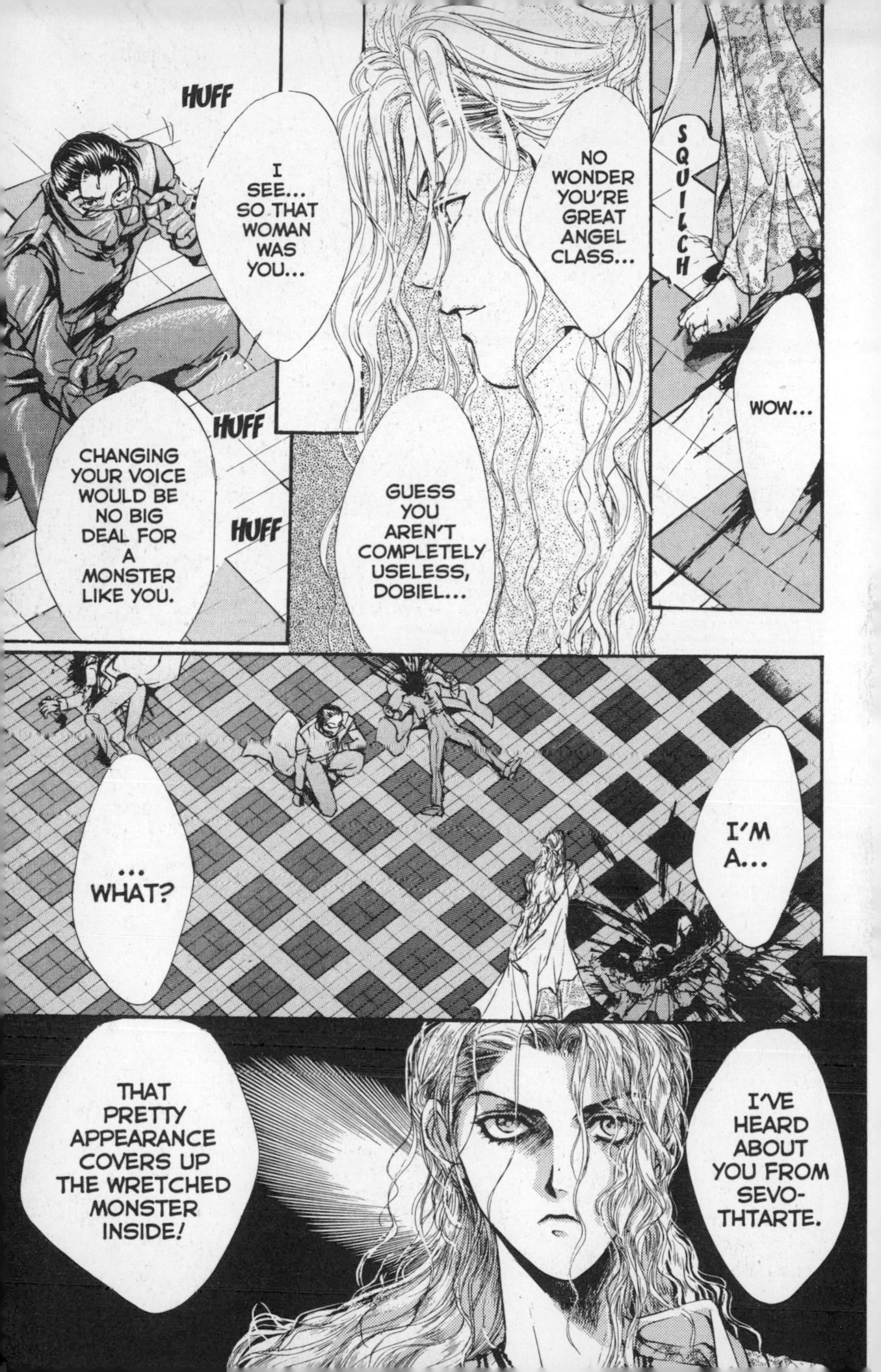
SQUILCH
WOW...
NO WONDER YOU'RE GREAT ANGEL CLASS...
GUESS YOU AREN'T COMPLETELY USELESS, DOBIEL...
HUFF
I SEE... SO THAT WOMAN WAS YOU...
HUFF
CHANGING YOUR VOICE WOULD BE NO BIG DEAL FOR A MONSTER LIKE YOU.
HUFF
I'M A...
...WHAT?
I'VE HEARD ABOUT YOU FROM SEVO-THTARTE.
THAT PRETTY APPEARANCE COVERS UP THE WRETCHED MONSTER INSIDE!

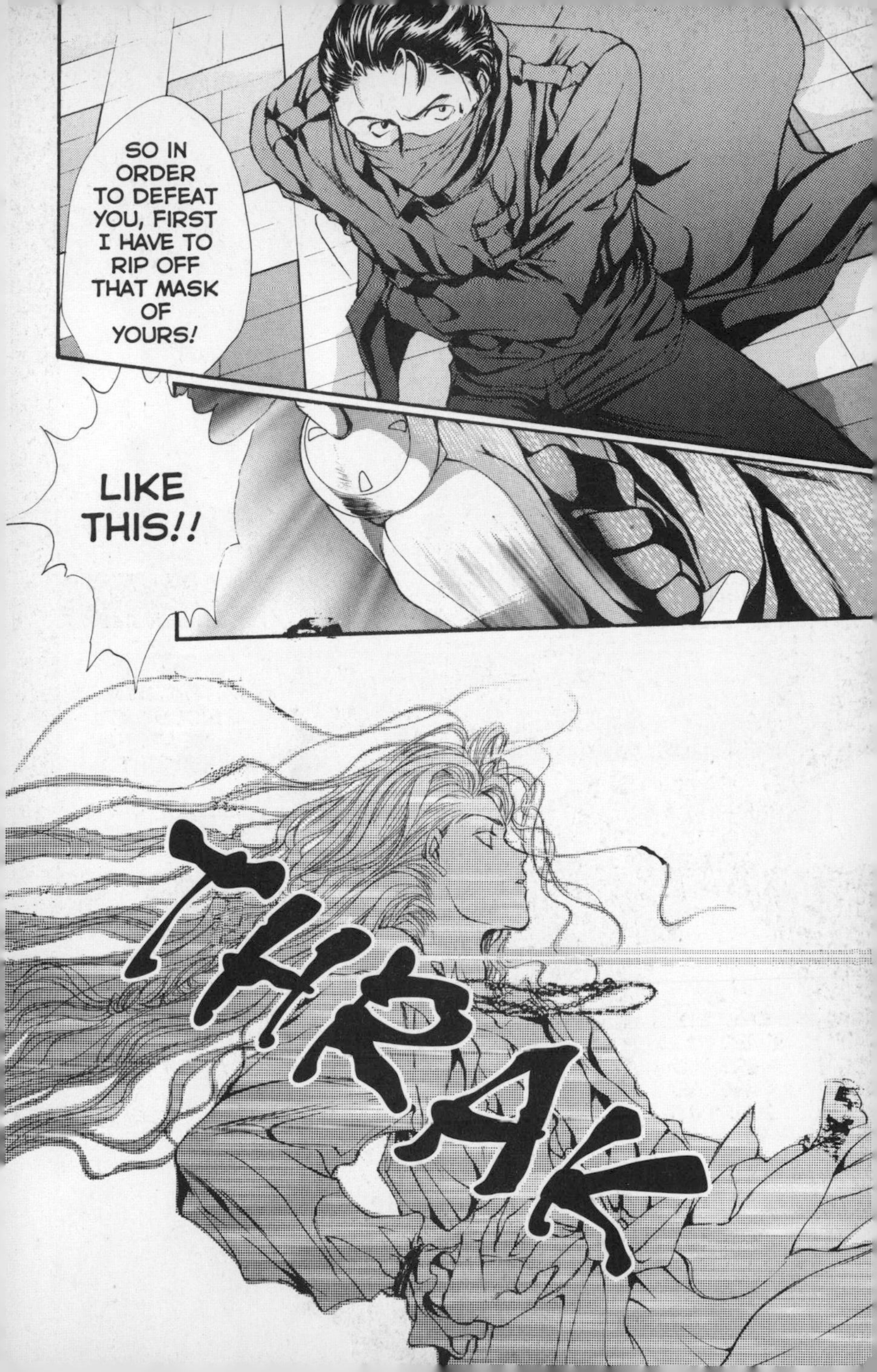
SO IN ORDER TO DEFEAT YOU, FIRST I HAVE TO RIP OFF THAT MASK OF YOURS!
LIKE THIS!!
THRAK

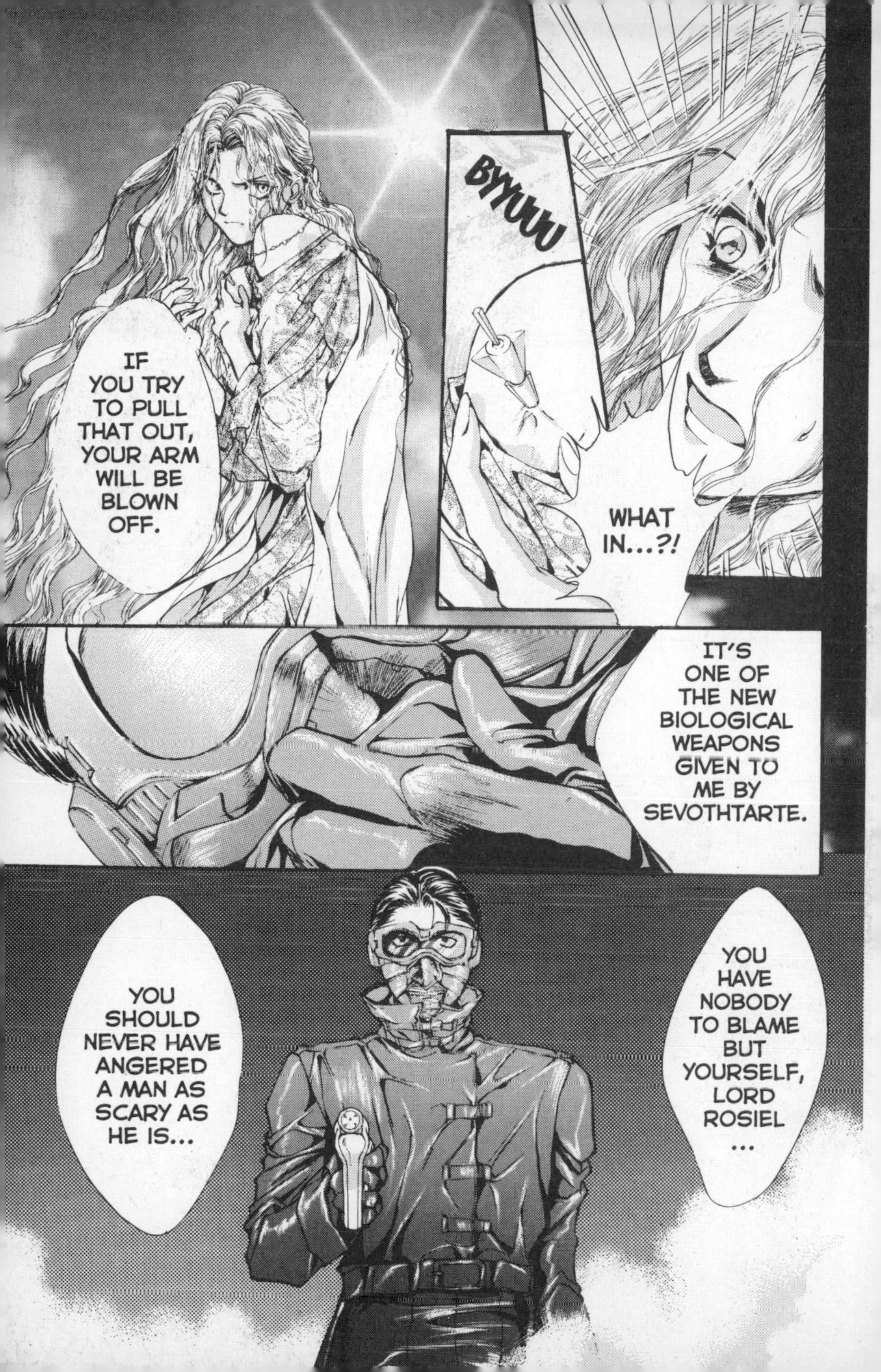
BYYUUU
WHAT IN...?!
IF YOU TRY TO PULL THAT OUT, YOUR ARM WILL BE BLOWN OFF.
IT'S ONE OF THE NEW BIOLOGICAL WEAPONS GIVEN TO ME BY SEVOTHTARTE.
YOU HAVE NOBODY TO BLAME BUT YOURSELF, LORD ROSIEL ...
YOU SHOULD NEVER HAVE ANGERED A MAN AS SCARY AS HE IS...

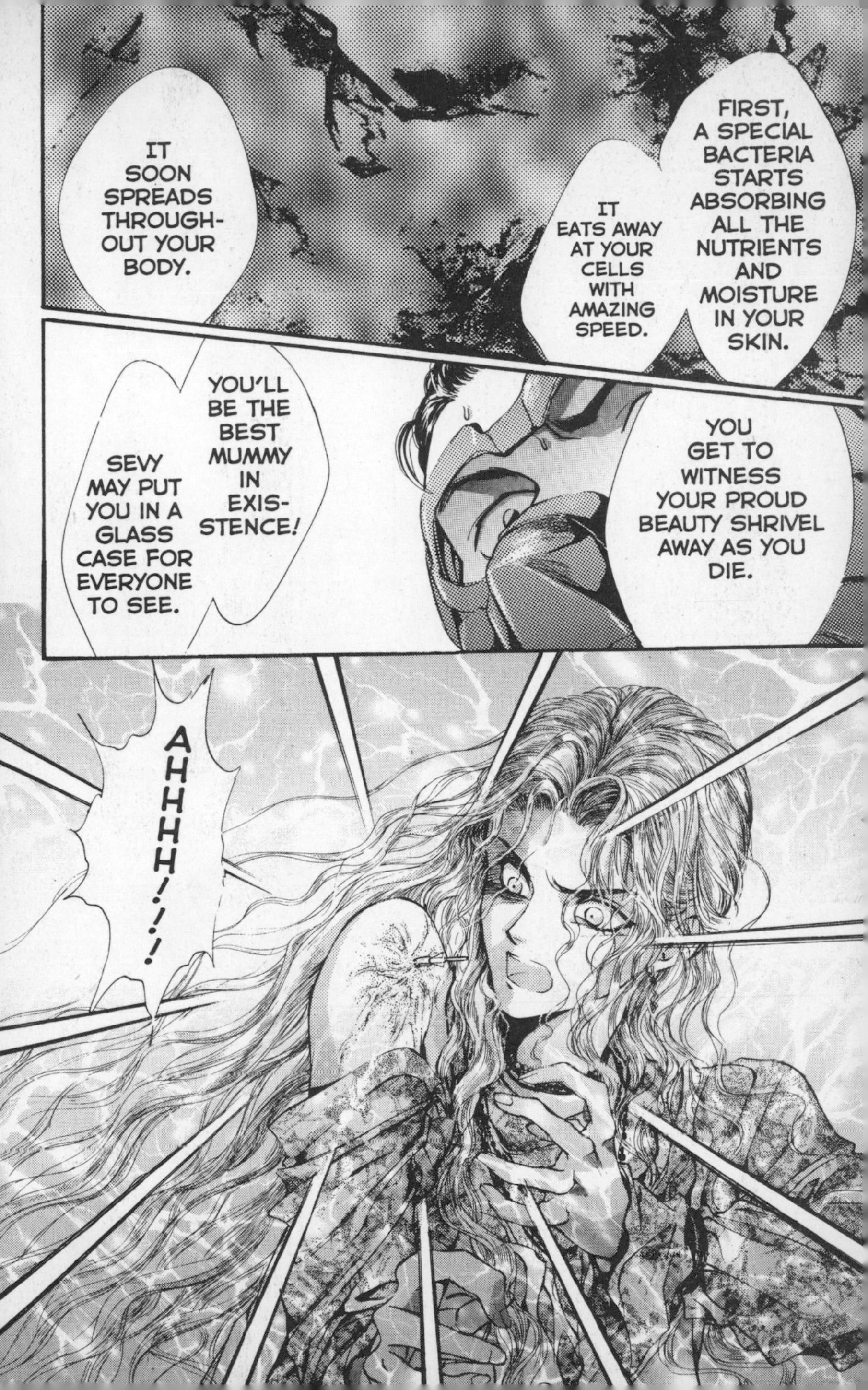
FIRST, A SPECIAL BACTERIA STARTS ABSORBING ALL THE NUTRIENTS AND MOISTURE IN YOUR SKIN.
IT EATS AWAY AT YOUR CELLS WITH AMAZING SPEED.
IT SOON SPREADS THROUGH-OUT YOUR BODY.
YOU GET TO WITNESS YOUR PROUD BEAUTY SHRIVEL AWAY AS YOU DIE.
YOU'LL BE THE BEST MUMMY IN EXIS-STENCE!
SEVY MAY PUT YOU IN A GLASS CASE FOR EVERYONE TO SEE.
AHHHH!!!!

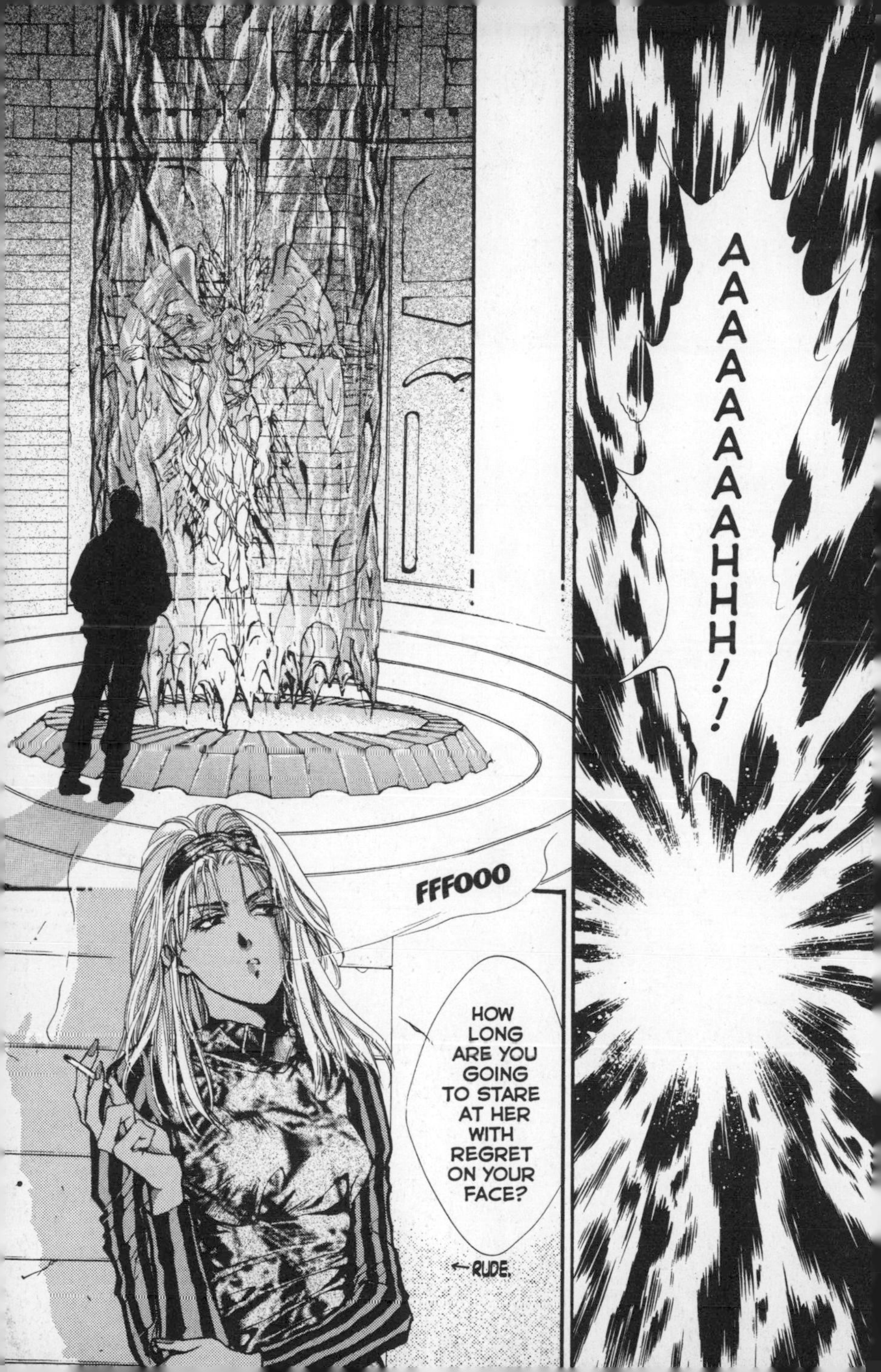
AAAAAAAAHHH!!
FFFOOO
HOW LONG ARE YOU GOING TO STARE AT HER WITH REGRET ON YOUR FACE?
←RUDE.

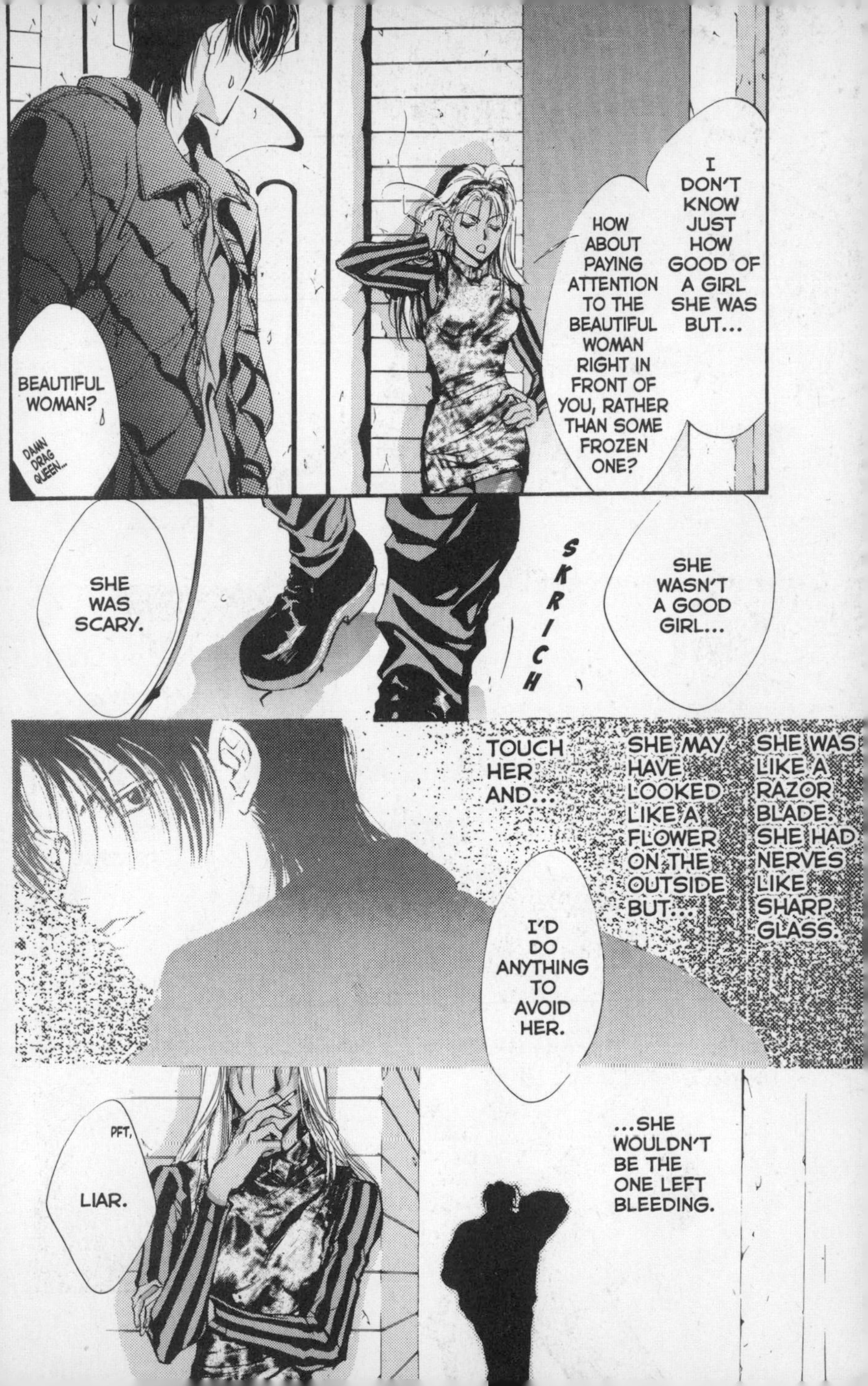
I DON'T KNOW JUST HOW GOOD OF A GIRL SHE WAS BUT...
HOW ABOUT PAYING ATTENTION TO THE BEAUTIFUL WOMAN RIGHT IN FRONT OF YOU, RATHER THAN SOME FROZEN ONE?
BEAUTIFUL WOMAN?
DAMN DRAG QUEEN...
SHE WASN'T A GOOD GIRL...
SKRICH
SHE WAS SCARY.
SHE WAS LIKE A RAZOR BLADE. SHE HAD NERVES LIKE SHARP GLASS.
SHE MAY HAVE LOOKED LIKE A FLOWER ON THE OUTSIDE BUT...
TOUCH HER AND...
I'D DO ANYTHING TO AVOID HER.
...SHE WOULDN'T BE THE ONE LEFT BLEEDING.
PFT,
LIAR.

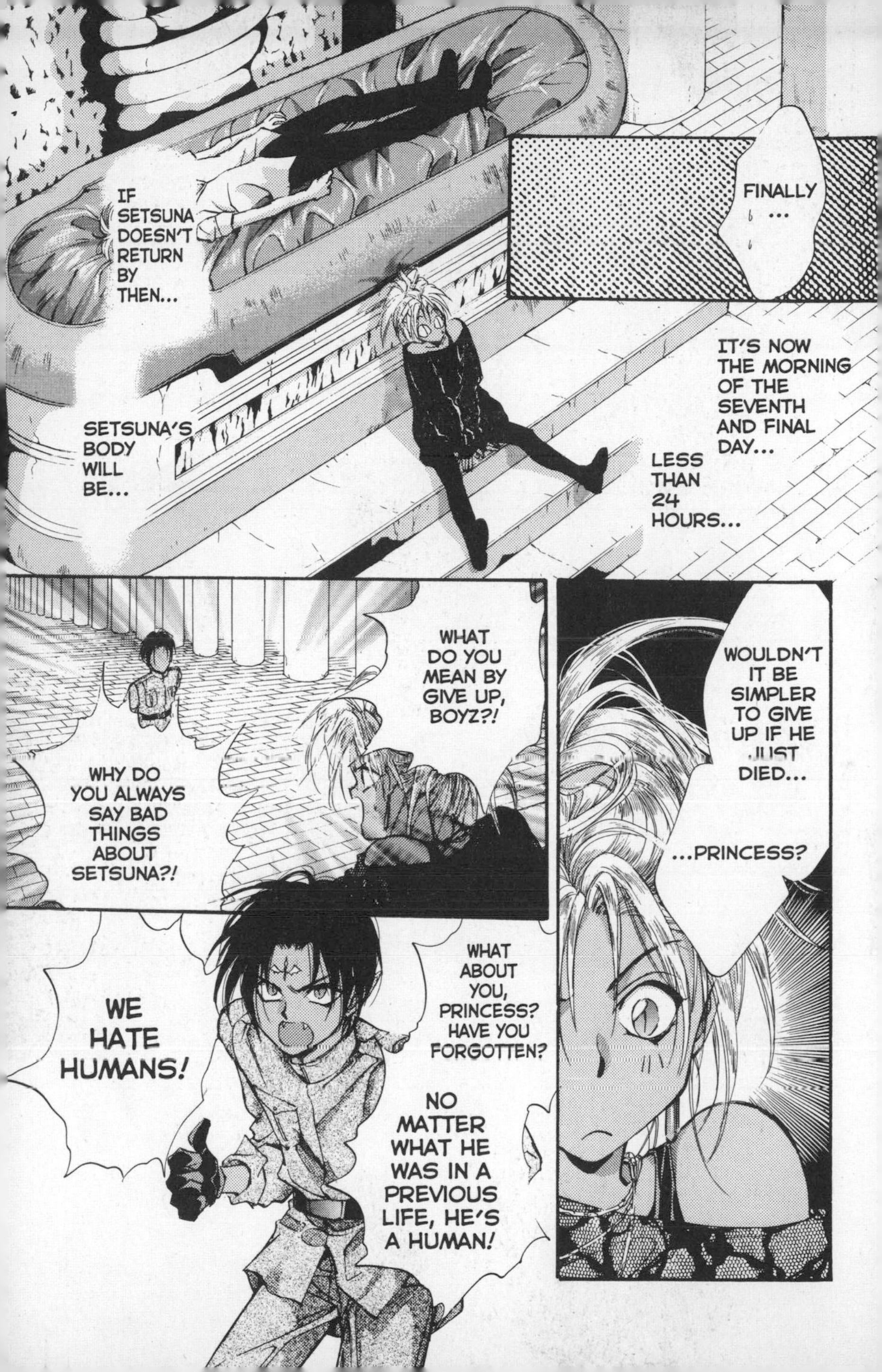
FINALLY ...
IT'S NOW THE MORNING OF THE SEVENTH AND FINAL DAY...
LESS THAN 24 HOURS...
IF SETSUNA DOESN'T RETURN BY THEN...
SETSUNA'S BODY WILL BE...
WOULDN'T IT BE SIMPLER TO GIVE UP IF HE JUST DIED...
...PRINCESS?
WHAT DO YOU MEAN BY GIVE UP, BOYZ?!
WHY DO YOU ALWAYS SAY BAD THINGS ABOUT SETSUNA?!
WHAT ABOUT YOU, PRINCESS? HAVE YOU FORGOTTEN?
NO MATTER WHAT HE WAS IN A PREVIOUS LIFE, HE'S A HUMAN!
WE HATE HUMANS!

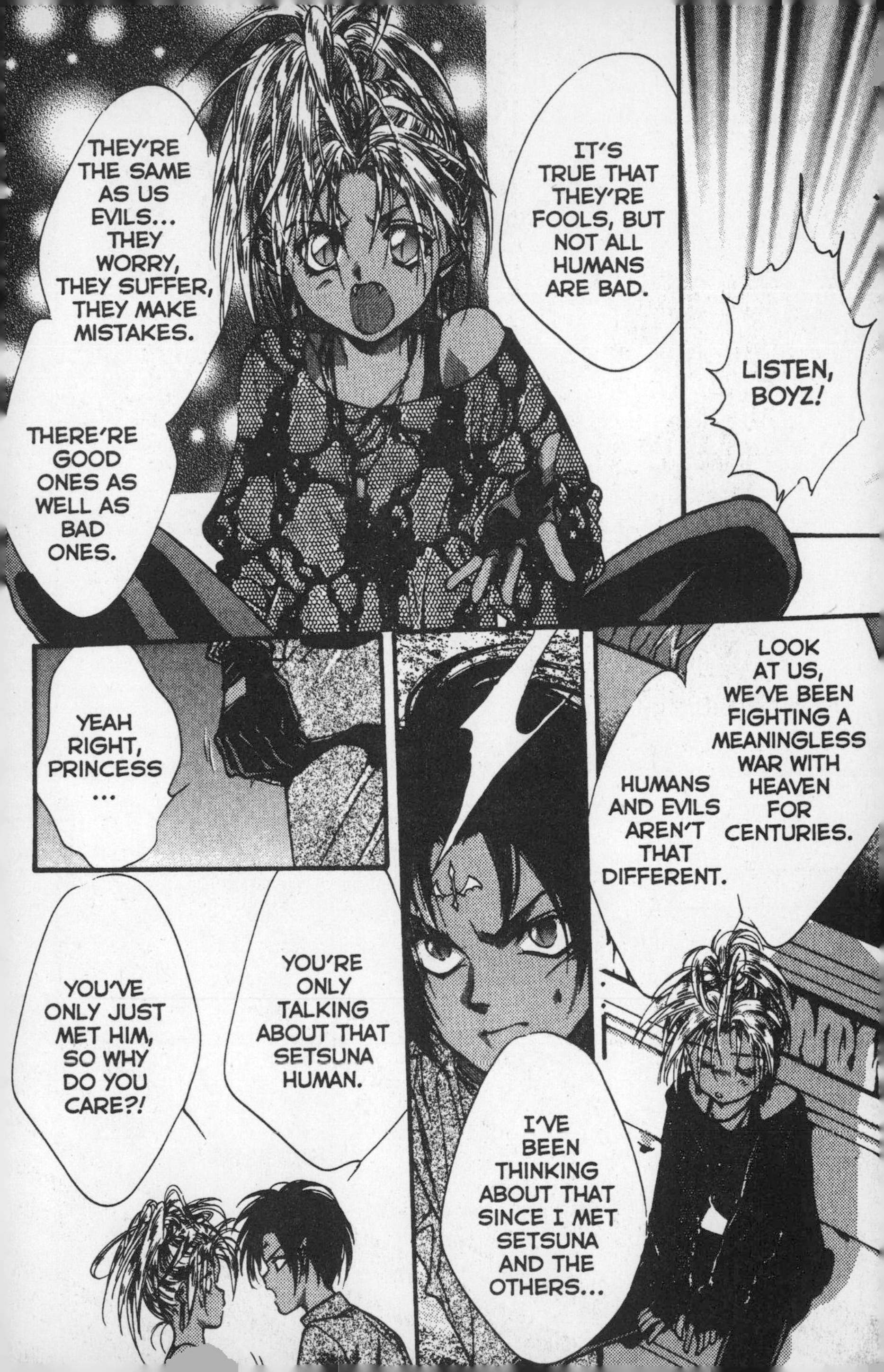
LISTEN, BOYZ!
IT'S TRUE THAT THEY'RE FOOLS, BUT NOT ALL HUMANS ARE BAD.
THEY'RE THE SAME AS US EVILS... THEY WORRY, THEY SUFFER, THEY MAKE MISTAKES.
THERE'RE GOOD ONES AS WELL AS BAD ONES.
LOOK AT US, WE'VE BEEN FIGHTING A MEANINGLESS WAR WITH HEAVEN FOR CENTURIES.
HUMANS AND EVILS AREN'T THAT DIFFERENT.
I'VE BEEN THINKING ABOUT THAT SINCE I MET SETSUNA AND THE OTHERS...
YEAH RIGHT, PRINCESS ...
YOU'RE ONLY TALKING ABOUT THAT SETSUNA HUMAN.
YOU'VE ONLY JUST MET HIM, SO WHY DO YOU CARE?!

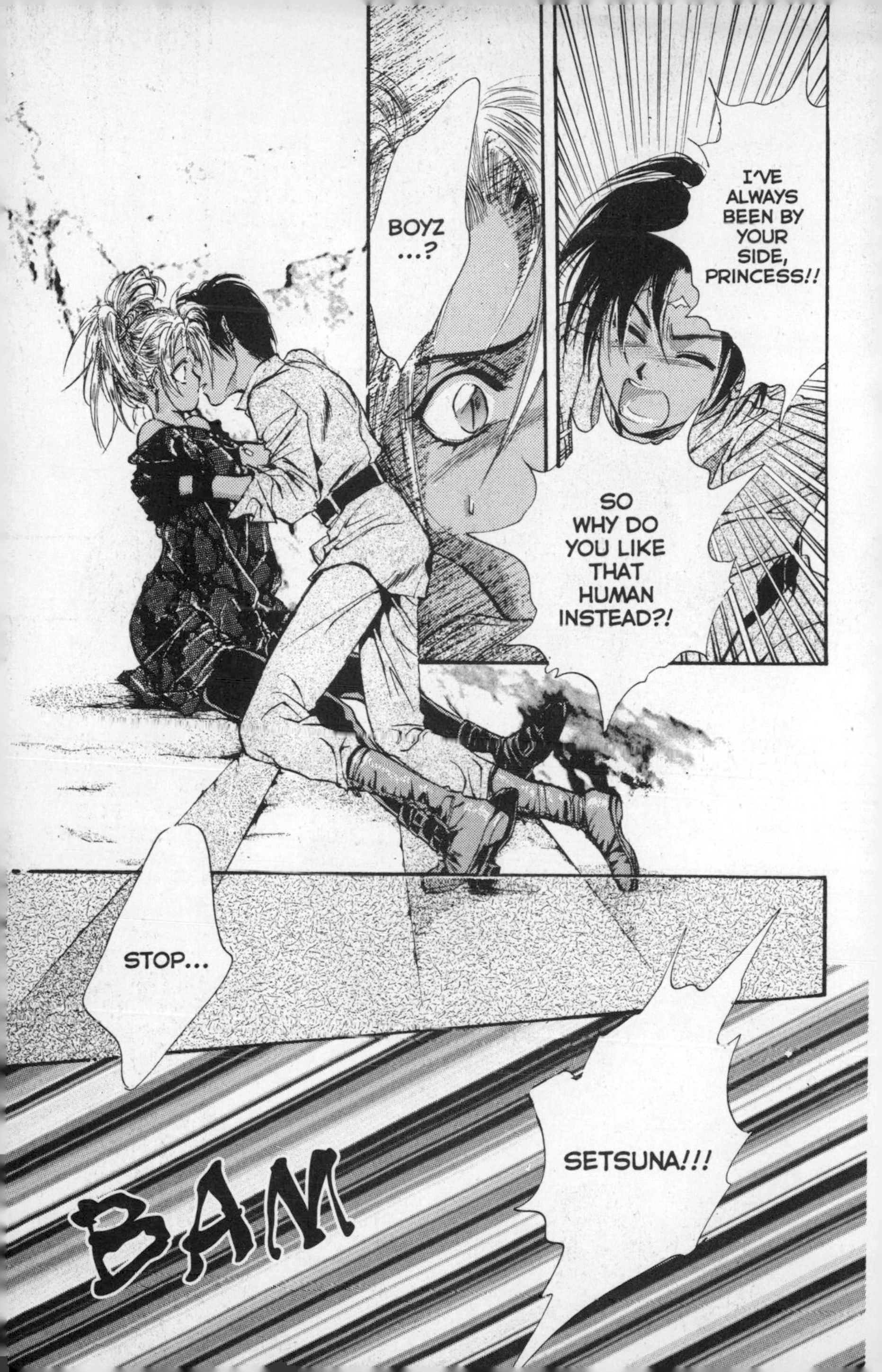
I'VE ALWAYS BEEN BY YOUR SIDE, PRINCESS!!
SO WHY DO YOU LIKE THAT HUMAN INSTEAD?!
BOYZ ...?
STOP...
SETSUNA!!!
BAM

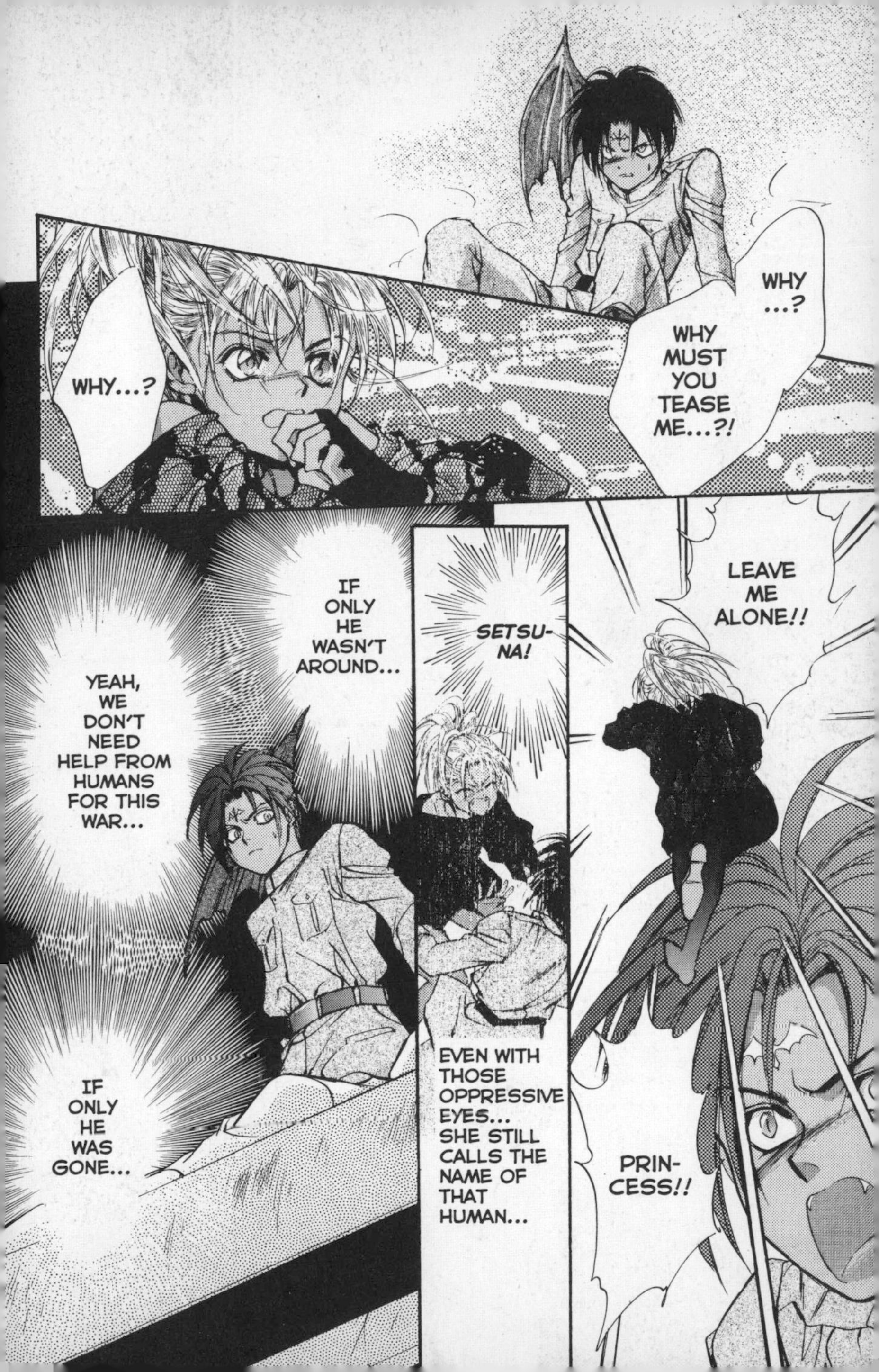
WHY ...?
WHY MUST YOU TEASE ME...?!
WHY...?
LEAVE ME ALONE!!
PRIN-CESS!!
SETSU-NA!
EVEN WITH THOSE OPPRESSIVE EYES... SHE STILL CALLS THE NAME OF THAT HUMAN...
IF ONLY HE WASN'T AROUND...
YEAH, WE DON'T NEED HELP FROM HUMANS FOR THIS WAR...
IF ONLY HE WAS GONE...

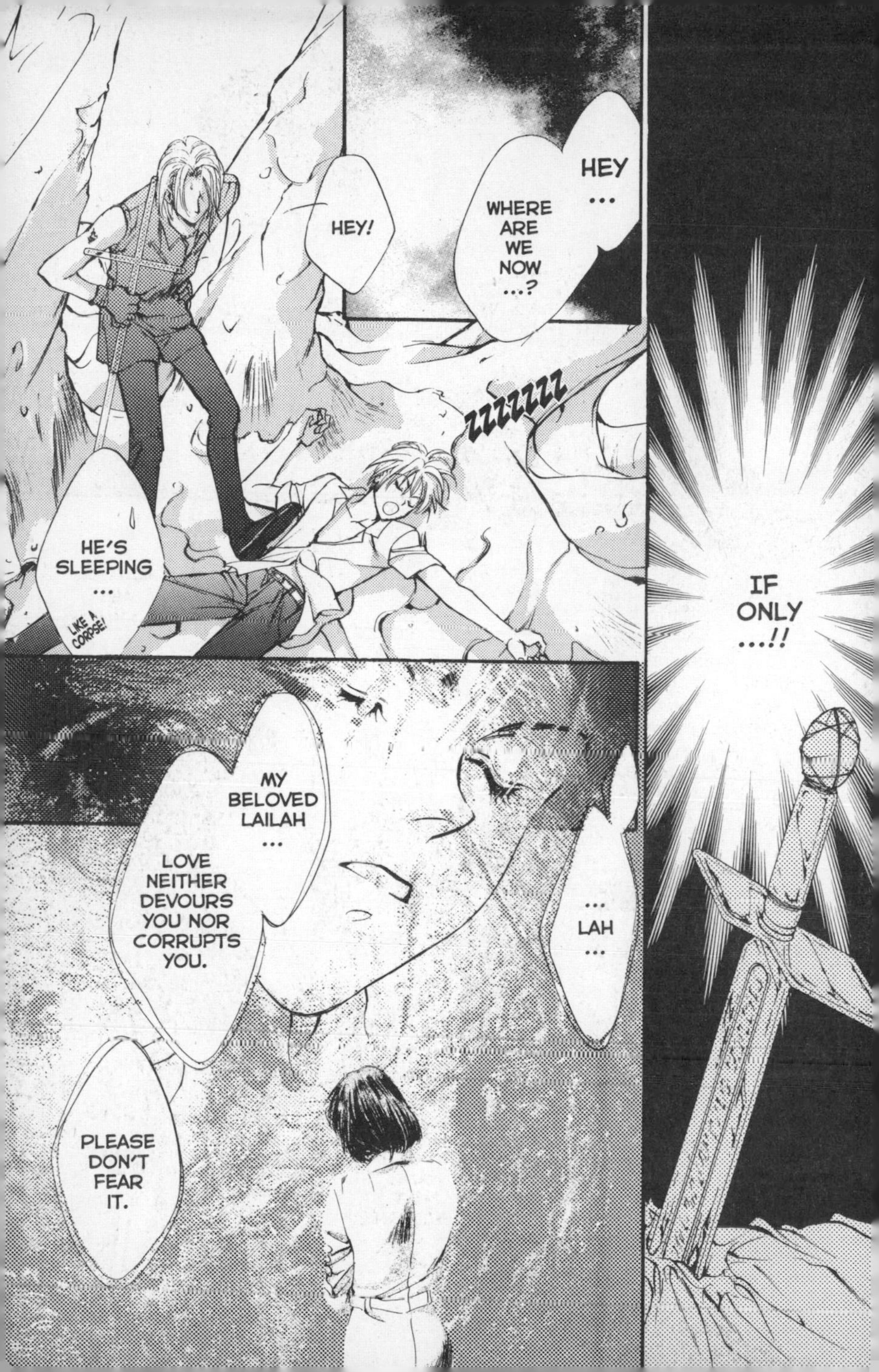
IF ONLY ...!!
HEY ...
WHERE ARE WE NOW ...?
HEY!
ZZZZZZZ
HE'S SLEEPING ...
LIKE A CORPSE!
... LAH ...
MY BELOVED LAILAH ...
LOVE NEITHER DEVOURS YOU NOR CORRUPTS YOU.
PLEASE DON'T FEAR IT.

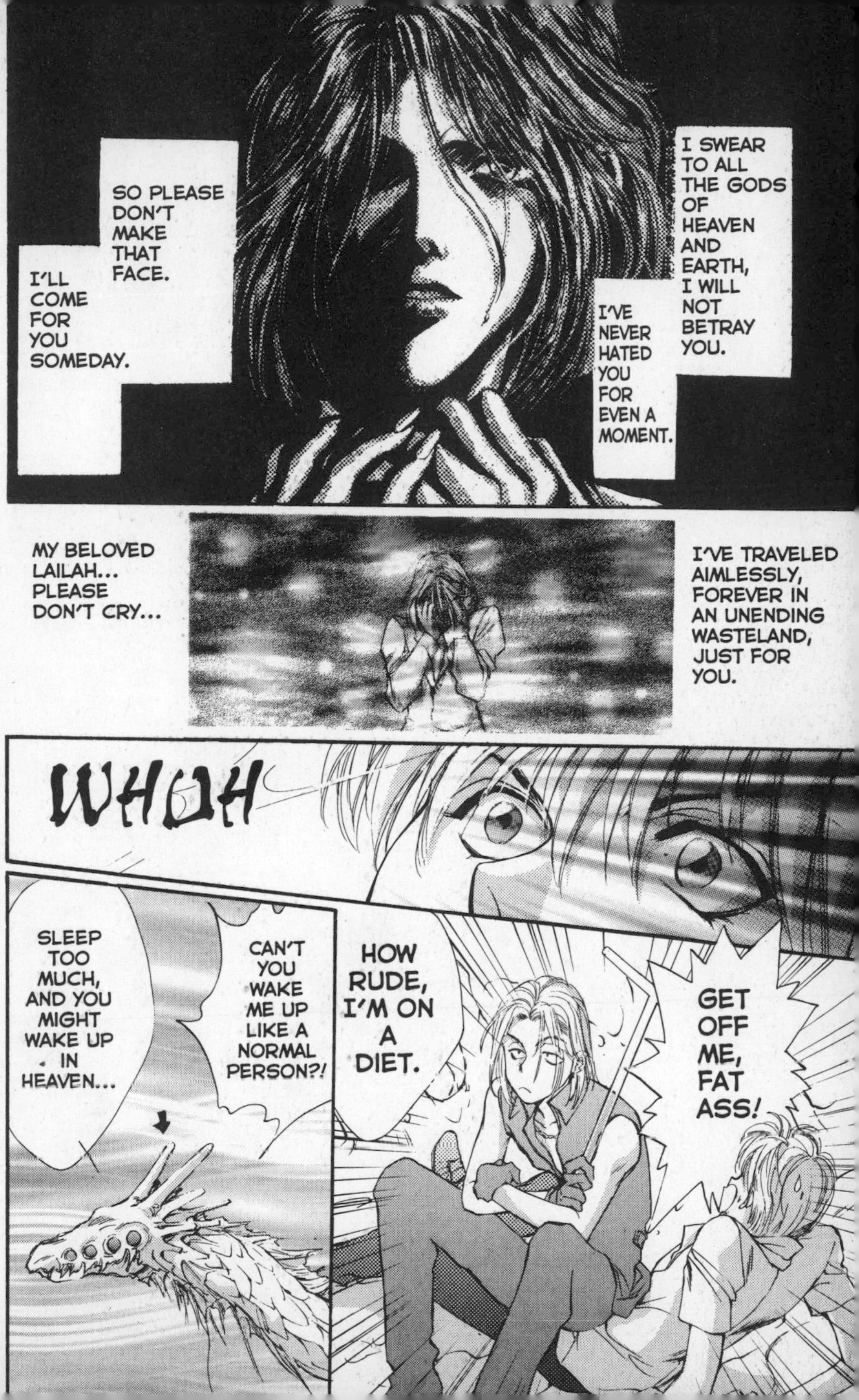
I SWEAR TO ALL THE GODS OF HEAVEN AND EARTH, I WILL NOT BETRAY YOU.
I'VE NEVER HATED YOU FOR EVEN A MOMENT.
SO PLEASE DON'T MAKE THAT FACE.
I'LL COME FOR YOU SOMEDAY.
I'VE TRAVELED AIMLESSLY, FOREVER IN AN UNENDING WASTELAND, JUST FOR YOU.
MY BELOVED LAILAH... PLEASE DON'T CRY...
WHOH
GET OFF ME, FAT ASS!
HOW RUDE, I'M ON A DIET.
CAN'T YOU WAKE ME UP LIKE A NORMAL PERSON?!
SLEEP TOO MUCH, AND YOU MIGHT WAKE UP IN HEAVEN...

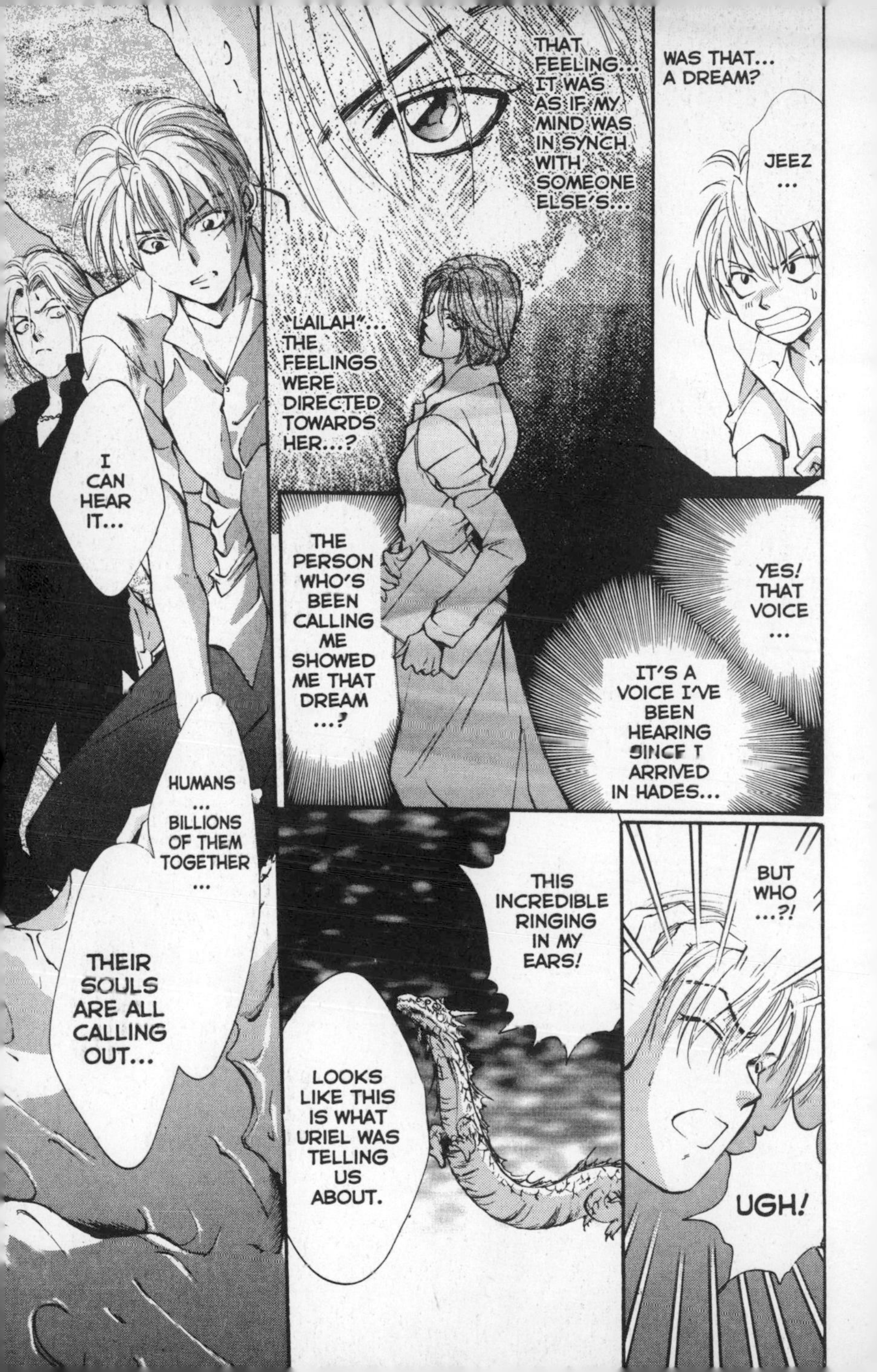
WAS THAT... A DREAM?
JEEZ ...
THAT FEELING... IT WAS AS IF MY MIND WAS IN SYNCH WITH SOMEONE ELSE'S...
"LAILAH"... THE FEELINGS WERE DIRECTED TOWARDS HER...?
YES! THAT VOICE ...
IT'S A VOICE I'VE BEEN HEARING SINCE I ARRIVED IN HADES...
THE PERSON WHO'S BEEN CALLING ME SHOWED ME THAT DREAM ...?
BUT WHO ...?!
UGH!
THIS INCREDIBLE RINGING IN MY EARS!
LOOKS LIKE THIS IS WHAT URIEL WAS TELLING US ABOUT.
I CAN HEAR IT...
HUMANS ... BILLIONS OF THEM TOGETHER ...
THEIR SOULS ARE ALL CALLING OUT...

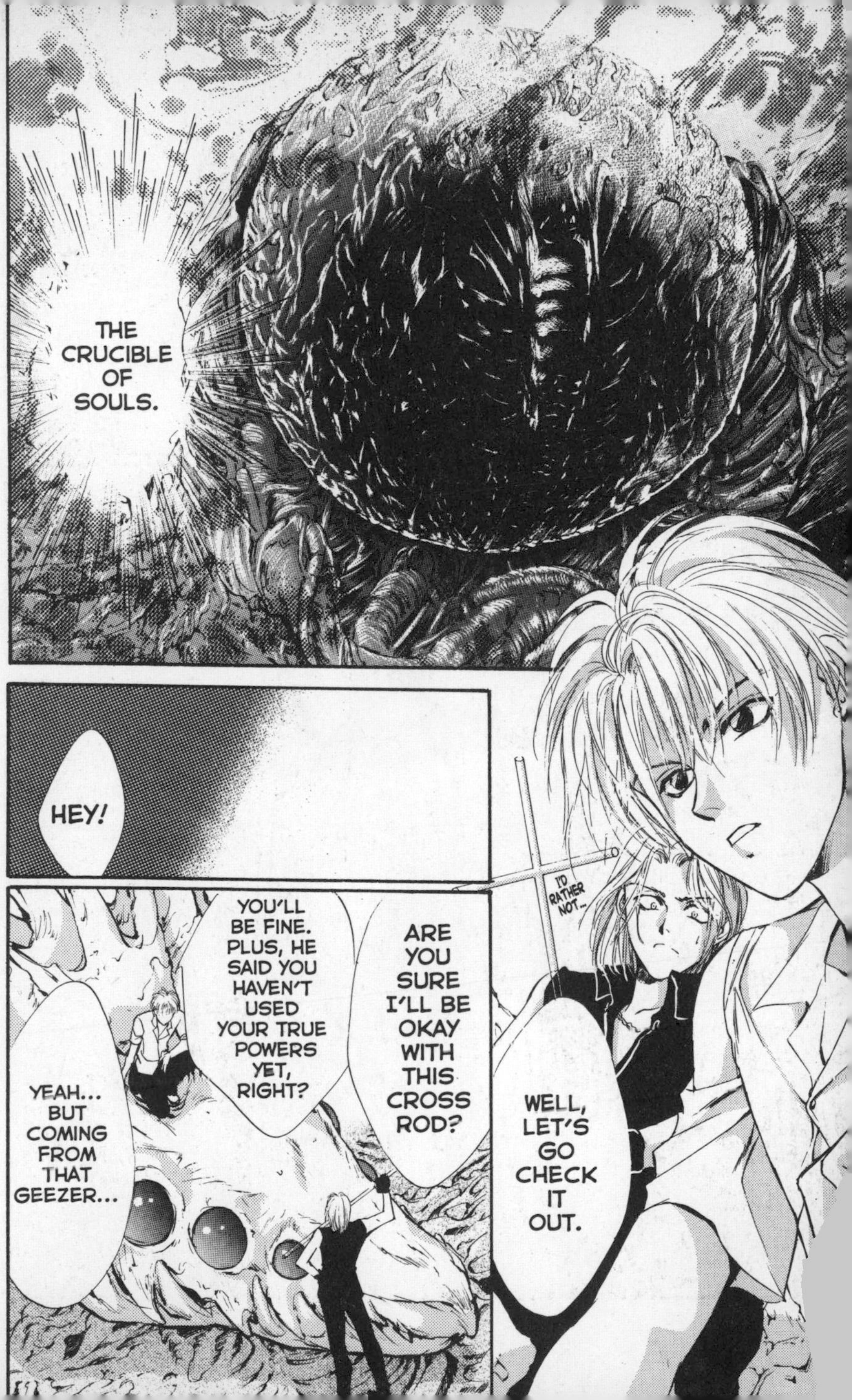
THE CRUCIBLE OF SOULS.
I'D RATHER NOT...
WELL, LET'S GO CHECK IT OUT.
HEY!
ARE YOU SURE I'LL BE OKAY WITH THIS CROSS ROD?
YOU'LL BE FINE. PLUS, HE SAID YOU HAVEN'T USED YOUR TRUE POWERS YET, RIGHT?
YEAH... BUT COMING FROM THAT GEEZER...

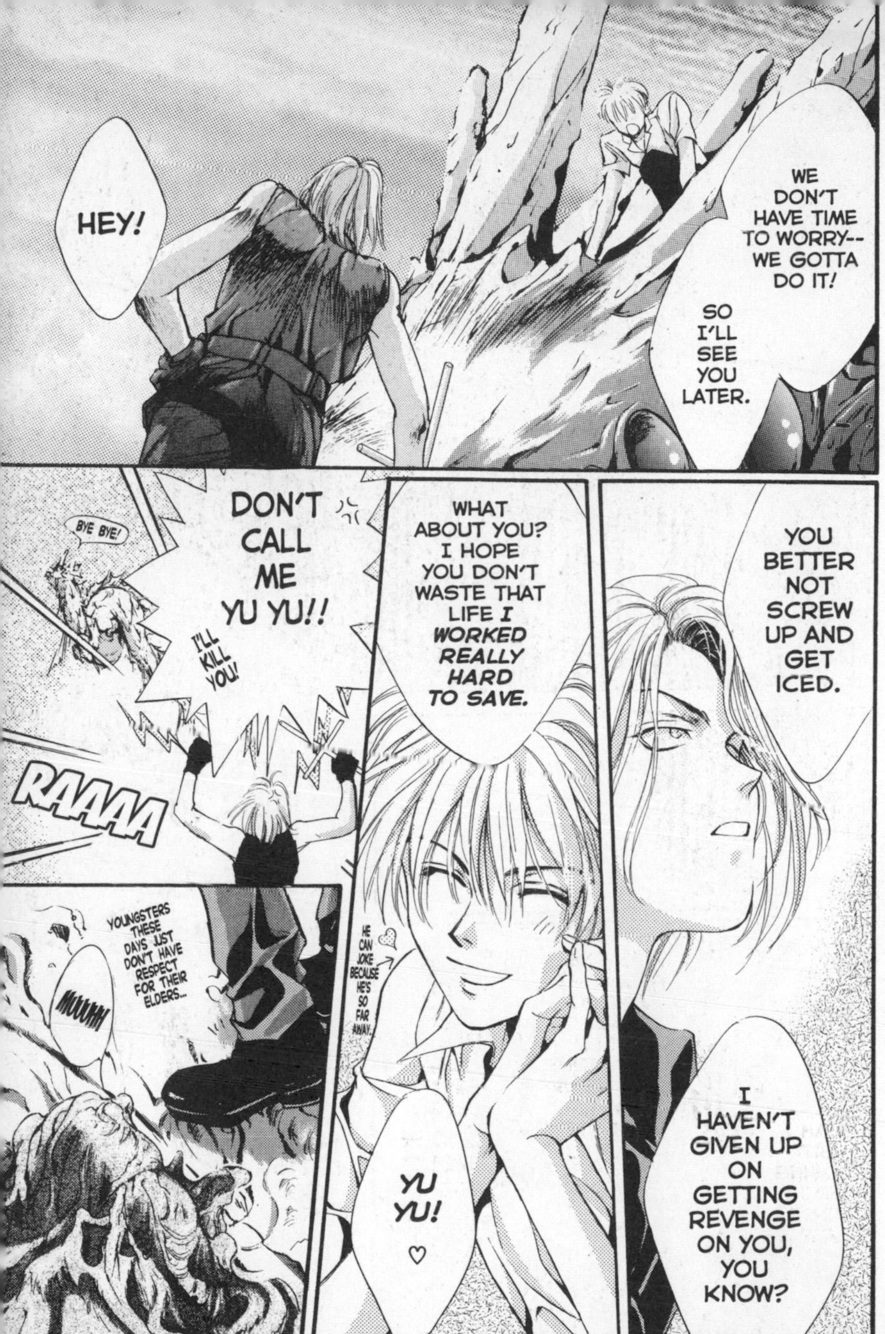
WE DON'T HAVE TIME TO WORRY-- WE GOTTA DO IT!
SO I'LL SEE YOU LATER.
HEY!
YOU BETTER NOT SCREW UP AND GET ICED.
I HAVEN'T GIVEN UP ON GETTING REVENGE ON YOU, YOU KNOW?
WHAT ABOUT YOU? I HOPE YOU DON'T WASTE THAT LIFE I WORKED REALLY HARD TO SAVE.
HE CAN JOKE BECAUSE HE'S SO FAR AWAY...
YU YU! ♡
DON'T CALL ME YU YU!!
BYE BYE!
I'LL KILL YOU!
RAAAAA
YOUNGSTERS THESE DAYS JUST DON'T HAVE RESPECT FOR THEIR ELDERS...

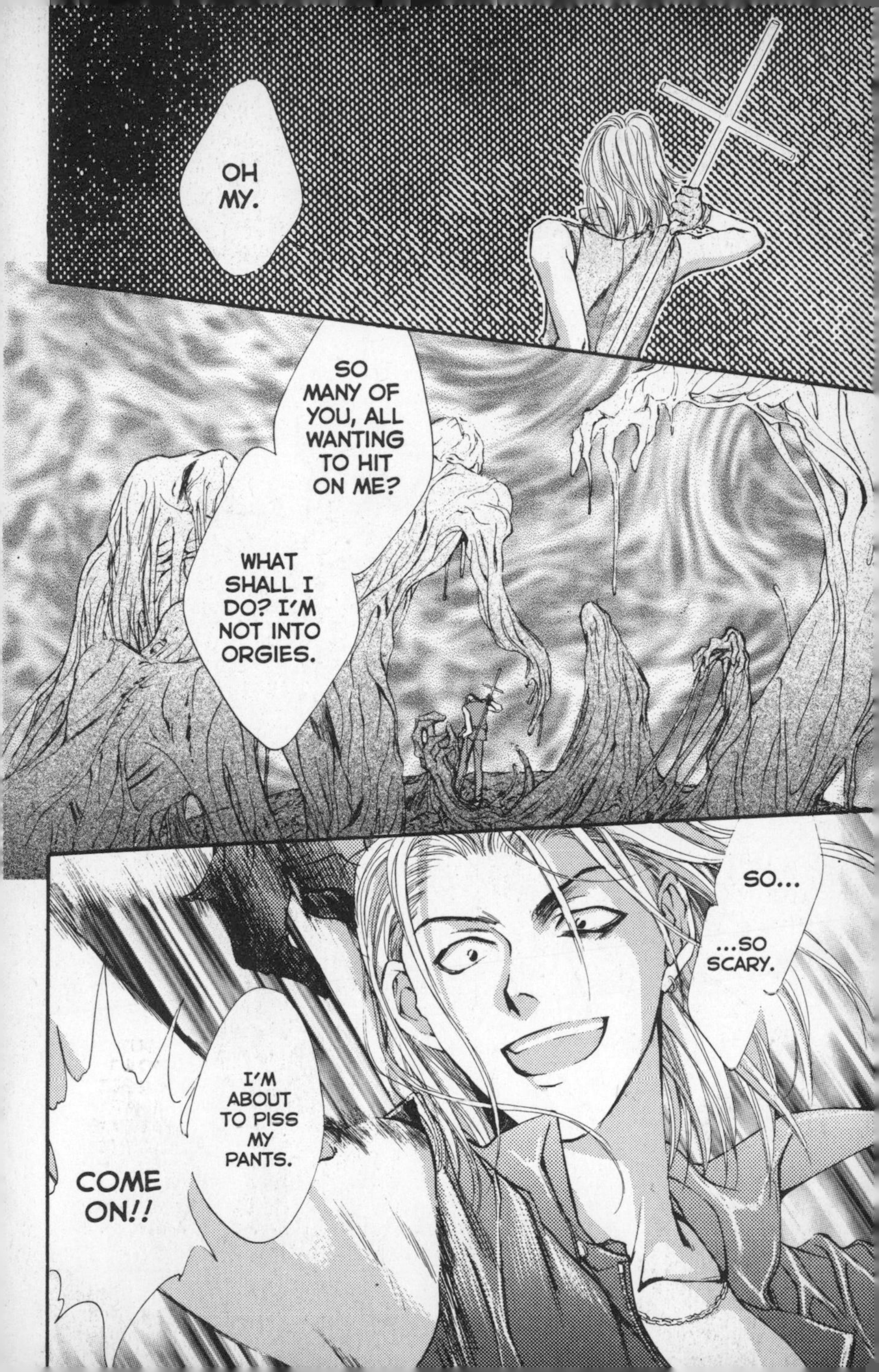
OH MY.
SO MANY OF YOU, ALL WANTING TO HIT ON ME?
WHAT SHALL I DO? I'M NOT INTO ORGIES.
SO...
...SO SCARY.
I'M ABOUT TO PISS MY PANTS.
COME ON!!

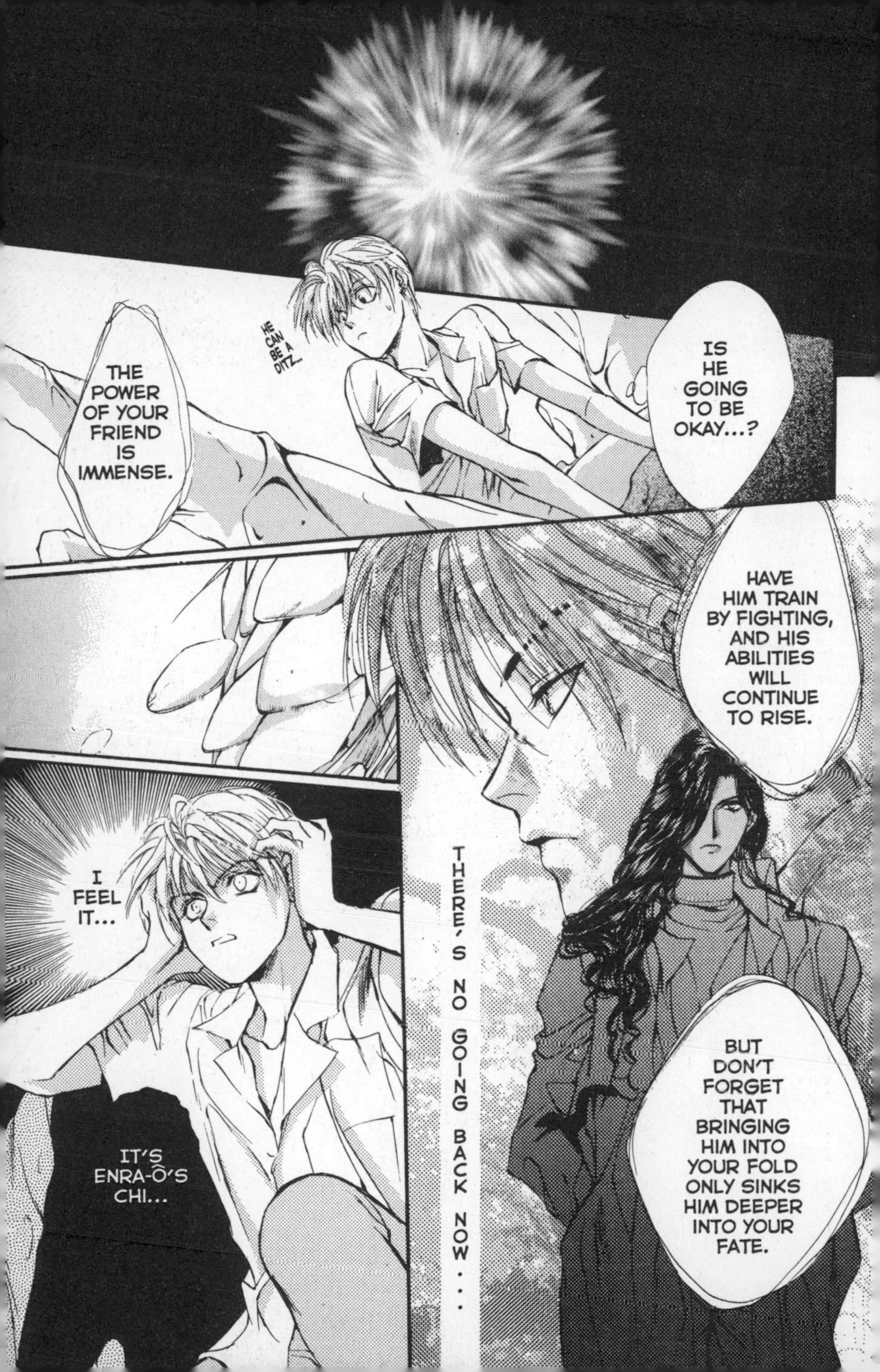
IS HE GOING TO BE OKAY...?
HE CAN BE A DITZ...
THE POWER OF YOUR FRIEND IS IMMENSE.
HAVE HIM TRAIN BY FIGHTING, AND HIS ABILITIES WILL CONTINUE TO RISE.
BUT DON'T FORGET THAT BRINGING HIM INTO YOUR FOLD ONLY SINKS HIM DEEPER INTO YOUR FATE.
THERE'S NO GOING BACK NOW...
I FEEL IT...
IT'S ENRA-Ô'S CHI...

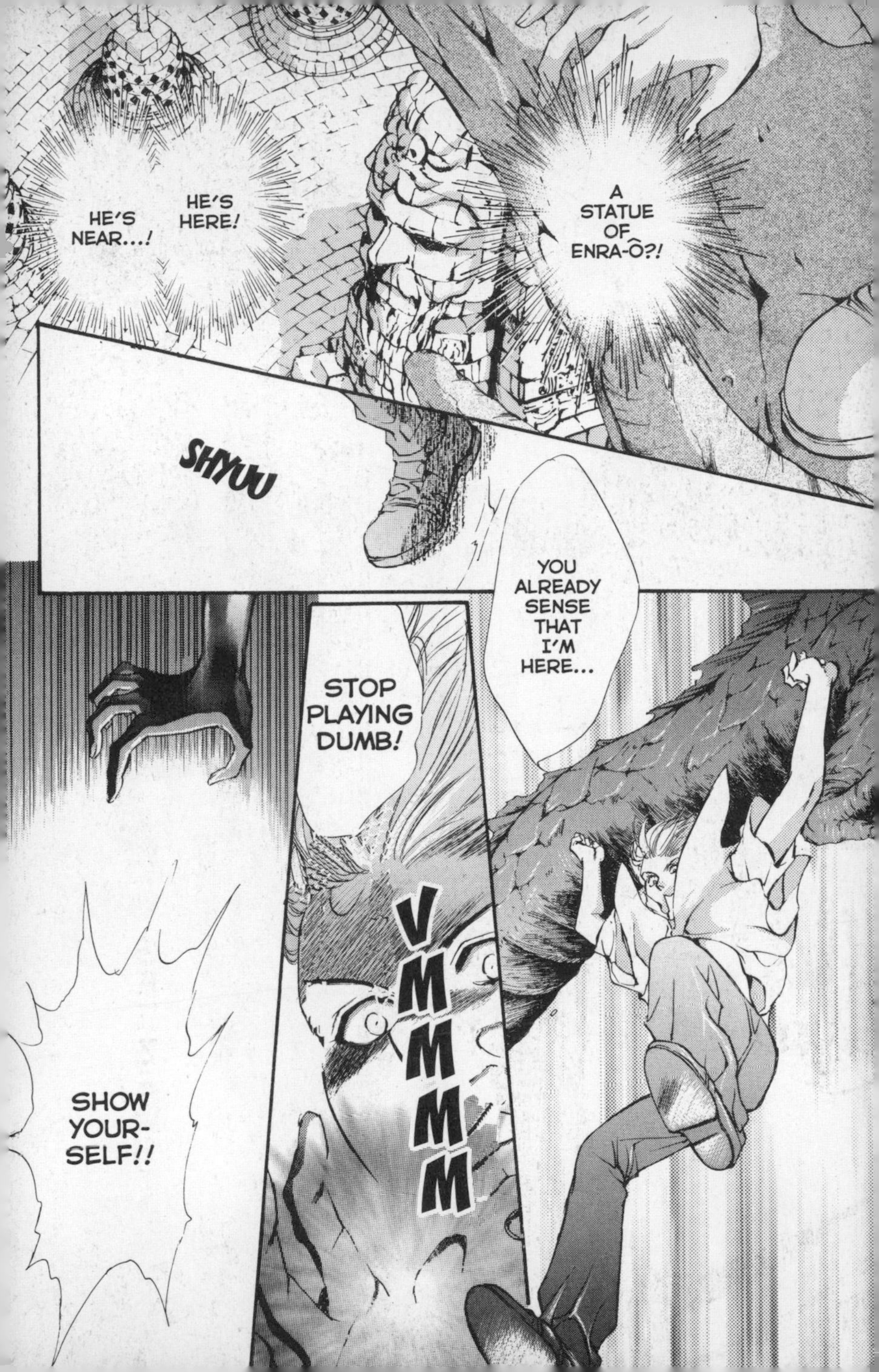
A STATUE OF ENRA-Ô?!
HE'S HERE!
HE'S NEAR...!
SHYUU
YOU ALREADY SENSE THAT I'M HERE...
STOP PLAYING DUMB!
VMMMM
SHOW YOUR-SELF!!

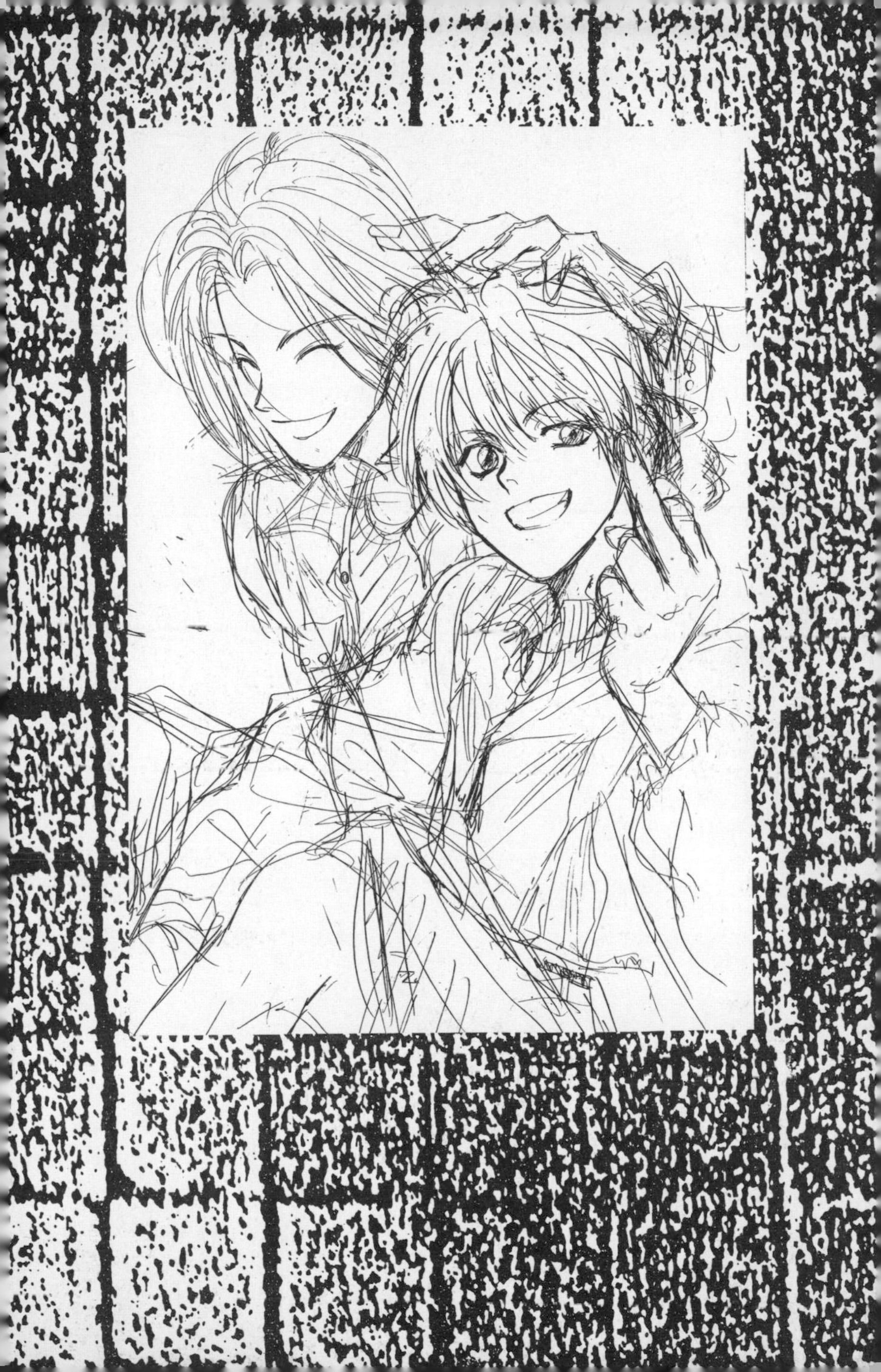

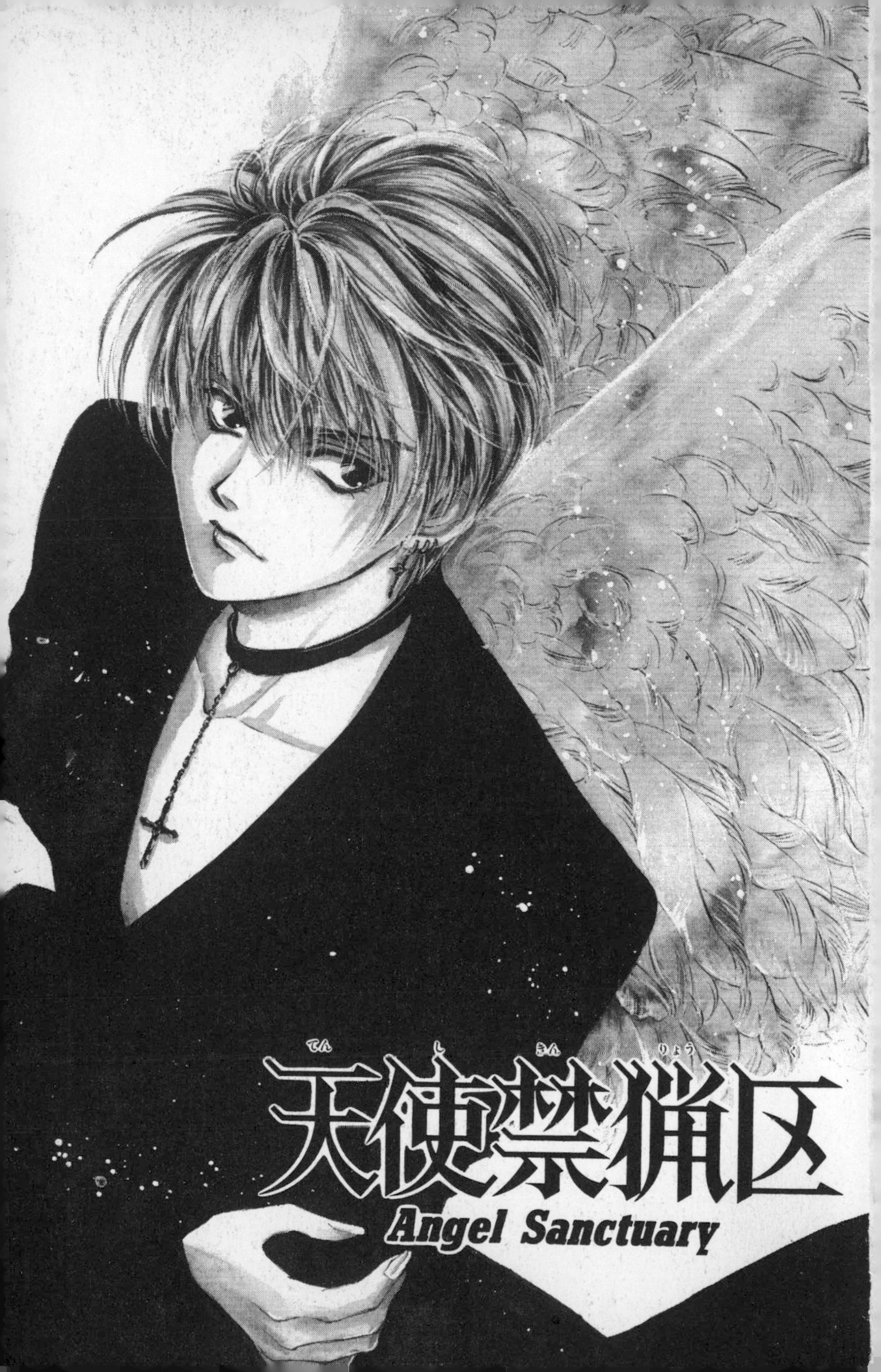
天使禁猟区
Angel Sanctuary

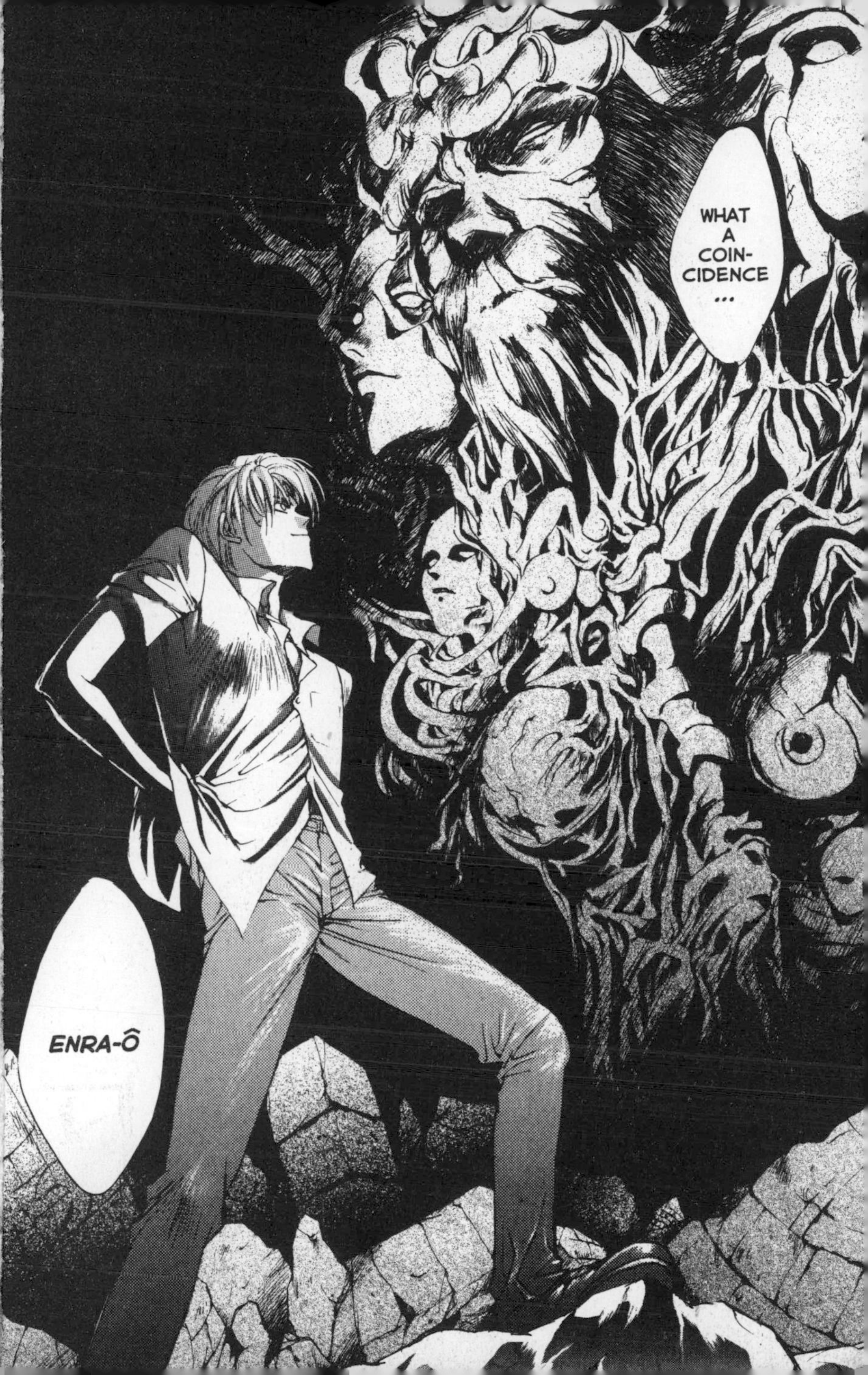
WHAT A COIN-CIDENCE ...
ENRA-Ô

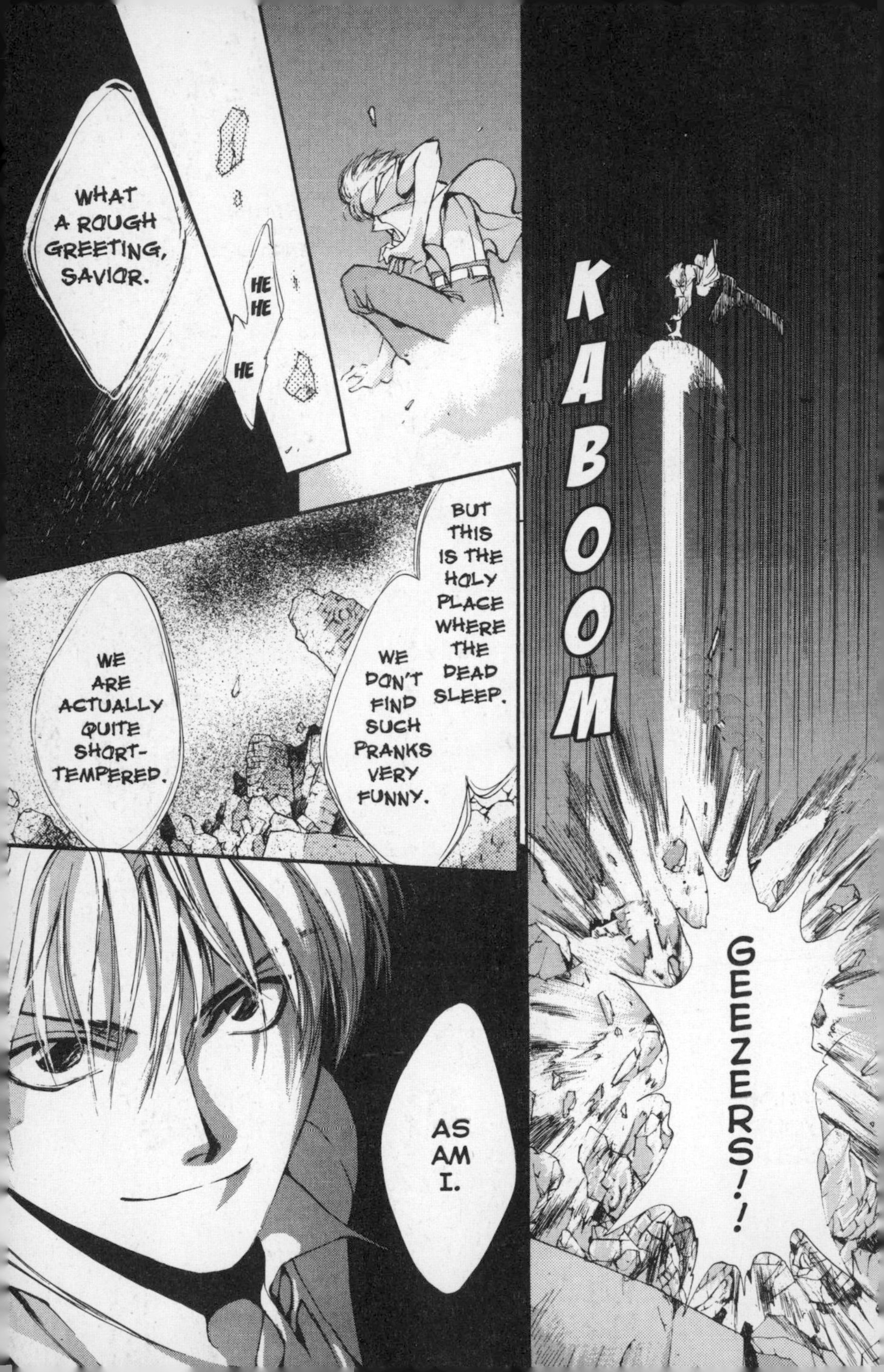
KABOOM
GEEZERS!!
HE HE HE
WHAT A ROUGH GREETING, SAVIOR.
BUT THIS IS THE HOLY PLACE WHERE THE DEAD SLEEP.
WE DON'T FIND SUCH PRANKS VERY FUNNY.
WE ARE ACTUALLY QUITE SHORT-TEMPERED.
AS AM I.

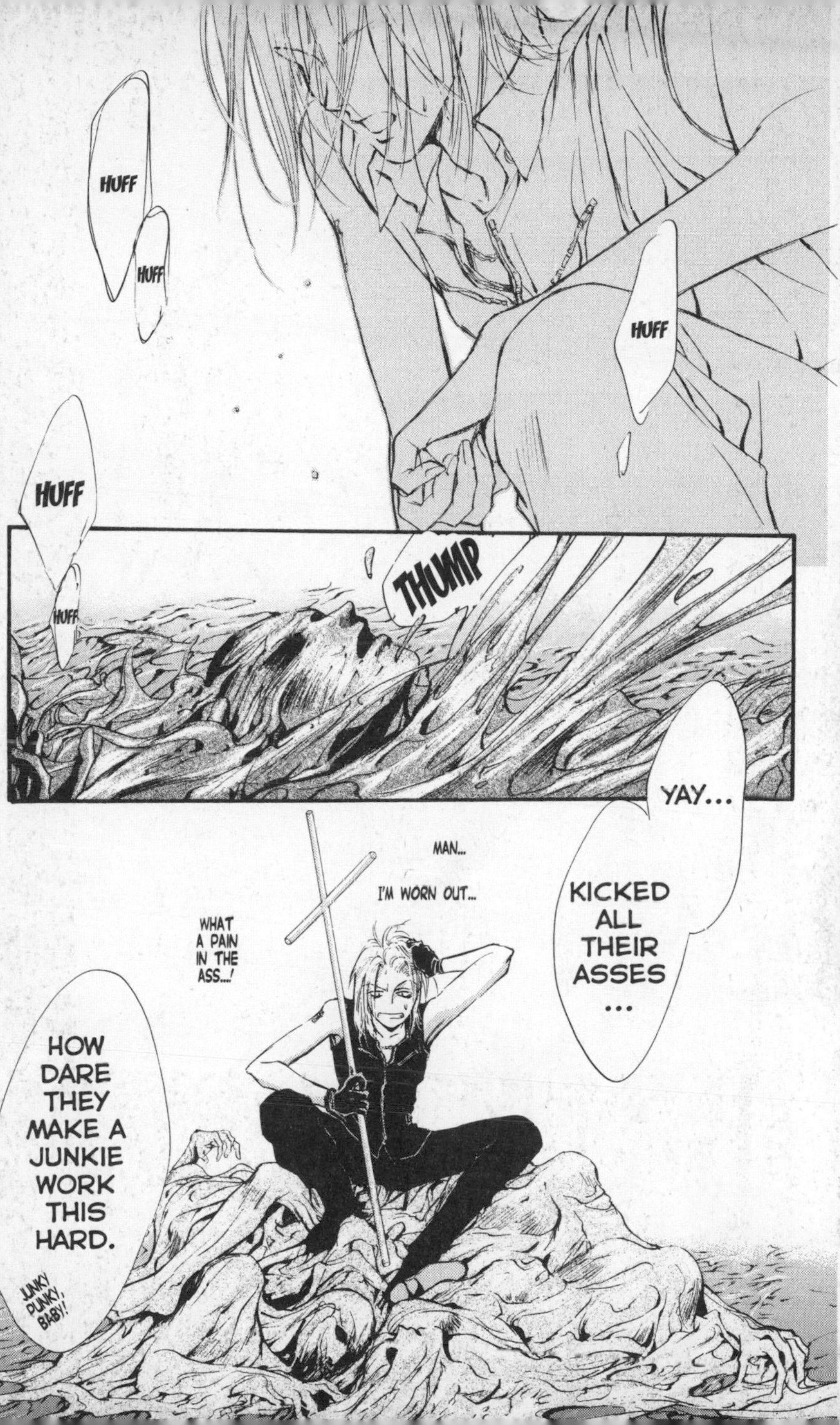
HUFF
HUFF
HUFF
HUFF
HUFF
THUMP
YAY... KICKED ALL THEIR ASSES...
MAN... I'M WORN OUT...
WHAT A PAIN IN THE ASS...!
HOW DARE THEY MAKE A JUNKIE WORK THIS HARD.
JUNKY PUNKY, BABY!

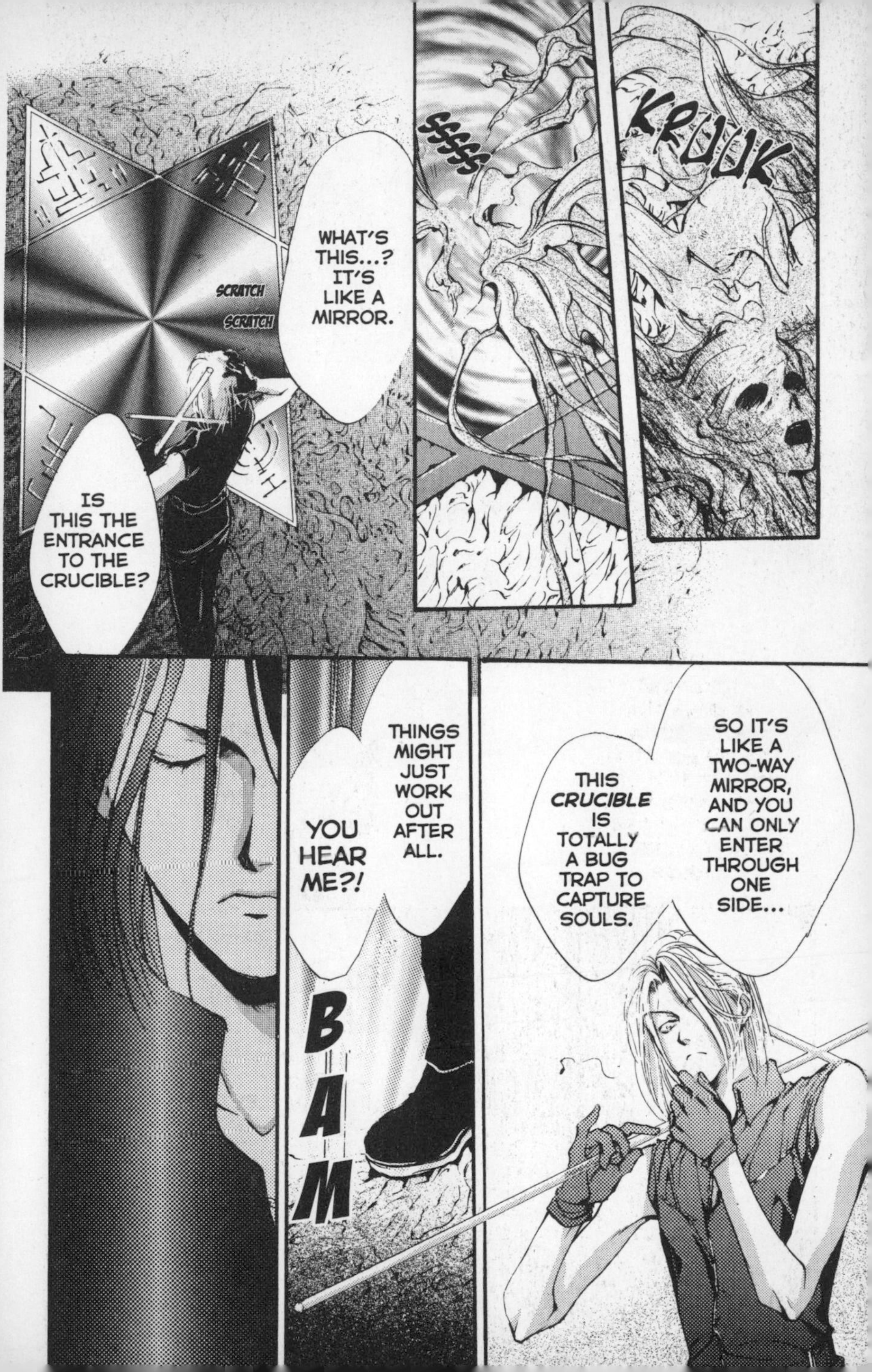
KRUUK
SSSSS
WHAT'S THIS...? IT'S LIKE A MIRROR.
SCRATCH
SCRATCH
IS THIS THE ENTRANCE TO THE CRUCIBLE?
SO IT'S LIKE A TWO-WAY MIRROR, AND YOU CAN ONLY ENTER THROUGH ONE SIDE...
THIS *CRUCIBLE* IS TOTALLY A BUG TRAP TO CAPTURE SOULS.
THINGS MIGHT JUST WORK OUT AFTER ALL.
YOU HEAR ME?!
BAM

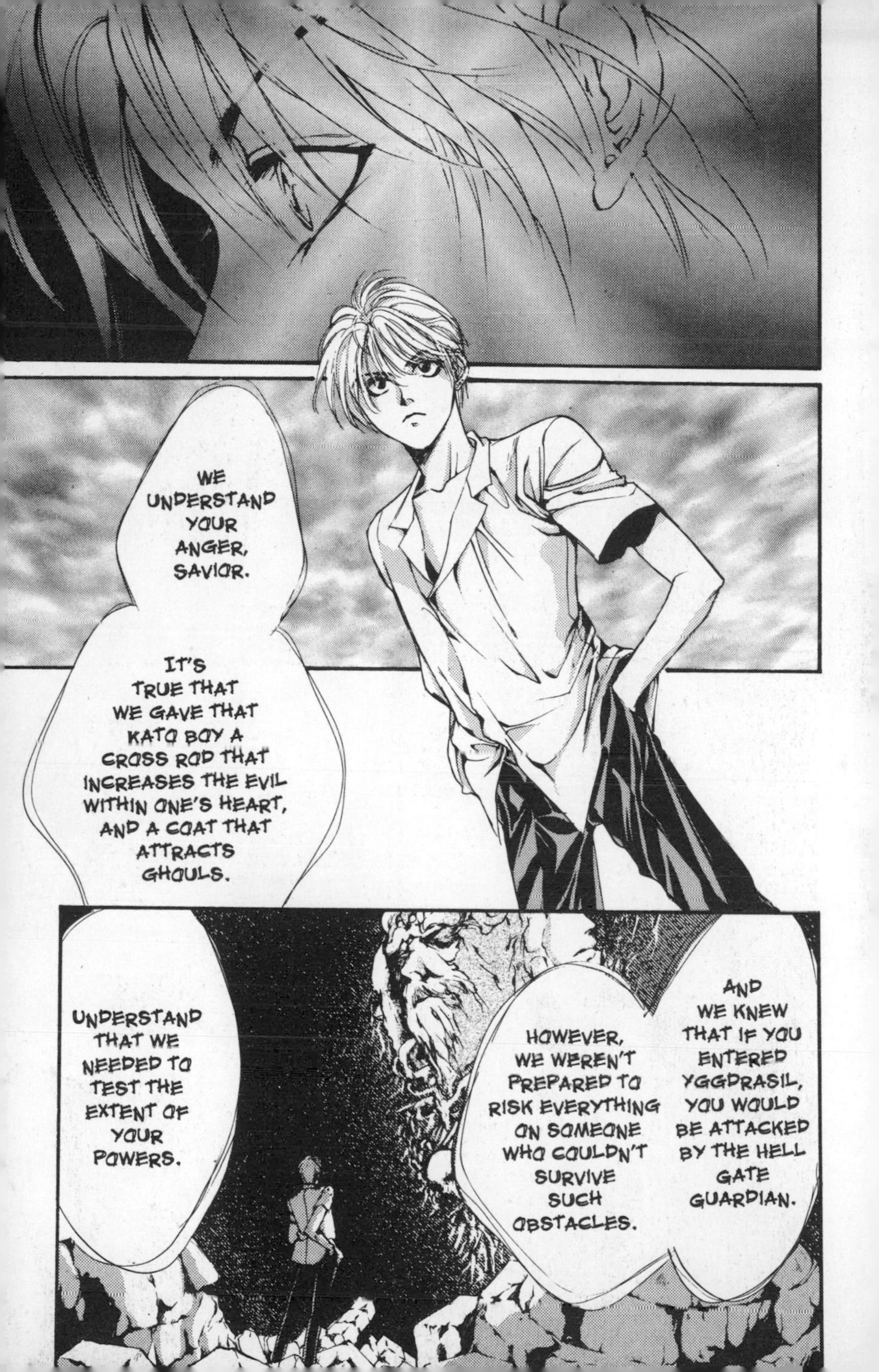
WE UNDERSTAND YOUR ANGER, SAVIOR.
IT'S TRUE THAT WE GAVE THAT KATO BOY A CROSS ROD THAT INCREASES THE EVIL WITHIN ONE'S HEART, AND A COAT THAT ATTRACTS GHOULS.
AND WE KNEW THAT IF YOU ENTERED YGGDRASIL, YOU WOULD BE ATTACKED BY THE HELL GATE GUARDIAN.
HOWEVER, WE WEREN'T PREPARED TO RISK EVERYTHING ON SOMEONE WHO COULDN'T SURVIVE SUCH OBSTACLES.
UNDERSTAND THAT WE NEEDED TO TEST THE EXTENT OF YOUR POWERS.

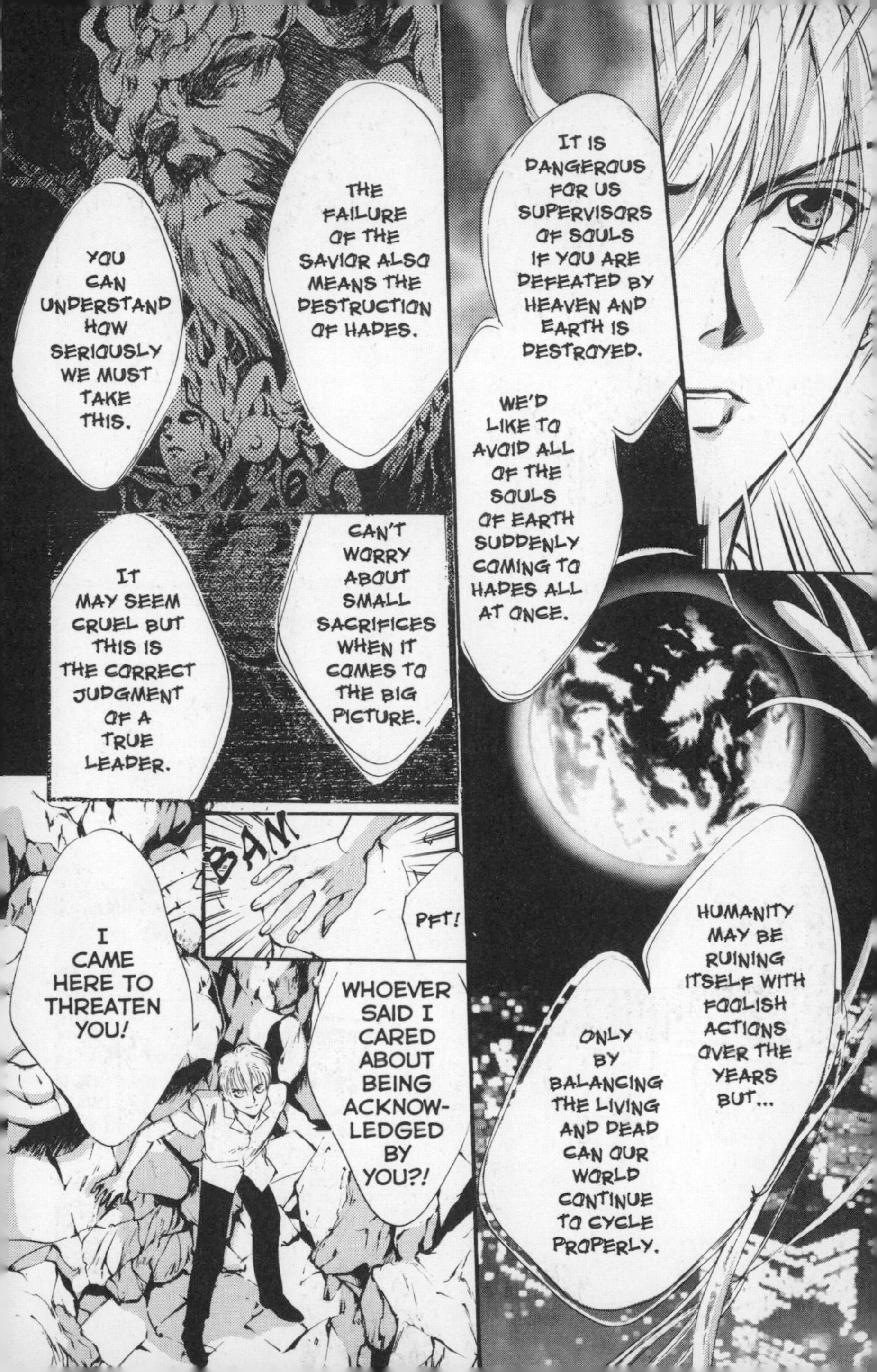
IT IS DANGEROUS FOR US SUPERVISORS OF SOULS IF YOU ARE DEFEATED BY HEAVEN AND EARTH IS DESTROYED.
WE'D LIKE TO AVOID ALL OF THE SOULS OF EARTH SUDDENLY COMING TO HADES ALL AT ONCE.
HUMANITY MAY BE RUINING ITSELF WITH FOOLISH ACTIONS OVER THE YEARS BUT...
ONLY BY BALANCING THE LIVING AND DEAD CAN OUR WORLD CONTINUE TO CYCLE PROPERLY.
THE FAILURE OF THE SAVIOR ALSO MEANS THE DESTRUCTION OF HADES.
YOU CAN UNDERSTAND HOW SERIOUSLY WE MUST TAKE THIS.
CAN'T WORRY ABOUT SMALL SACRIFICES WHEN IT COMES TO THE BIG PICTURE.
IT MAY SEEM CRUEL BUT THIS IS THE CORRECT JUDGMENT OF A TRUE LEADER.
BAM
PFT!
WHOEVER SAID I CARED ABOUT BEING ACKNOW-LEDGED BY YOU?!
I CAME HERE TO THREATEN YOU!

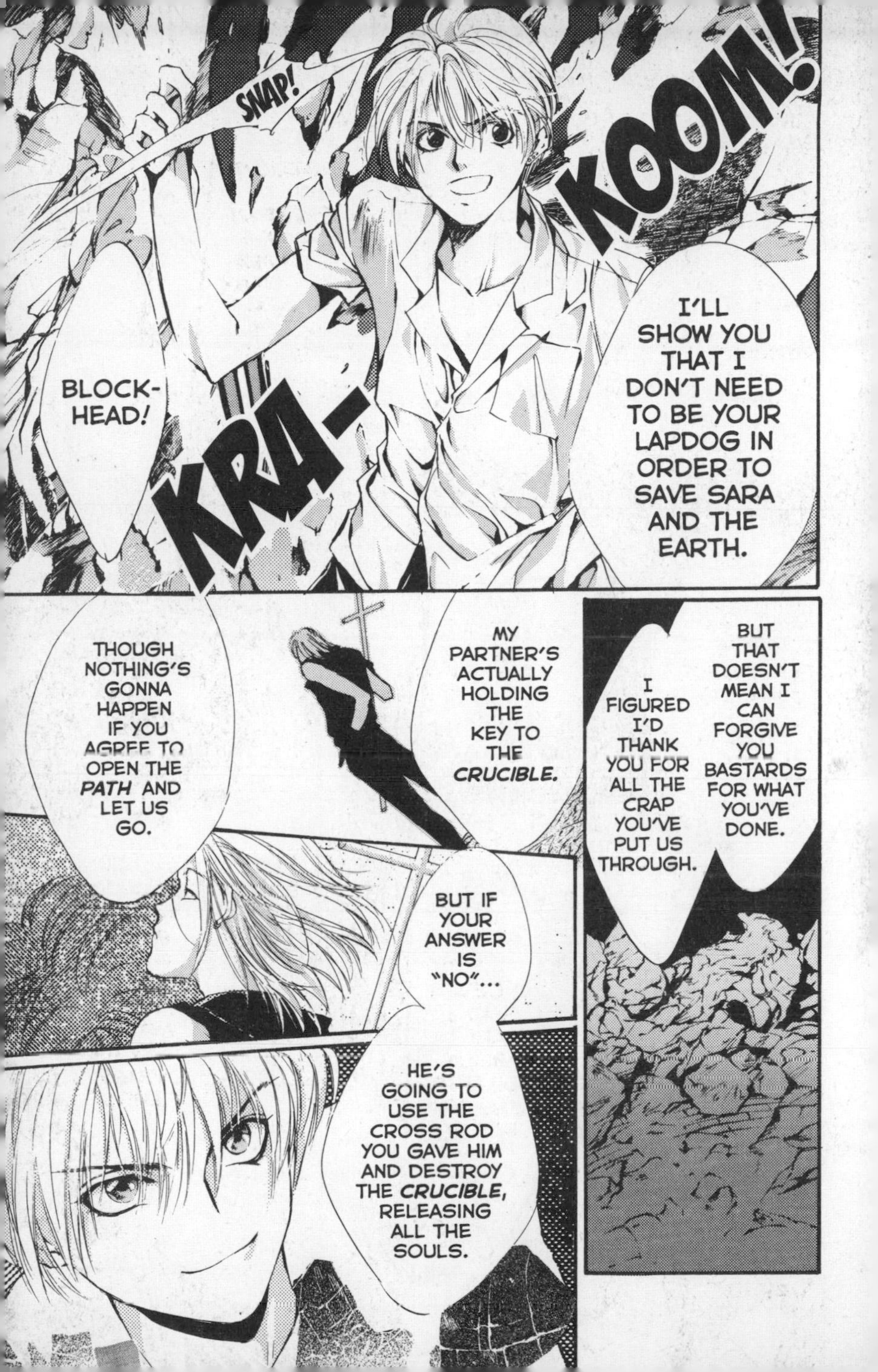
SNAP!
KRA-KOOM!
I'LL SHOW YOU THAT I DON'T NEED TO BE YOUR LAPDOG IN ORDER TO SAVE SARA AND THE EARTH.
BLOCK-HEAD!
I FIGURED I'D THANK YOU FOR ALL THE CRAP YOU'VE PUT US THROUGH.
BUT THAT DOESN'T MEAN I CAN FORGIVE YOU BASTARDS FOR WHAT YOU'VE DONE.
MY PARTNER'S ACTUALLY HOLDING THE KEY TO THE *CRUCIBLE.*
THOUGH NOTHING'S GONNA HAPPEN IF YOU AGREE TO OPEN THE *PATH* AND LET US GO.
BUT IF YOUR ANSWER IS "NO"...
HE'S GOING TO USE THE CROSS ROD YOU GAVE HIM AND DESTROY THE *CRUCIBLE*, RELEASING ALL THE SOULS.

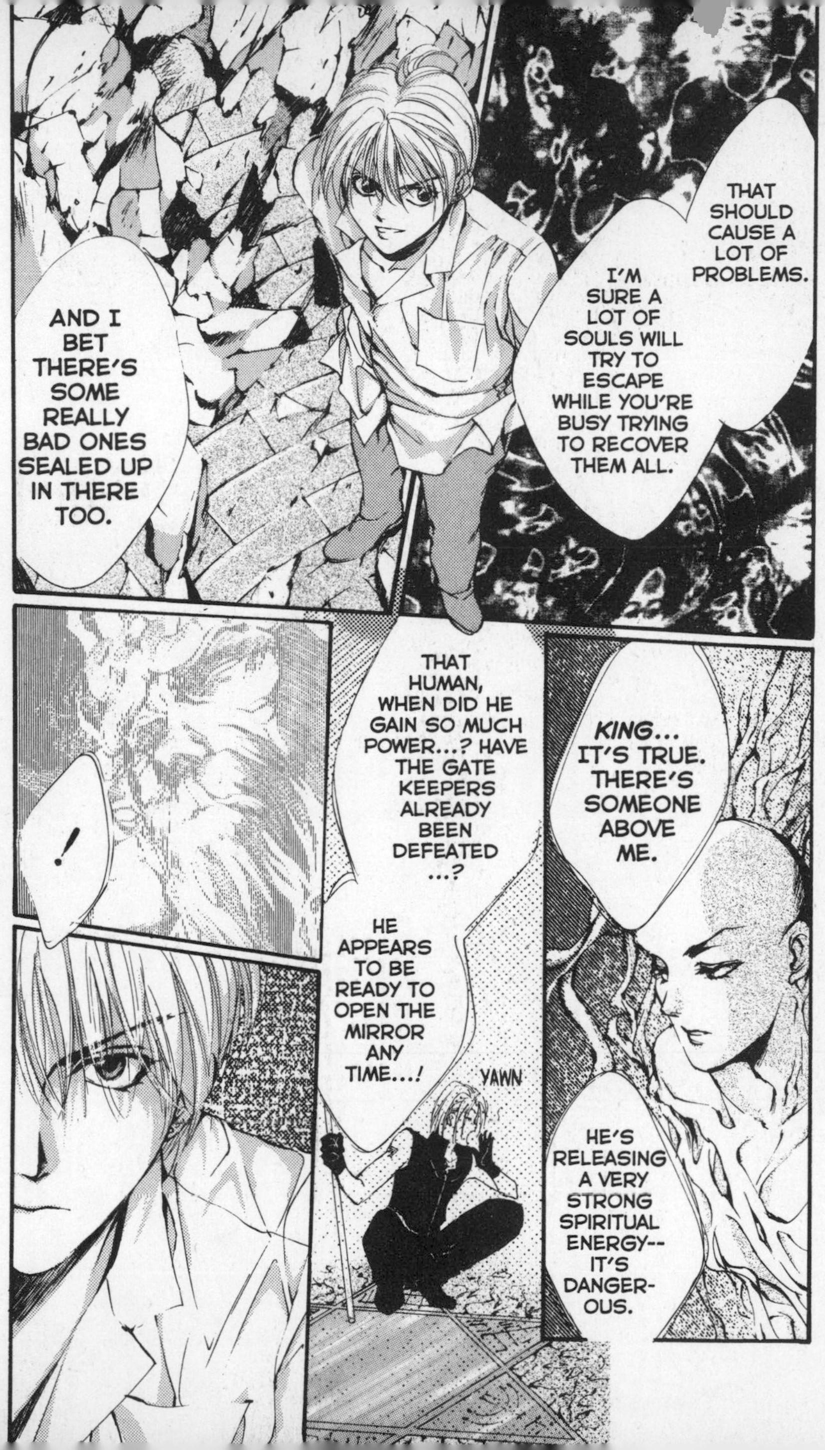
THAT SHOULD CAUSE A LOT OF PROBLEMS.
I'M SURE A LOT OF SOULS WILL TRY TO ESCAPE WHILE YOU'RE BUSY TRYING TO RECOVER THEM ALL.
AND I BET THERE'S SOME REALLY BAD ONES SEALED UP IN THERE TOO.
KING... IT'S TRUE. THERE'S SOMEONE ABOVE ME.
HE'S RELEASING A VERY STRONG SPIRITUAL ENERGY--IT'S DANGEROUS.
THAT HUMAN, WHEN DID HE GAIN SO MUCH POWER...? HAVE THE GATE KEEPERS ALREADY BEEN DEFEATED ...?
HE APPEARS TO BE READY TO OPEN THE MIRROR ANY TIME...!
YAWN
!

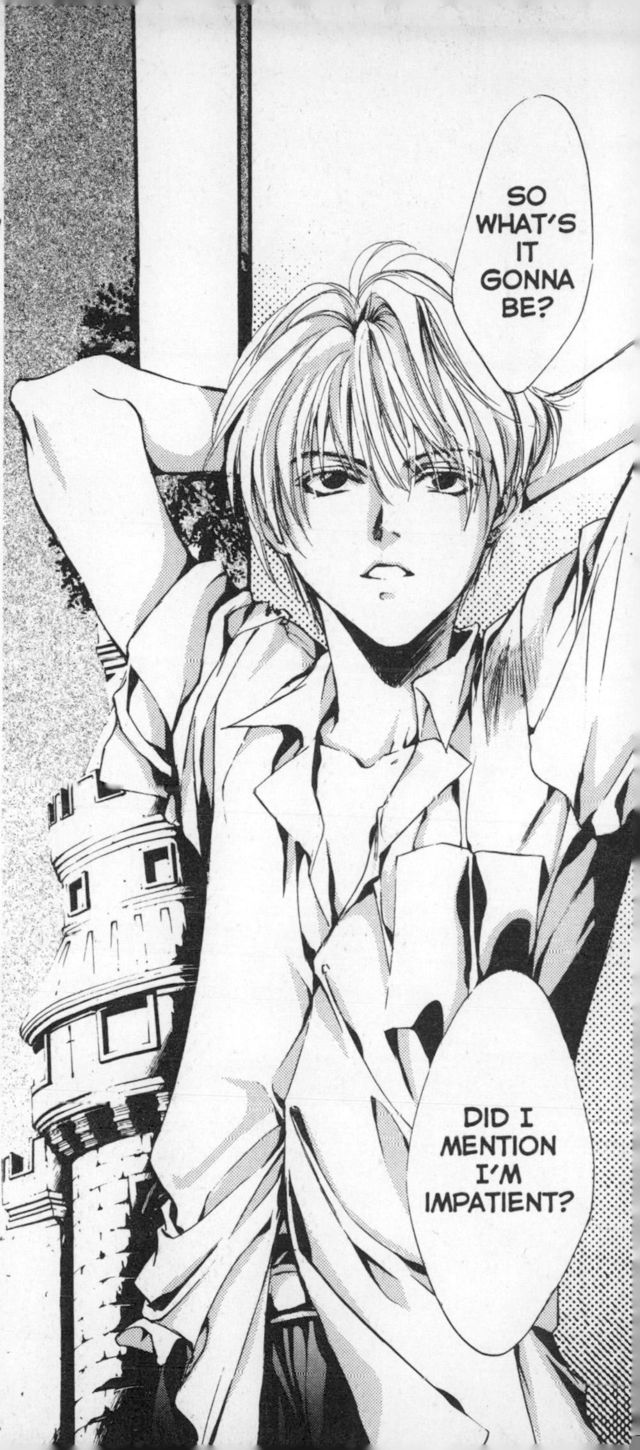
SO WHAT'S IT GONNA BE?
DID I MENTION I'M IMPATIENT?

"Yuki! Is you brain all right?! Are you alive?!" I've felt like yelling that to myself as I created this chapter. Huh? Why is that? Well, I can't tell you just yet... I'll reveal it in the next chapter, though. This chapter seems more about Rosiel than Setsuna. What is he doing? He may be my child, but sometimes he acts on his own. I don't remember raising him to be such a naughty child... oh wait, I do...! Anyway, that "Enra-Ô"!! There's so many lines to draw, I hate him! Why did I pick such a tiresome design? Oh what a pain... This whole Hades saga was very difficult, seriously.

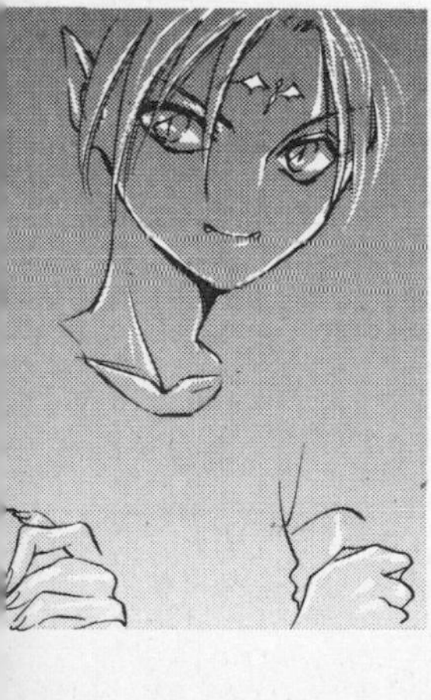

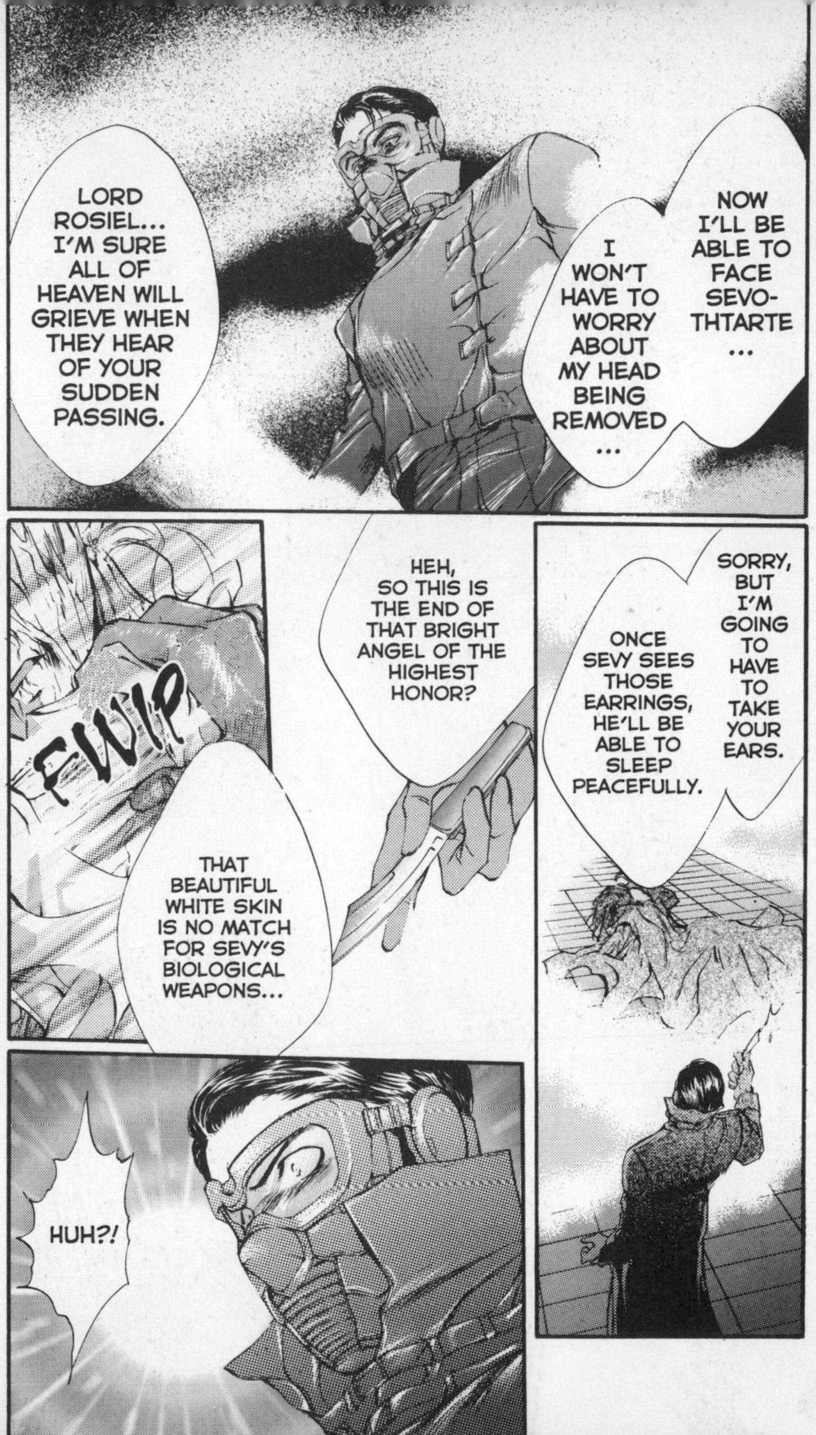
NOW I'LL BE ABLE TO FACE SEVOTHTARTE...
I WON'T HAVE TO WORRY ABOUT MY HEAD BEING REMOVED...
LORD ROSIEL... I'M SURE ALL OF HEAVEN WILL GRIEVE WHEN THEY HEAR OF YOUR SUDDEN PASSING.
SORRY, BUT I'M GOING TO HAVE TO TAKE YOUR EARS.
ONCE SEVY SEES THOSE EARRINGS, HE'LL BE ABLE TO SLEEP PEACEFULLY.
HEH, SO THIS IS THE END OF THAT BRIGHT ANGEL OF THE HIGHEST HONOR?
FWIP
THAT BEAUTIFUL WHITE SKIN IS NO MATCH FOR SEVY'S BIOLOGICAL WEAPONS...
HUH?!

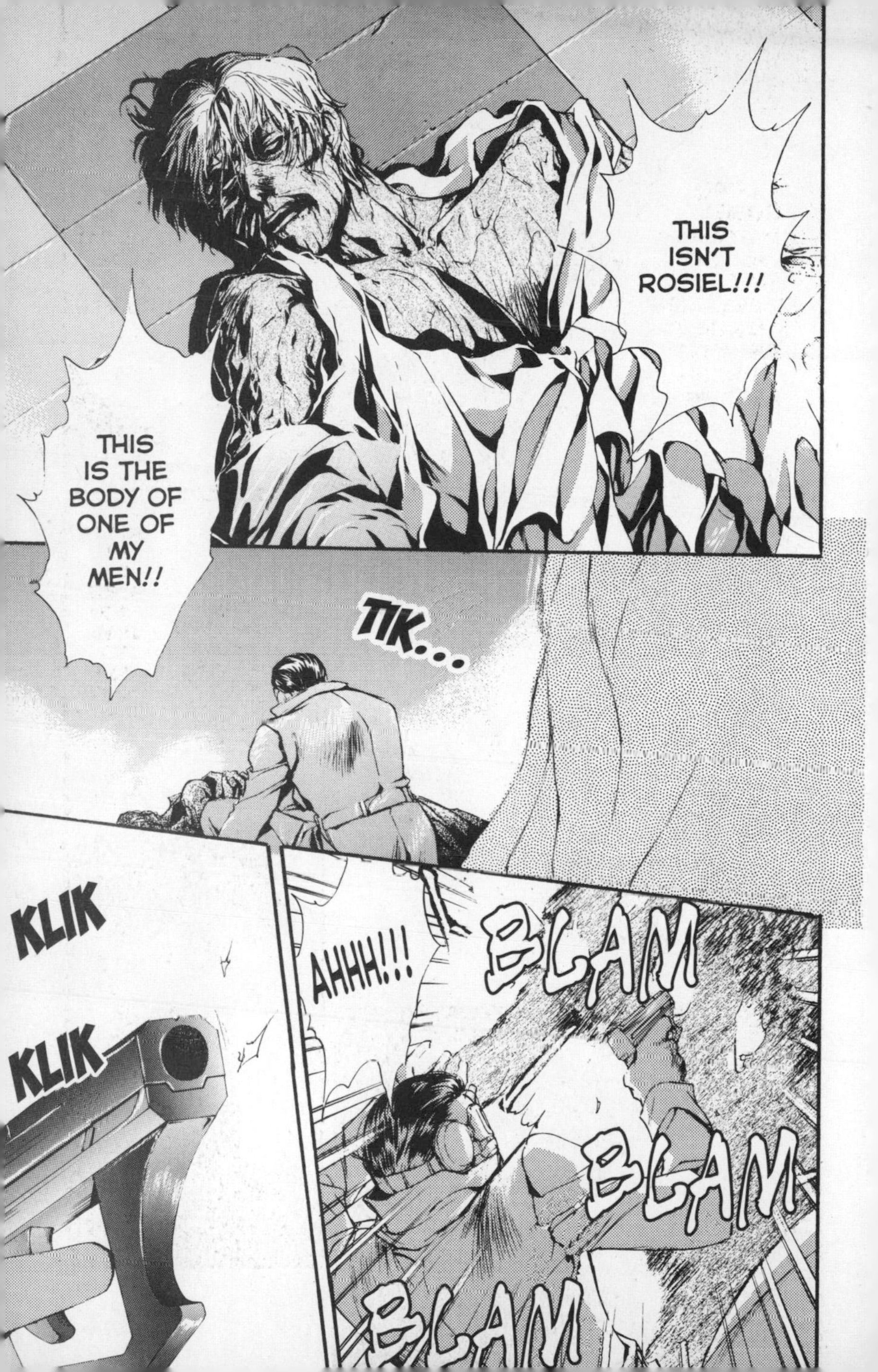
THIS ISN'T ROSIEL!!!
THIS IS THE BODY OF ONE OF MY MEN!!
TIK...
BLAM
AHHH!!!
BLAM
BLAM
KLIK
KLIK

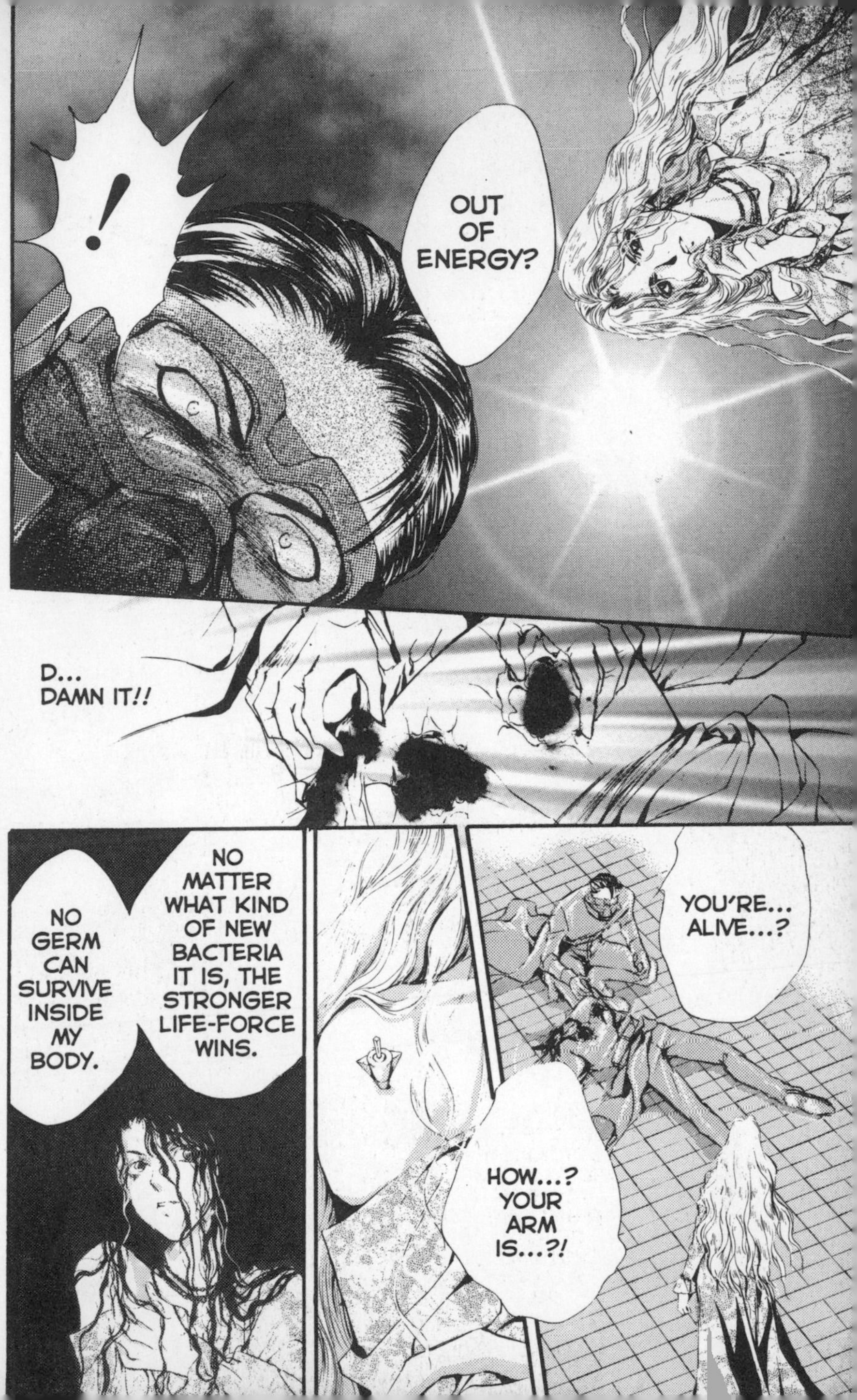
OUT OF ENERGY?
!
D... DAMN IT!!
YOU'RE... ALIVE...?
HOW...? YOUR ARM IS...?!
NO MATTER WHAT KIND OF NEW BACTERIA IT IS, THE STRONGER LIFE-FORCE WINS.
NO GERM CAN SURVIVE INSIDE MY BODY.

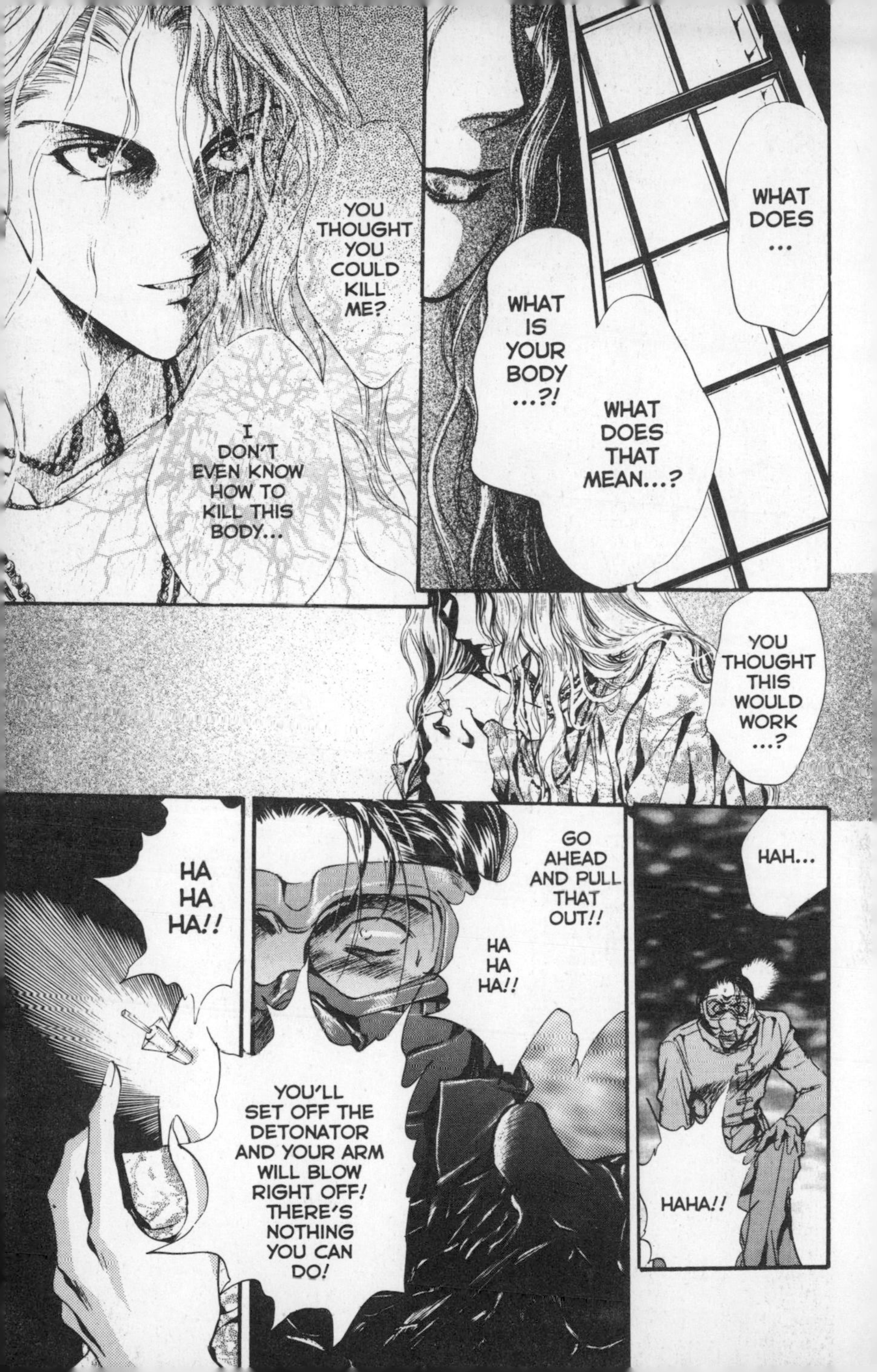
WHAT DOES ...
WHAT IS YOUR BODY ...?!
WHAT DOES THAT MEAN...?
YOU THOUGHT YOU COULD KILL ME?
I DON'T EVEN KNOW HOW TO KILL THIS BODY...
YOU THOUGHT THIS WOULD WORK ...?
HAH...
HAHA!!
GO AHEAD AND PULL THAT OUT!!
HA HA HA!!
HA HA HA!!
YOU'LL SET OFF THE DETONATOR AND YOUR ARM WILL BLOW RIGHT OFF! THERE'S NOTHING YOU CAN DO!

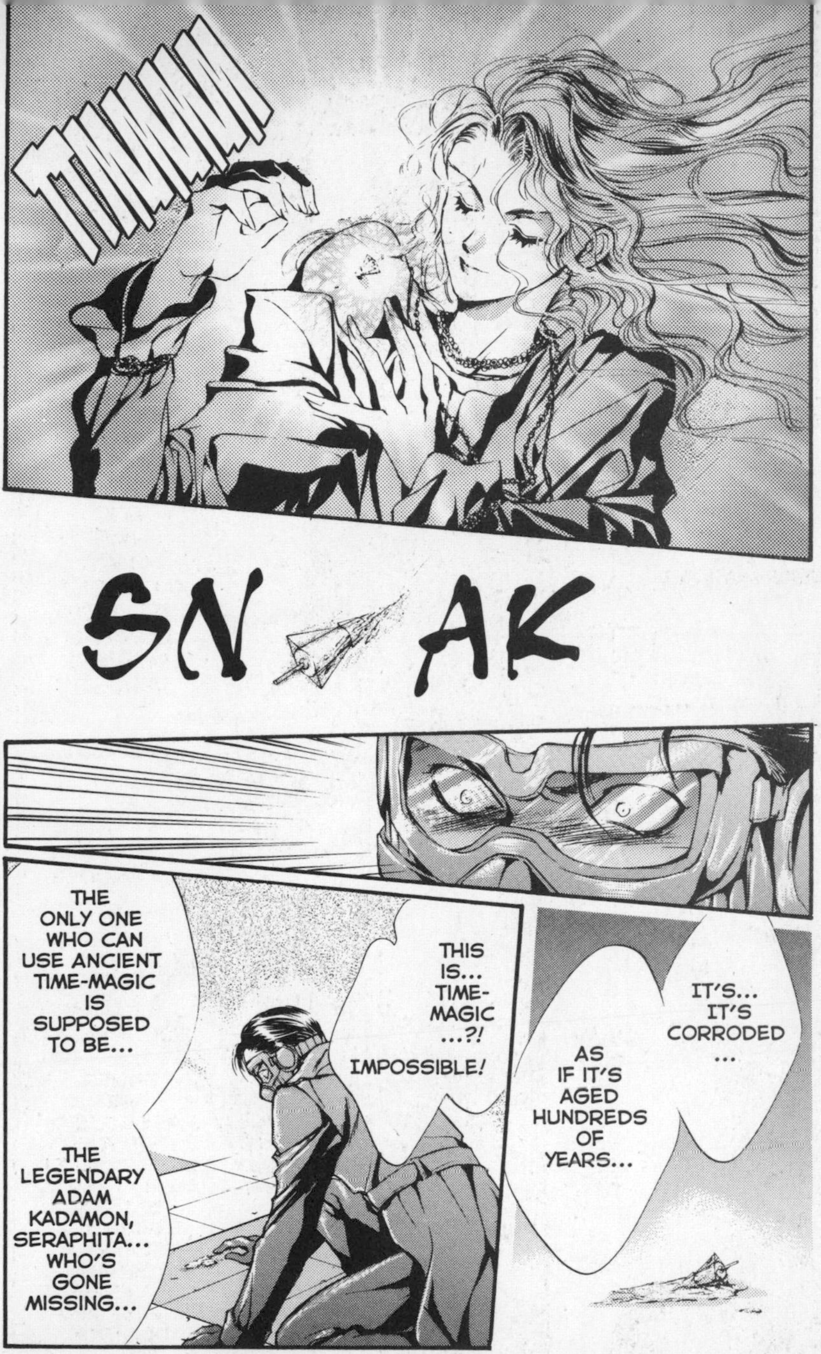
SN AK
IT'S... IT'S CORRODED...
AS IF IT'S AGED HUNDREDS OF YEARS...
THIS IS... TIME-MAGIC...?! IMPOSSIBLE!
THE ONLY ONE WHO CAN USE ANCIENT TIME-MAGIC IS SUPPOSED TO BE...
THE LEGENDARY ADAM KADAMON, SERAPHITA... WHO'S GONE MISSING...

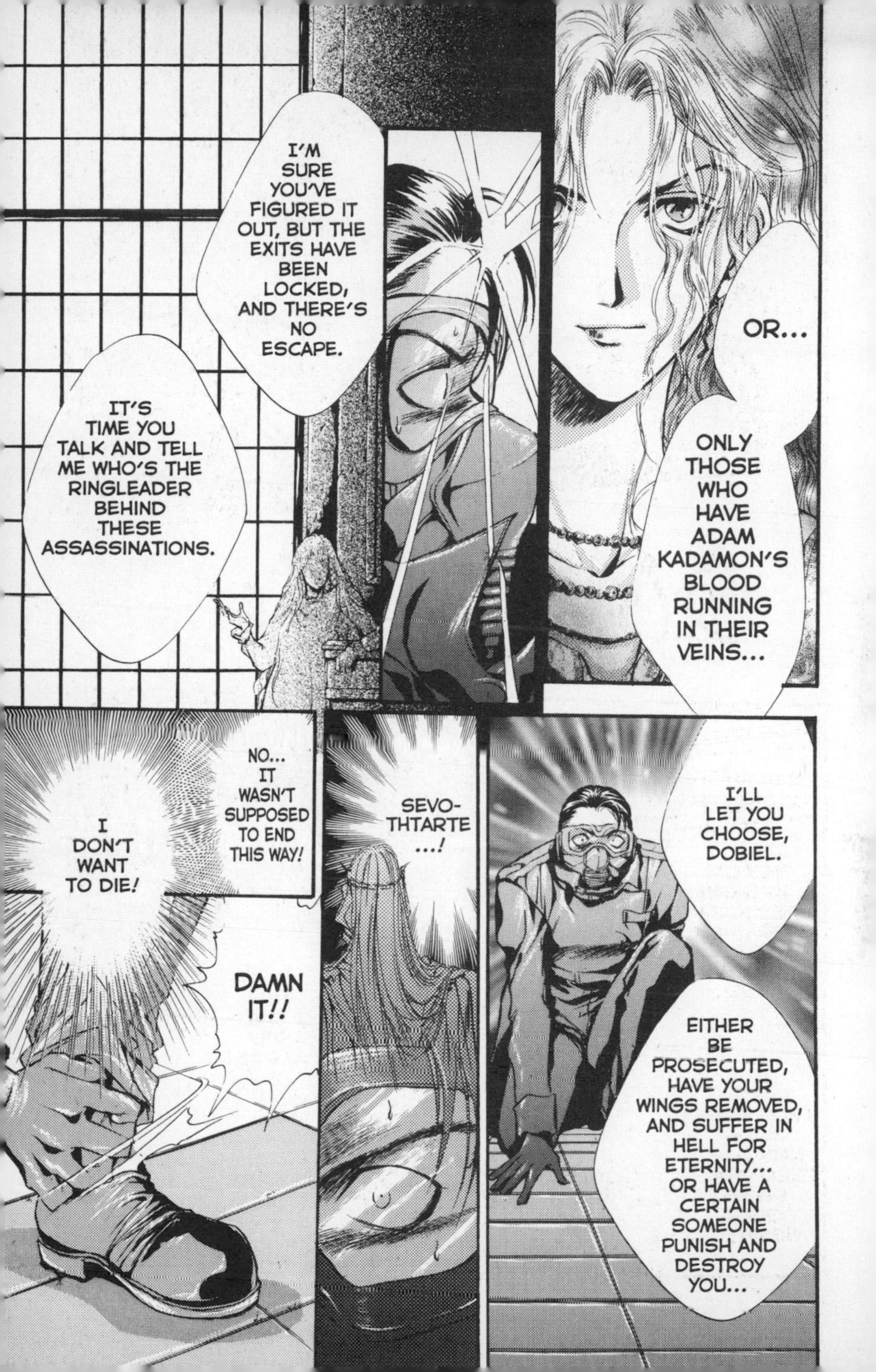
OR...
ONLY THOSE WHO HAVE ADAM KADAMON'S BLOOD RUNNING IN THEIR VEINS...
I'M SURE YOU'VE FIGURED IT OUT, BUT THE EXITS HAVE BEEN LOCKED, AND THERE'S NO ESCAPE.
IT'S TIME YOU TALK AND TELL ME WHO'S THE RINGLEADER BEHIND THESE ASSASSINATIONS.
I'LL LET YOU CHOOSE, DOBIEL.
EITHER BE PROSECUTED, HAVE YOUR WINGS REMOVED, AND SUFFER IN HELL FOR ETERNITY... OR HAVE A CERTAIN SOMEONE PUNISH AND DESTROY YOU...
SEVOTHTARTE ...!
NO... IT WASN'T SUPPOSED TO END THIS WAY!
I DON'T WANT TO DIE!
DAMN IT!!

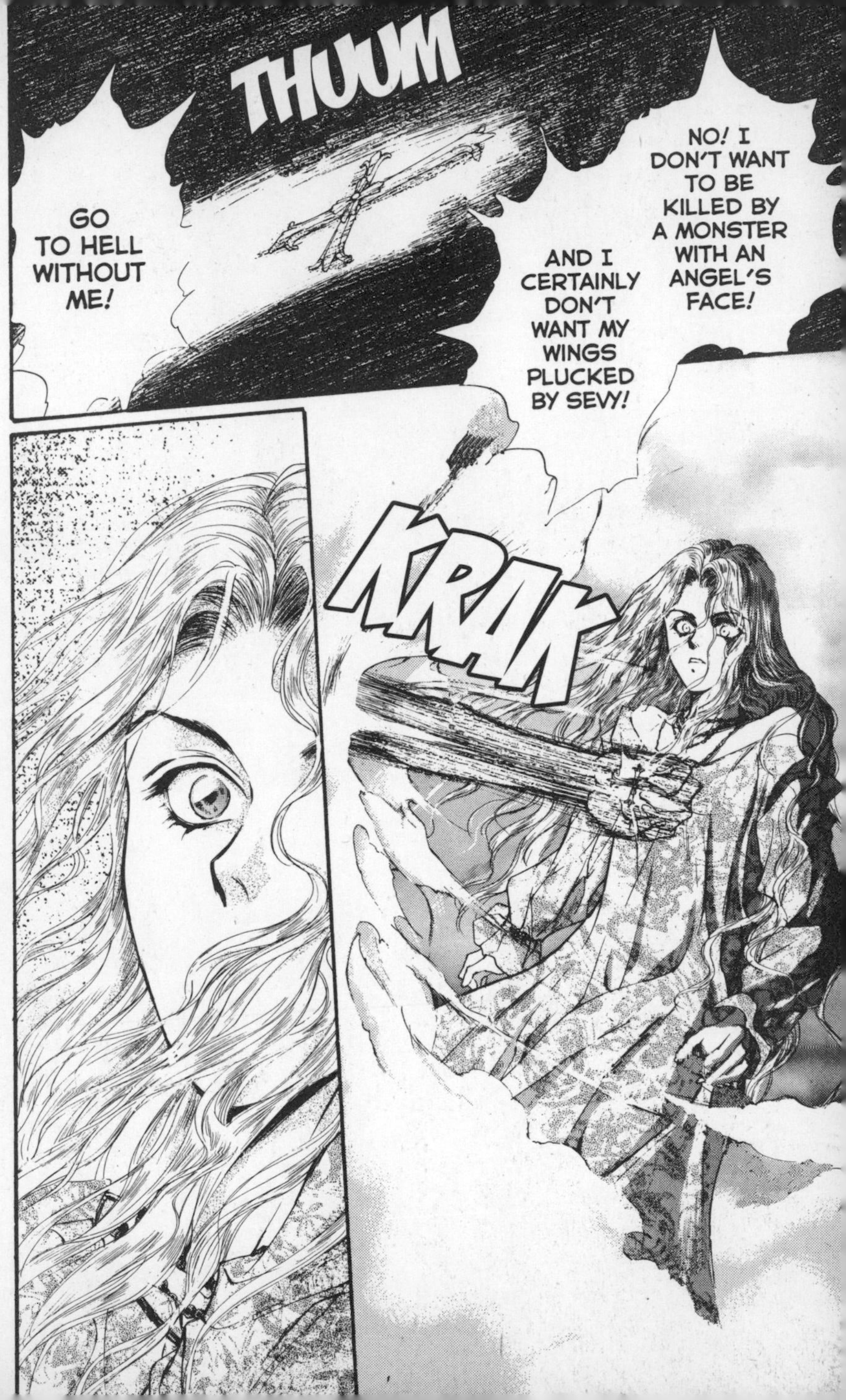
THUUM
NO! I DON'T WANT TO BE KILLED BY A MONSTER WITH AN ANGEL'S FACE!
AND I CERTAINLY DON'T WANT MY WINGS PLUCKED BY SEVY!
GO TO HELL WITHOUT ME!
KRAK

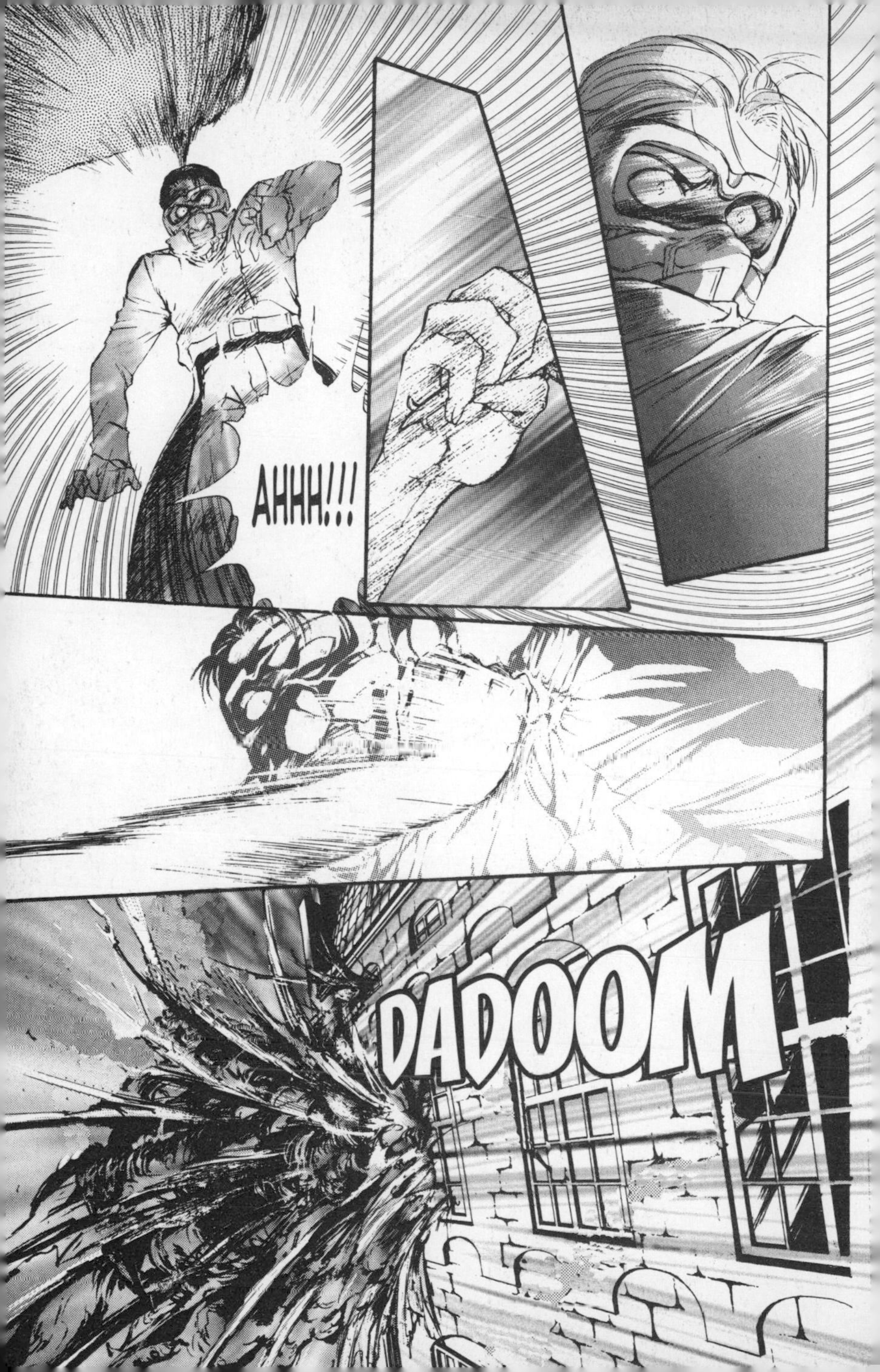
AHHH!!!
DADOOM

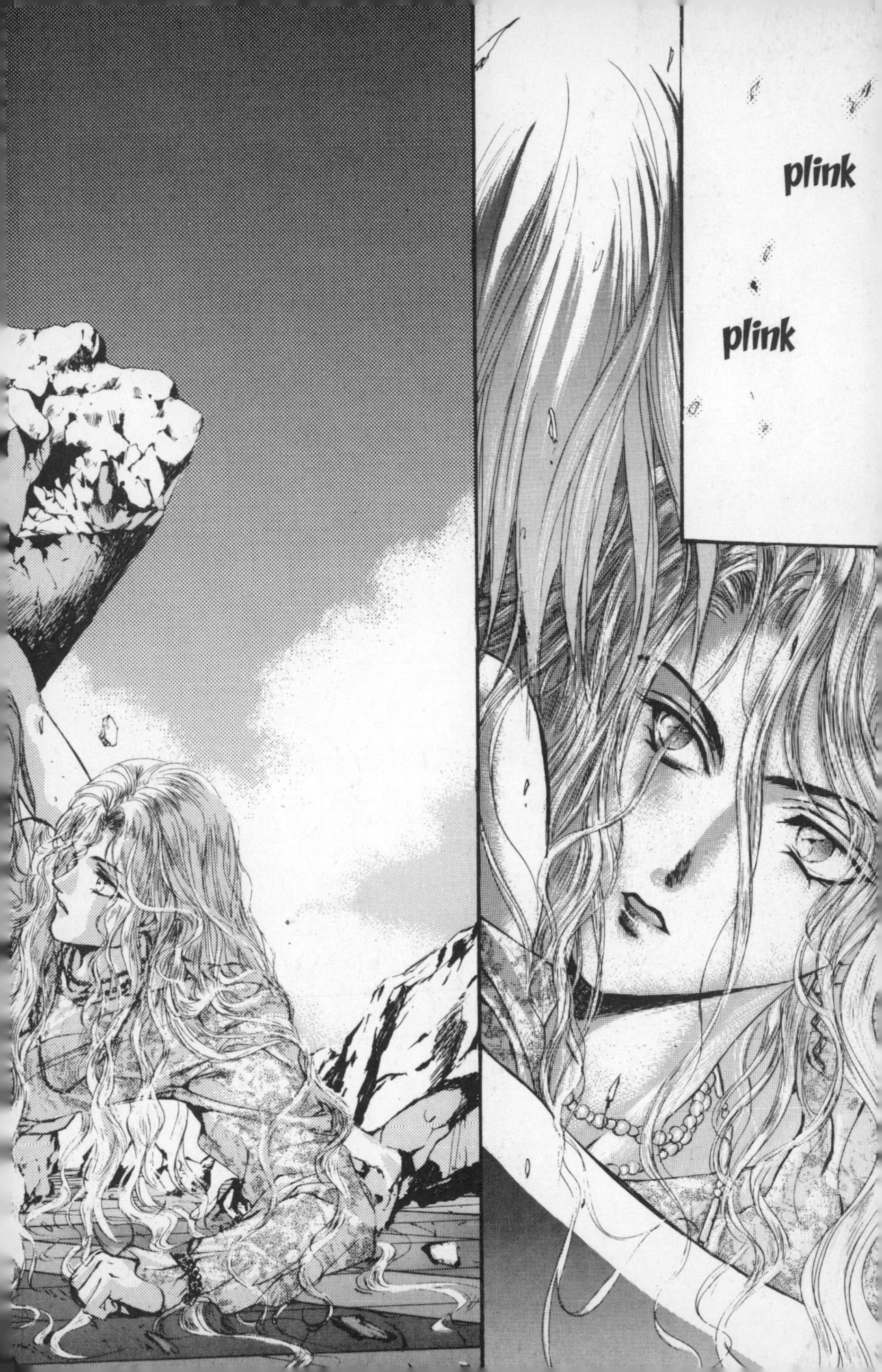
plink
plink

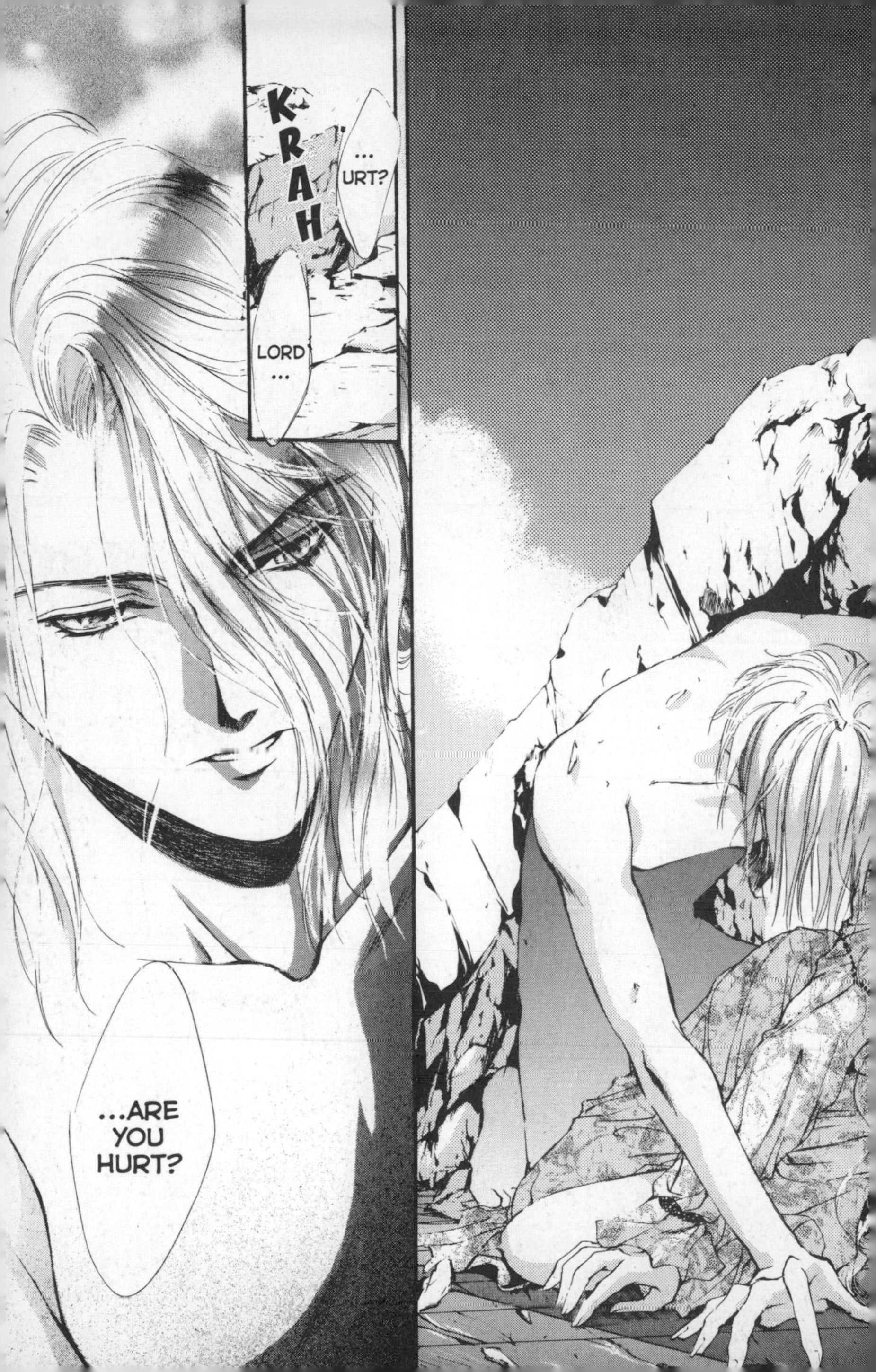

... URT?
KRAH
LORD ...
...ARE YOU HURT?

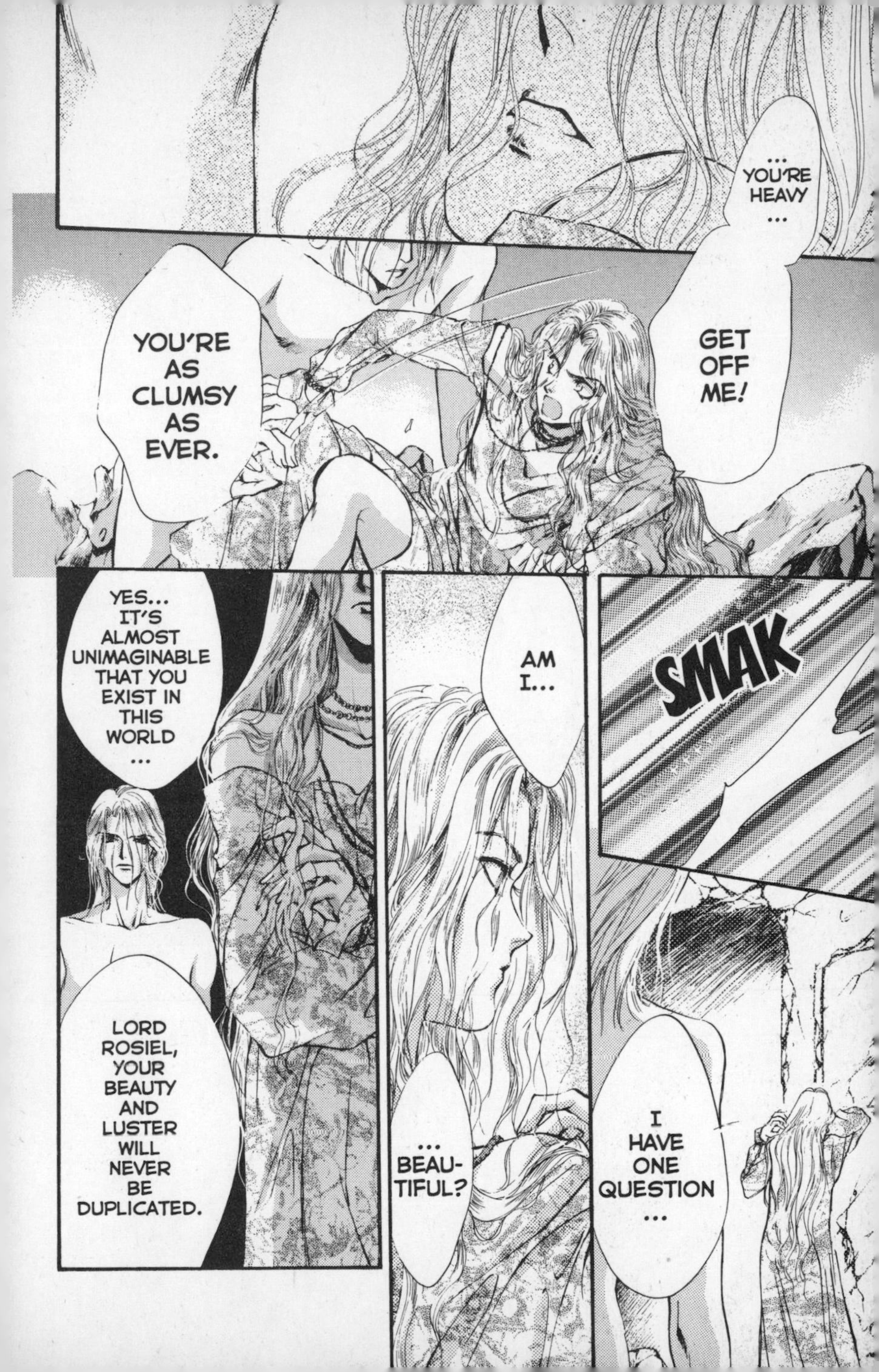
... YOU'RE HEAVY ...
GET OFF ME!
YOU'RE AS CLUMSY AS EVER.
SMAK
I HAVE ONE QUESTION ...
AM I...
... BEAUTIFUL?
YES... IT'S ALMOST UNIMAGINABLE THAT YOU EXIST IN THIS WORLD ...
LORD ROSIEL, YOUR BEAUTY AND LUSTER WILL NEVER BE DUPLICATED.

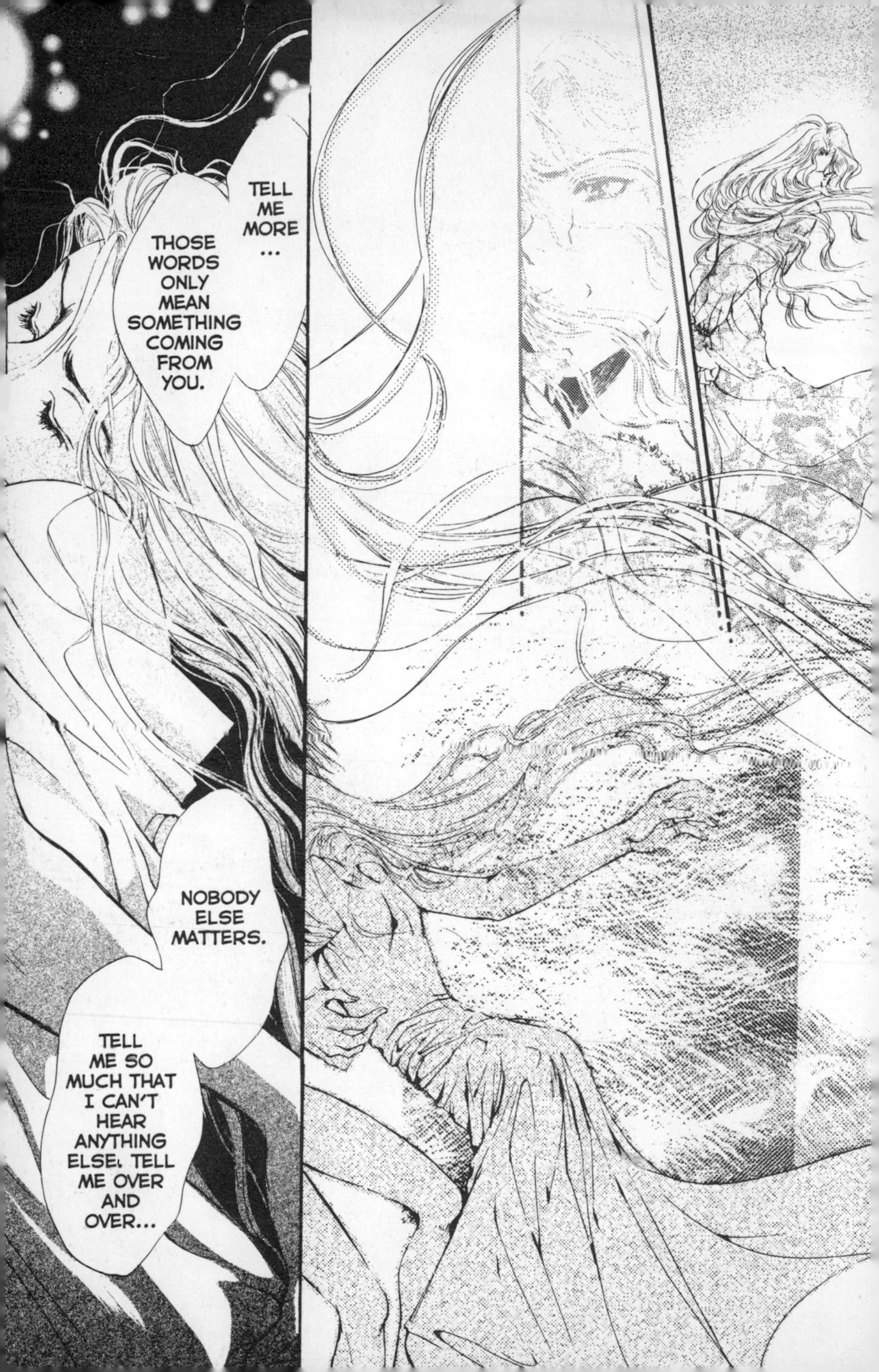
TELL ME MORE...
THOSE WORDS ONLY MEAN SOMETHING COMING FROM YOU.
NOBODY ELSE MATTERS.
TELL ME SO MUCH THAT I CAN'T HEAR ANYTHING ELSE, TELL ME OVER AND OVER...

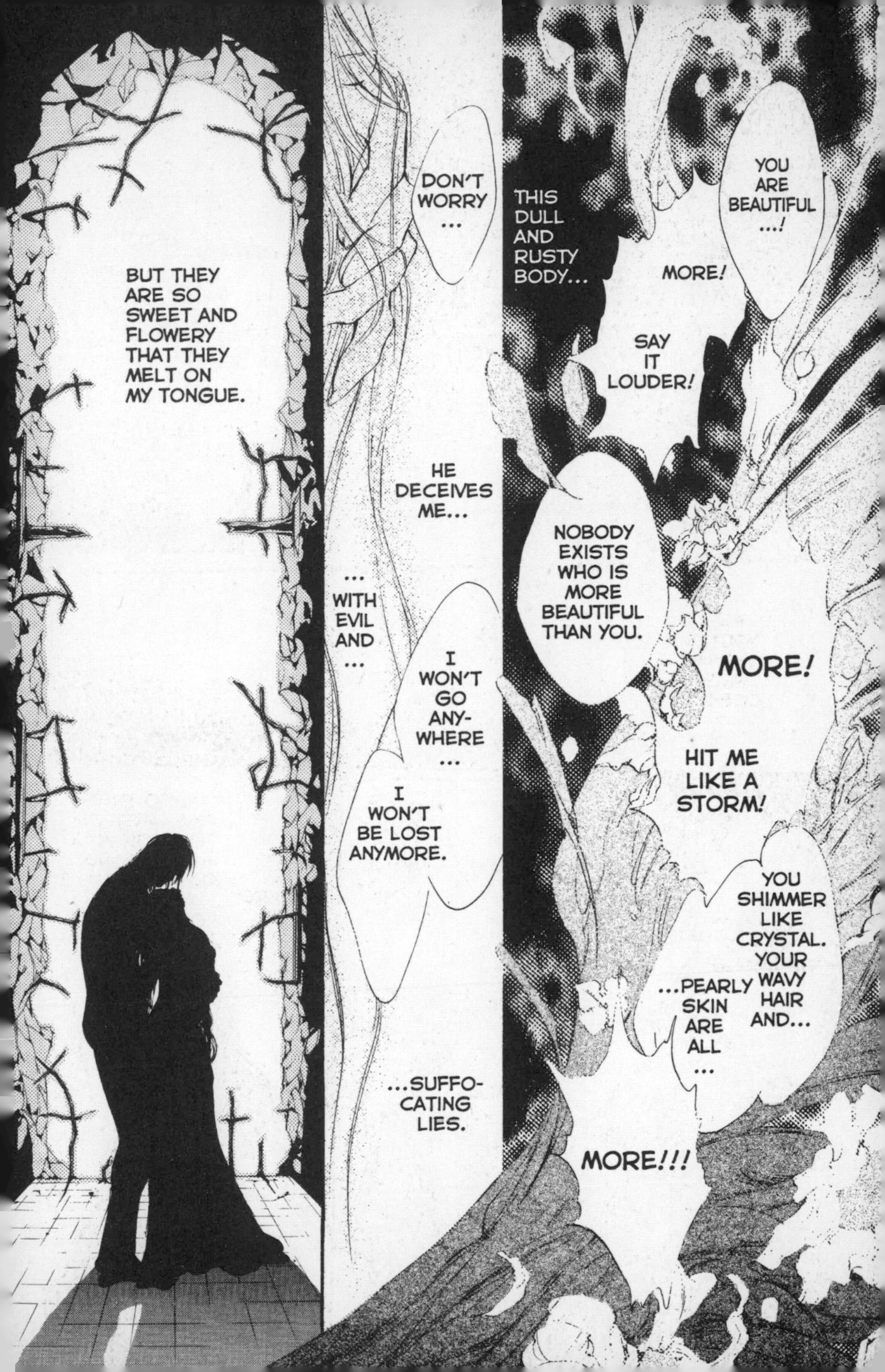
YOU ARE BEAUTIFUL ...!
THIS DULL AND RUSTY BODY...
MORE!
SAY IT LOUDER!
NOBODY EXISTS WHO IS MORE BEAUTIFUL THAN YOU.
MORE!
HIT ME LIKE A STORM!
YOU SHIMMER LIKE CRYSTAL. YOUR WAVY HAIR AND...
...PEARLY SKIN ARE ALL ...
MORE!!!
DON'T WORRY ...
HE DECEIVES ME...
... WITH EVIL AND ...
I WON'T GO ANY-WHERE ...
I WON'T BE LOST ANYMORE.
...SUFFO-CATING LIES.
BUT THEY ARE SO SWEET AND FLOWERY THAT THEY MELT ON MY TONGUE.

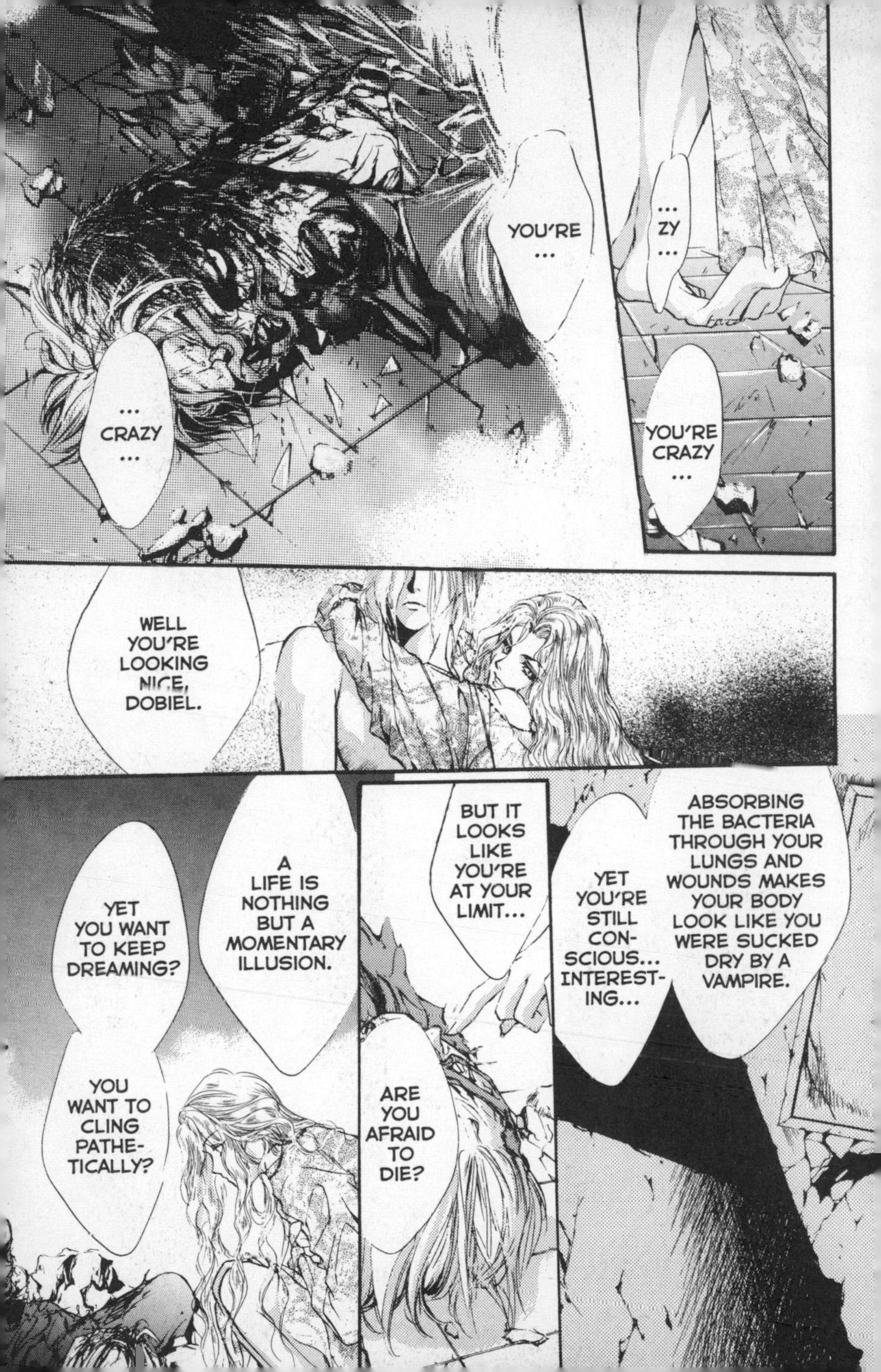
...ZY...
YOU'RE CRAZY...
YOU'RE...
...CRAZY...
WELL YOU'RE LOOKING NICE, DOBIEL.
ABSORBING THE BACTERIA THROUGH YOUR LUNGS AND WOUNDS MAKES YOUR BODY LOOK LIKE YOU WERE SUCKED DRY BY A VAMPIRE.
YET YOU'RE STILL CON-SCIOUS... INTEREST-ING...
BUT IT LOOKS LIKE YOU'RE AT YOUR LIMIT...
ARE YOU AFRAID TO DIE?
A LIFE IS NOTHING BUT A MOMENTARY ILLUSION.
YET YOU WANT TO KEEP DREAMING?
YOU WANT TO CLING PATHE-TICALLY?

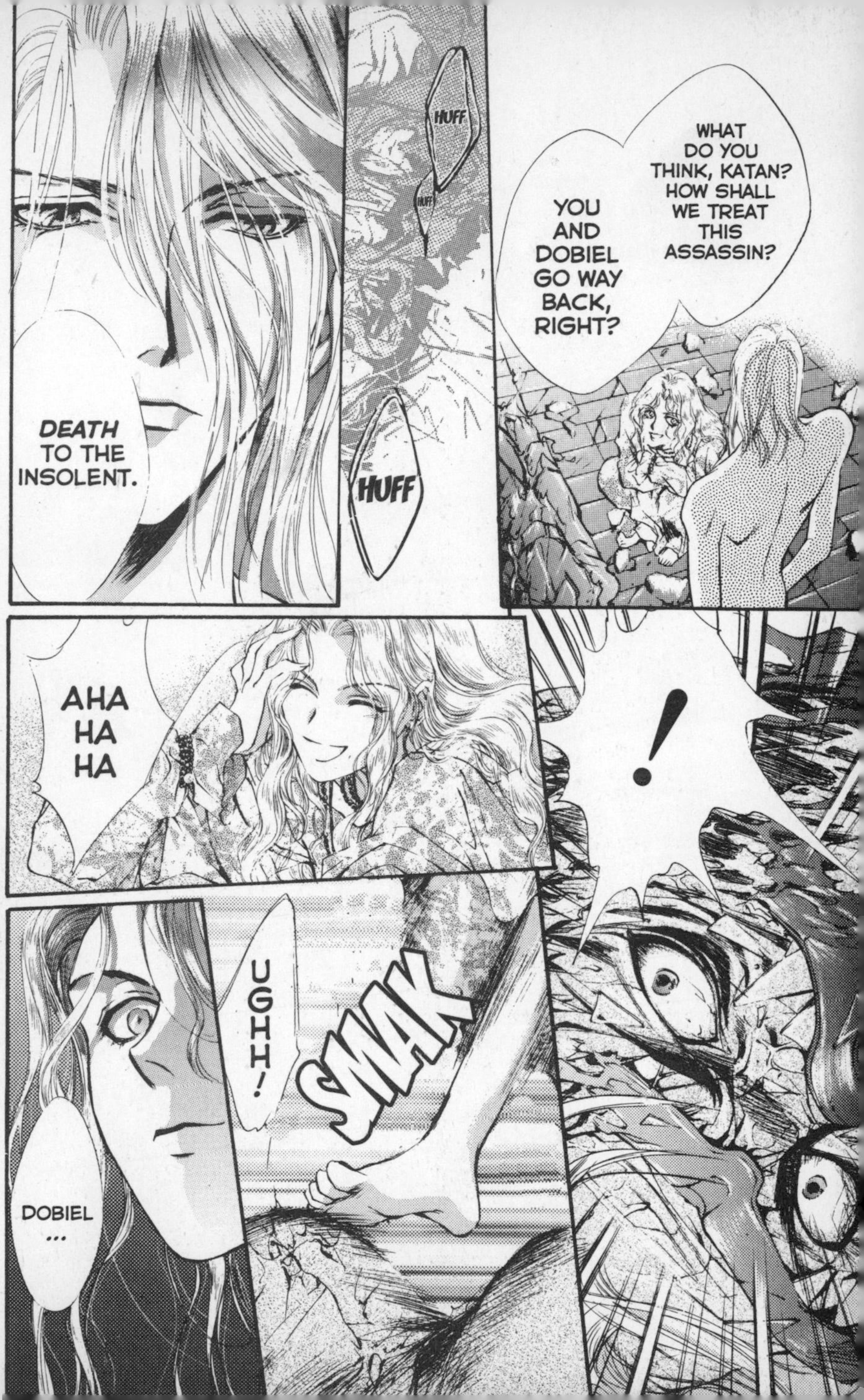
WHAT DO YOU THINK, KATAN? HOW SHALL WE TREAT THIS ASSASSIN?
YOU AND DOBIEL GO WAY BACK, RIGHT?
HUFF
HUFF
HUFF
DEATH TO THE INSOLENT.
!
AHA HA HA
SMAK
UGHH!
DOBIEL ...

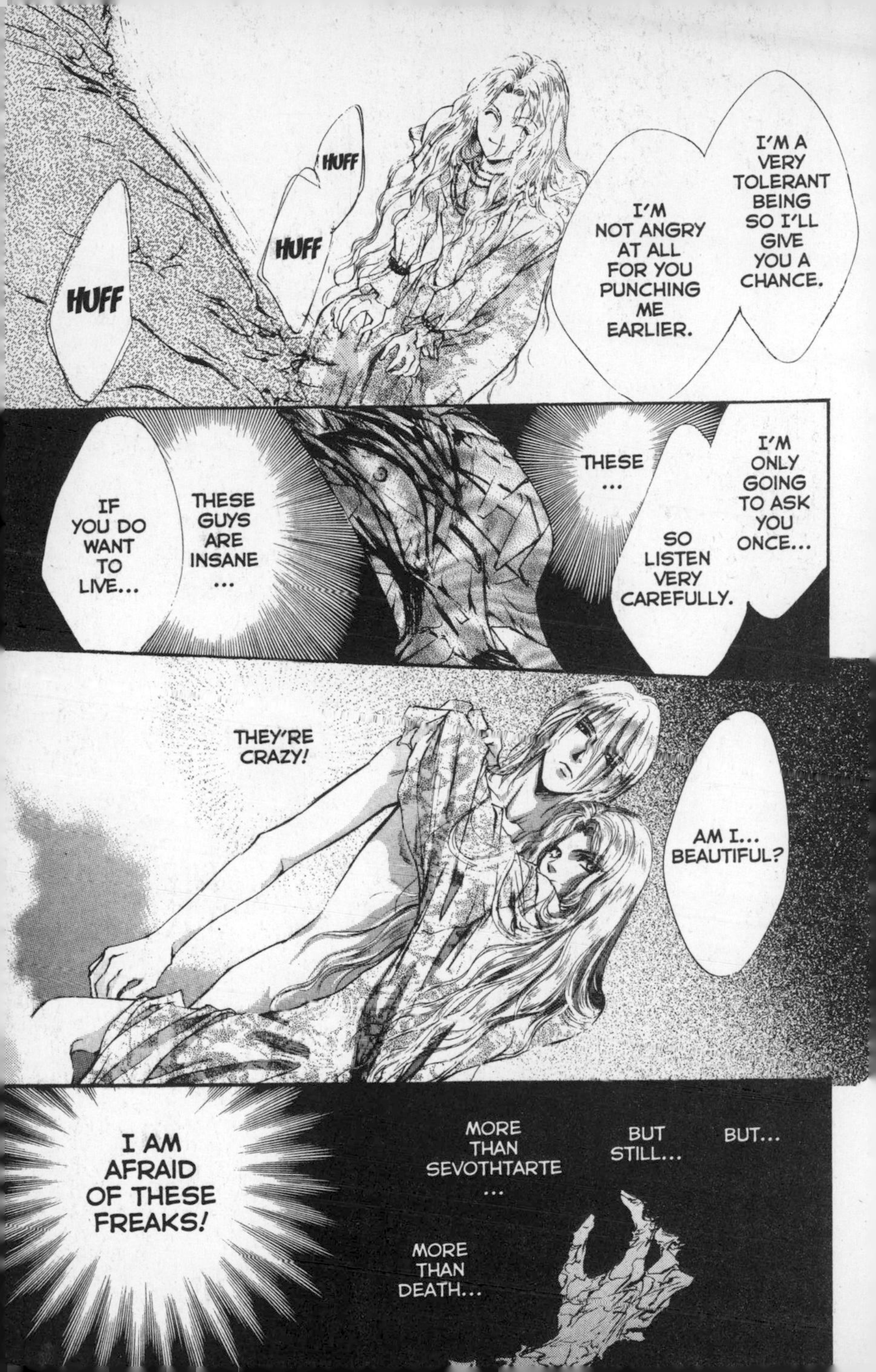
I'M A VERY TOLERANT BEING SO I'LL GIVE YOU A CHANCE.
I'M NOT ANGRY AT ALL FOR YOU PUNCHING ME EARLIER.
HUFF
HUFF
HUFF
I'M ONLY GOING TO ASK YOU ONCE...
SO LISTEN VERY CAREFULLY.
THESE ...
THESE GUYS ARE INSANE ...
IF YOU DO WANT TO LIVE...
AM I... BEAUTIFUL?
THEY'RE CRAZY!
BUT...
BUT STILL...
MORE THAN SEVOTHTARTE ...
MORE THAN DEATH...
I AM AFRAID OF THESE FREAKS!

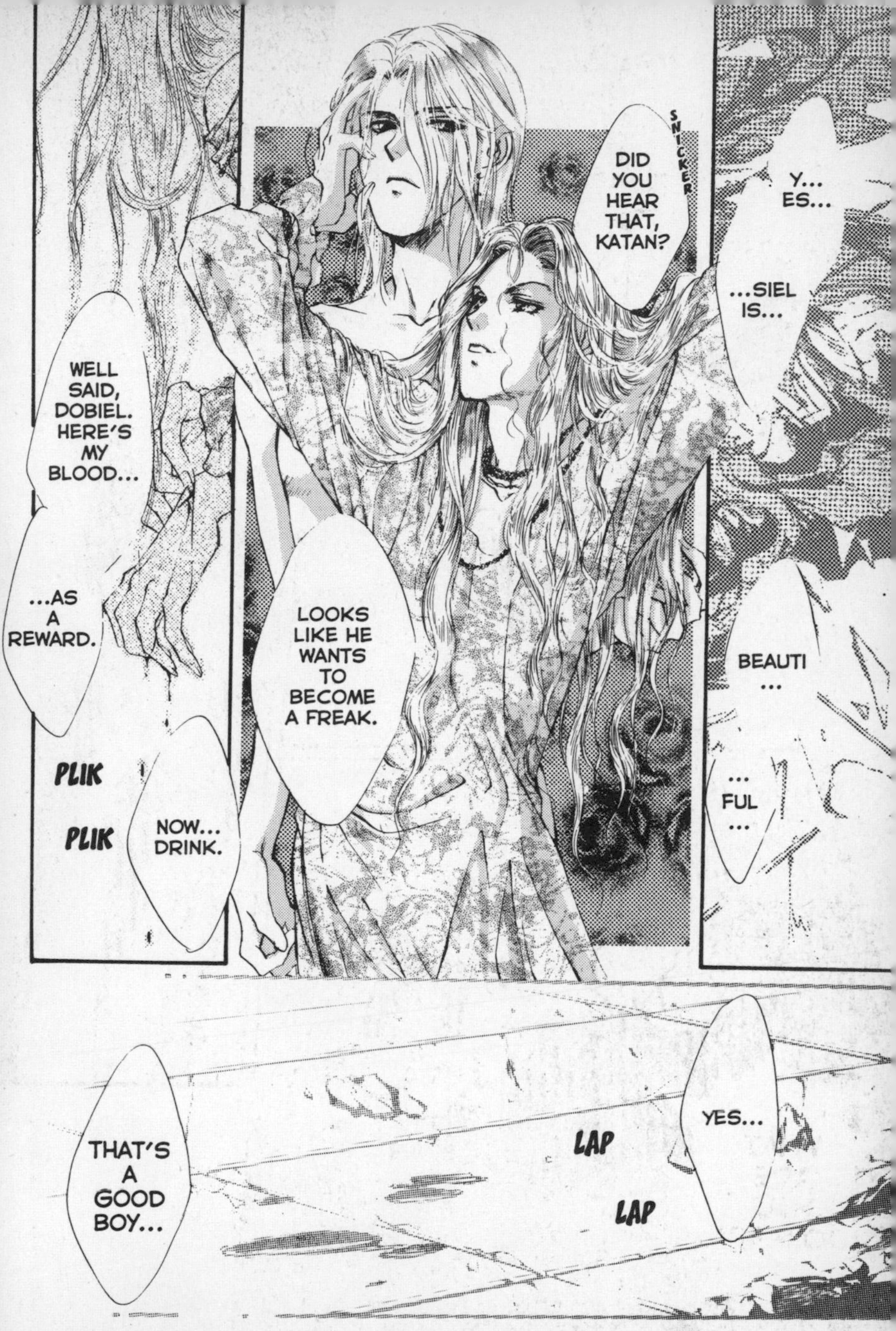
Y... ES...
...SIEL IS...
BEAUTI ...
... FUL ...
SNICKER
DID YOU HEAR THAT, KATAN?
LOOKS LIKE HE WANTS TO BECOME A FREAK.
WELL SAID, DOBIEL. HERE'S MY BLOOD...
...AS A REWARD.
PLIK
PLIK
NOW... DRINK.
YES...
LAP
LAP
THAT'S A GOOD BOY...

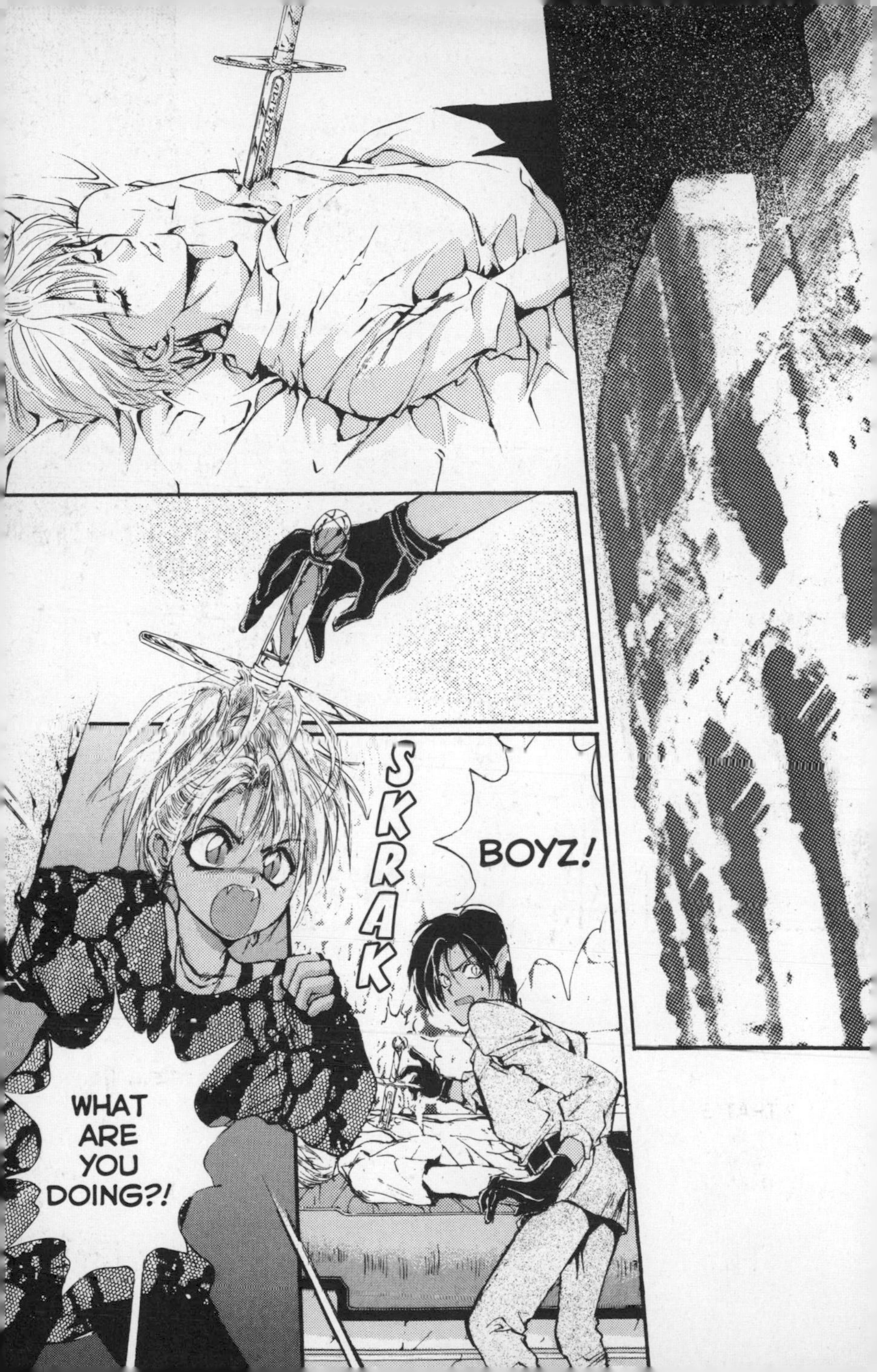
SKRAK
BOYZ!
WHAT ARE YOU DOING?!

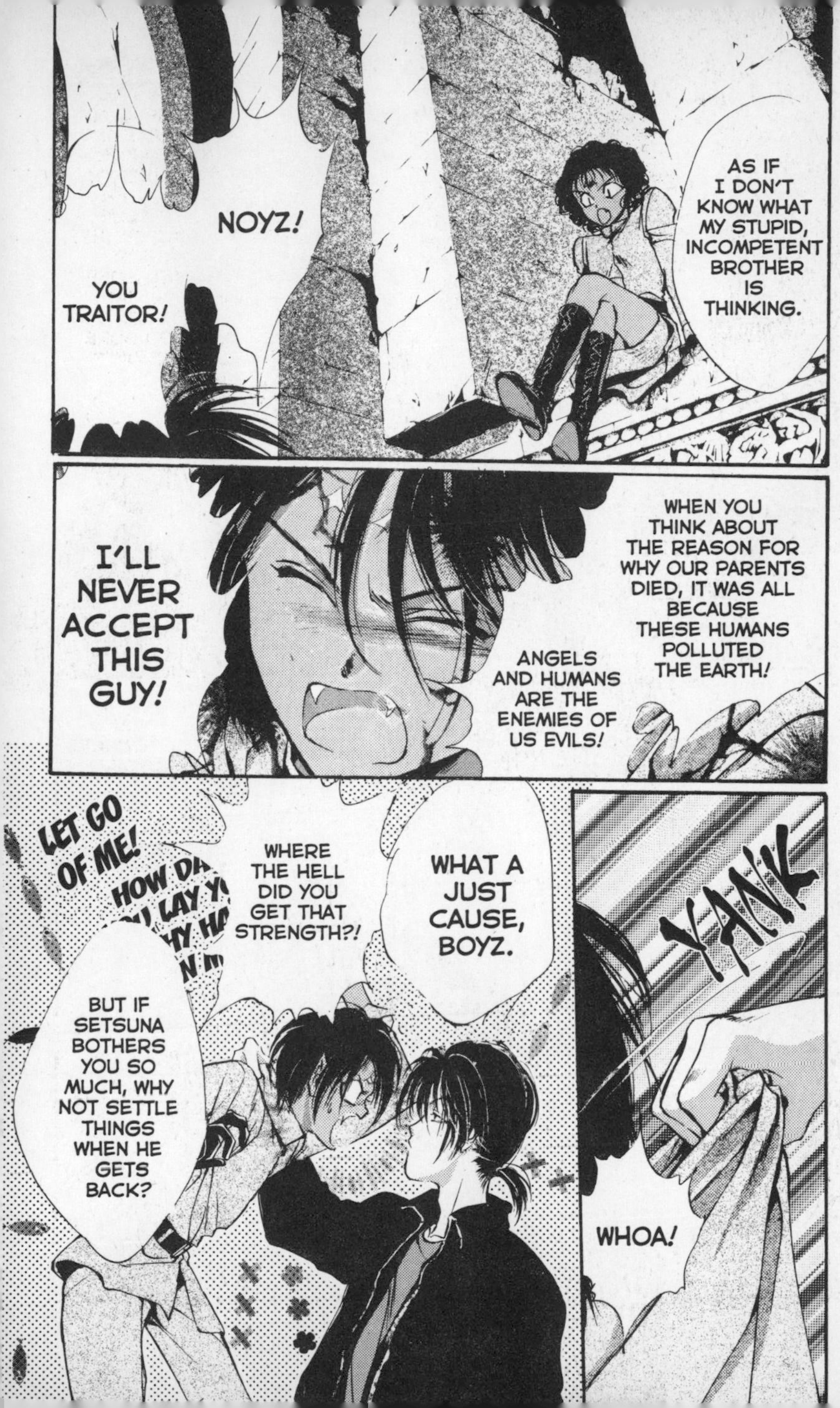
AS IF I DON'T KNOW WHAT MY STUPID, INCOMPETENT BROTHER IS THINKING.
NOYZ!
YOU TRAITOR!
WHEN YOU THINK ABOUT THE REASON FOR WHY OUR PARENTS DIED, IT WAS ALL BECAUSE THESE HUMANS POLLUTED THE EARTH!
ANGELS AND HUMANS ARE THE ENEMIES OF US EVILS!
I'LL NEVER ACCEPT THIS GUY!
YANK
WHOA!
WHAT A JUST CAUSE, BOYZ.
WHERE THE HELL DID YOU GET THAT STRENGTH?!
LET GO OF ME!
BUT IF SETSUNA BOTHERS YOU SO MUCH, WHY NOT SETTLE THINGS WHEN HE GETS BACK?

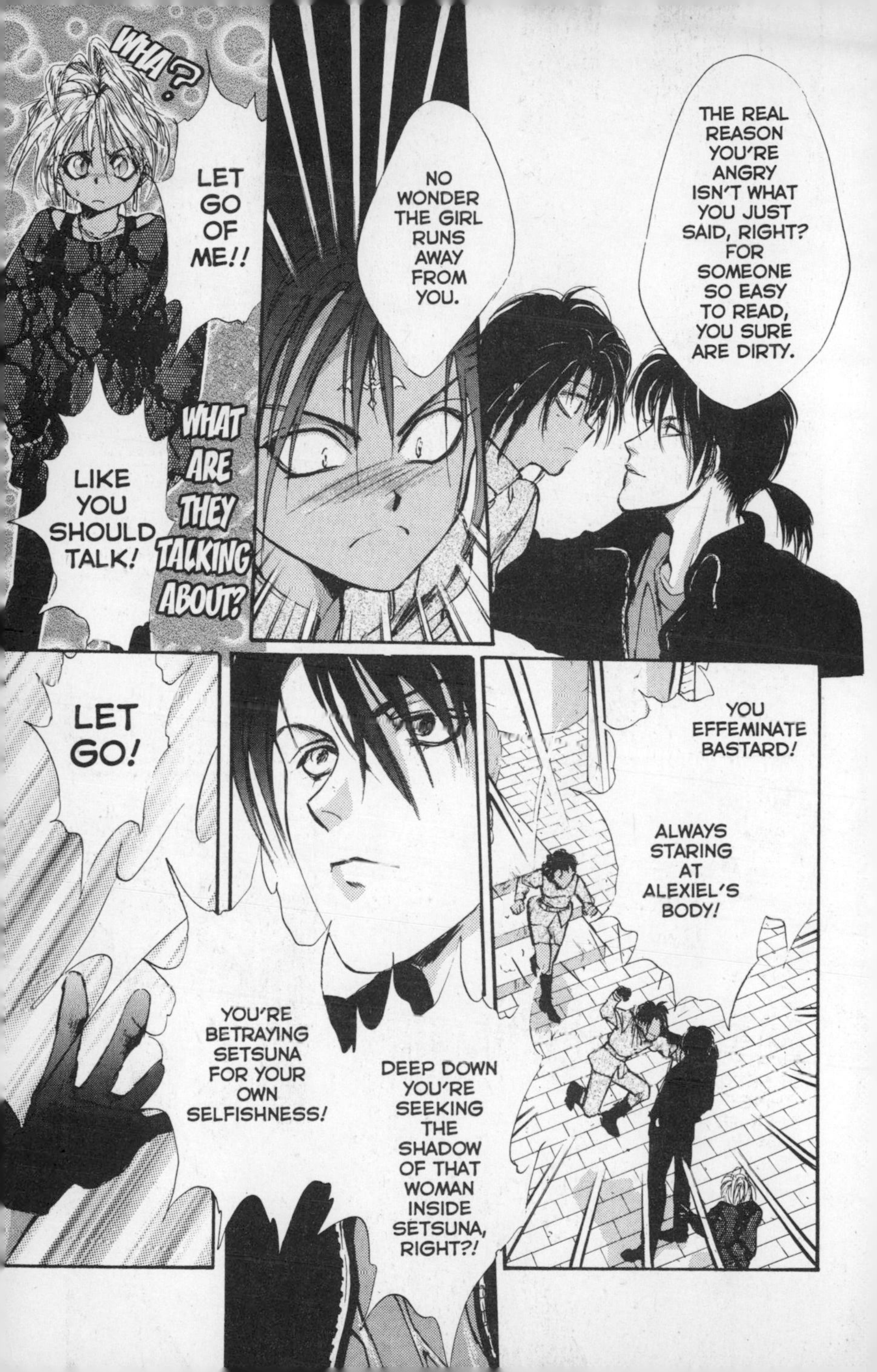
THE REAL REASON YOU'RE ANGRY ISN'T WHAT YOU JUST SAID, RIGHT? FOR SOMEONE SO EASY TO READ, YOU SURE ARE DIRTY.
NO WONDER THE GIRL RUNS AWAY FROM YOU.
WHA?
LET GO OF ME!!
LIKE YOU SHOULD TALK!
WHAT ARE THEY TALKING ABOUT?
YOU EFFEMINATE BASTARD!
ALWAYS STARING AT ALEXIEL'S BODY!
DEEP DOWN YOU'RE SEEKING THE SHADOW OF THAT WOMAN INSIDE SETSUNA, RIGHT?!
YOU'RE BETRAYING SETSUNA FOR YOUR OWN SELFISHNESS!
LET GO!

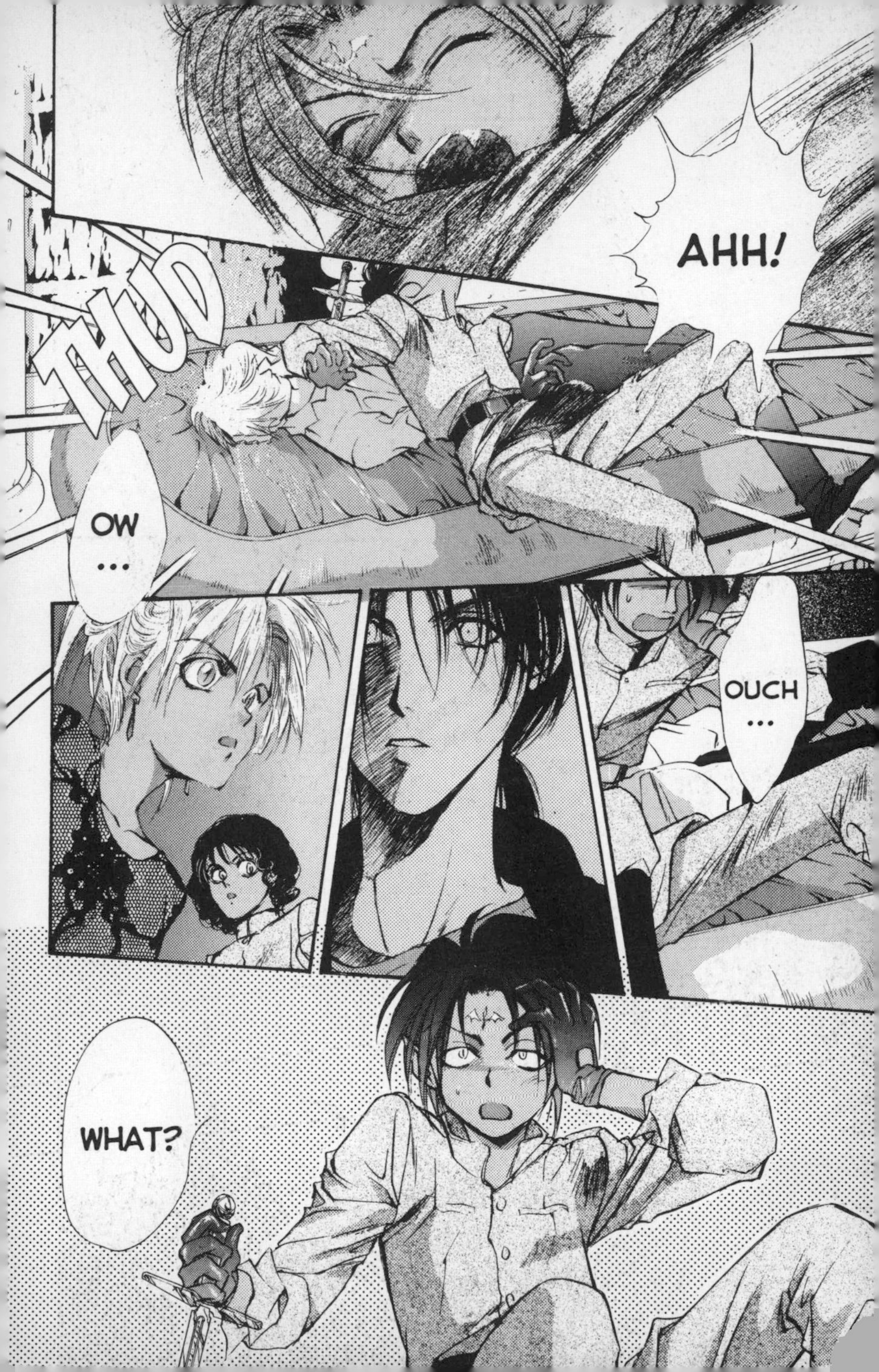
AHH!
THUD
OW ...
OUCH ...
WHAT?

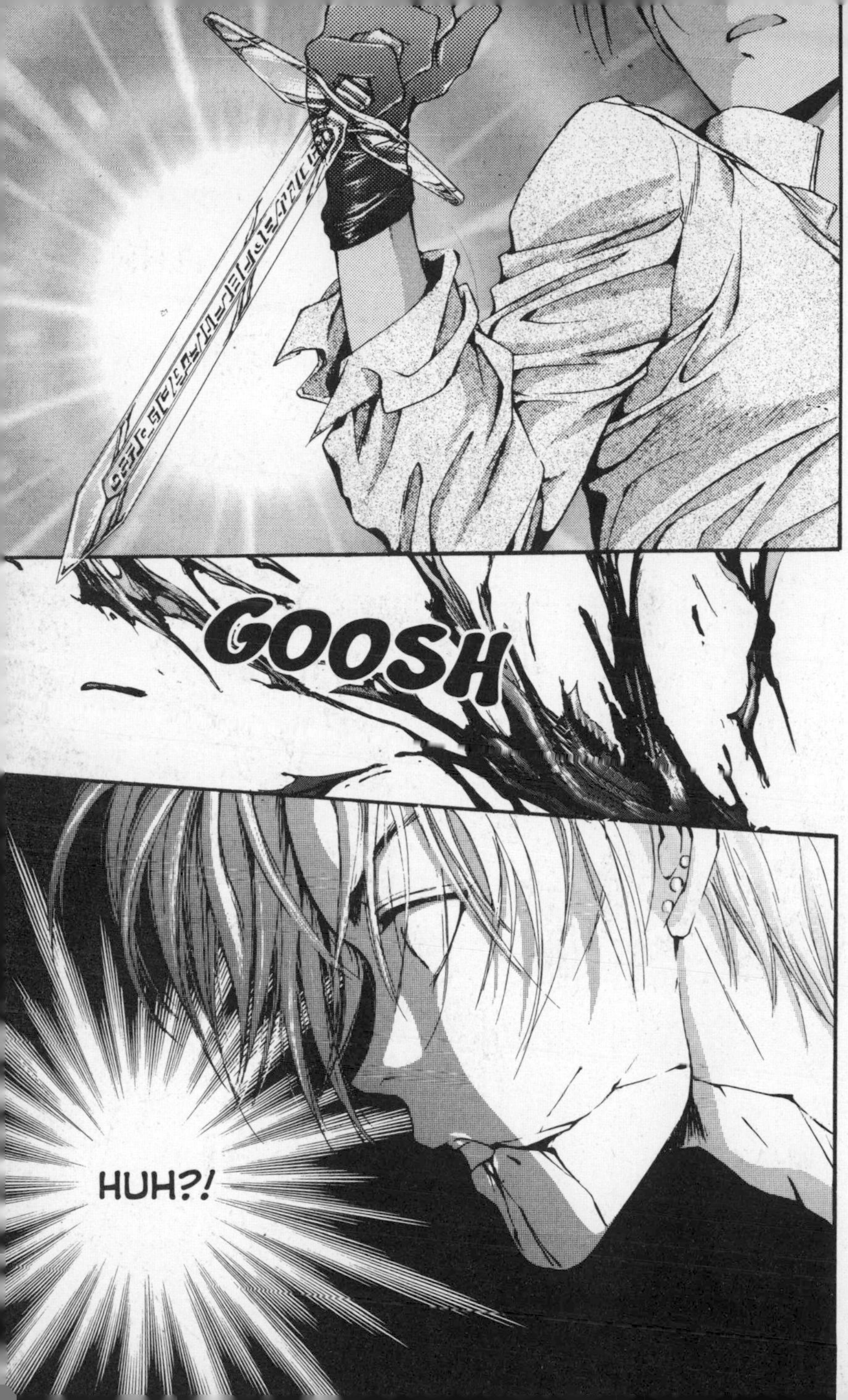
GOOSH
HUH?!

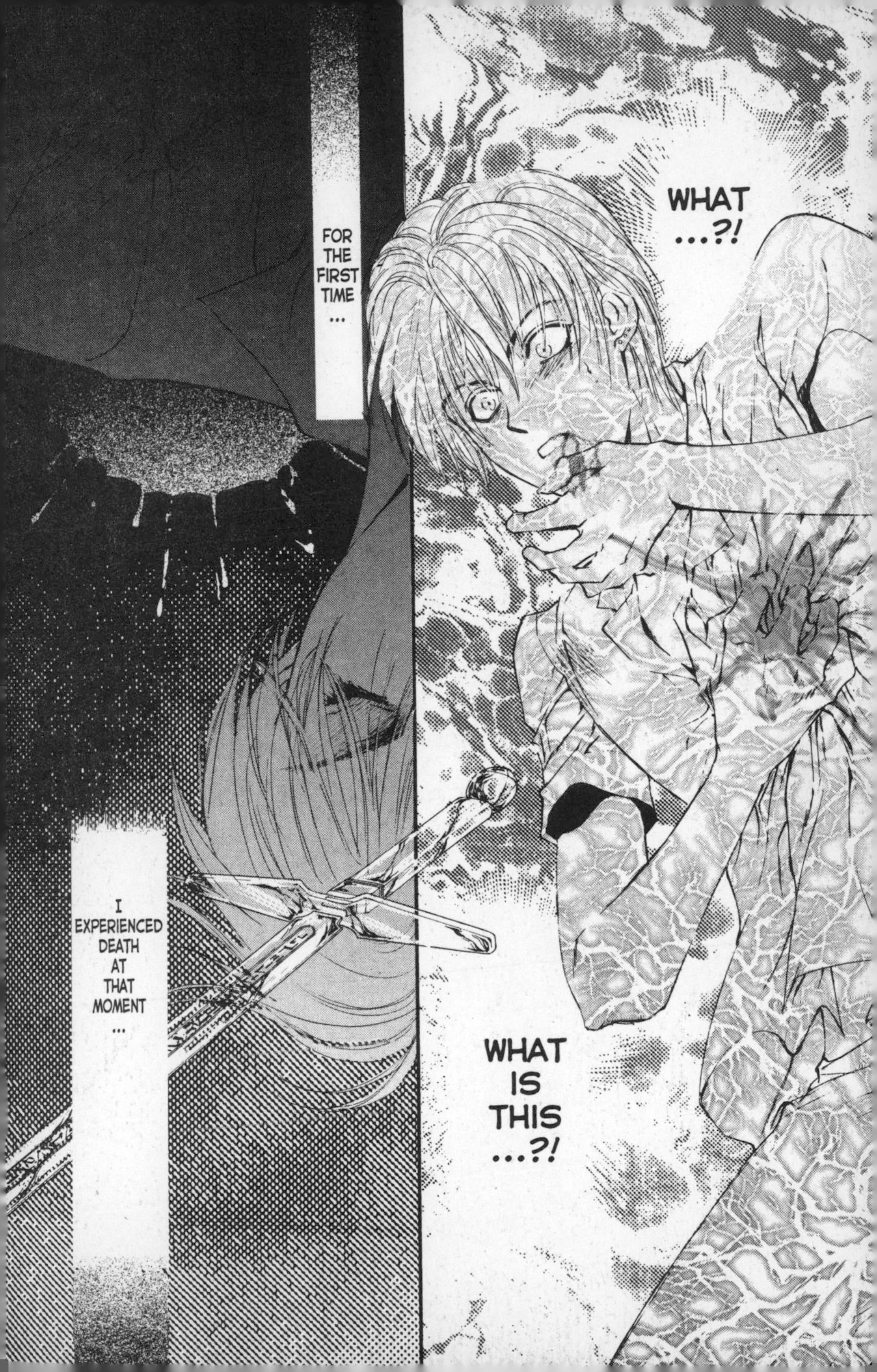
WHAT ...?!
WHAT IS THIS ...?!
FOR THE FIRST TIME ...
I EXPERIENCED DEATH AT THAT MOMENT ...

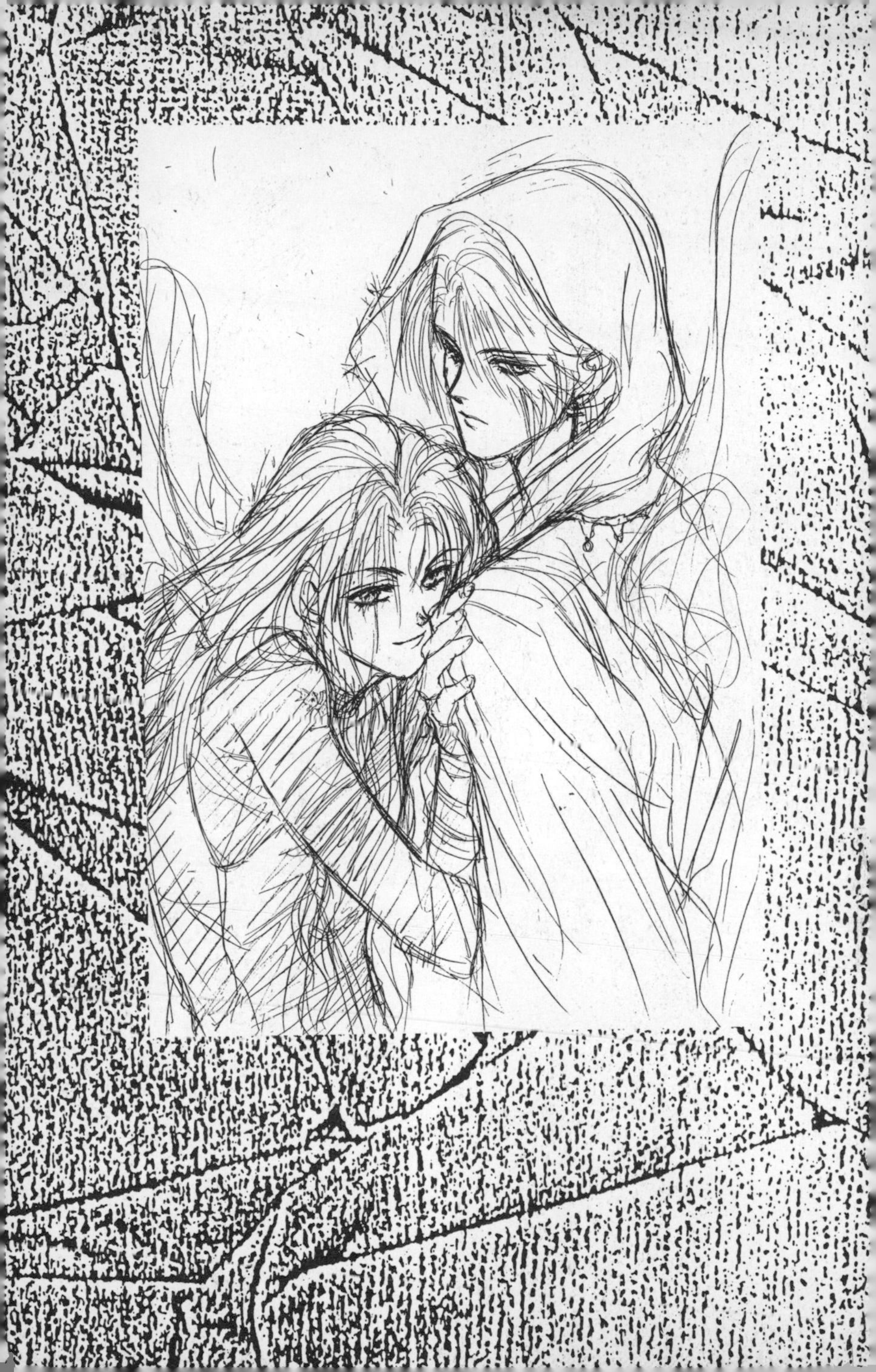

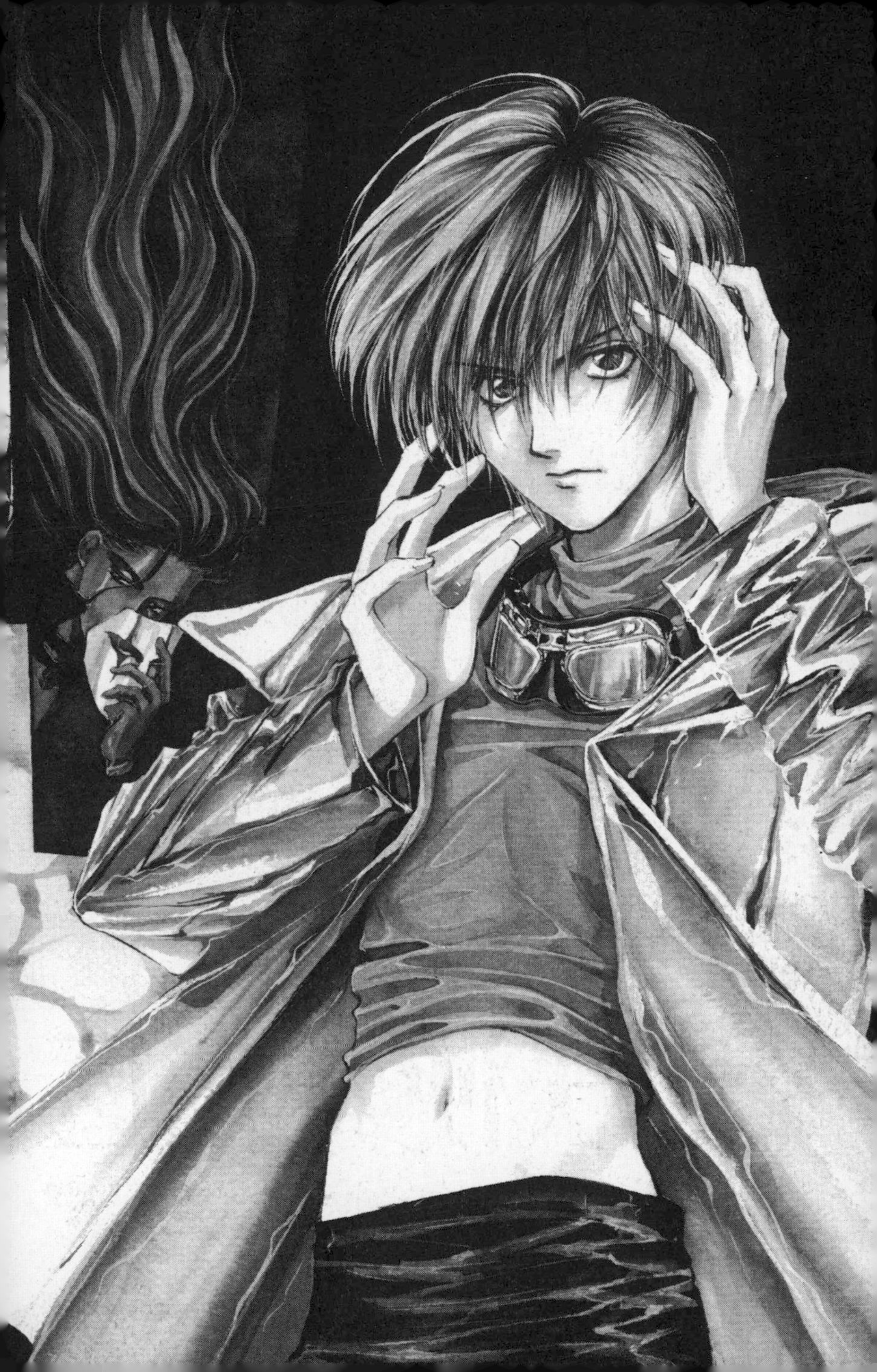

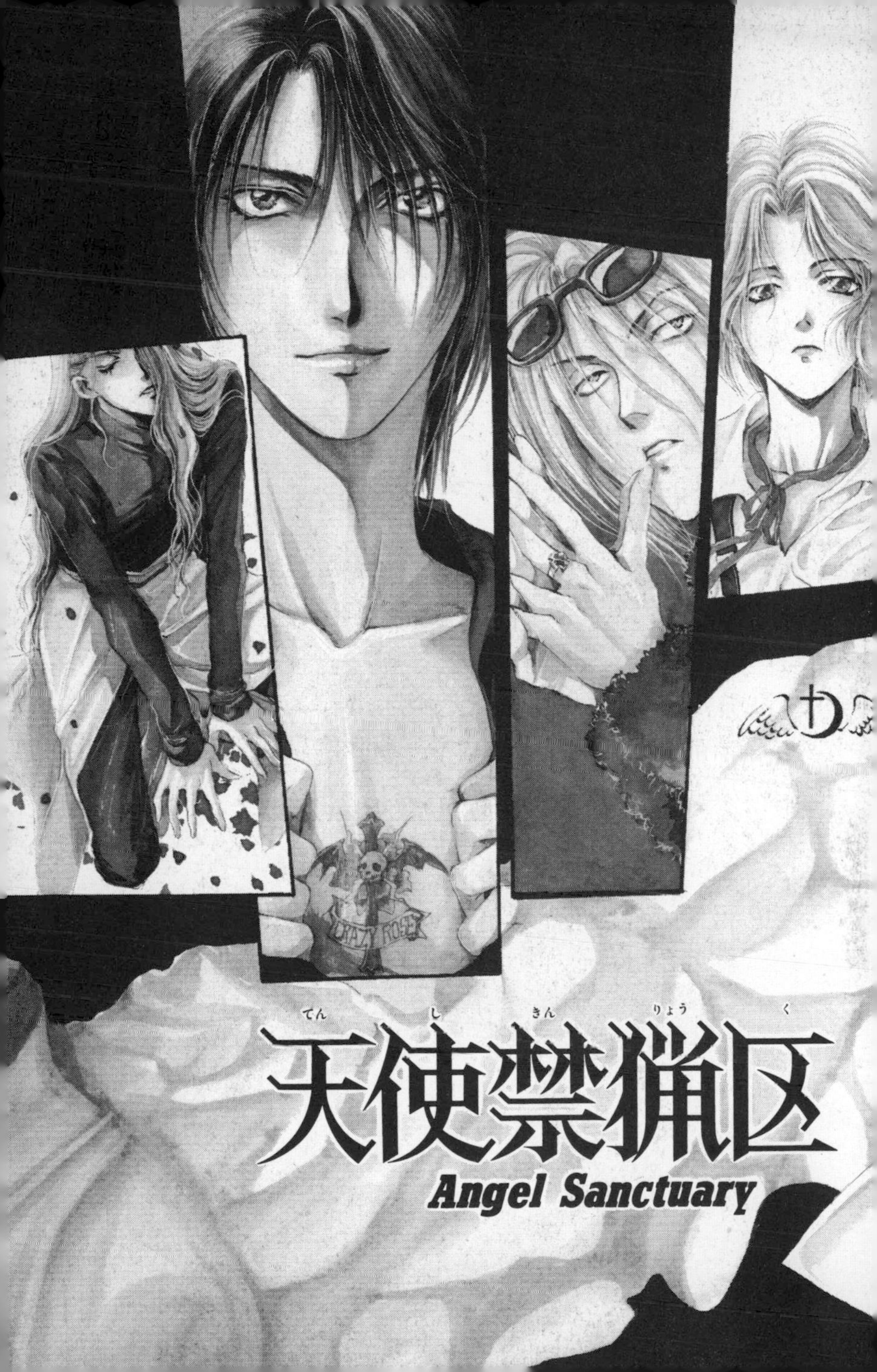
CRAZY ROSE
天使禁猟区
Angel Sanctuary

[redacted]

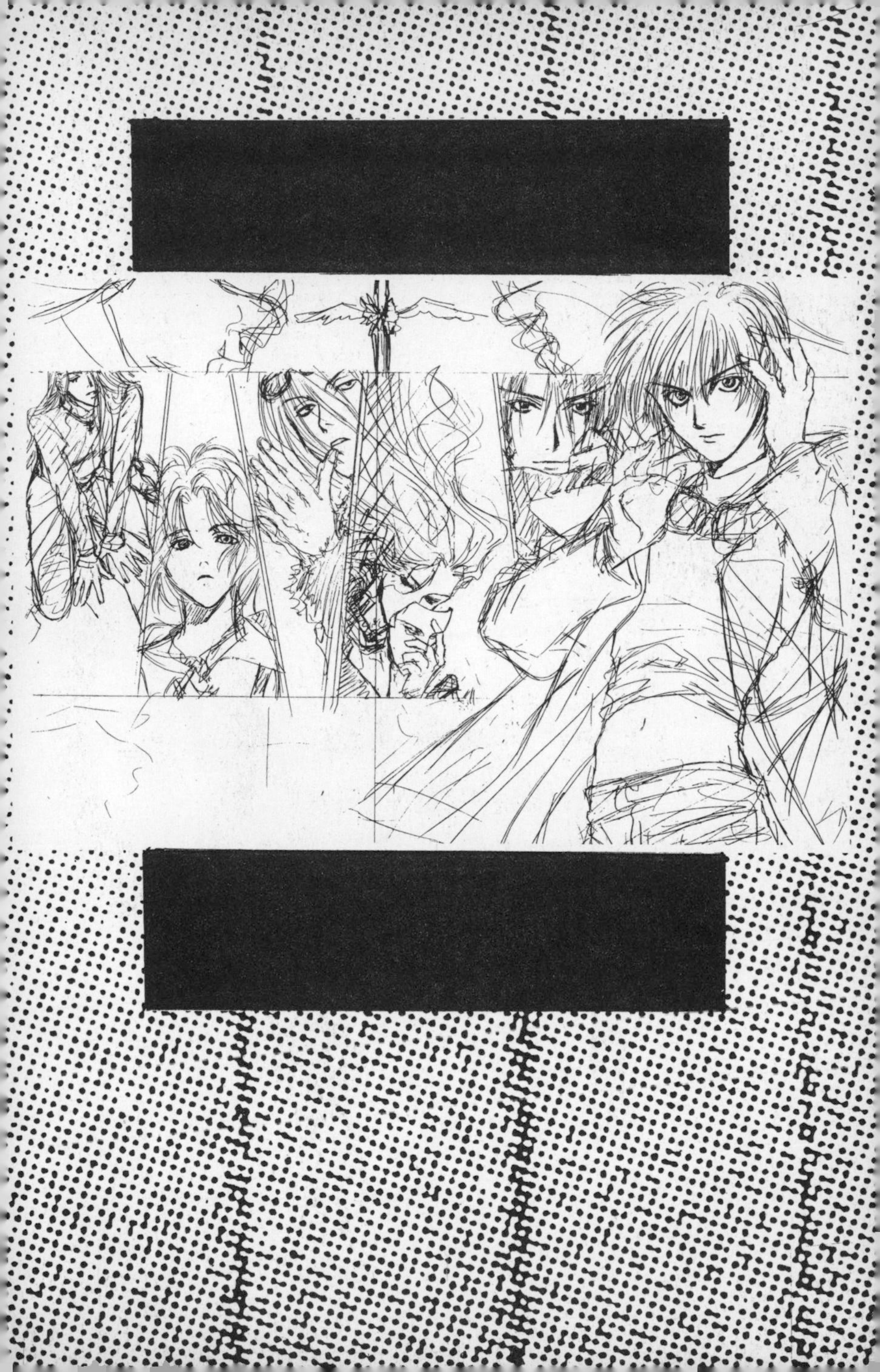

[redacted]

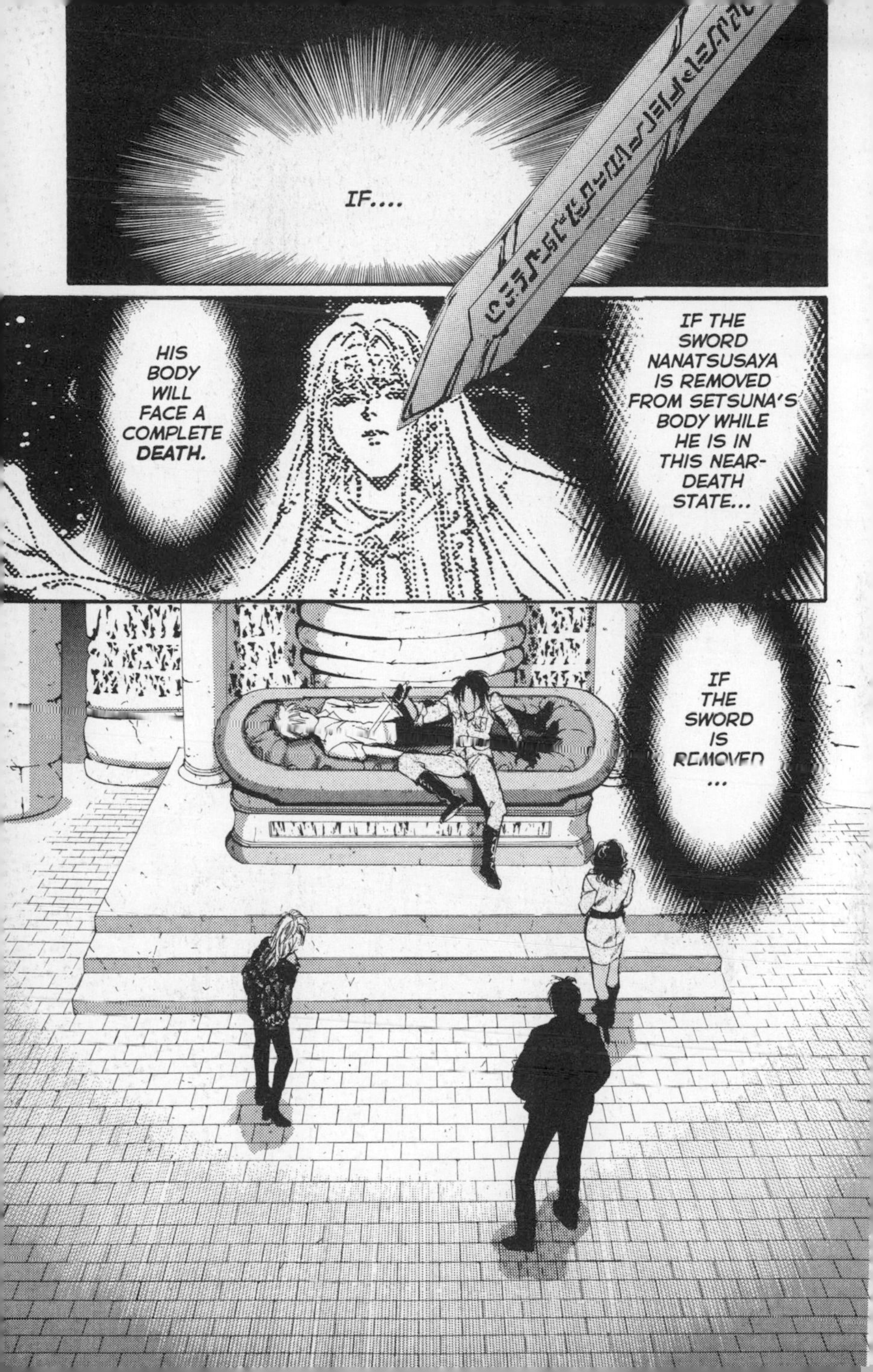
IF....
IF THE SWORD NANATSUSAYA IS REMOVED FROM SETSUNA'S BODY WHILE HE IS IN THIS NEAR-DEATH STATE...
HIS BODY WILL FACE A COMPLETE DEATH.
IF THE SWORD IS REMOVED ...

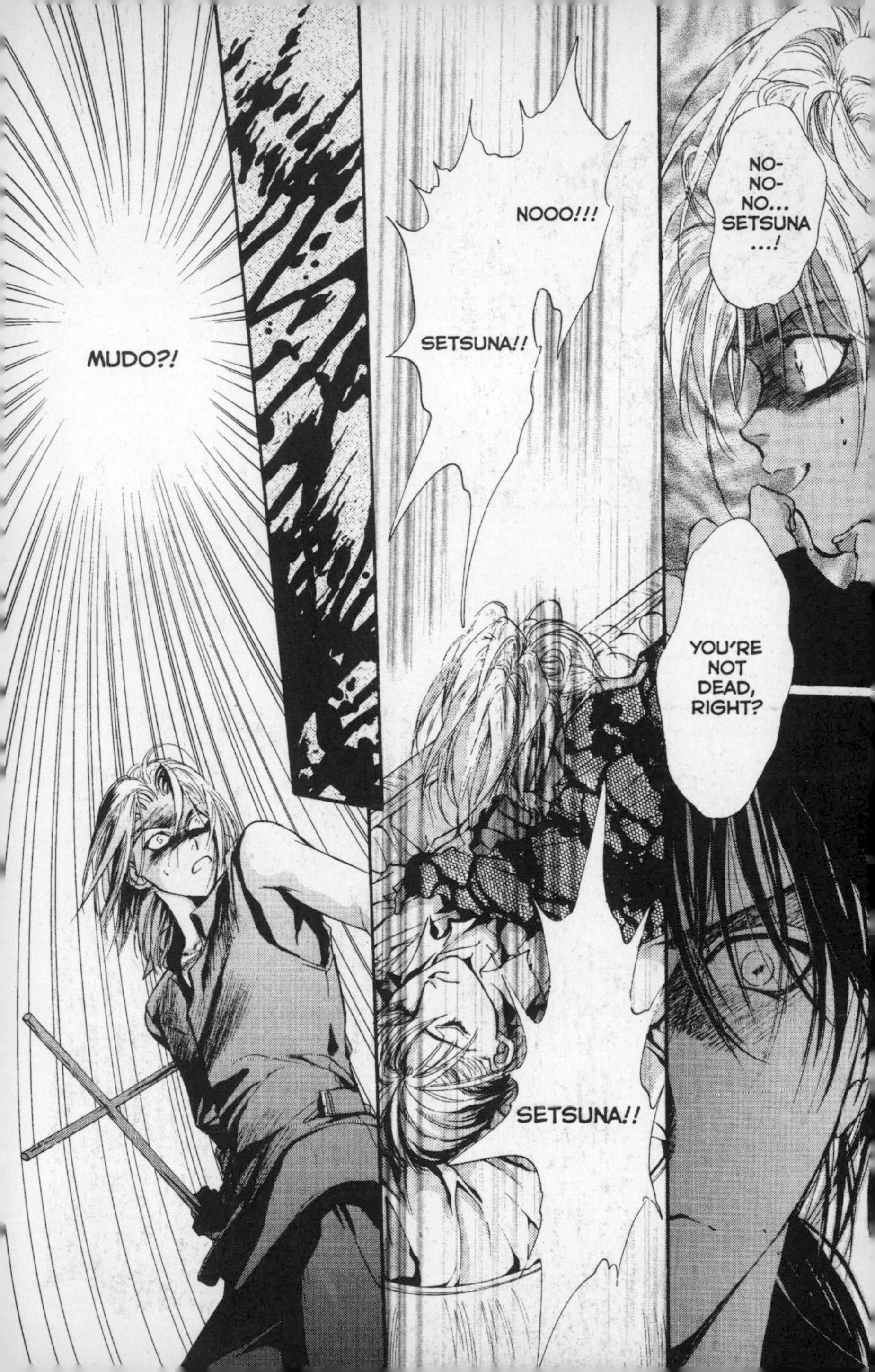
NO- NO- NO... SETSUNA ...!
YOU'RE NOT DEAD, RIGHT?
NOOO!!!
SETSUNA!!
SETSUNA!!
MUDO?!

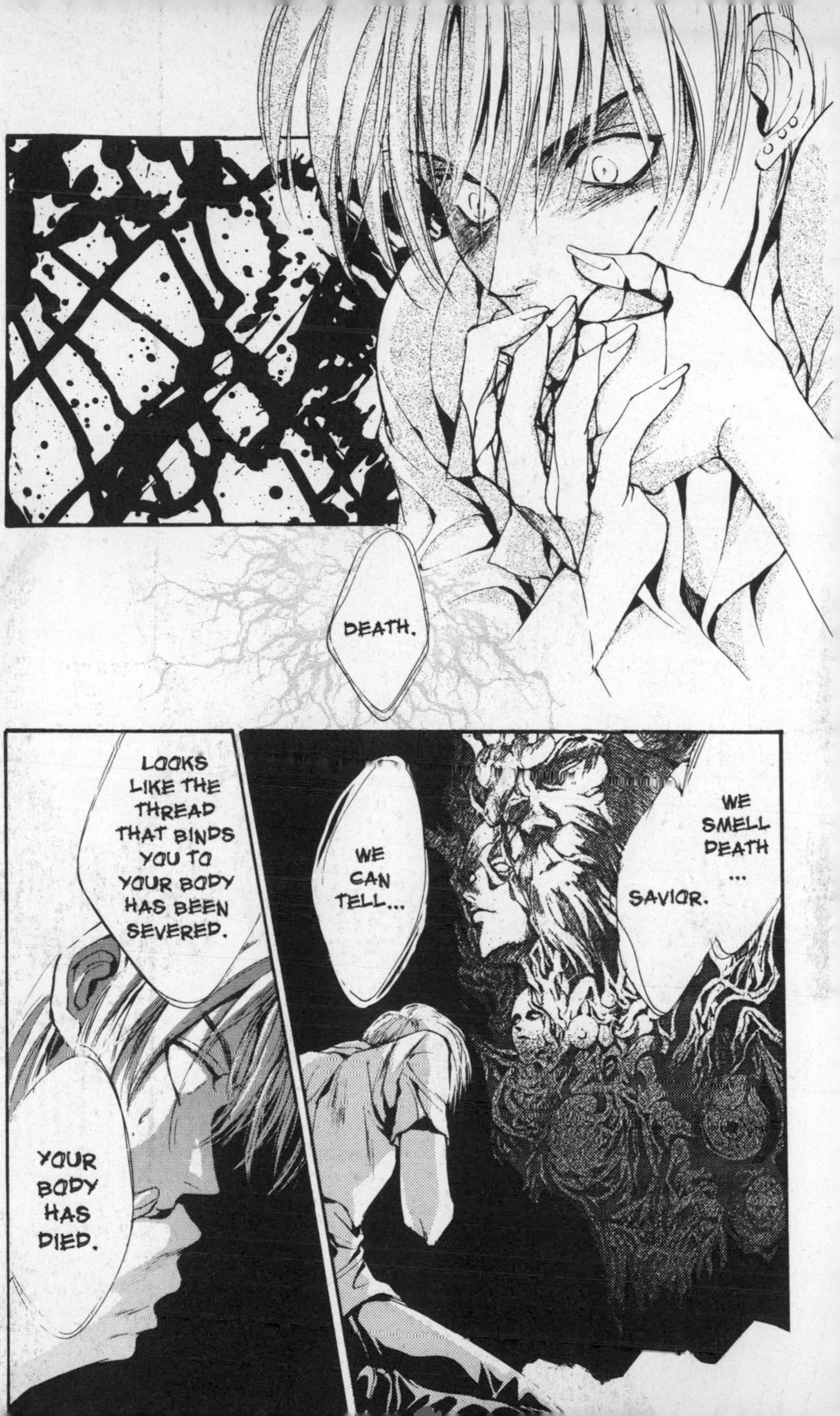
DEATH.
WE SMELL DEATH ...
SAVIOR.
WE CAN TELL...
LOOKS LIKE THE THREAD THAT BINDS YOU TO YOUR BODY HAS BEEN SEVERED.
YOUR BODY HAS DIED.

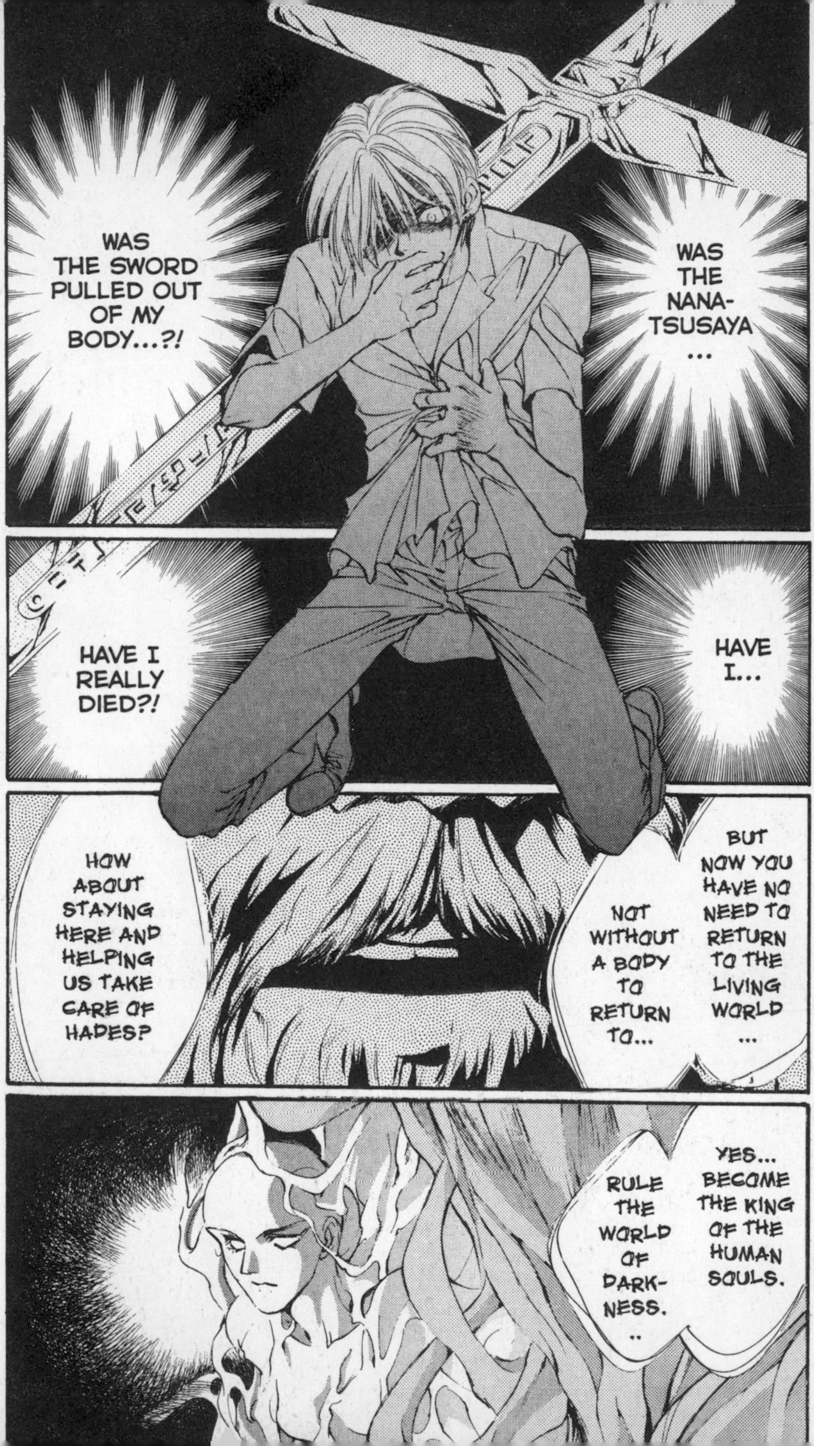
WAS THE NANA-TSUSAYA...
WAS THE SWORD PULLED OUT OF MY BODY...?!
HAVE I...
HAVE I REALLY DIED?!
BUT NOW YOU HAVE NO NEED TO RETURN TO THE LIVING WORLD...
NOT WITHOUT A BODY TO RETURN TO...
HOW ABOUT STAYING HERE AND HELPING US TAKE CARE OF HADES?
YES... BECOME THE KING OF THE HUMAN SOULS.
RULE THE WORLD OF DARKNESS...

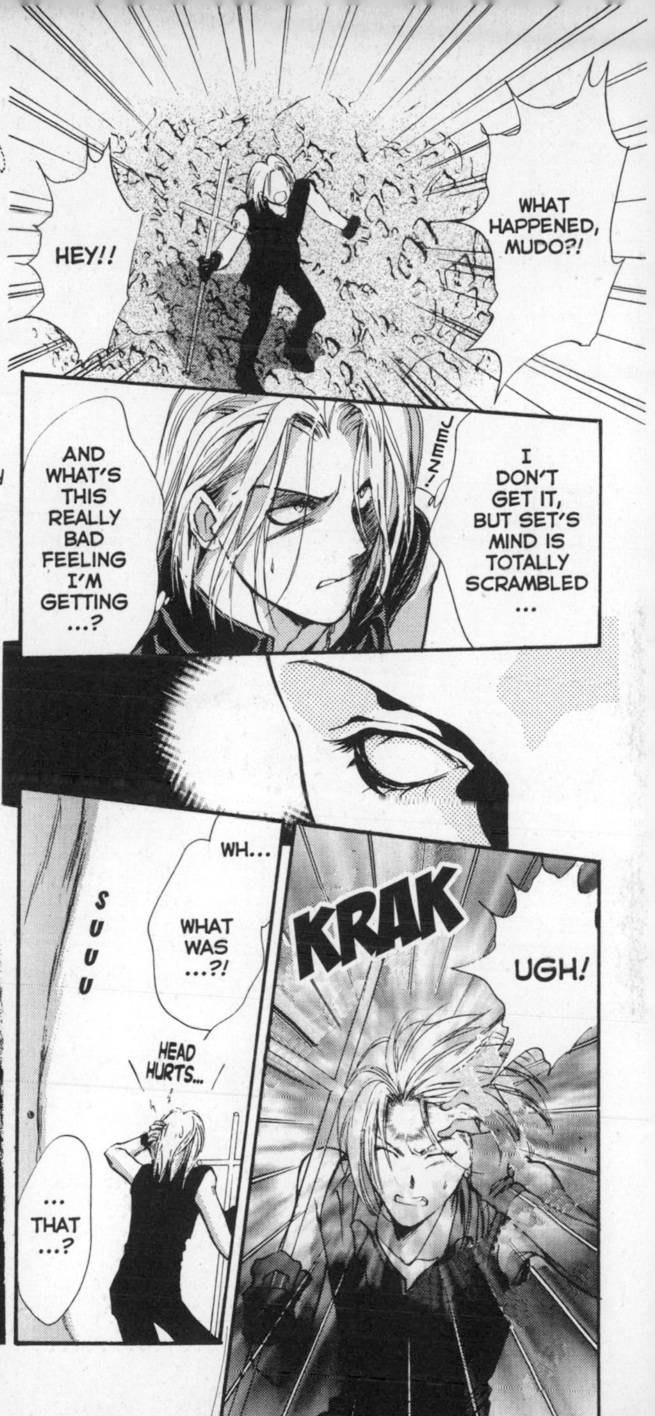
WHAT HAPPENED, MUDO?!
HEY!!
I DON'T GET IT, BUT SET'S MIND IS TOTALLY SCRAMBLED ...
JEN!
AND WHAT'S THIS REALLY BAD FEELING I'M GETTING ...?
KRAK
UGH!
WH...
WHAT WAS ...?!
SUUU
HEAD HURTS...
... THAT ...?

Hello! Did everyone see the embrace between Rosiel and Katan in the last chapter? Did you get dizzy? Almost faint? I did! Oh, how embarrassing... What am I drawing? At first I was going to have Katan save Rosiel in a normal way but I thought that since Katan was just reborn into a new body, it would be weird if he was wearing clothes. I got a lot of comments like "Put some clothes on!!" and "I'm sad you turned Katan into a pervert." (Why does that make him a pervert...?) Also...

(to be continued)

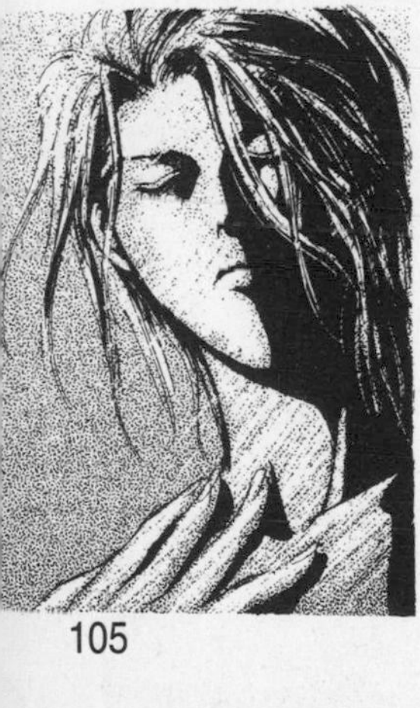

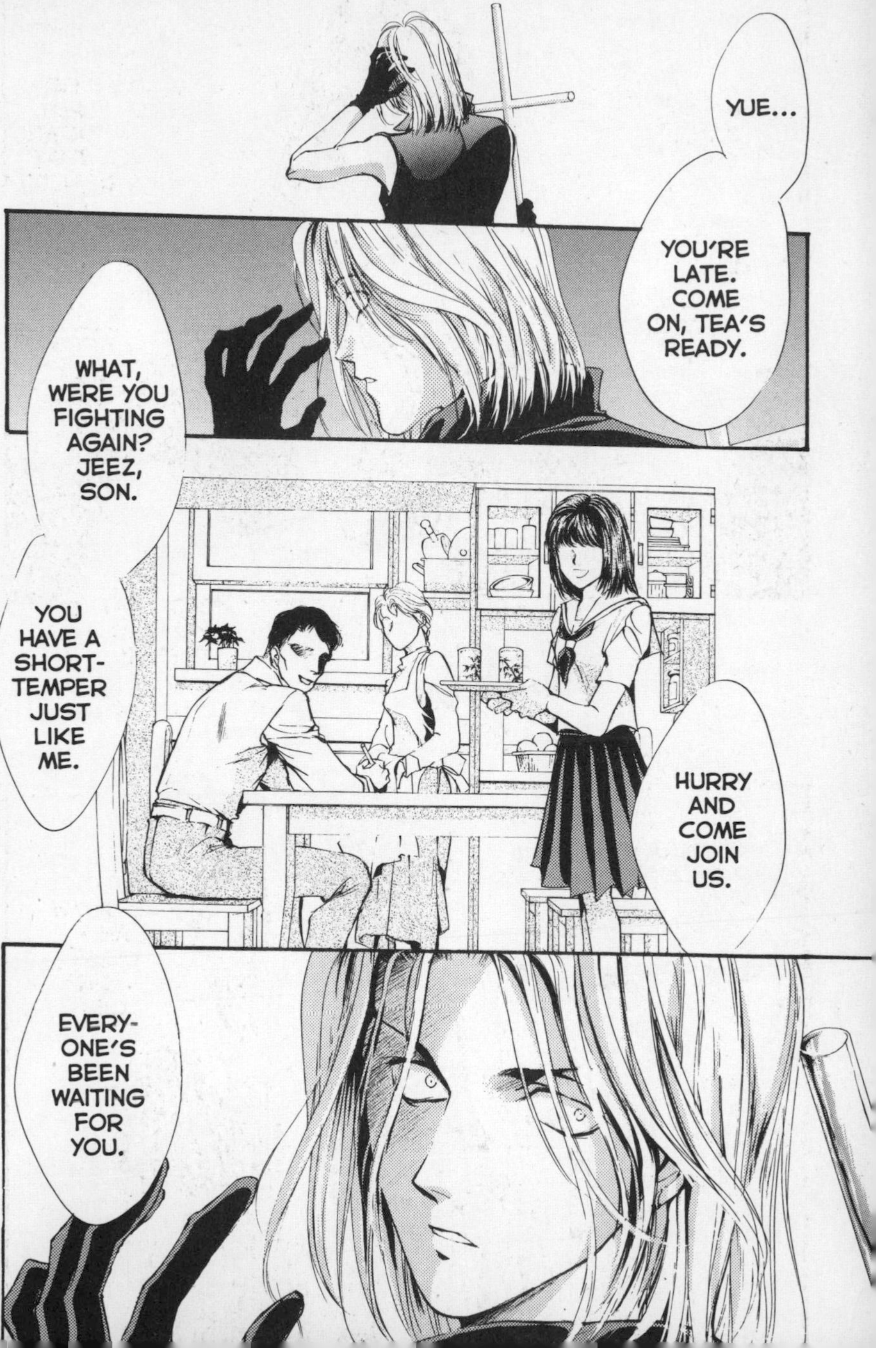
YUE...
YOU'RE LATE. COME ON, TEA'S READY.
WHAT, WERE YOU FIGHTING AGAIN? JEEZ, SON.
YOU HAVE A SHORT-TEMPER JUST LIKE ME.
HURRY AND COME JOIN US.
EVERY-ONE'S BEEN WAITING FOR YOU.

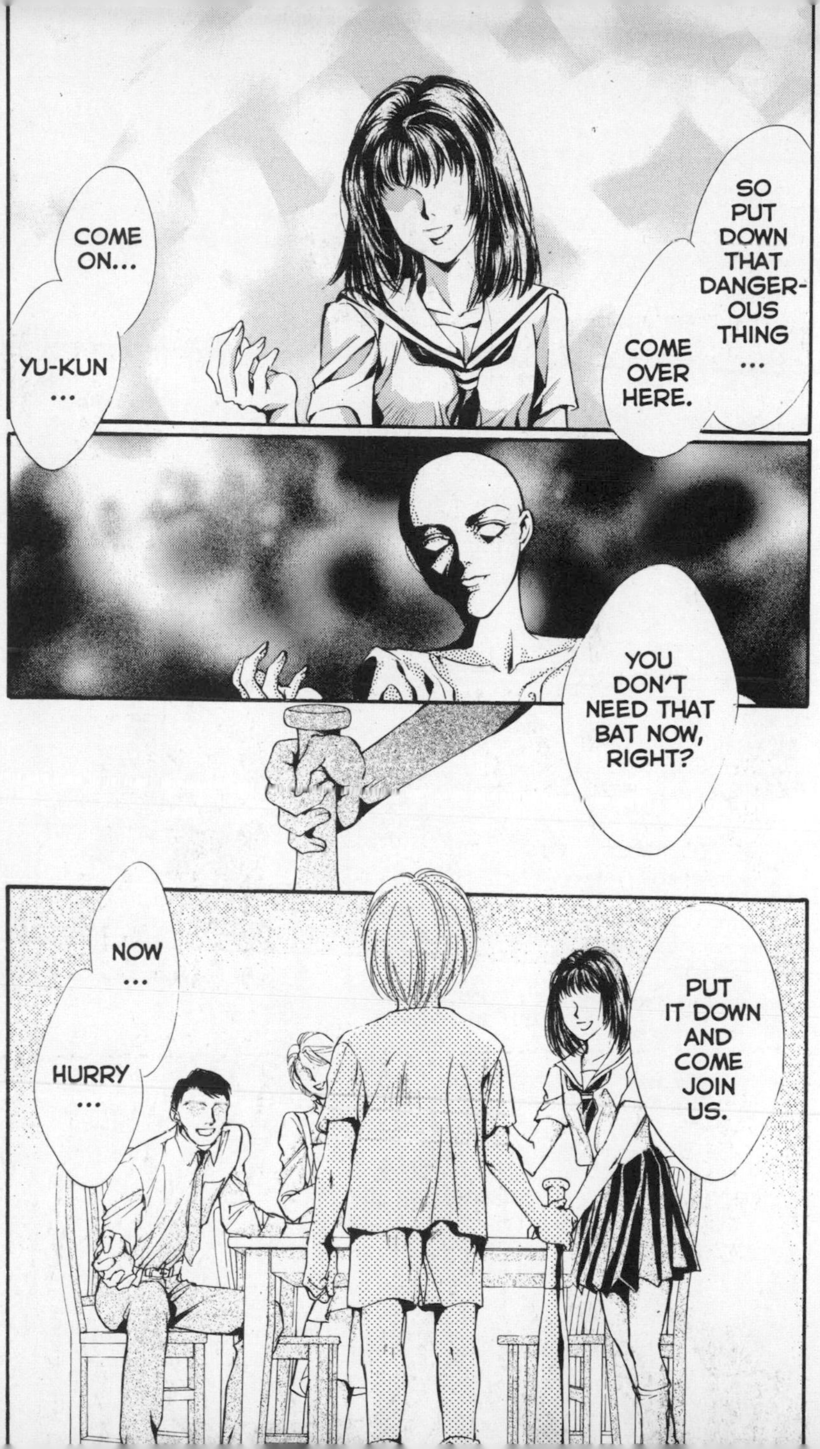
SO PUT DOWN THAT DANGER-OUS THING ...
COME OVER HERE.
COME ON...
YU-KUN ...
YOU DON'T NEED THAT BAT NOW, RIGHT?
PUT IT DOWN AND COME JOIN US.
NOW ...
HURRY ...

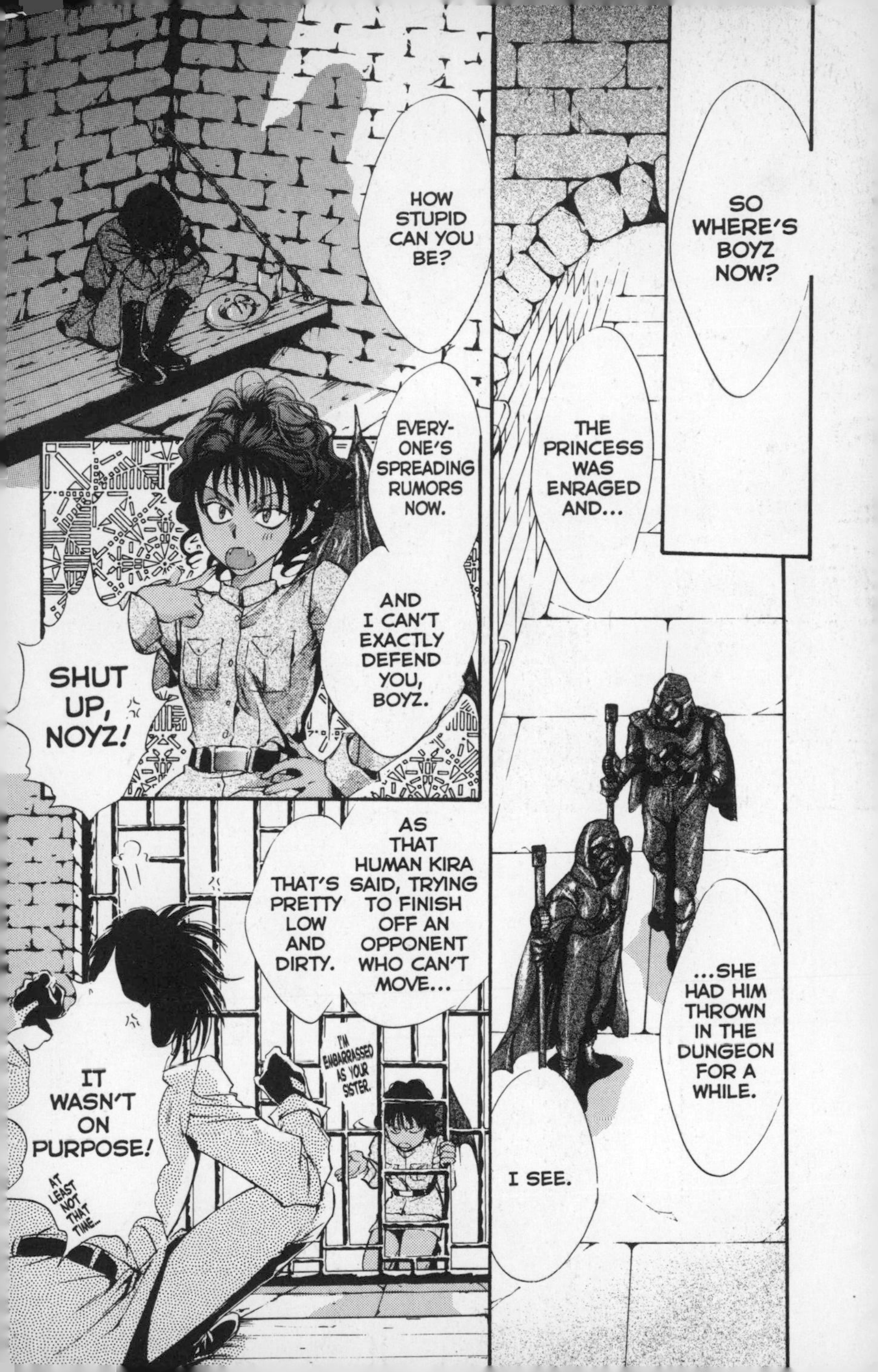
SO WHERE'S BOYZ NOW?
THE PRINCESS WAS ENRAGED AND...
...SHE HAD HIM THROWN IN THE DUNGEON FOR A WHILE.
I SEE.
HOW STUPID CAN YOU BE?
EVERY-ONE'S SPREADING RUMORS NOW.
AND I CAN'T EXACTLY DEFEND YOU, BOYZ.
SHUT UP, NOYZ!
AS THAT HUMAN KIRA SAID, TRYING TO FINISH OFF AN OPPONENT WHO CAN'T MOVE...
THAT'S PRETTY LOW AND DIRTY.
I'M EMBARRASSED AS YOUR SISTER.
IT WASN'T ON PURPOSE!
AT LEAST NOT THAT TIME.

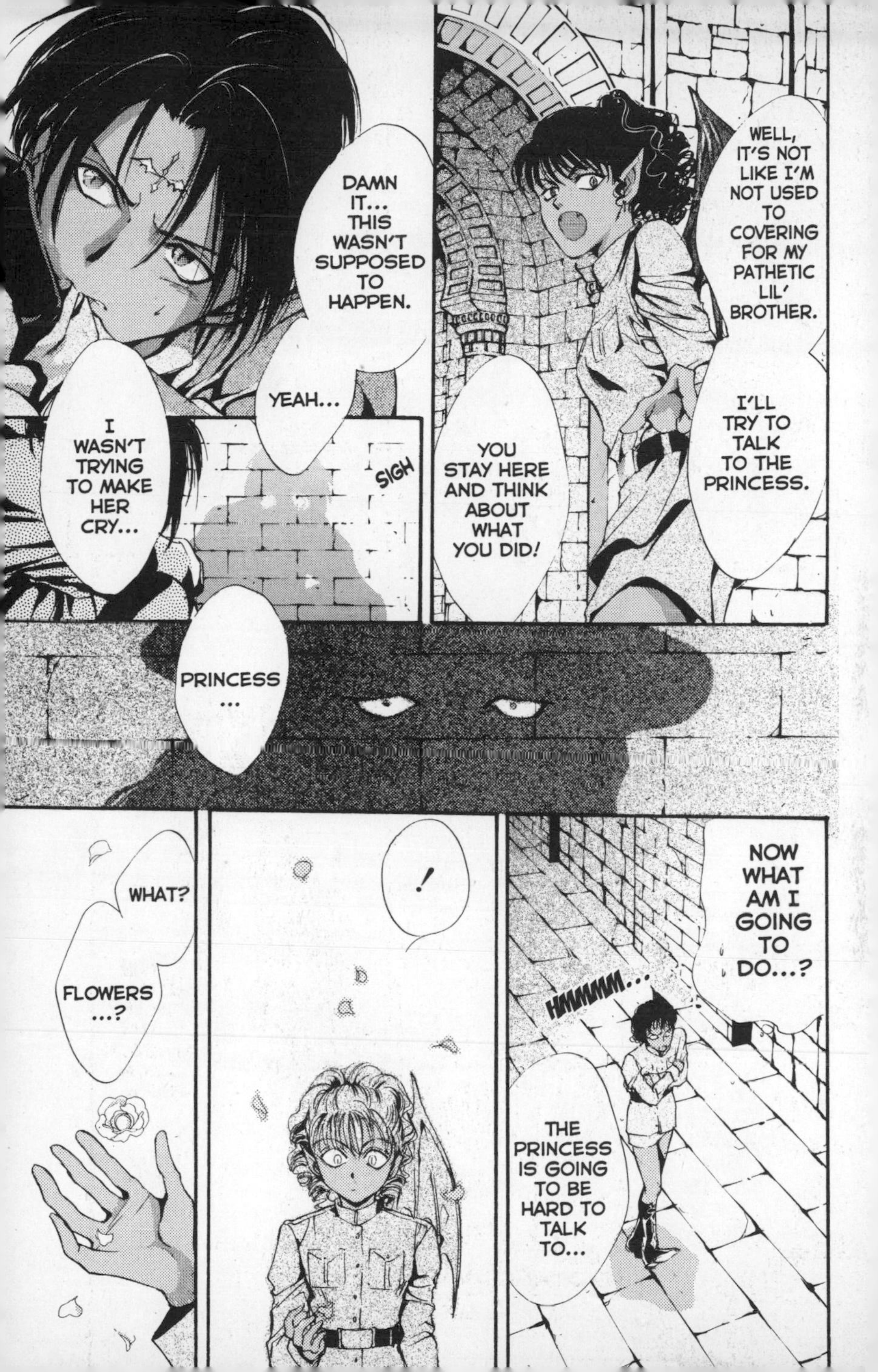
WELL, IT'S NOT LIKE I'M NOT USED TO COVERING FOR MY PATHETIC LIL' BROTHER.
I'LL TRY TO TALK TO THE PRINCESS.
YOU STAY HERE AND THINK ABOUT WHAT YOU DID!
DAMN IT... THIS WASN'T SUPPOSED TO HAPPEN.
YEAH...
SIGH
I WASN'T TRYING TO MAKE HER CRY...
PRINCESS...
NOW WHAT AM I GOING TO DO...?
HMMMM...
THE PRINCESS IS GOING TO BE HARD TO TALK TO...
!
WHAT?
FLOWERS...?

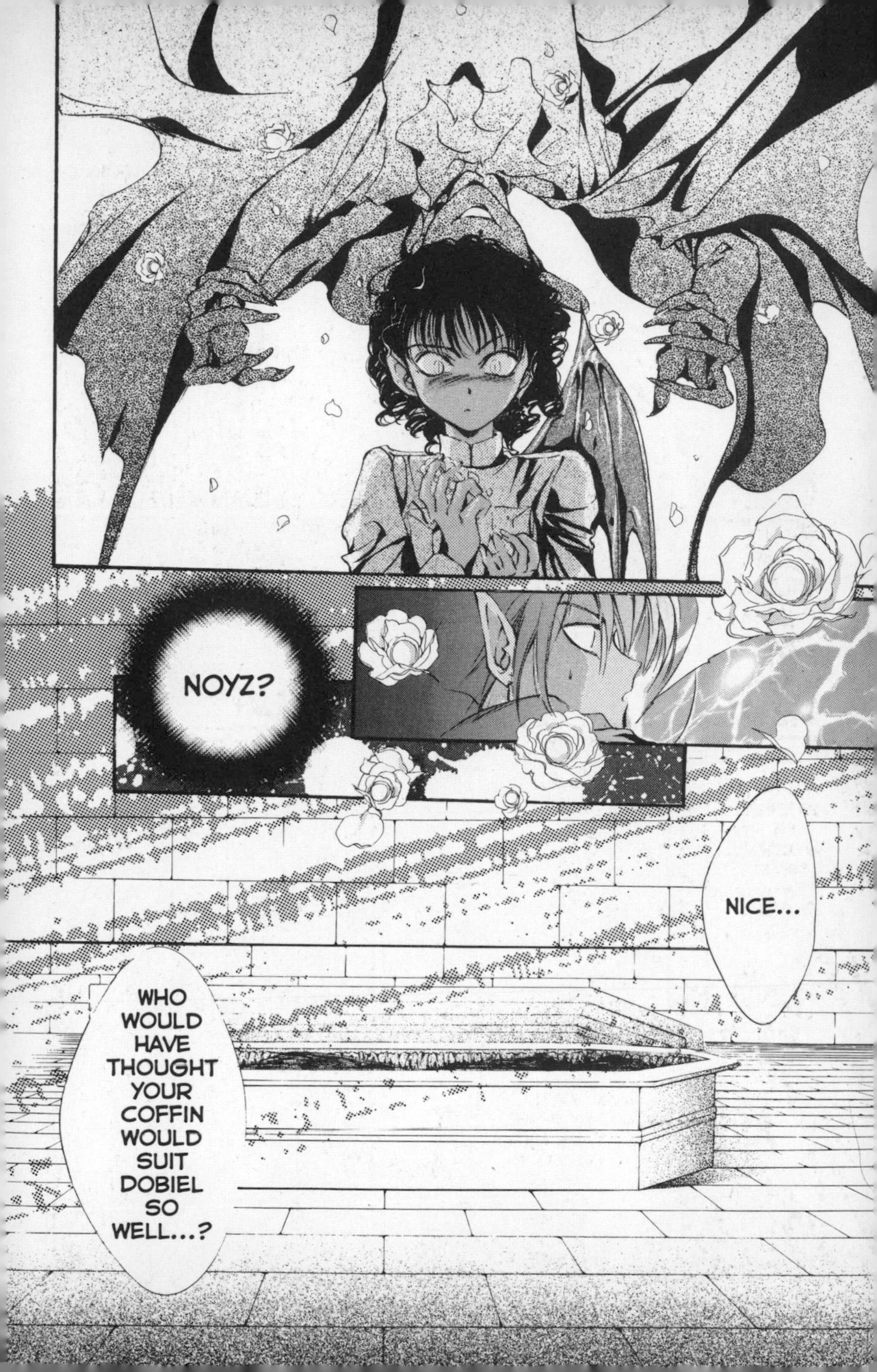
NOYZ?
NICE...
WHO WOULD HAVE THOUGHT YOUR COFFIN WOULD SUIT DOBIEL SO WELL...?

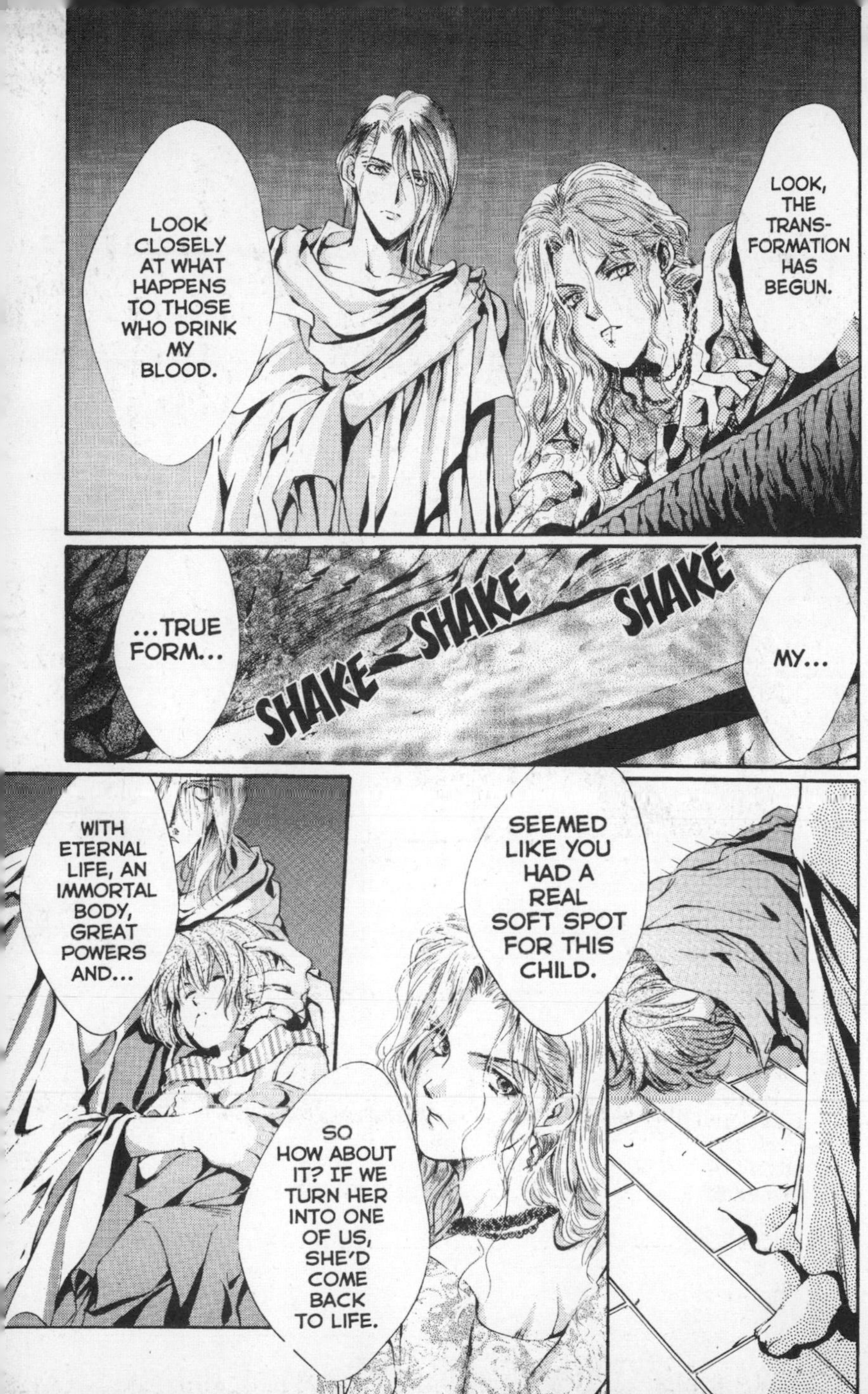
LOOK, THE TRANS-FORMATION HAS BEGUN.
LOOK CLOSELY AT WHAT HAPPENS TO THOSE WHO DRINK MY BLOOD.
MY...
SHAKE SHAKE SHAKE SHAKE
...TRUE FORM...
SEEMED LIKE YOU HAD A REAL SOFT SPOT FOR THIS CHILD.
SO HOW ABOUT IT? IF WE TURN HER INTO ONE OF US, SHE'D COME BACK TO LIFE.
WITH ETERNAL LIFE, AN IMMORTAL BODY, GREAT POWERS AND...

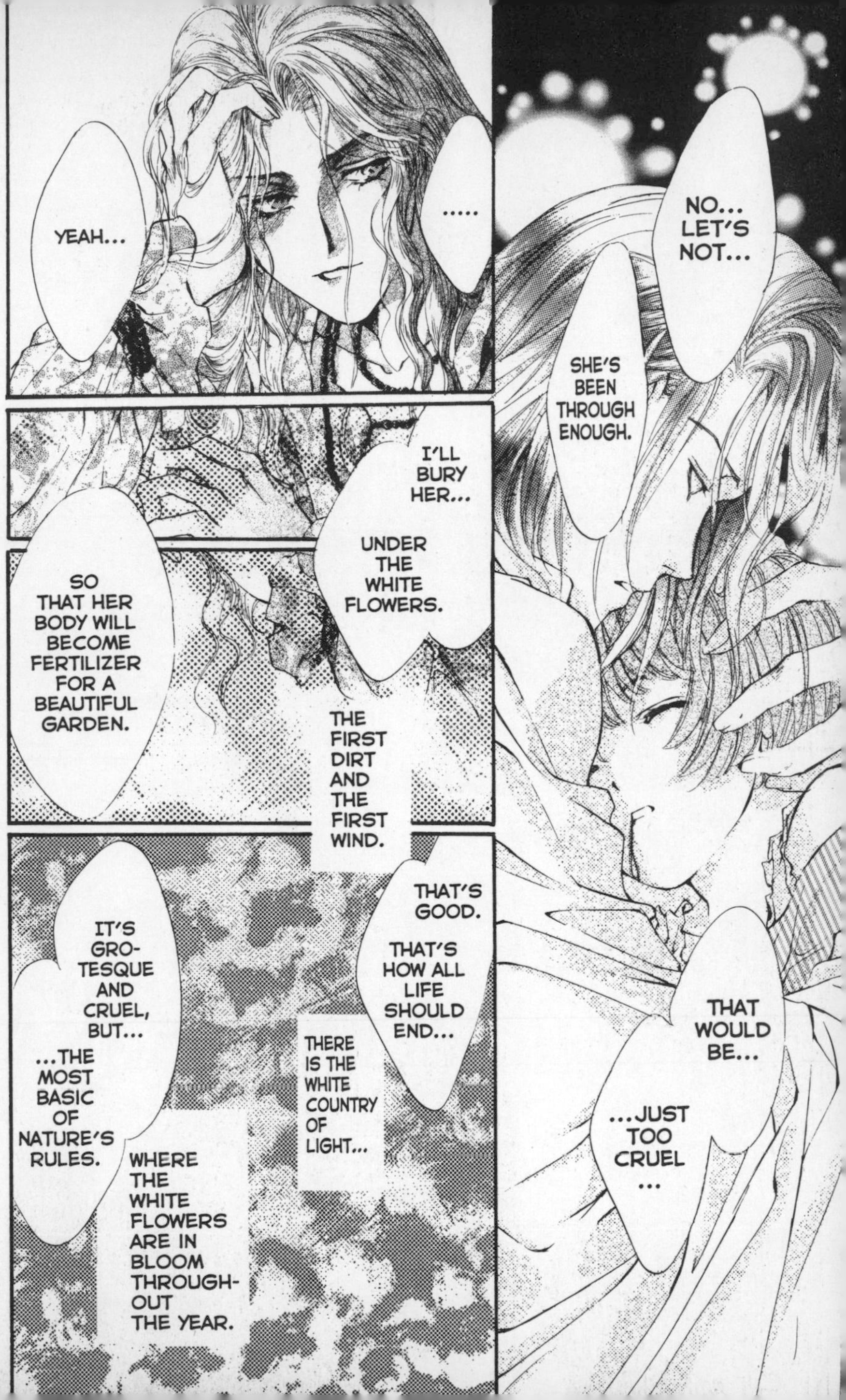
NO... LET'S NOT...
SHE'S BEEN THROUGH ENOUGH.
THAT WOULD BE...
...JUST TOO CRUEL ...
.....
YEAH...
I'LL BURY HER...
UNDER THE WHITE FLOWERS.
SO THAT HER BODY WILL BECOME FERTILIZER FOR A BEAUTIFUL GARDEN.
THE FIRST DIRT AND THE FIRST WIND.
THAT'S GOOD.
THAT'S HOW ALL LIFE SHOULD END...
IT'S GRO-TESQUE AND CRUEL, BUT...
...THE MOST BASIC OF NATURE'S RULES.
THERE IS THE WHITE COUNTRY OF LIGHT...
WHERE THE WHITE FLOWERS ARE IN BLOOM THROUGH-OUT THE YEAR.

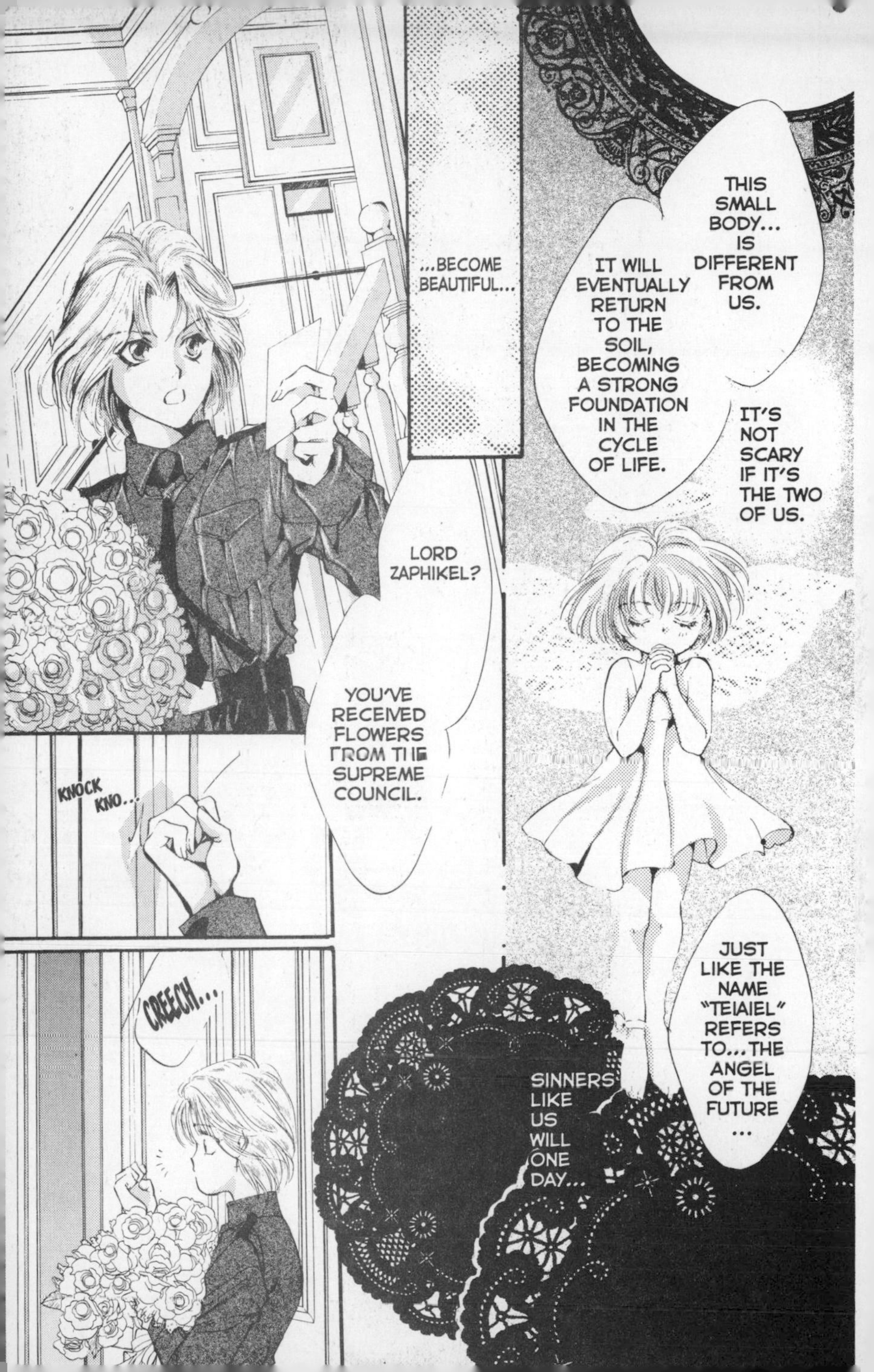
THIS SMALL BODY... IS DIFFERENT FROM US.
IT WILL EVENTUALLY RETURN TO THE SOIL, BECOMING A STRONG FOUNDATION IN THE CYCLE OF LIFE.
IT'S NOT SCARY IF IT'S THE TWO OF US.
JUST LIKE THE NAME "TEIAIEL" REFERS TO... THE ANGEL OF THE FUTURE ...
SINNERS LIKE US WILL ONE DAY...
...BECOME BEAUTIFUL...
LORD ZAPHIKEL?
YOU'VE RECEIVED FLOWERS FROM THE SUPREME COUNCIL.
KNOCK KNO...
CREECH...

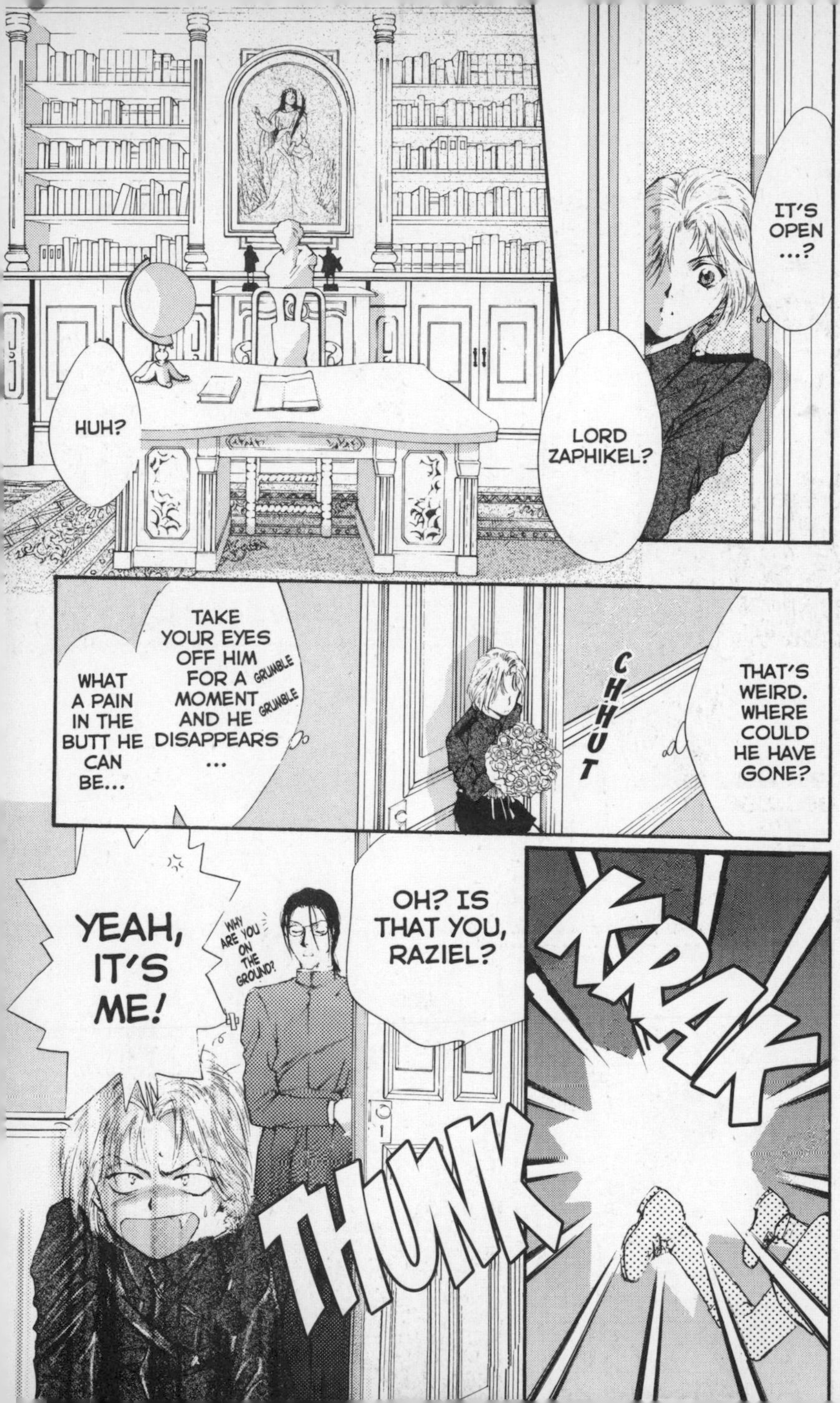
IT'S OPEN ...?
LORD ZAPHIKEL?
HUH?
THAT'S WEIRD. WHERE COULD HE HAVE GONE?
CHHUT
TAKE YOUR EYES OFF HIM FOR A MOMENT AND HE DISAPPEARS ...
GRUMBLE GRUMBLE
WHAT A PAIN IN THE BUTT HE CAN BE...
KRAK
THUNK
OH? IS THAT YOU, RAZIEL?
WHY ARE YOU ON THE GROUND?
YEAH, IT'S ME!

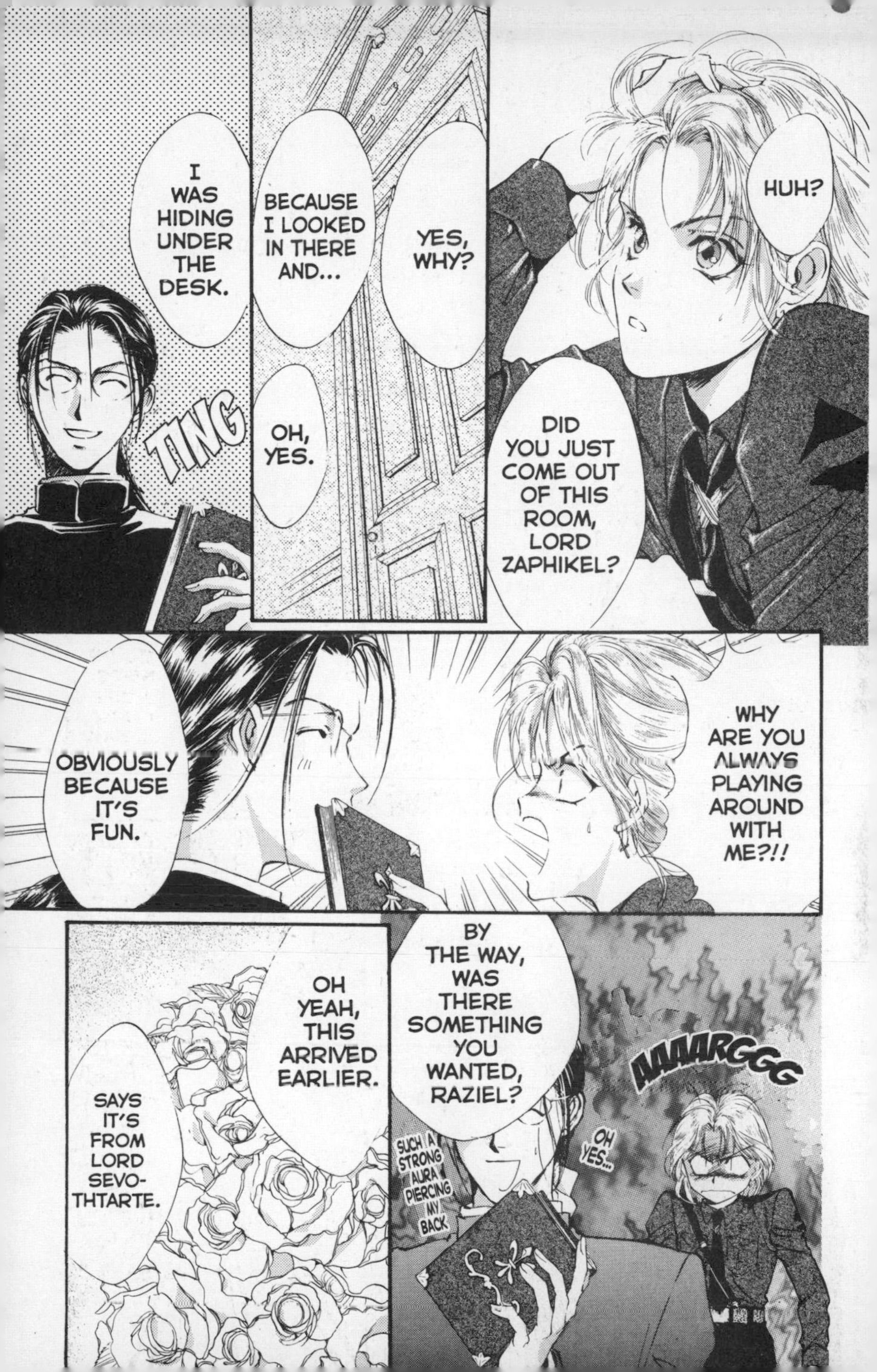
HUH?
DID YOU JUST COME OUT OF THIS ROOM, LORD ZAPHIKEL?
YES, WHY?
BECAUSE I LOOKED IN THERE AND...
OH, YES.
I WAS HIDING UNDER THE DESK.
TING
WHY ARE YOU ALWAYS PLAYING AROUND WITH ME?!!
OBVIOUSLY BECAUSE IT'S FUN.
BY THE WAY, WAS THERE SOMETHING YOU WANTED, RAZIEL?
AAAARGGG
OH YES...
SUCH A STRONG AURA PIERCING MY BACK
OH YEAH, THIS ARRIVED EARLIER.
SAYS IT'S FROM LORD SEVOTHTARTE.

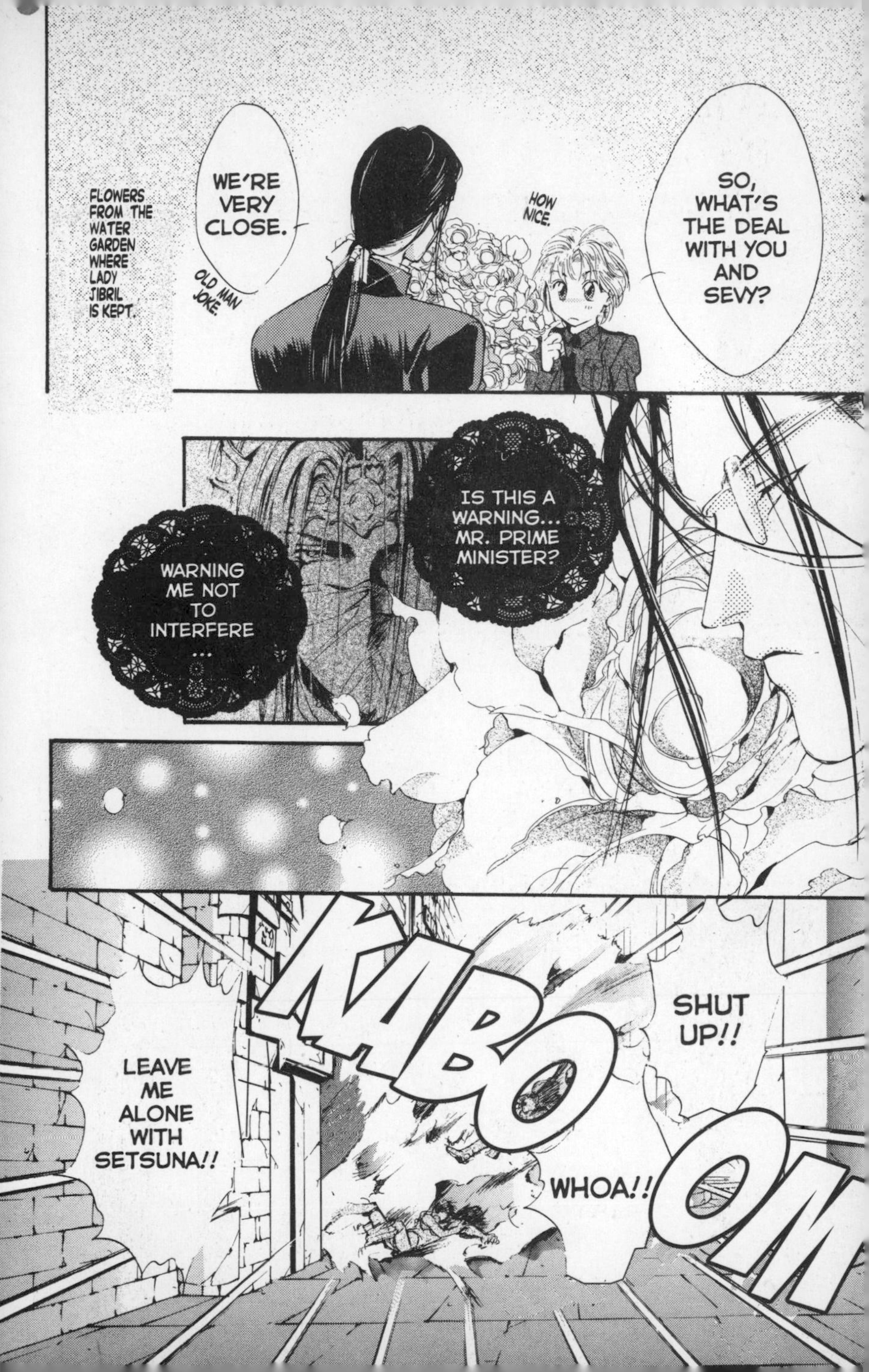
SO, WHAT'S THE DEAL WITH YOU AND SEVY?
HOW NICE.
WE'RE VERY CLOSE.
OLD MAN JOKE.
FLOWERS FROM THE WATER GARDEN WHERE LADY JIBRIL IS KEPT.
IS THIS A WARNING... MR. PRIME MINISTER?
WARNING ME NOT TO INTERFERE ...
SHUT UP!!
KABOOM
LEAVE ME ALONE WITH SETSUNA!!
WHOA!!

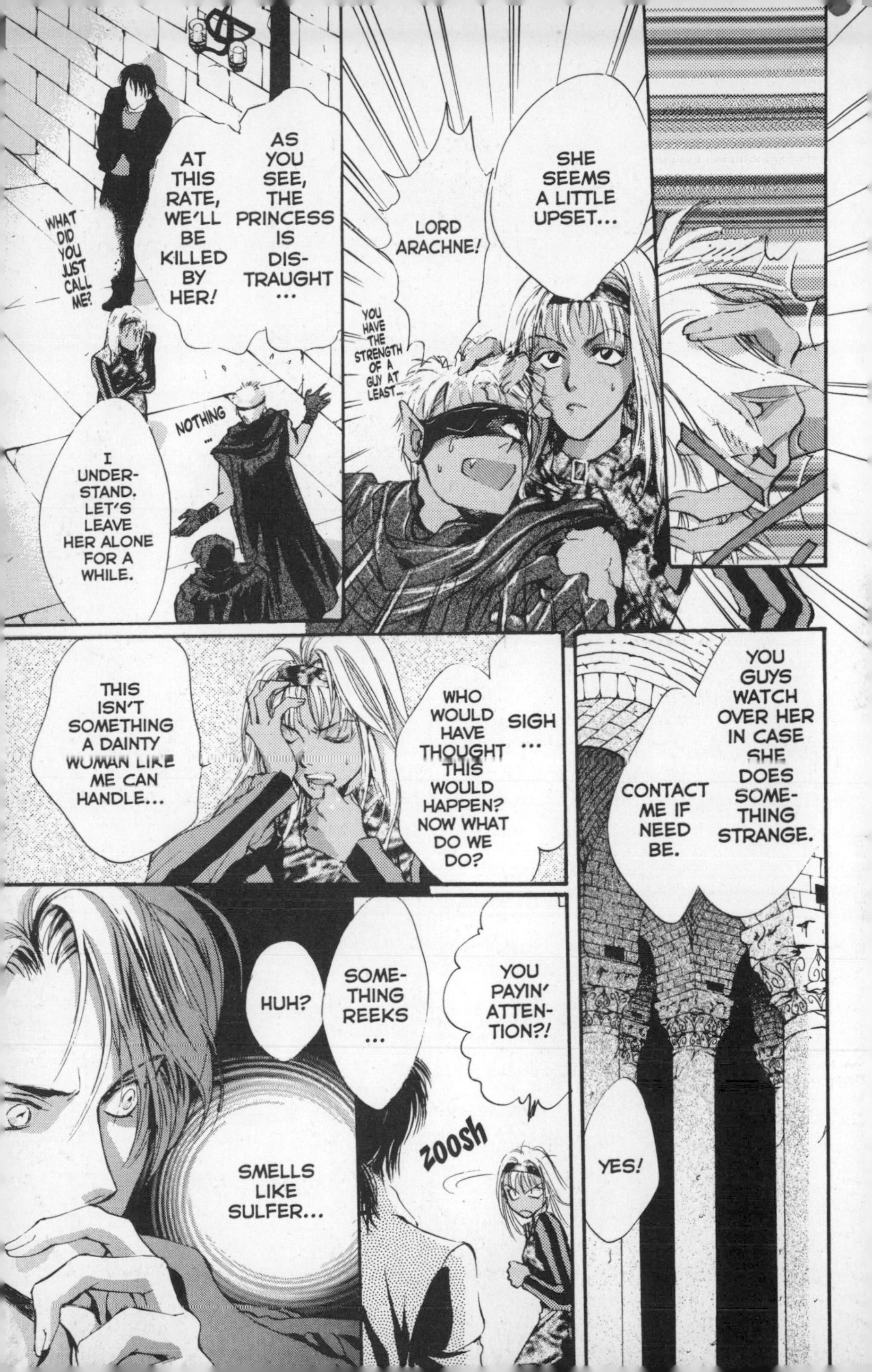
SHE SEEMS A LITTLE UPSET...
LORD ARACHNE!
YOU HAVE THE STRENGTH OF A GUY AT LEAST...
AS YOU SEE, THE PRINCESS IS DIS-TRAUGHT...
AT THIS RATE, WE'LL BE KILLED BY HER!
WHAT DID YOU JUST CALL ME?
NOTHING...
I UNDER-STAND. LET'S LEAVE HER ALONE FOR A WHILE.
YOU GUYS WATCH OVER HER IN CASE SHE DOES SOME-THING STRANGE.
CONTACT ME IF NEED BE.
YES!
SIGH...
WHO WOULD HAVE THOUGHT THIS WOULD HAPPEN? NOW WHAT DO WE DO?
THIS ISN'T SOMETHING A DAINTY WOMAN LIKE ME CAN HANDLE...
YOU PAYIN' ATTEN-TION?!
SOME-THING REEKS...
HUH?
zoosh
SMELLS LIKE SULFER...

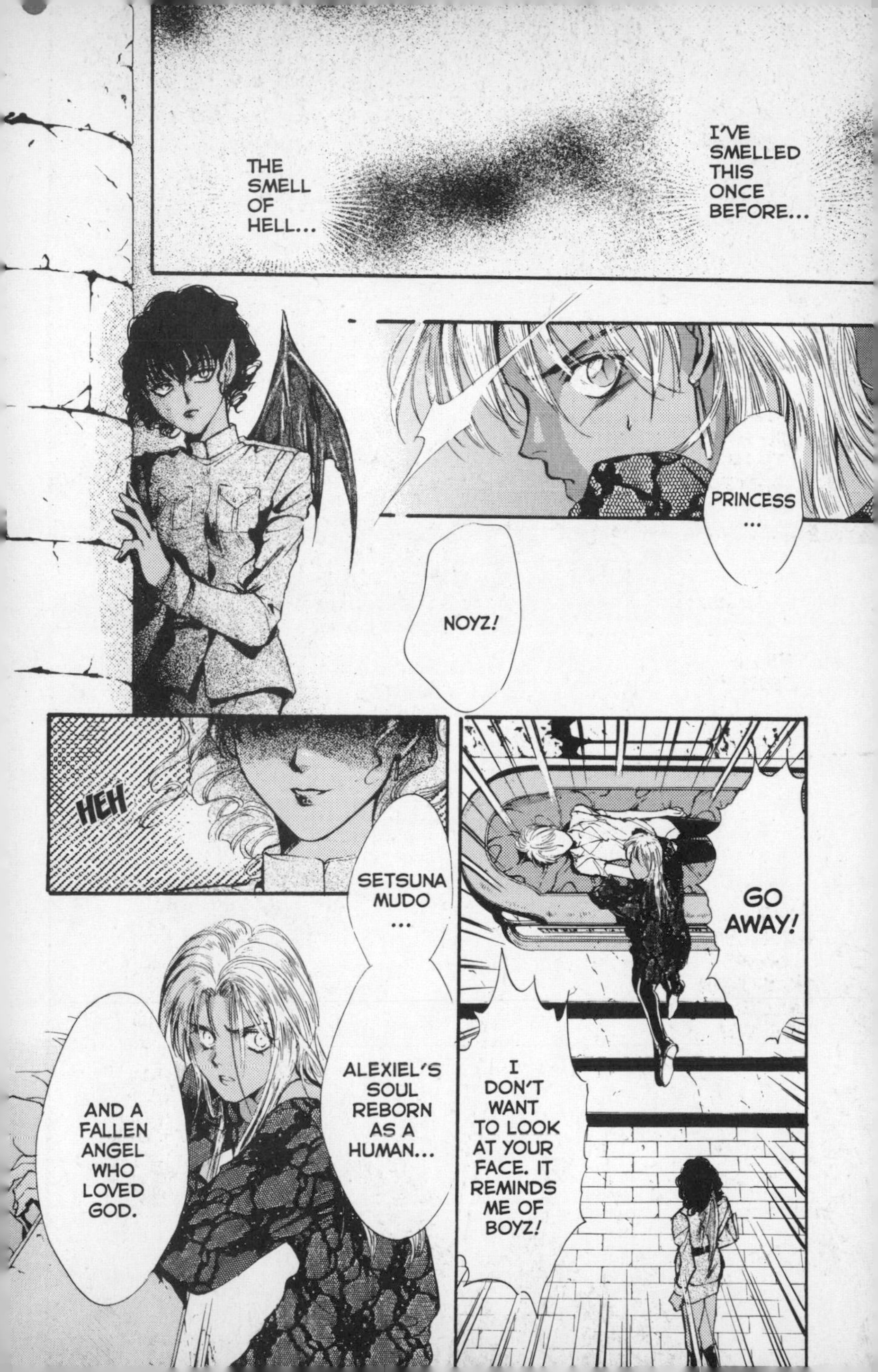
I'VE SMELLED THIS ONCE BEFORE...
THE SMELL OF HELL...
PRINCESS ...
NOYZ!
GO AWAY!
I DON'T WANT TO LOOK AT YOUR FACE. IT REMINDS ME OF BOYZ!
HEH
SETSUNA MUDO ...
ALEXIEL'S SOUL REBORN AS A HUMAN...
AND A FALLEN ANGEL WHO LOVED GOD.

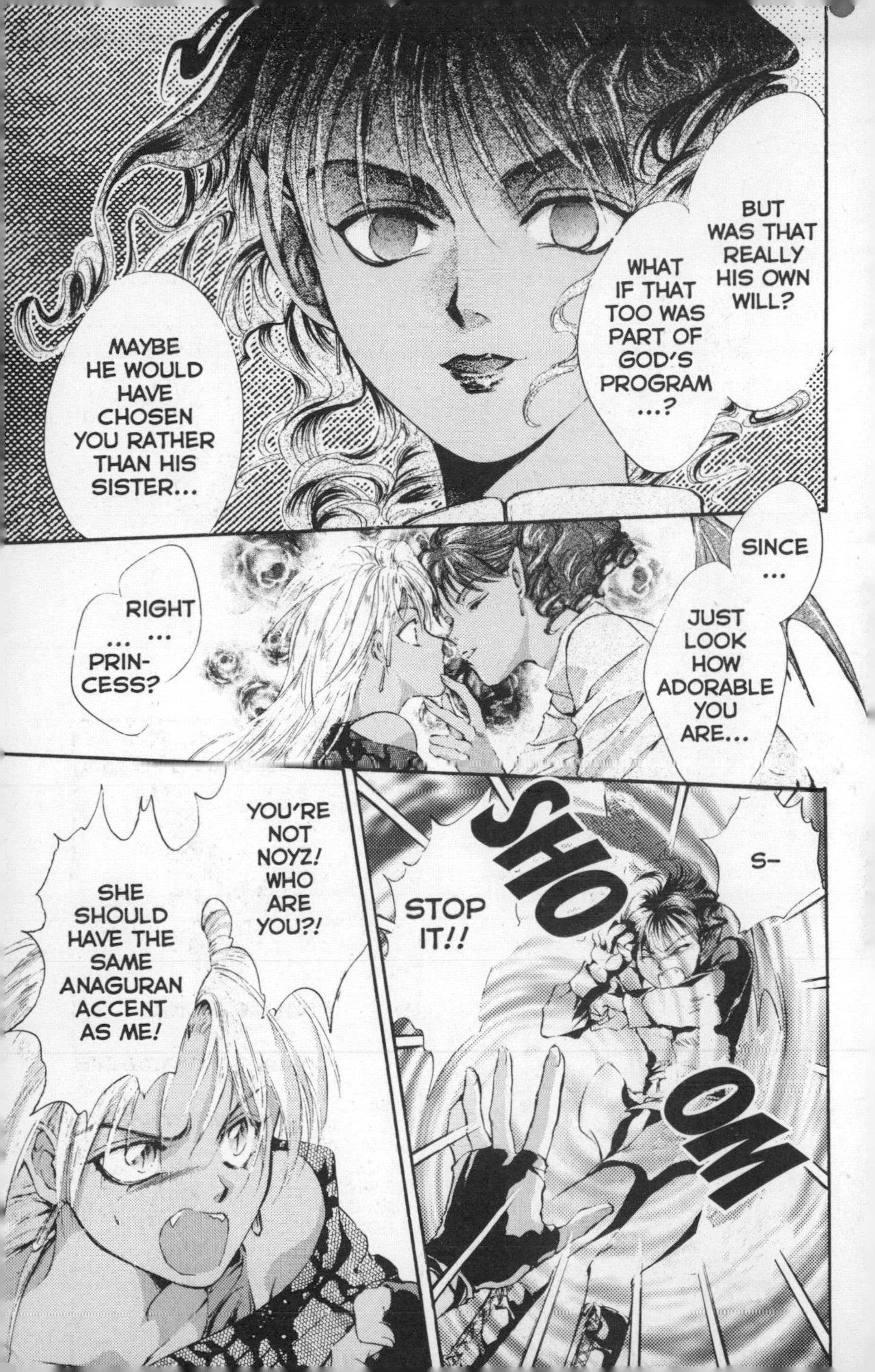
BUT WAS THAT REALLY HIS OWN WILL?
WHAT IF THAT TOO WAS PART OF GOD'S PROGRAM ...?
MAYBE HE WOULD HAVE CHOSEN YOU RATHER THAN HIS SISTER...
SINCE ...
JUST LOOK HOW ADORABLE YOU ARE...
RIGHT ... ... PRIN-CESS?
S–
SHOOM
STOP IT!!
YOU'RE NOT NOYZ! WHO ARE YOU?!
SHE SHOULD HAVE THE SAME ANAGURAN ACCENT AS ME!

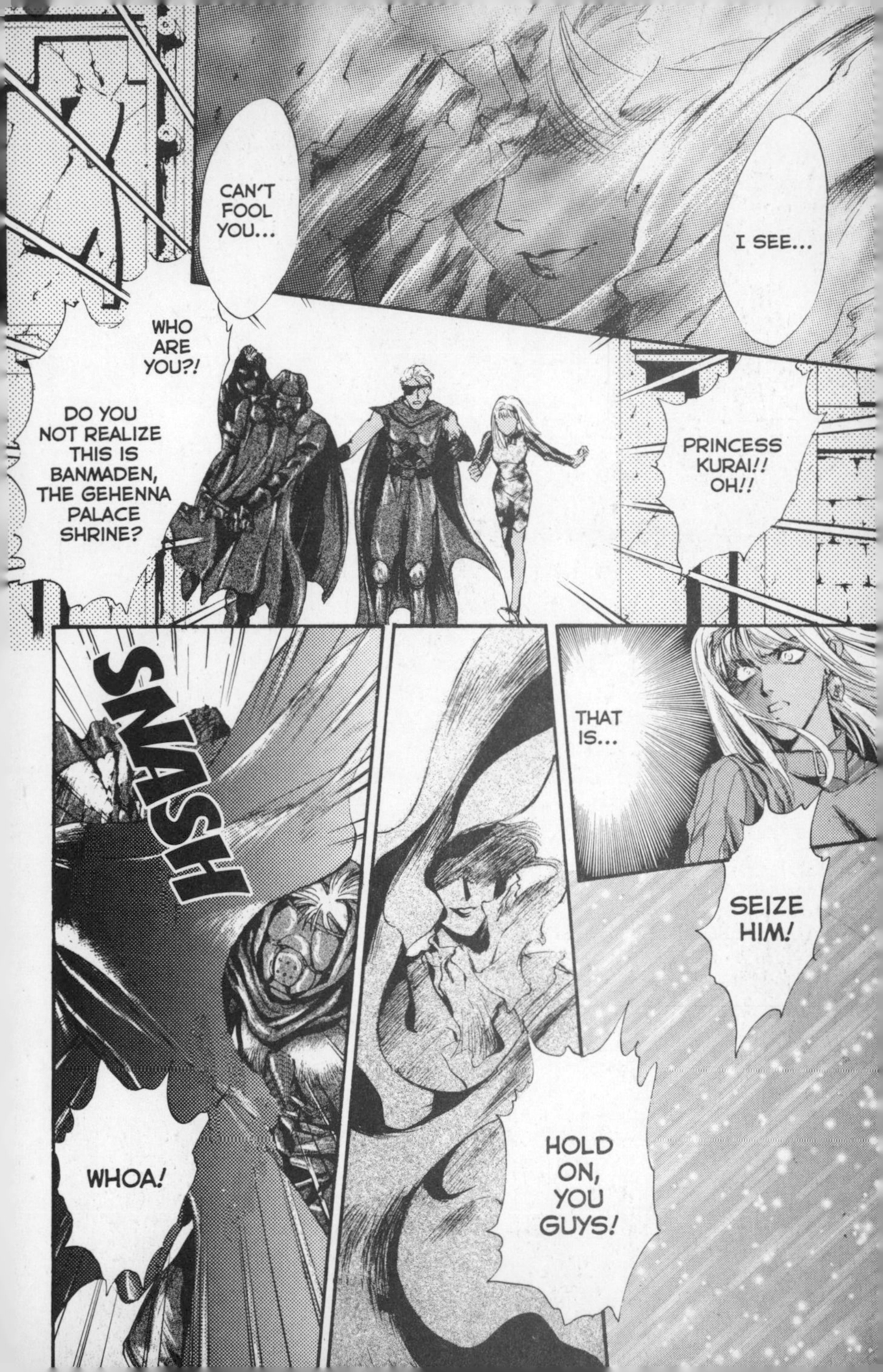
I SEE...
CAN'T FOOL YOU...
PRINCESS KURAI!! OH!!
WHO ARE YOU?!
DO YOU NOT REALIZE THIS IS BANMADEN, THE GEHENNA PALACE SHRINE?
THAT IS...
SEIZE HIM!
HOLD ON, YOU GUYS!
SMASH!
WHOA!

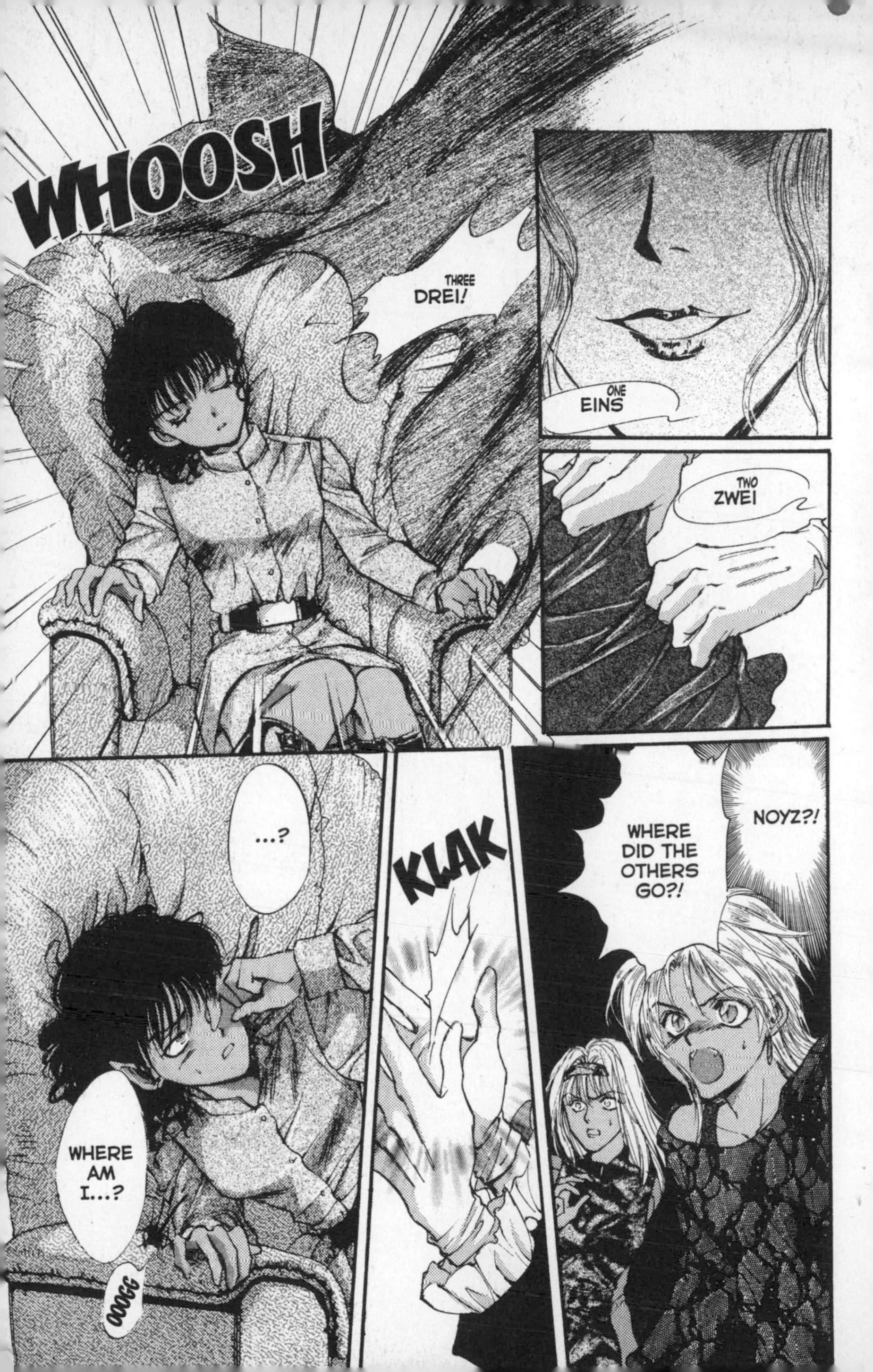
ONE
EINS
TWO
ZWEI
WHOOSH
THREE
DREI!
NOYZ?!
WHERE DID THE OTHERS GO?!
KLAK
...?
WHERE AM I...?
OOOGG

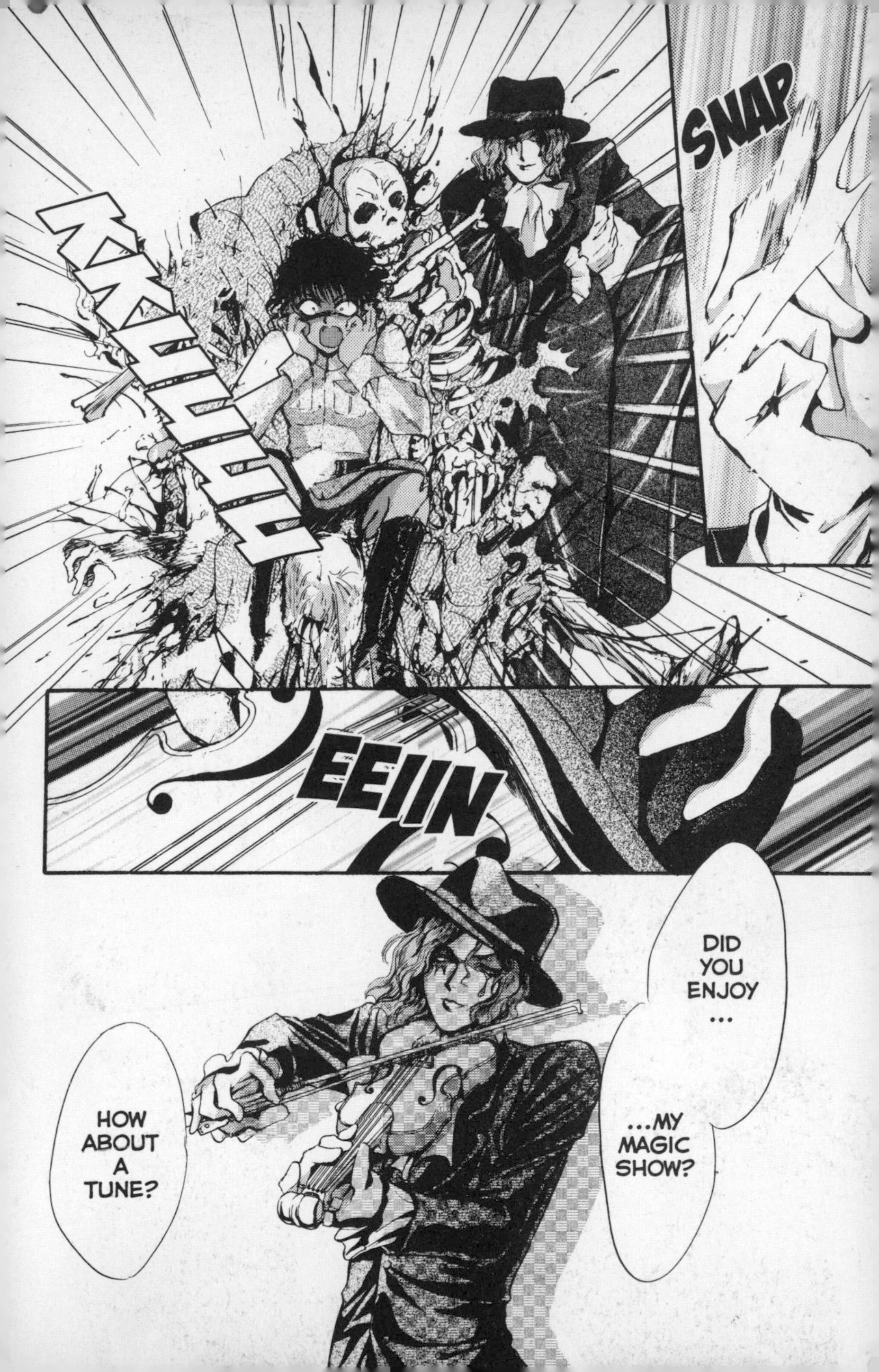
SNAP
EEIIN
DID YOU ENJOY ...
...MY MAGIC SHOW?
HOW ABOUT A TUNE?

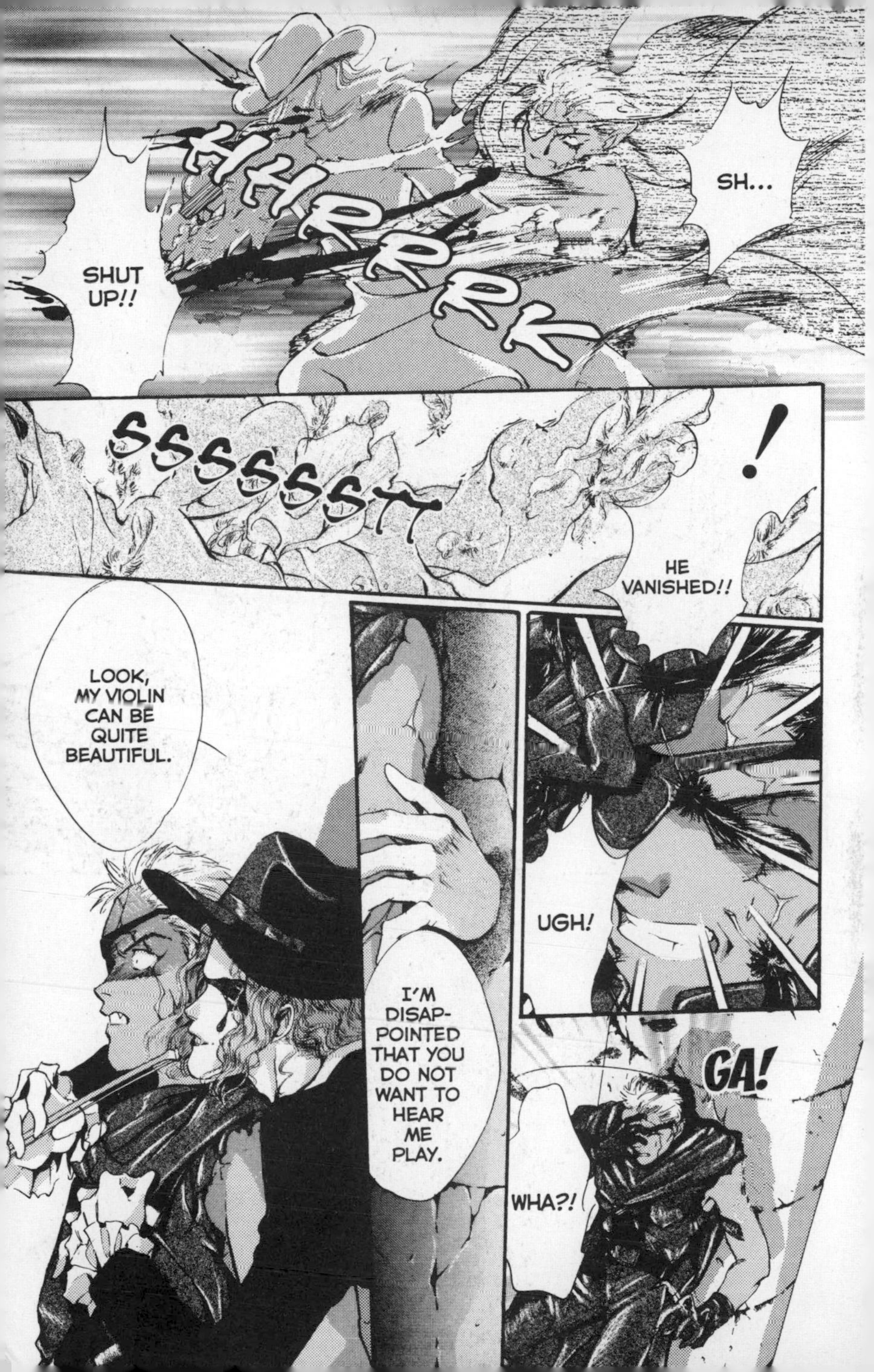
SH...
HHRRRK
SHUT UP!!
!
SSSSSSTT
HE VANISHED!!
UGH!
GA!
WHA?!
LOOK, MY VIOLIN CAN BE QUITE BEAUTIFUL.
I'M DISAP-POINTED THAT YOU DO NOT WANT TO HEAR ME PLAY.

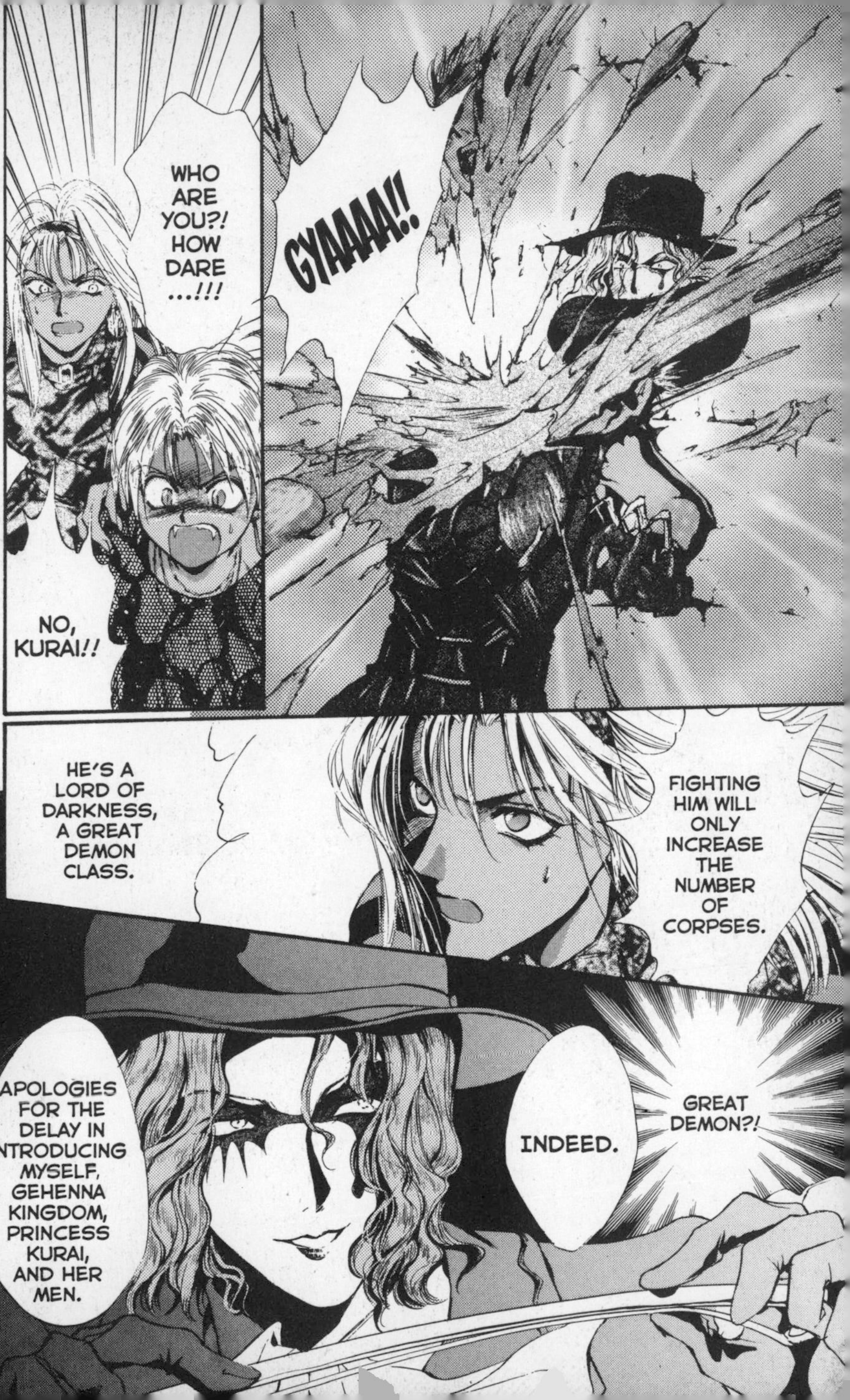
GYAAAA!!
WHO ARE YOU?! HOW DARE ...!!!
NO, KURAI!!
FIGHTING HIM WILL ONLY INCREASE THE NUMBER OF CORPSES.
HE'S A LORD OF DARKNESS, A GREAT DEMON CLASS.
GREAT DEMON?!
INDEED.
APOLOGIES FOR THE DELAY IN INTRODUCING MYSELF, GEHENNA KINGDOM, PRINCESS KURAI, AND HER MEN.

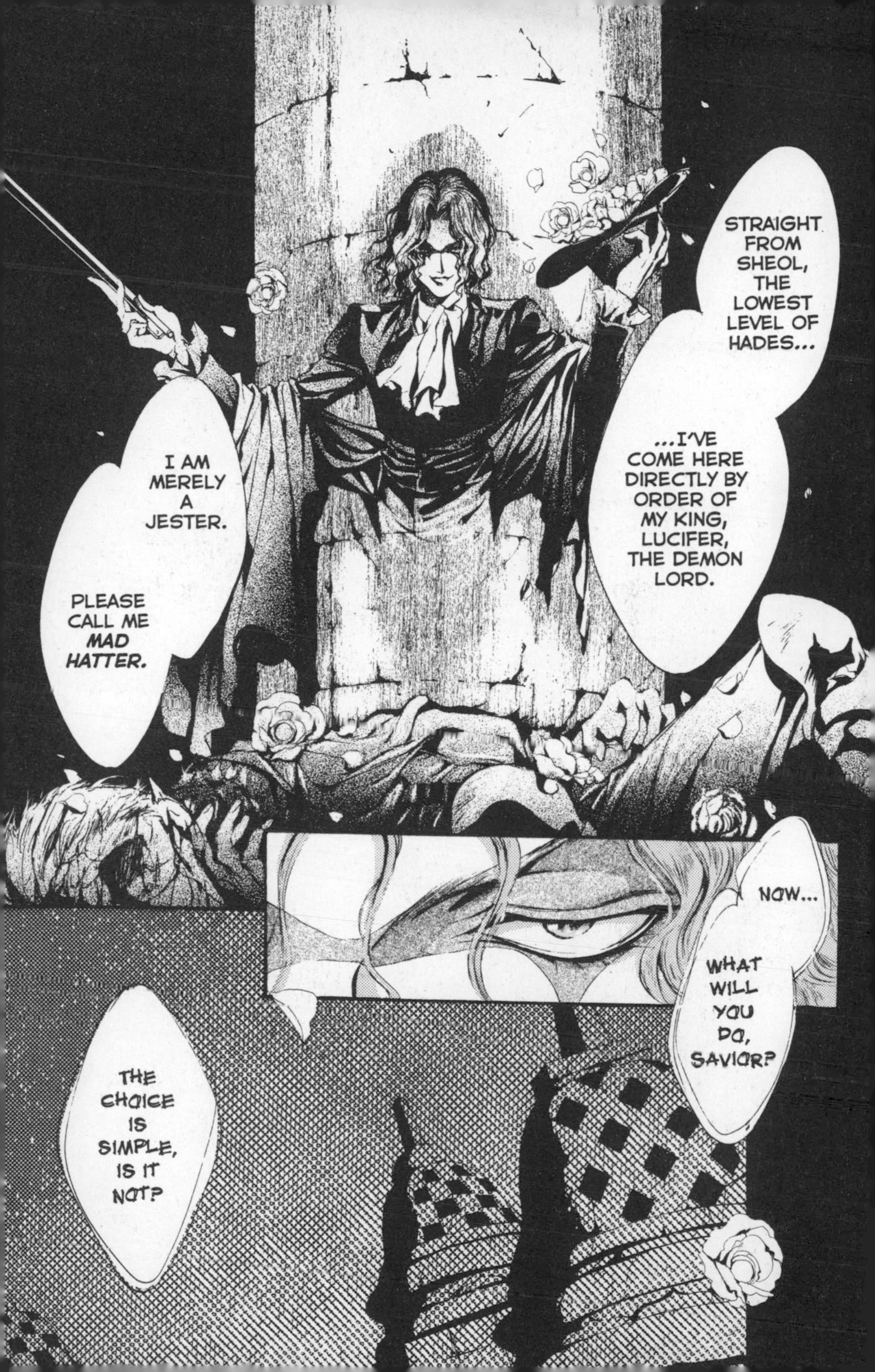
STRAIGHT FROM SHEOL, THE LOWEST LEVEL OF HADES...
...I'VE COME HERE DIRECTLY BY ORDER OF MY KING, LUCIFER, THE DEMON LORD.
I AM MERELY A JESTER.
PLEASE CALL ME MAD HATTER.
NOW...
WHAT WILL YOU DO, SAVIOR?
THE CHOICE IS SIMPLE, IS IT NOT?

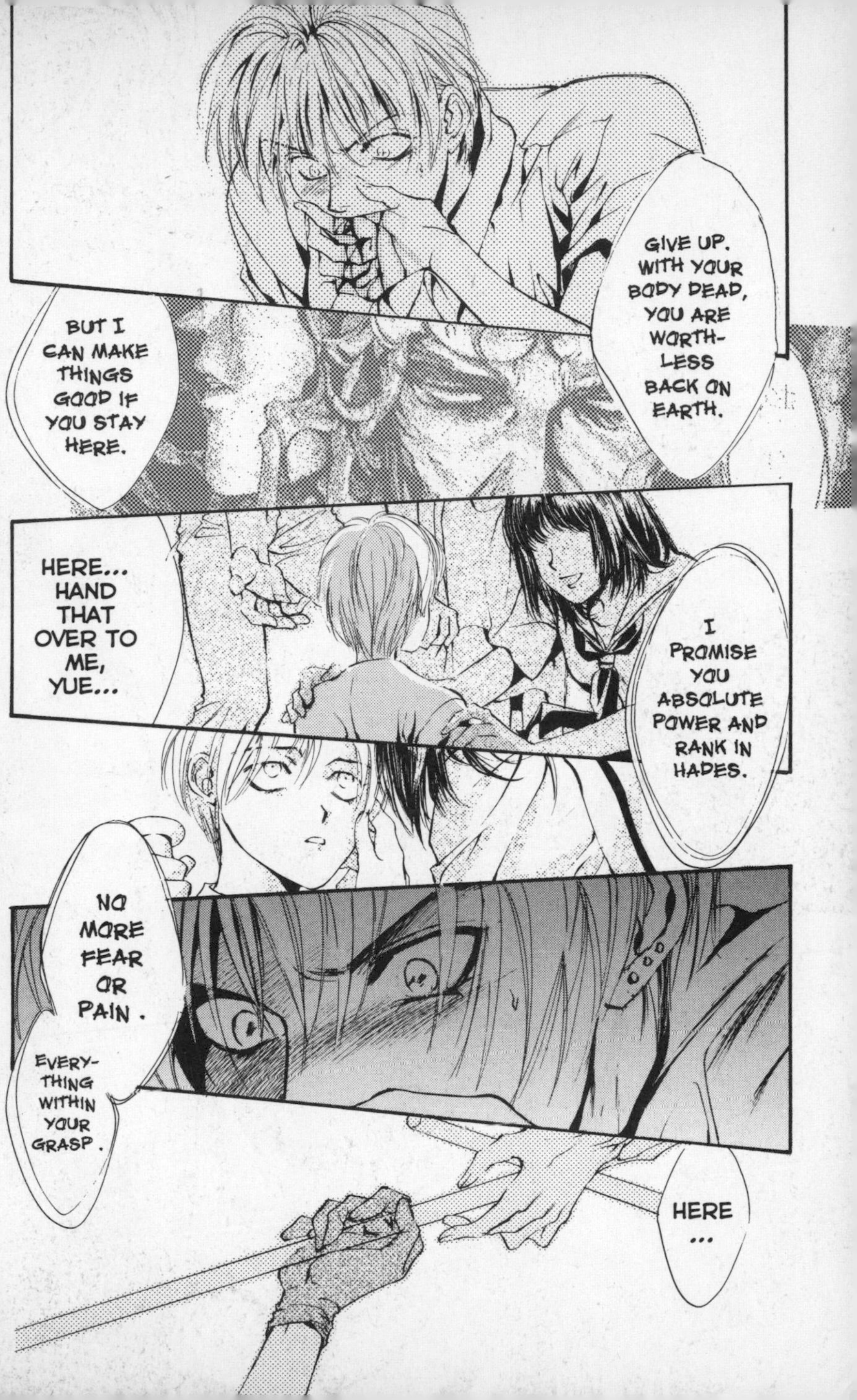
GIVE UP. WITH YOUR BODY DEAD, YOU ARE WORTH-LESS BACK ON EARTH.
BUT I CAN MAKE THINGS GOOD IF YOU STAY HERE.
I PROMISE YOU ABSOLUTE POWER AND RANK IN HADES.
HERE... HAND THAT OVER TO ME, YUE...
NO MORE FEAR OR PAIN.
EVERY-THING WITHIN YOUR GRASP.
HERE ...

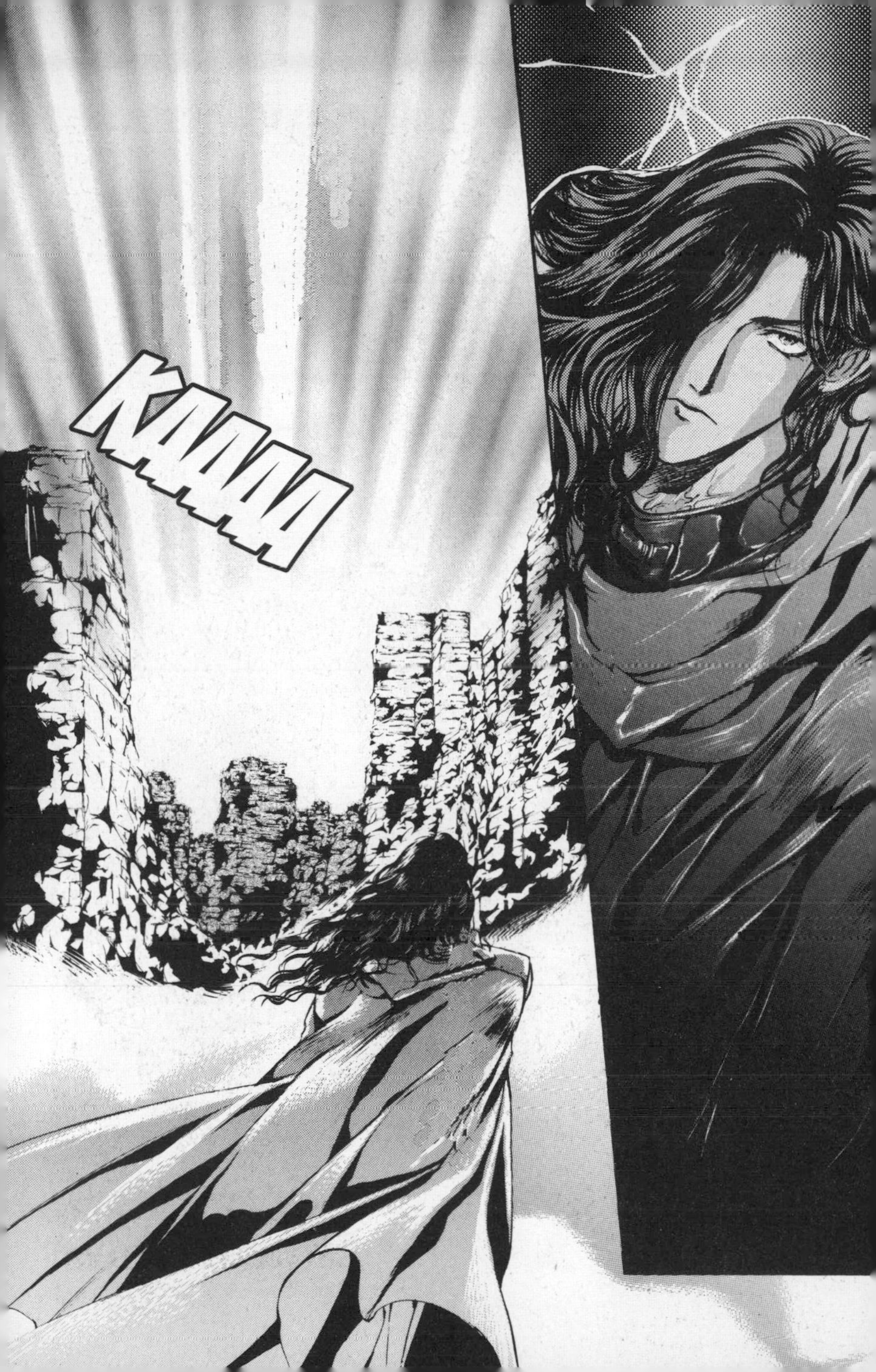
KADAA

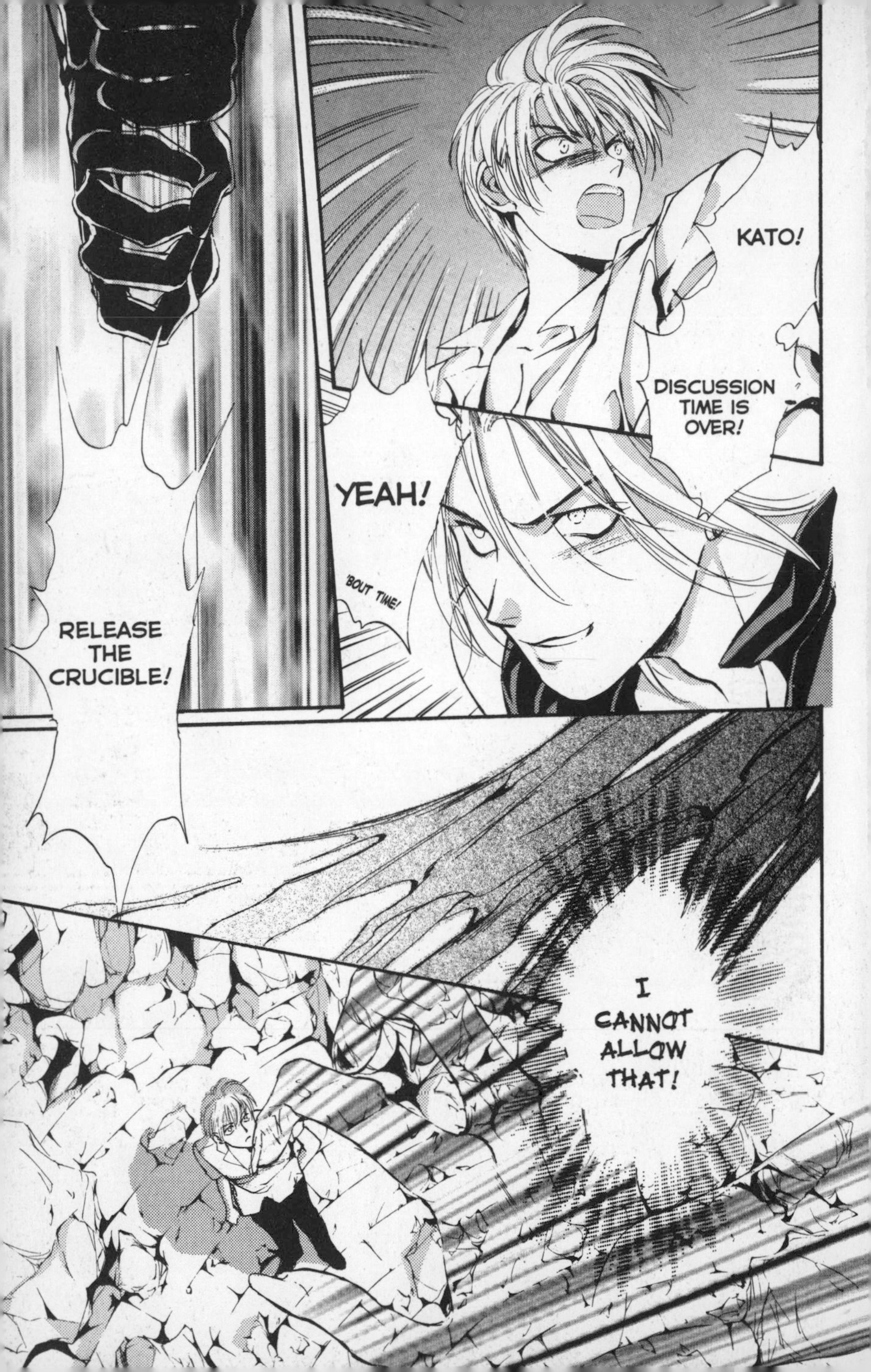
KATO!
DISCUSSION TIME IS OVER!
YEAH!
'BOUT TIME!
RELEASE THE CRUCIBLE!
I CANNOT ALLOW THAT!

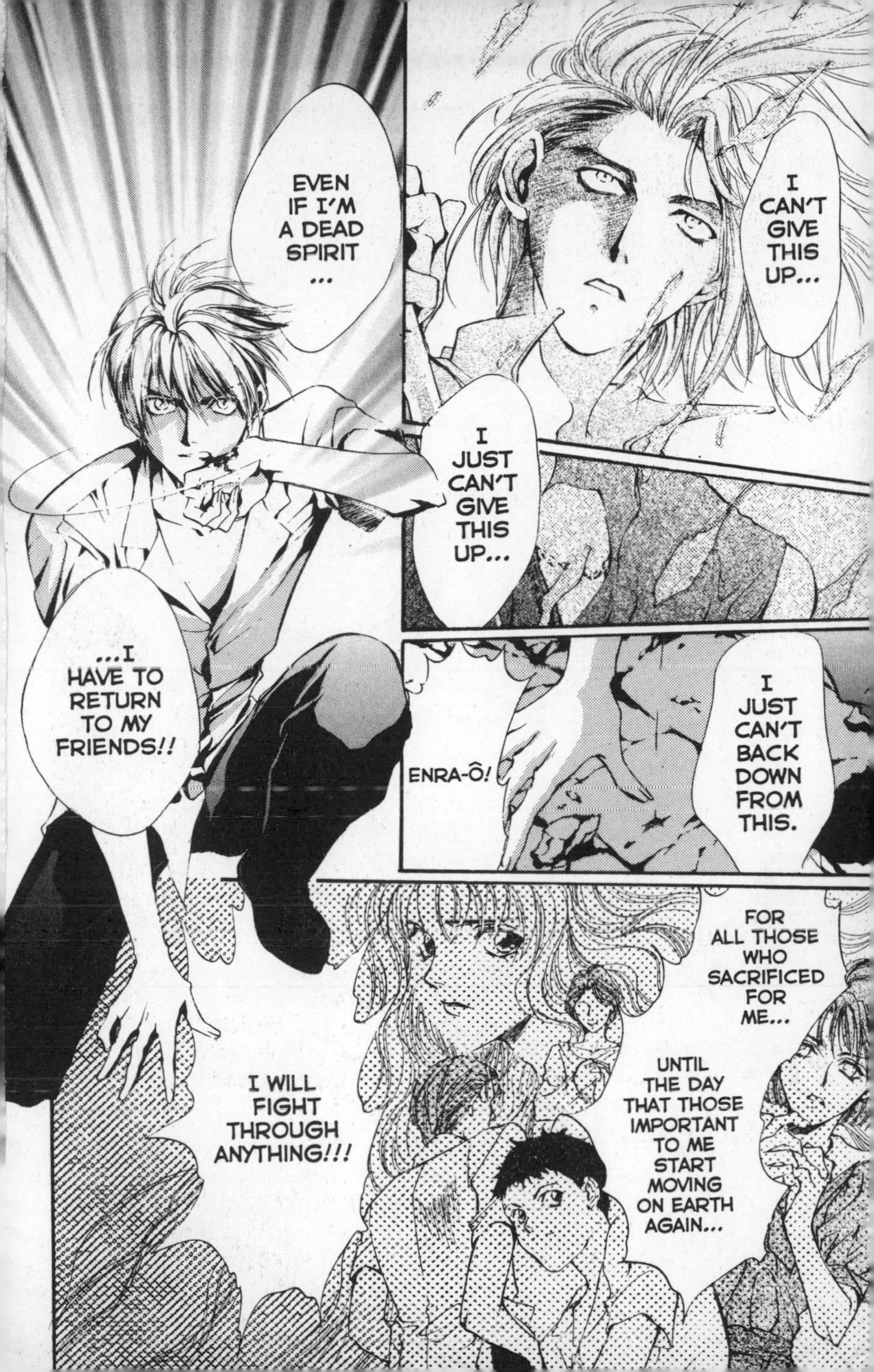
I CAN'T GIVE THIS UP...
I JUST CAN'T GIVE THIS UP...
I JUST CAN'T BACK DOWN FROM THIS.
ENRA-Ô!
EVEN IF I'M A DEAD SPIRIT ...
...I HAVE TO RETURN TO MY FRIENDS!!
FOR ALL THOSE WHO SACRIFICED FOR ME...
UNTIL THE DAY THAT THOSE IMPORTANT TO ME START MOVING ON EARTH AGAIN...
I WILL FIGHT THROUGH ANYTHING!!!

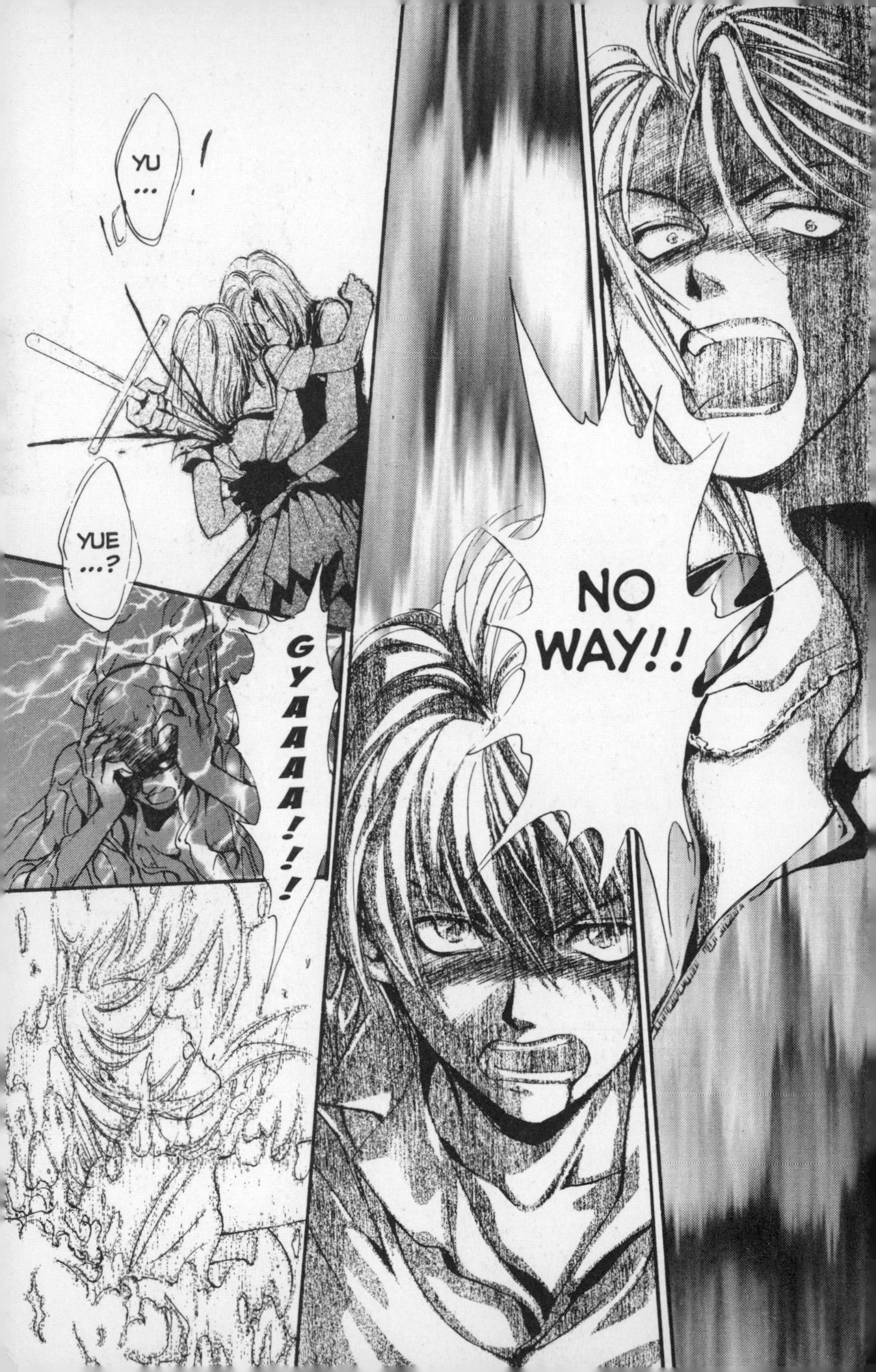
NO WAY!!
YU...
YUE...?
GYAAAAA!!!

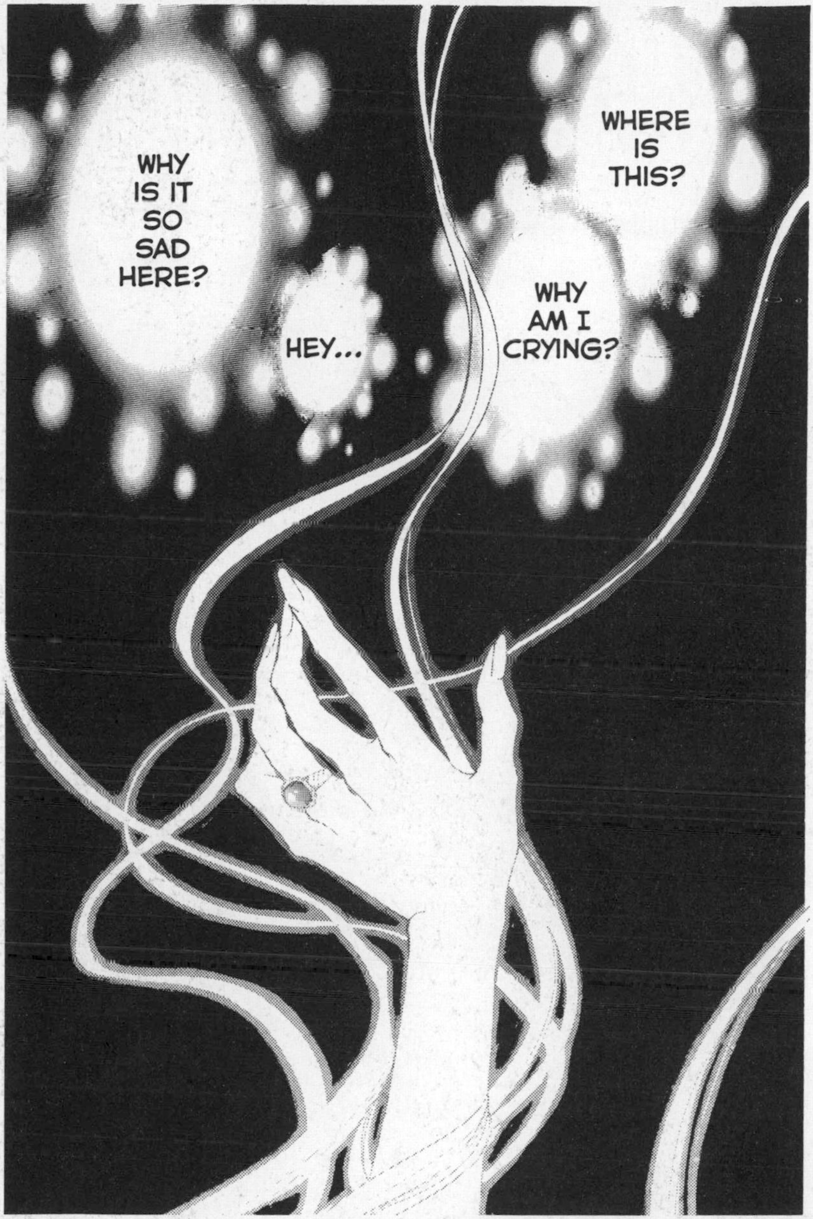
WHERE IS THIS?
WHY AM I CRYING?
HEY...
WHY IS IT SO SAD HERE?

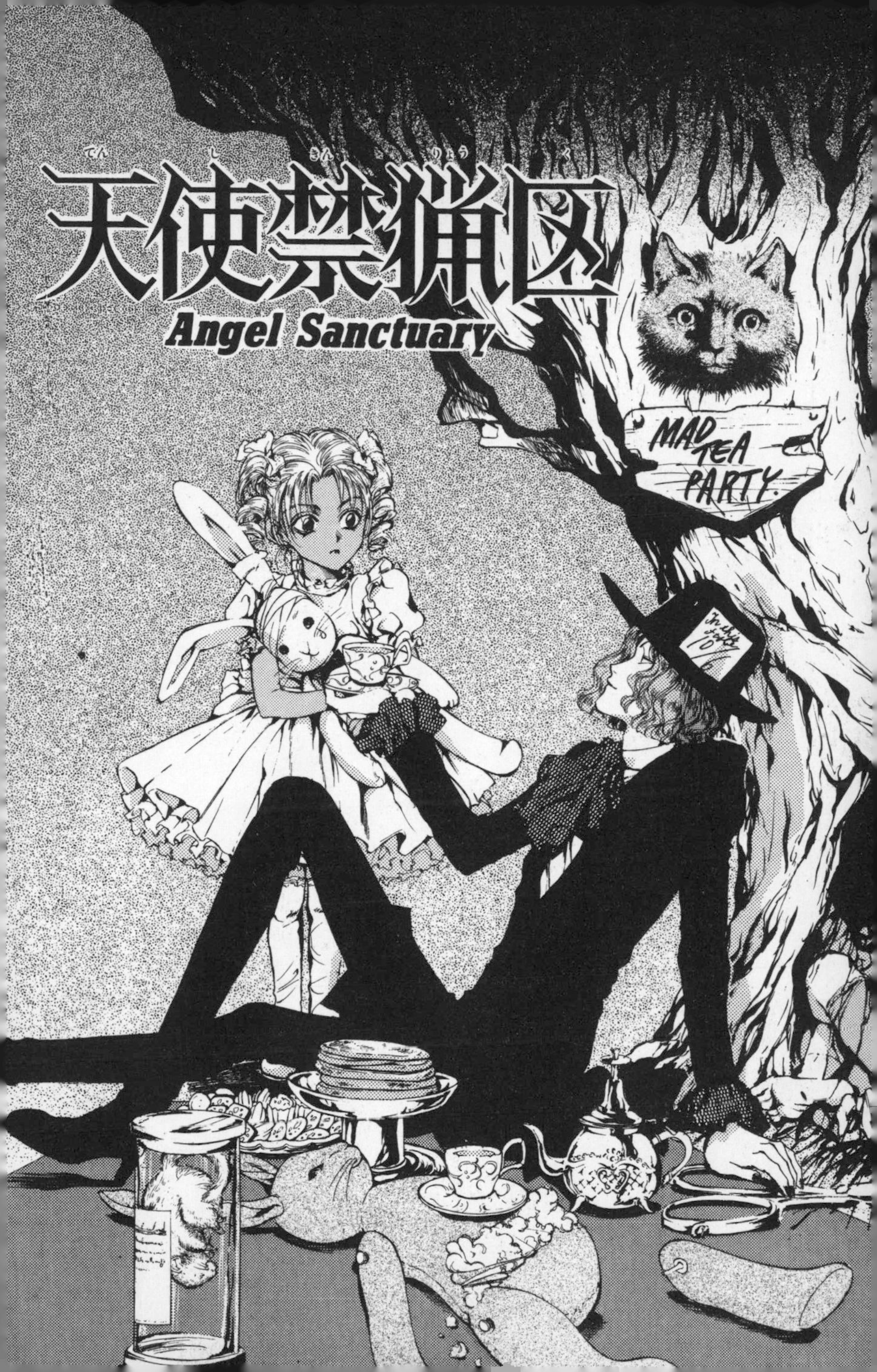
天使禁猟区
Angel Sanctuary
MAD TEA PARTY

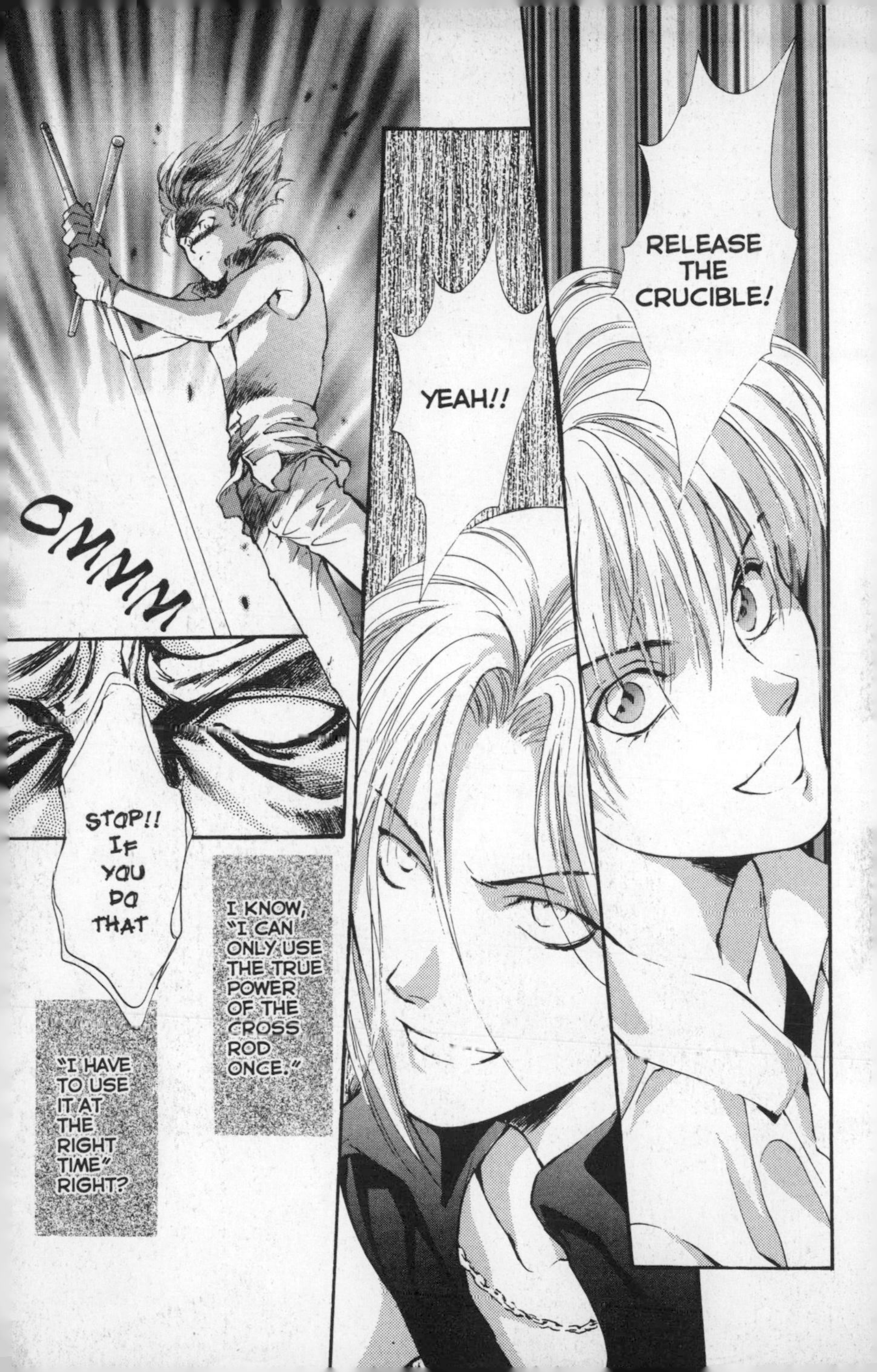
RELEASE THE CRUCIBLE!
YEAH!!
OMMM
STOP!! IF YOU DO THAT
I KNOW, "I CAN ONLY USE THE TRUE POWER OF THE CROSS ROD ONCE."
"I HAVE TO USE IT AT THE RIGHT TIME" RIGHT?

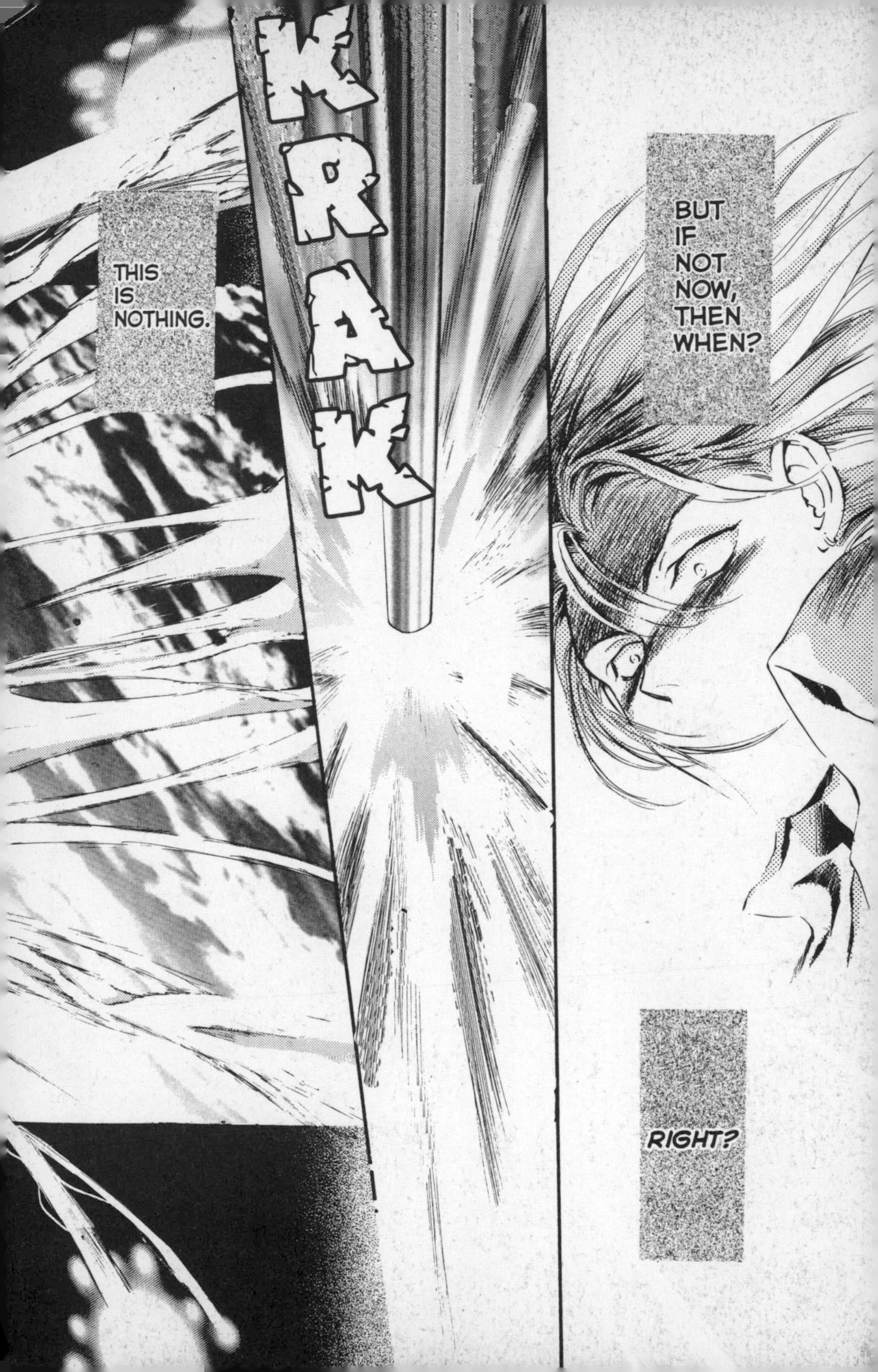
BUT IF NOT NOW, THEN WHEN?
RIGHT?
KRAK
THIS IS NOTHING.

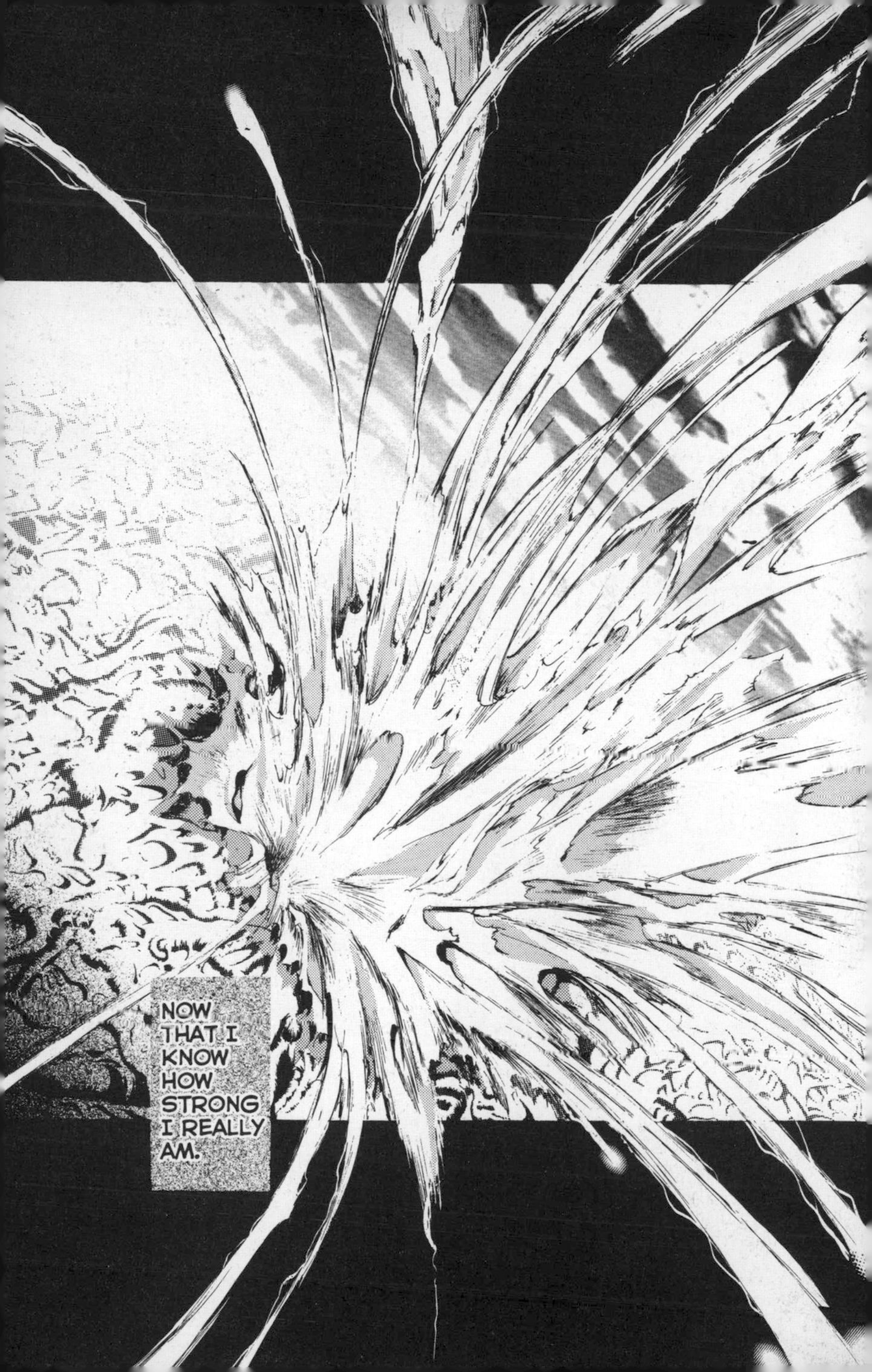
NOW THAT I KNOW HOW STRONG I REALLY AM.

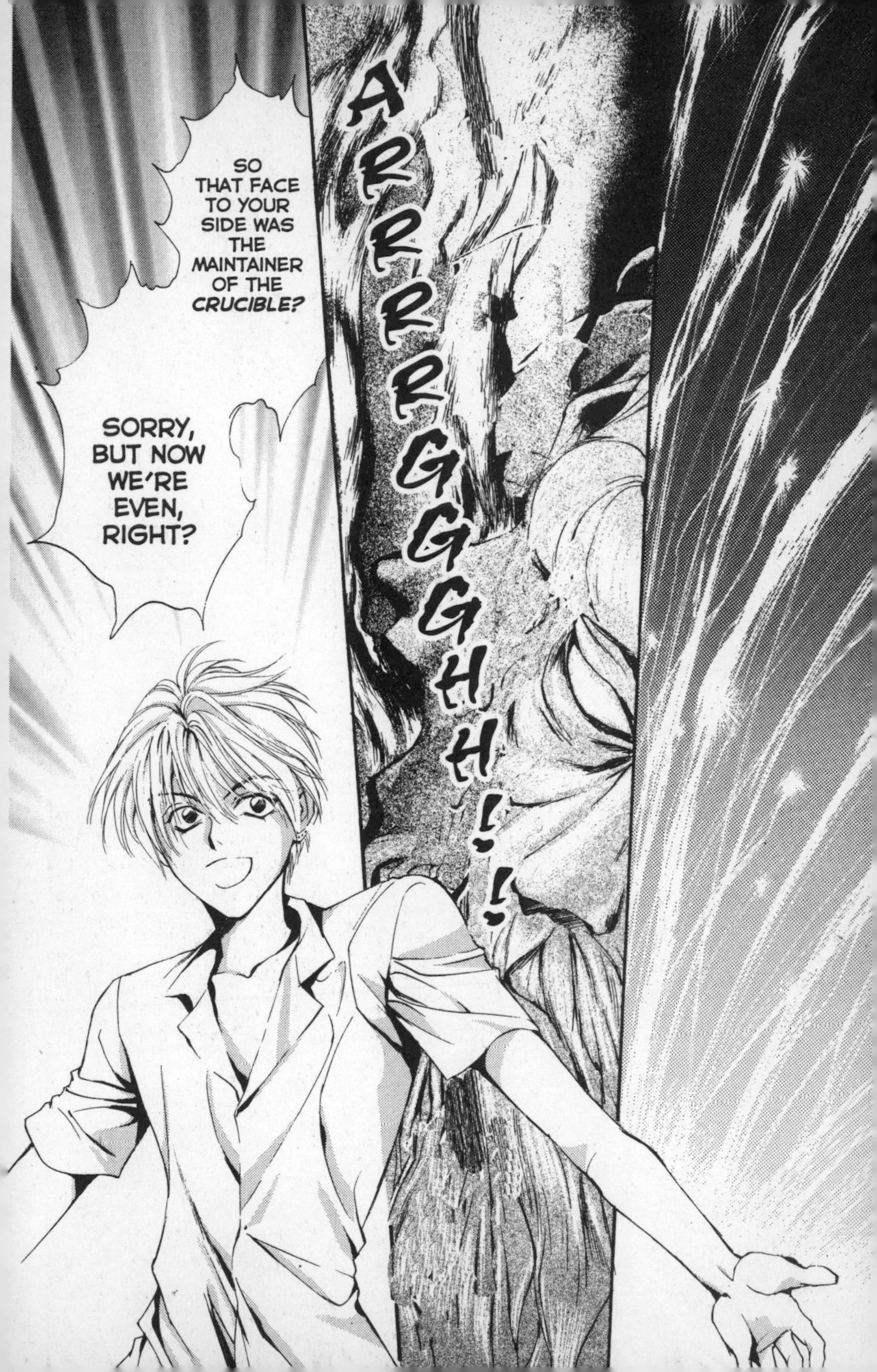
ARRRRRGGGGHH!!
SO THAT FACE TO YOUR SIDE WAS THE MAINTAINER OF THE *CRUCIBLE*?
SORRY, BUT NOW WE'RE EVEN, RIGHT?

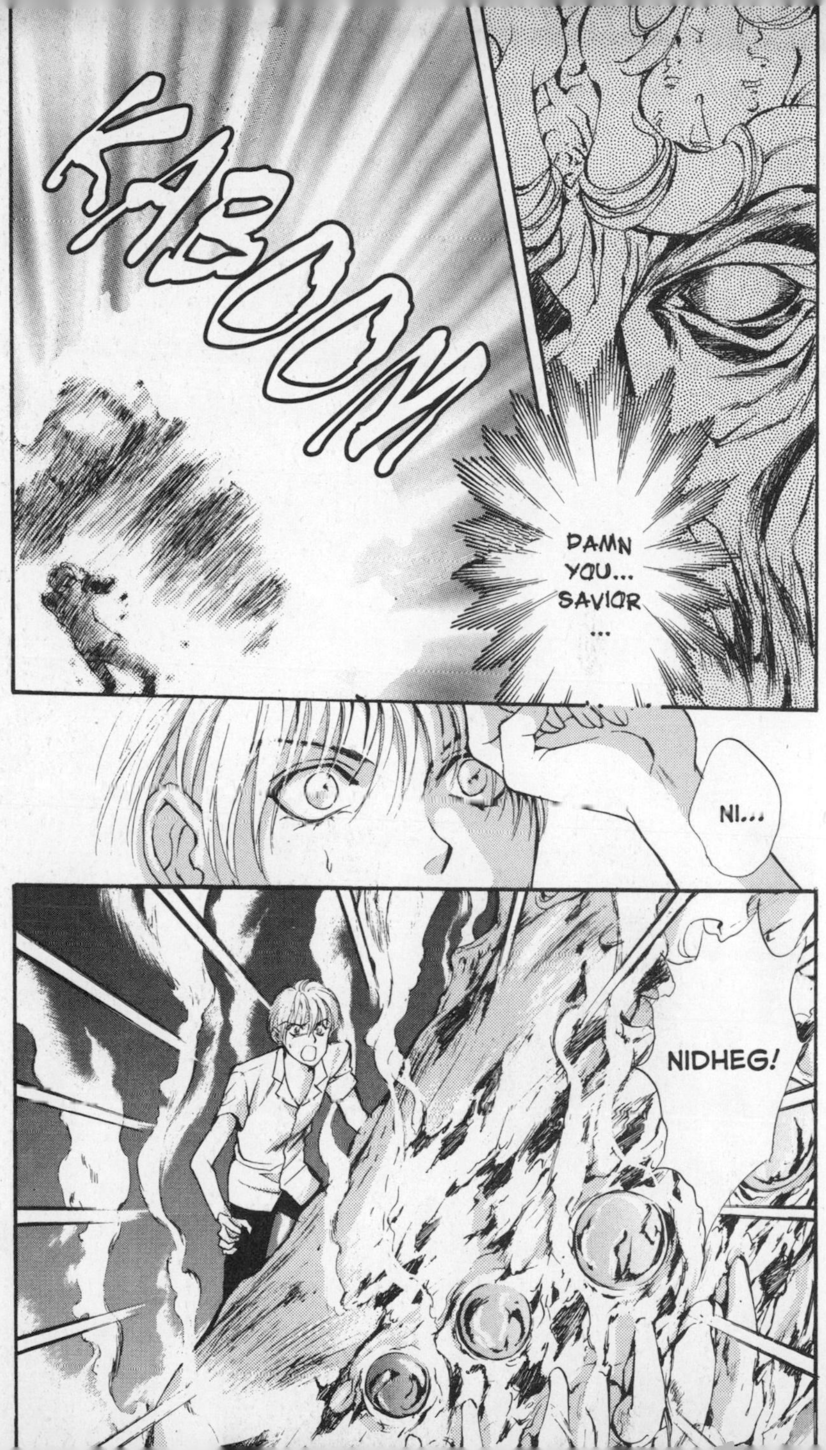
DAMN YOU... SAVIOR ...
KABOOM
NI...
NIDHEG!

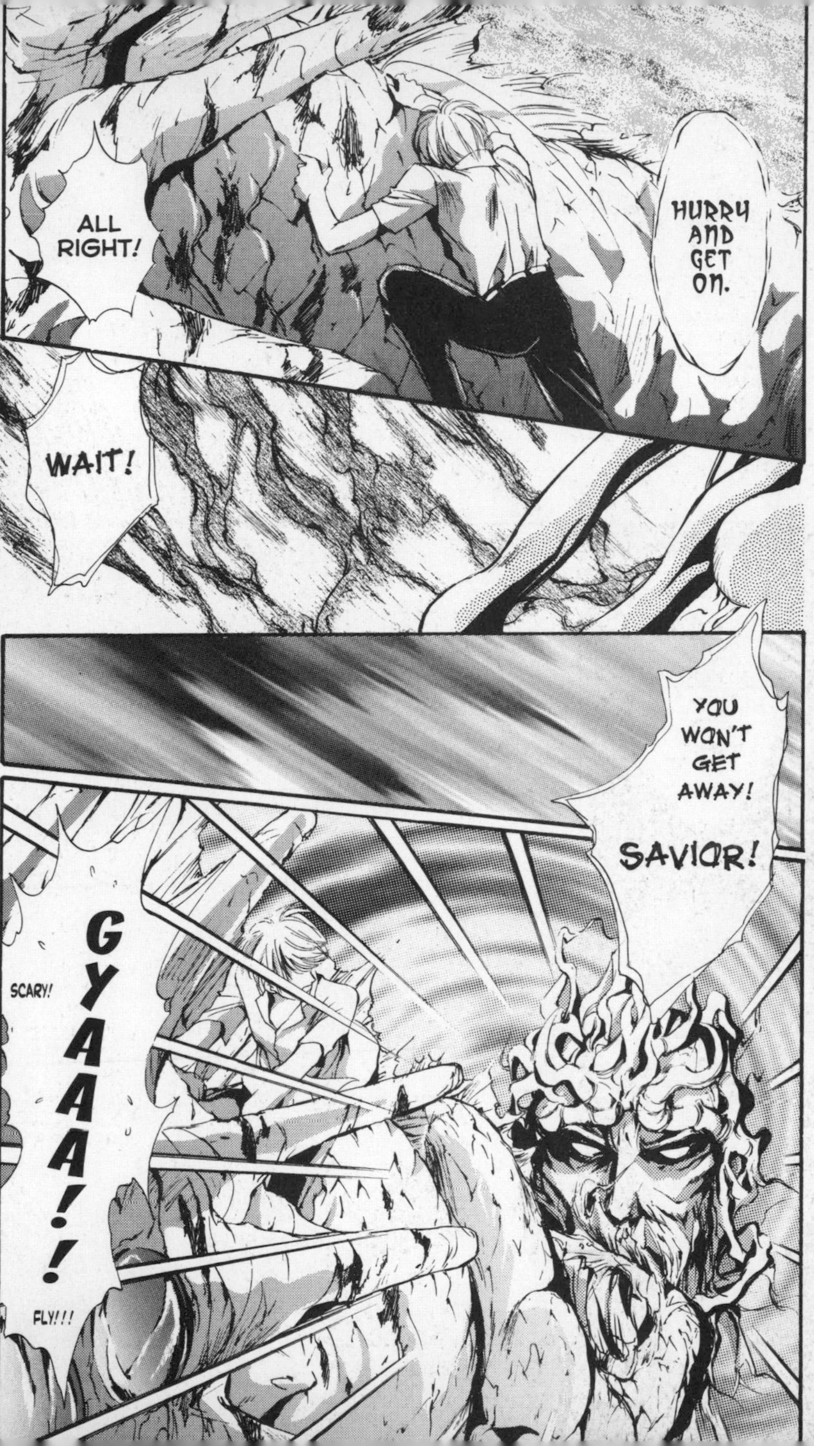
HURRY AND GET ON.
ALL RIGHT!
WAIT!
YOU WON'T GET AWAY!
SAVIOR!
GYAAAA!!!
SCARY!
FLY!!!

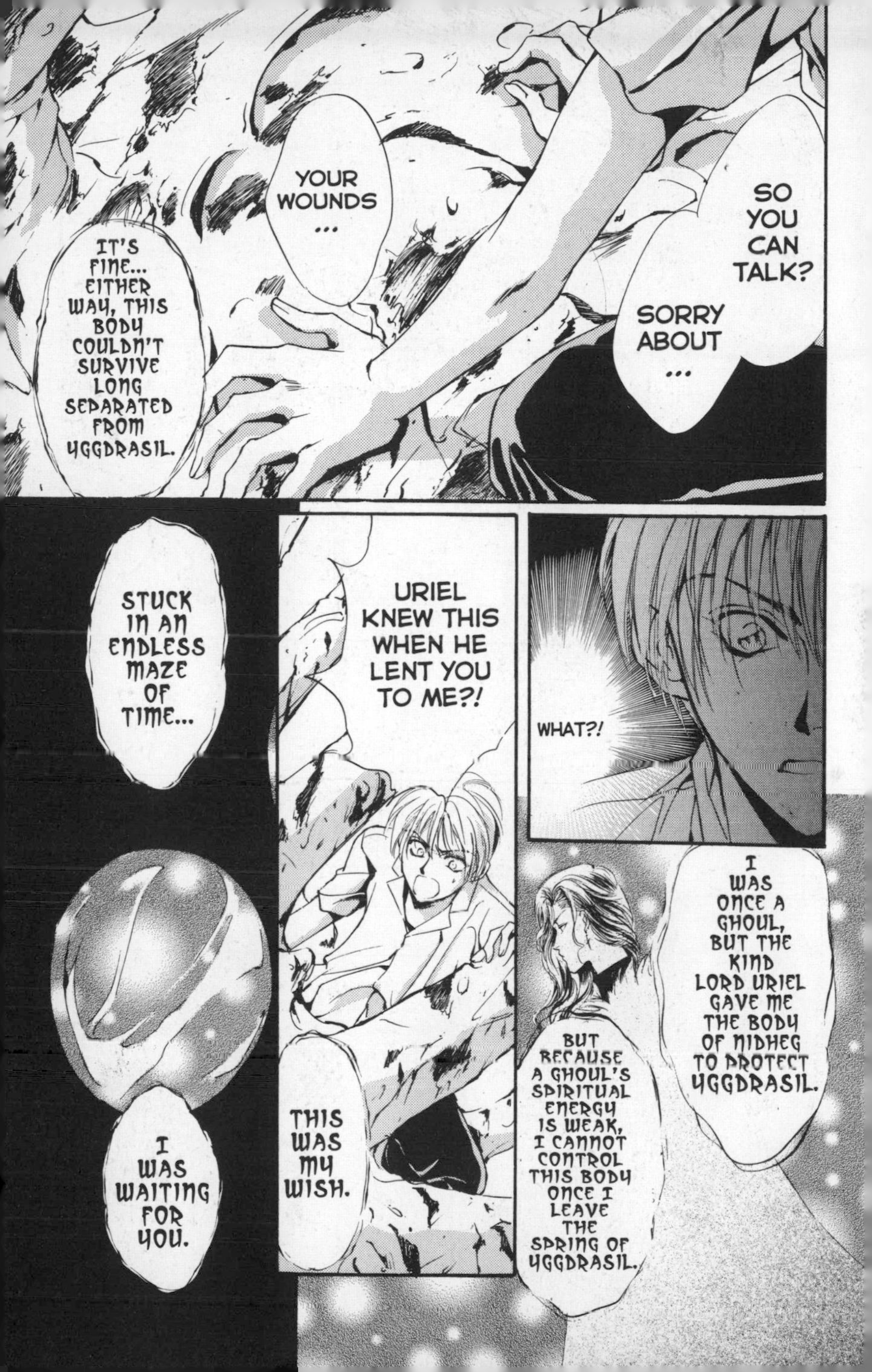
SO YOU CAN TALK?
SORRY ABOUT ...
YOUR WOUNDS ...
IT'S FINE... EITHER WAY, THIS BODY COULDN'T SURVIVE LONG SEPARATED FROM YGGDRASIL.
WHAT?!
I WAS ONCE A GHOUL, BUT THE KIND LORD URIEL GAVE ME THE BODY OF NIDHEG TO PROTECT YGGDRASIL.
BUT BECAUSE A GHOUL'S SPIRITUAL ENERGY IS WEAK, I CANNOT CONTROL THIS BODY ONCE I LEAVE THE SPRING OF YGGDRASIL.
URIEL KNEW THIS WHEN HE LENT YOU TO ME?!
THIS WAS MY WISH.
STUCK IN AN ENDLESS MAZE OF TIME...
I WAS WAITING FOR YOU.

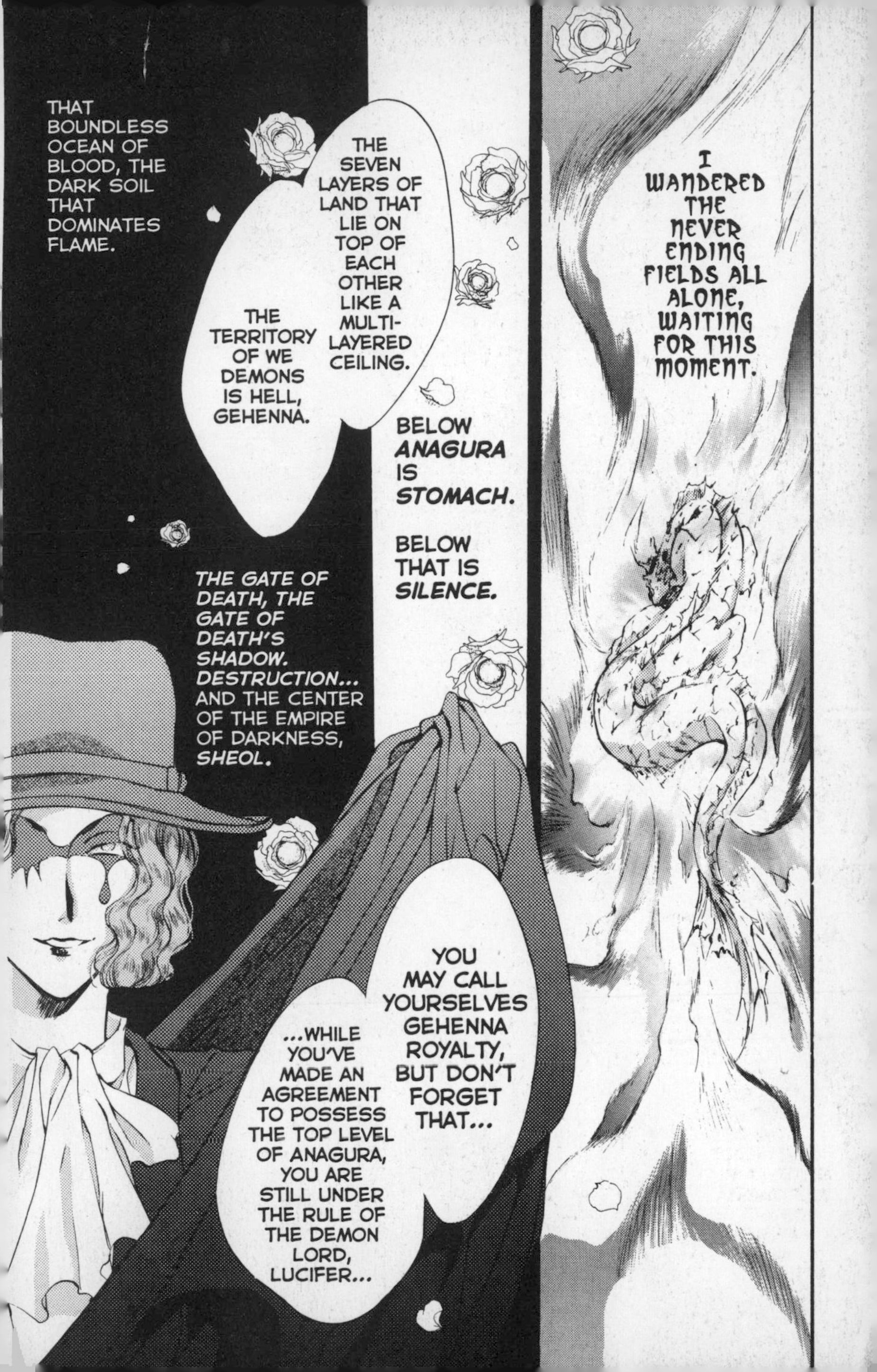
I WANDERED THE NEVER ENDING FIELDS ALL ALONE, WAITING FOR THIS MOMENT.
THE SEVEN LAYERS OF LAND THAT LIE ON TOP OF EACH OTHER LIKE A MULTI-LAYERED CEILING.
THAT BOUNDLESS OCEAN OF BLOOD, THE DARK SOIL THAT DOMINATES FLAME.
THE TERRITORY OF WE DEMONS IS HELL, GEHENNA.
BELOW *ANAGURA* IS *STOMACH*.
BELOW THAT IS *SILENCE*.
THE GATE OF DEATH, THE GATE OF DEATH'S SHADOW. DESTRUCTION... AND THE CENTER OF THE EMPIRE OF DARKNESS, *SHEOL*.
YOU MAY CALL YOURSELVES GEHENNA ROYALTY, BUT DON'T FORGET THAT...
...WHILE YOU'VE MADE AN AGREEMENT TO POSSESS THE TOP LEVEL OF ANAGURA, YOU ARE STILL UNDER THE RULE OF THE DEMON LORD, LUCIFER...

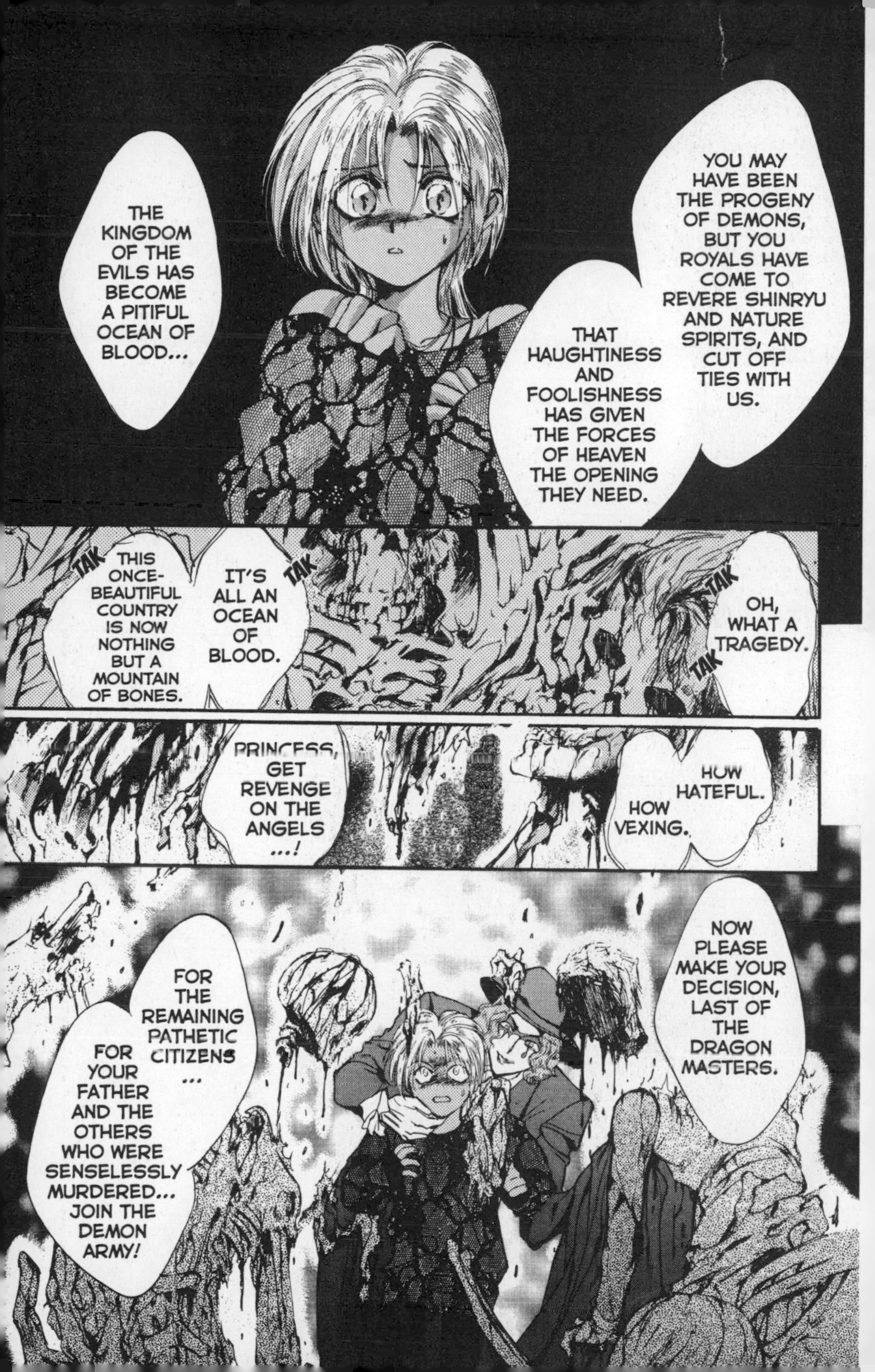
YOU MAY HAVE BEEN THE PROGENY OF DEMONS, BUT YOU ROYALS HAVE COME TO REVERE SHINRYU AND NATURE SPIRITS, AND CUT OFF TIES WITH US.
THAT HAUGHTINESS AND FOOLISHNESS HAS GIVEN THE FORCES OF HEAVEN THE OPENING THEY NEED.
THE KINGDOM OF THE EVILS HAS BECOME A PITIFUL OCEAN OF BLOOD...
TAK
TAK
OH, WHAT A TRAGEDY.
TAK
IT'S ALL AN OCEAN OF BLOOD.
TAK
THIS ONCE-BEAUTIFUL COUNTRY IS NOW NOTHING BUT A MOUNTAIN OF BONES.
HOW HATEFUL.
HOW VEXING.
PRINCESS, GET REVENGE ON THE ANGELS ...!
NOW PLEASE MAKE YOUR DECISION, LAST OF THE DRAGON MASTERS.
FOR THE REMAINING PATHETIC CITIZENS ...
FOR YOUR FATHER AND THE OTHERS WHO WERE SENSELESSLY MURDERED... JOIN THE DEMON ARMY!

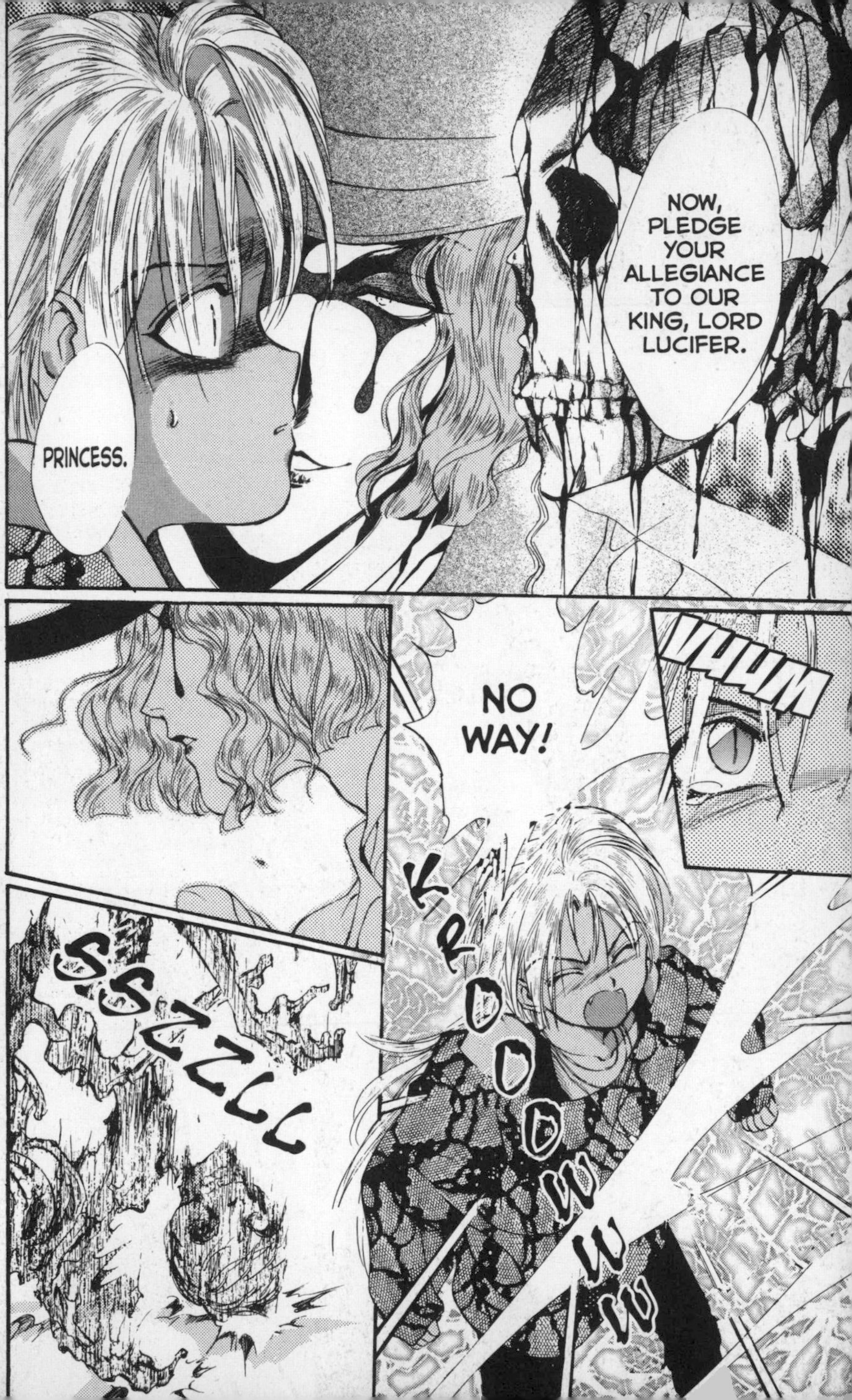
NOW, PLEDGE YOUR ALLEGIANCE TO OUR KING, LORD LUCIFER.
PRINCESS.
VUUM
NO WAY!
KRDDDWWW
SSZZZLLL

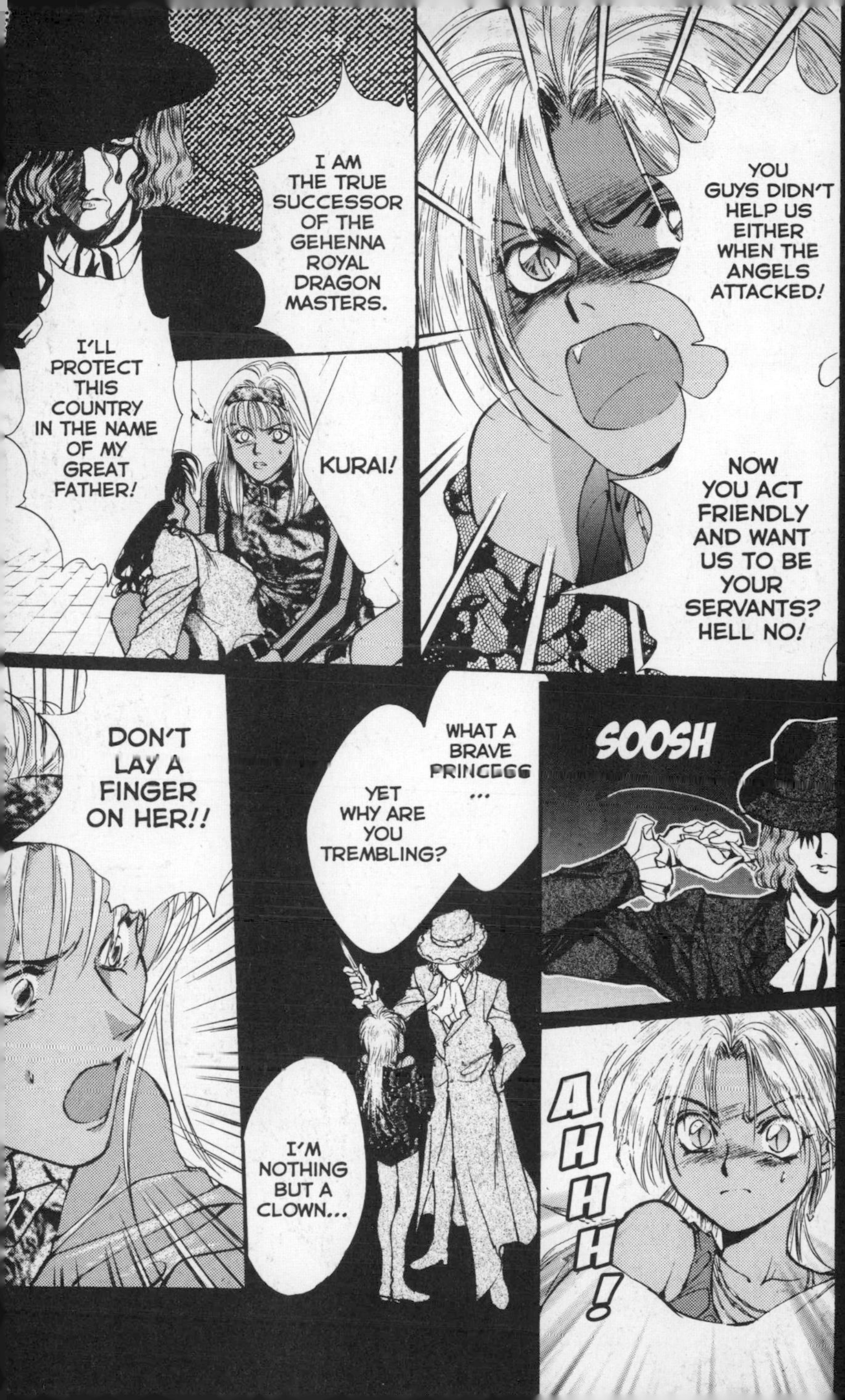
YOU GUYS DIDN'T HELP US EITHER WHEN THE ANGELS ATTACKED!
NOW YOU ACT FRIENDLY AND WANT US TO BE YOUR SERVANTS? HELL NO!
I AM THE TRUE SUCCESSOR OF THE GEHENNA ROYAL DRAGON MASTERS.
I'LL PROTECT THIS COUNTRY IN THE NAME OF MY GREAT FATHER!
KURAI!
SOOSH
AHHHH!
WHAT A BRAVE PRINCESS ...
YET WHY ARE YOU TREMBLING?
I'M NOTHING BUT A CLOWN...
DON'T LAY A FINGER ON HER!!

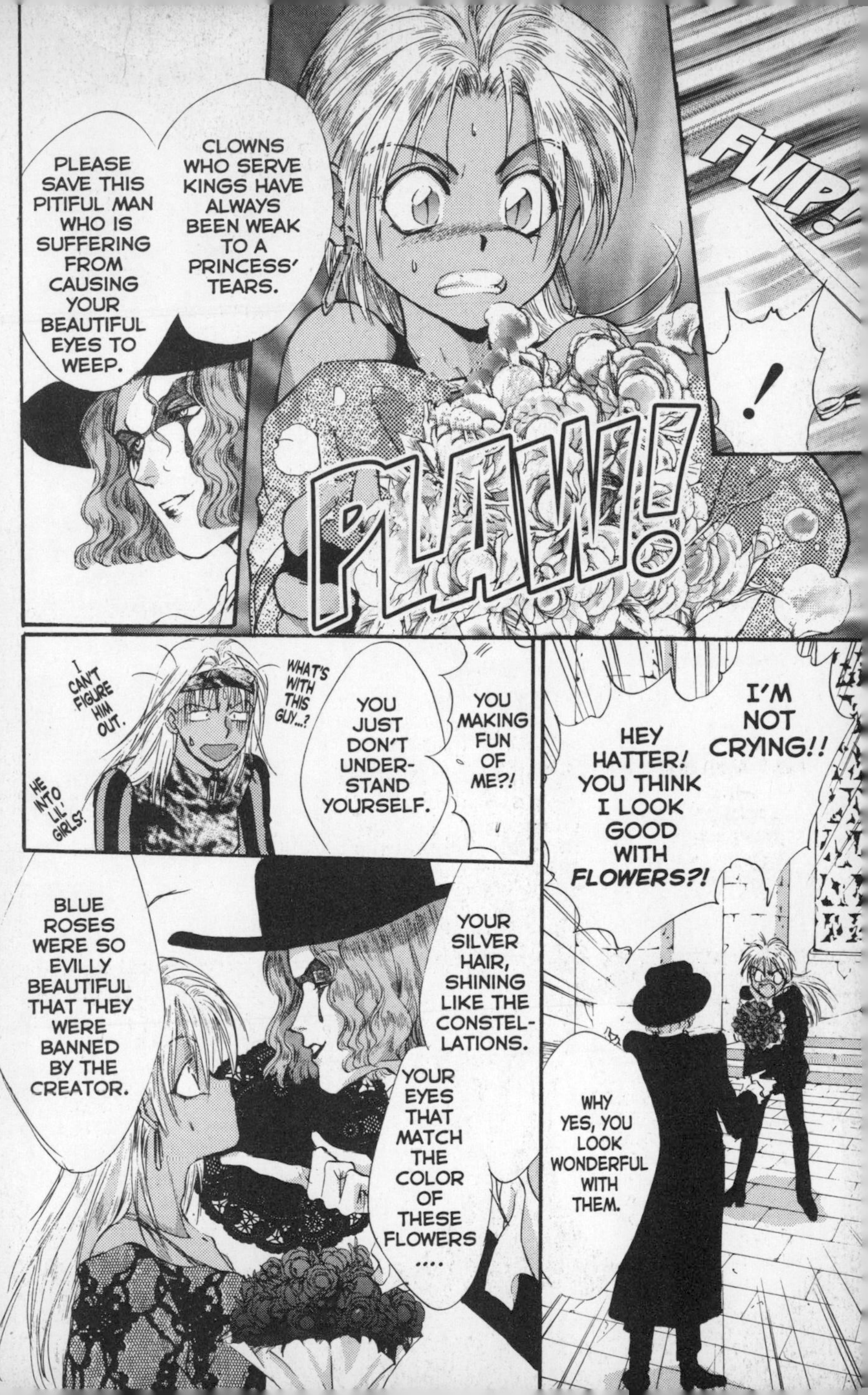
FWIP!
!
PLAW!
CLOWNS WHO SERVE KINGS HAVE ALWAYS BEEN WEAK TO A PRINCESS' TEARS.
PLEASE SAVE THIS PITIFUL MAN WHO IS SUFFERING FROM CAUSING YOUR BEAUTIFUL EYES TO WEEP.
I'M NOT CRYING!!
HEY HATTER! YOU THINK I LOOK GOOD WITH FLOWERS?!
WHY YES, YOU LOOK WONDERFUL WITH THEM.
YOU MAKING FUN OF ME?!
YOU JUST DON'T UNDER-STAND YOURSELF.
WHAT'S WITH THIS GUY...?
I CAN'T FIGURE HIM OUT.
HE INTO LIL' GIRLS?
YOUR SILVER HAIR, SHINING LIKE THE CONSTEL-LATIONS.
YOUR EYES THAT MATCH THE COLOR OF THESE FLOWERS ....
BLUE ROSES WERE SO EVILLY BEAUTIFUL THAT THEY WERE BANNED BY THE CREATOR.

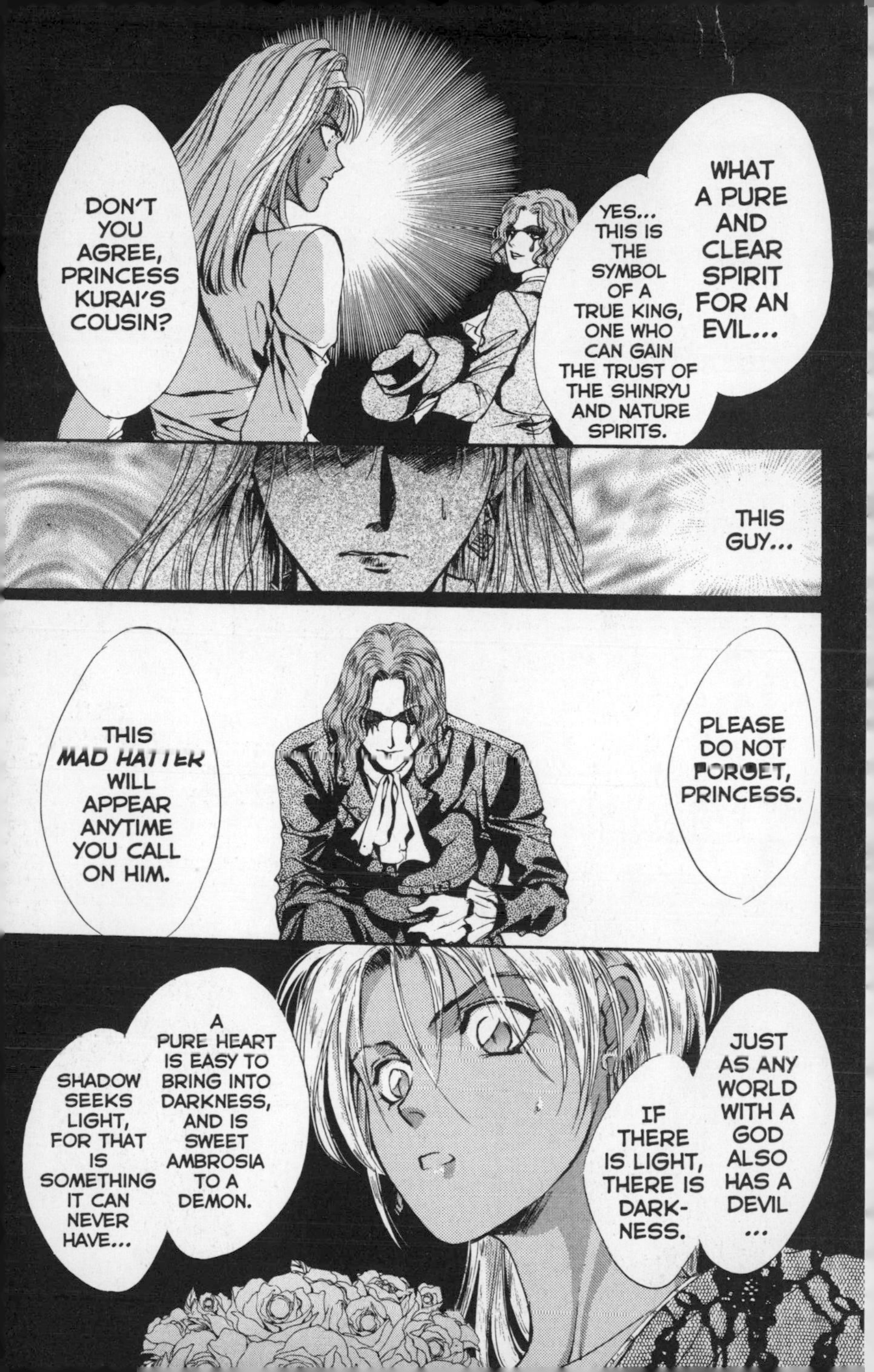
WHAT A PURE AND CLEAR SPIRIT FOR AN EVIL...
YES... THIS IS THE SYMBOL OF A TRUE KING, ONE WHO CAN GAIN THE TRUST OF THE SHINRYU AND NATURE SPIRITS.
DON'T YOU AGREE, PRINCESS KURAI'S COUSIN?
THIS GUY...
PLEASE DO NOT FORGET, PRINCESS.
THIS *MAD HATTER* WILL APPEAR ANYTIME YOU CALL ON HIM.
JUST AS ANY WORLD WITH A GOD ALSO HAS A DEVIL ...
IF THERE IS LIGHT, THERE IS DARK-NESS.
A PURE HEART IS EASY TO BRING INTO DARKNESS, AND IS SWEET AMBROSIA TO A DEMON.
SHADOW SEEKS LIGHT, FOR THAT IS SOMETHING IT CAN NEVER HAVE...

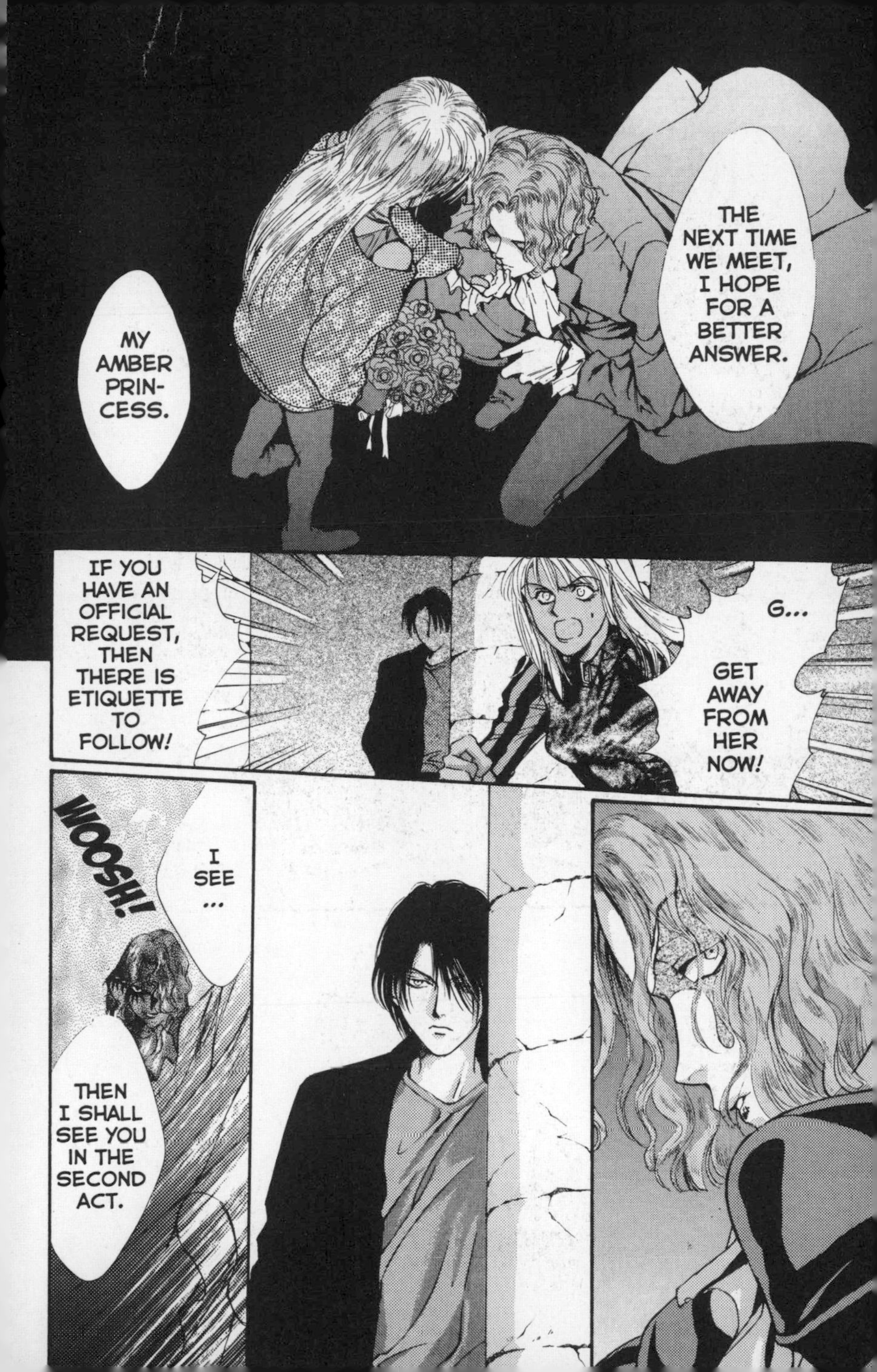
THE NEXT TIME WE MEET, I HOPE FOR A BETTER ANSWER.
MY AMBER PRIN-CESS.
G...
GET AWAY FROM HER NOW!
IF YOU HAVE AN OFFICIAL REQUEST, THEN THERE IS ETIQUETTE TO FOLLOW!
WOOSH!
I SEE ...
THEN I SHALL SEE YOU IN THE SECOND ACT.

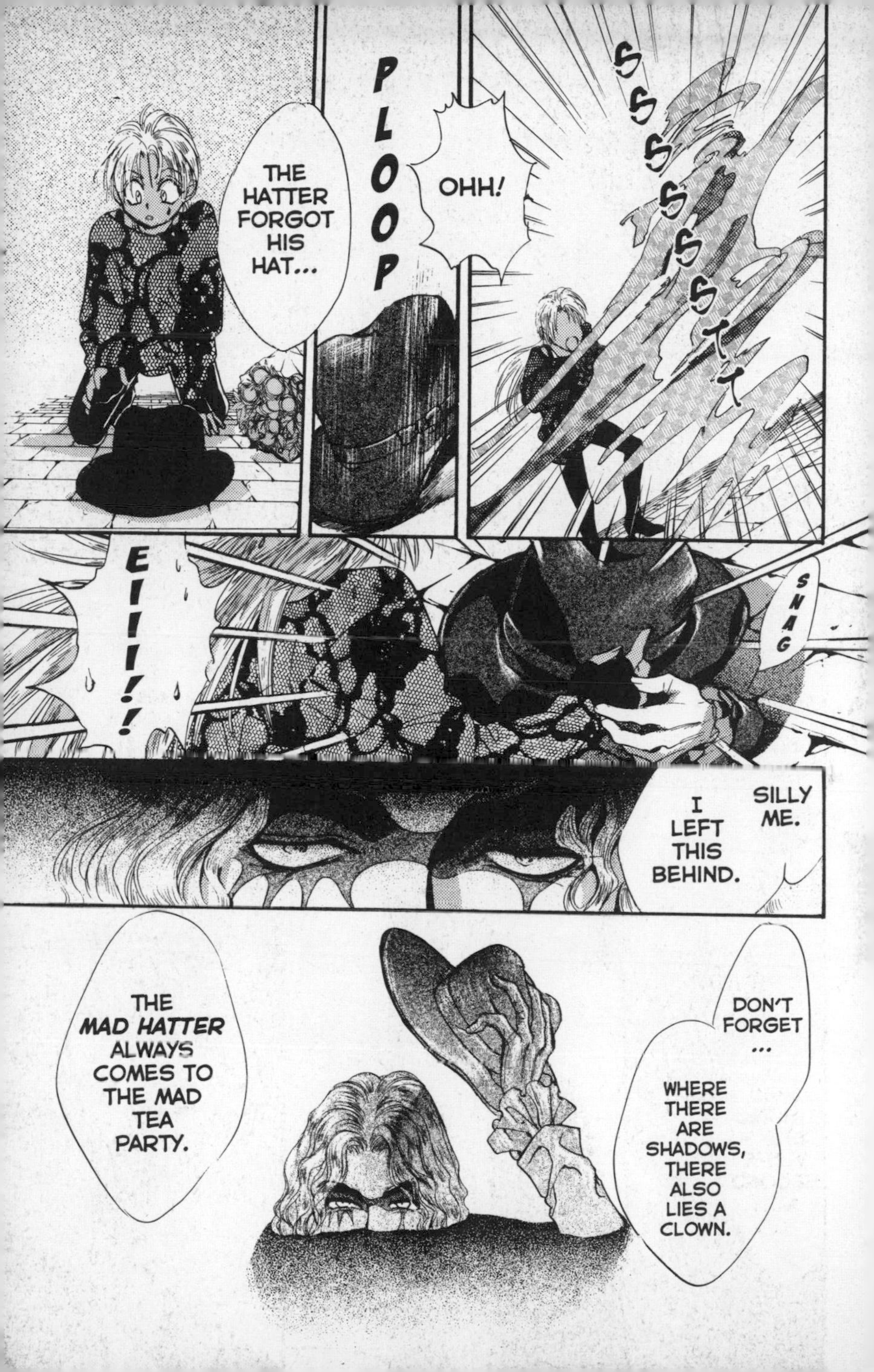
SSSSSSTT
OHH!
PLOOP
THE HATTER FORGOT HIS HAT...
SNAG
EIIII!!!
SILLY ME.
I LEFT THIS BEHIND.
DON'T FORGET ...
WHERE THERE ARE SHADOWS, THERE ALSO LIES A CLOWN.
THE *MAD HATTER* ALWAYS COMES TO THE MAD TEA PARTY.

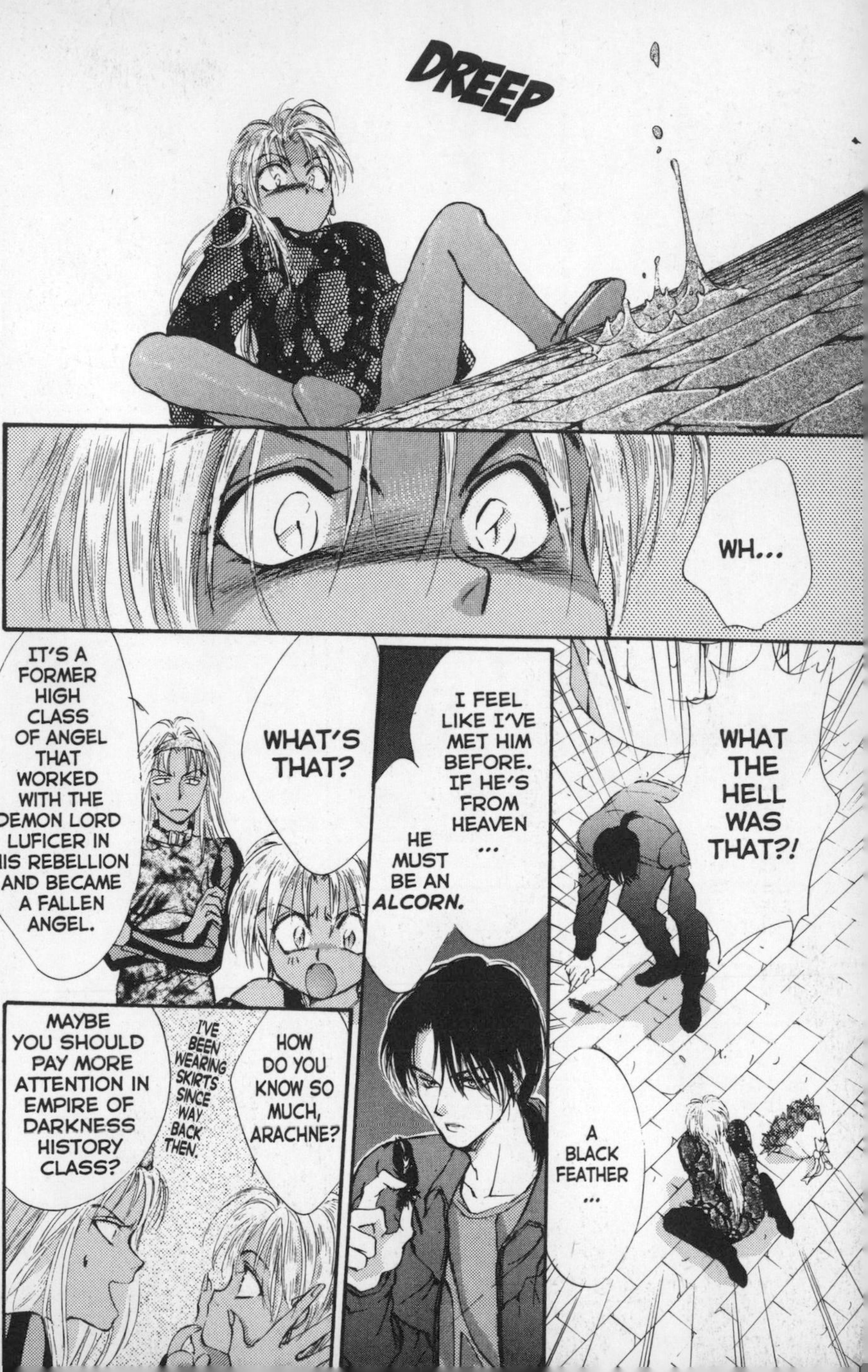
DREEP
WH...
WHAT THE HELL WAS THAT?!
A BLACK FEATHER ...
I FEEL LIKE I'VE MET HIM BEFORE. IF HE'S FROM HEAVEN ...
HE MUST BE AN *ALCORN.*
WHAT'S THAT?
IT'S A FORMER HIGH CLASS OF ANGEL THAT WORKED WITH THE DEMON LORD LUFICER IN HIS REBELLION AND BECAME A FALLEN ANGEL.
HOW DO YOU KNOW SO MUCH, ARACHNE?
I'VE BEEN WEARING SKIRTS SINCE WAY BACK THEN.
MAYBE YOU SHOULD PAY MORE ATTENTION IN EMPIRE OF DARKNESS HISTORY CLASS?

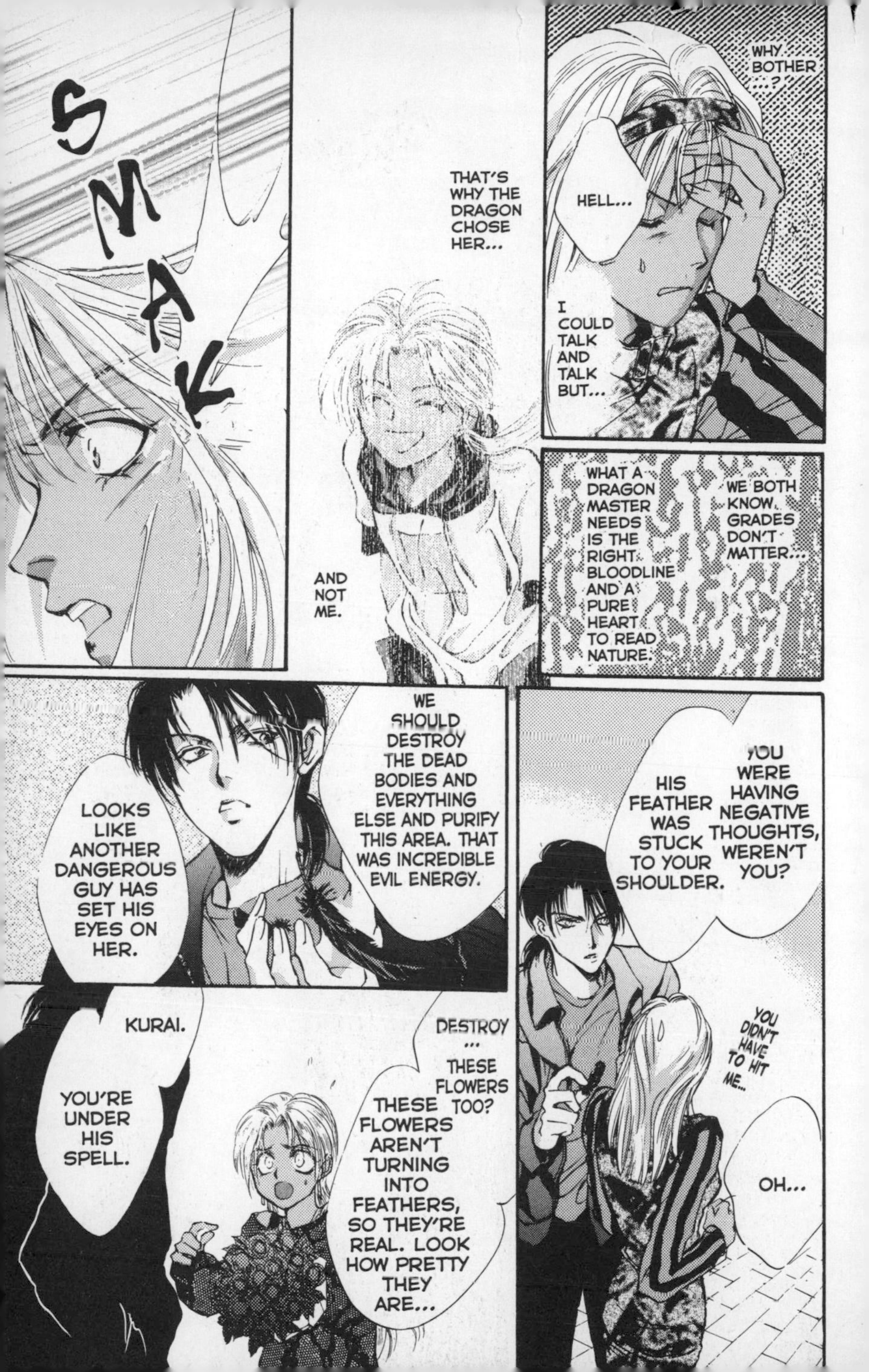
WHY BOTHER ...?
HELL...
I COULD TALK AND TALK BUT...
WE BOTH KNOW, GRADES DON'T MATTER...
WHAT A DRAGON MASTER NEEDS IS THE RIGHT BLOODLINE AND A PURE HEART TO READ NATURE.
THAT'S WHY THE DRAGON CHOSE HER...
AND NOT ME.
SMAK
YOU WERE HAVING NEGATIVE THOUGHTS, WEREN'T YOU?
HIS FEATHER WAS STUCK TO YOUR SHOULDER.
YOU DIDN'T HAVE TO HIT ME...
OH...
WE SHOULD DESTROY THE DEAD BODIES AND EVERYTHING ELSE AND PURIFY THIS AREA. THAT WAS INCREDIBLE EVIL ENERGY.
LOOKS LIKE ANOTHER DANGEROUS GUY HAS SET HIS EYES ON HER.
DESTROY ... THESE FLOWERS TOO?
THESE FLOWERS AREN'T TURNING INTO FEATHERS, SO THEY'RE REAL. LOOK HOW PRETTY THEY ARE...
KURAI.
YOU'RE UNDER HIS SPELL.

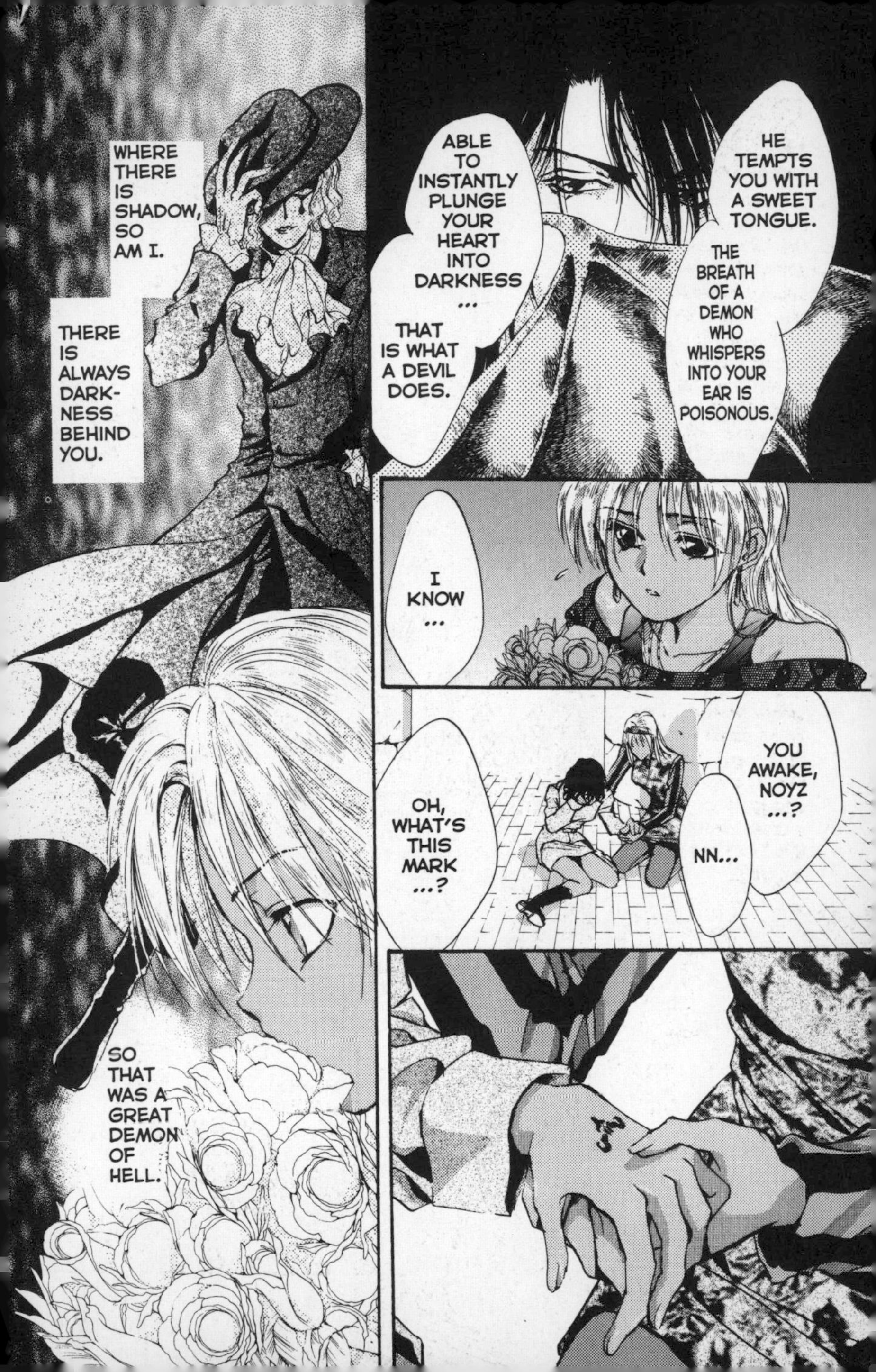
HE TEMPTS YOU WITH A SWEET TONGUE.
THE BREATH OF A DEMON WHO WHISPERS INTO YOUR EAR IS POISONOUS.
ABLE TO INSTANTLY PLUNGE YOUR HEART INTO DARKNESS ...
THAT IS WHAT A DEVIL DOES.
I KNOW ...
YOU AWAKE, NOYZ ...?
NN...
OH, WHAT'S THIS MARK ...?
WHERE THERE IS SHADOW, SO AM I.
THERE IS ALWAYS DARK-NESS BEHIND YOU.
SO THAT WAS A GREAT DEMON OF HELL.

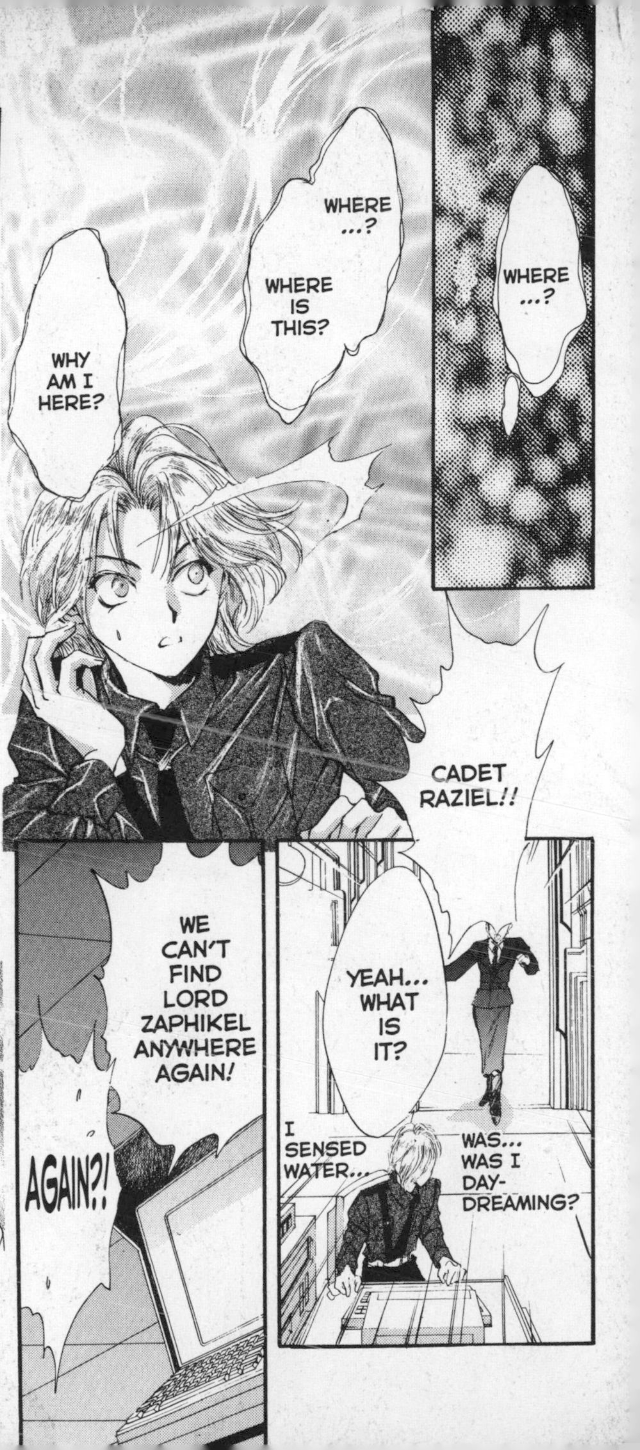
WHERE ...?
WHERE ...?
WHERE IS THIS?
WHY AM I HERE?
CADET RAZIEL!!
YEAH... WHAT IS IT?
WAS... WAS I DAY-DREAMING?
I SENSED WATER...
WE CAN'T FIND LORD ZAPHIKEL ANYWHERE AGAIN!
AGAIN?!

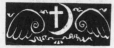

continuation--So I received many letters like "The scene was so scandalous that it knocked DobiDobi (aka Dobiel) out!" And immediately asking the man who saved you "Am I beautiful?" He must be insane... When Dobiel said "These two are crazy." I wanted to write "That's what everyone thinks." My editor started to say that when he saw this scene he thought "This is..." but then he noticed how red and embarrassed I was so he didn't mention anything. Thank you! Don't think that I was getting all excited drawing that... But I did draw it anyway...

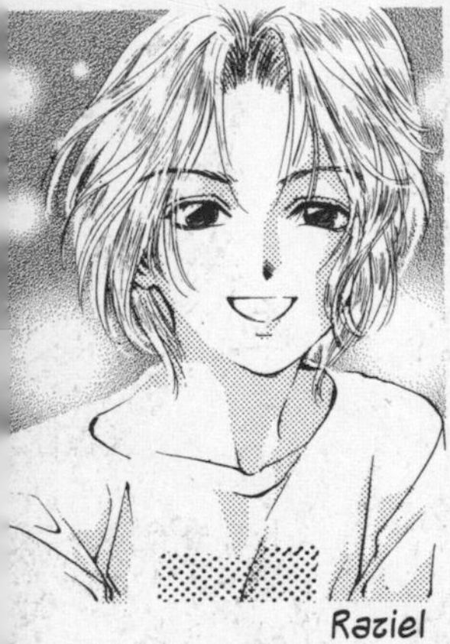

Raziel

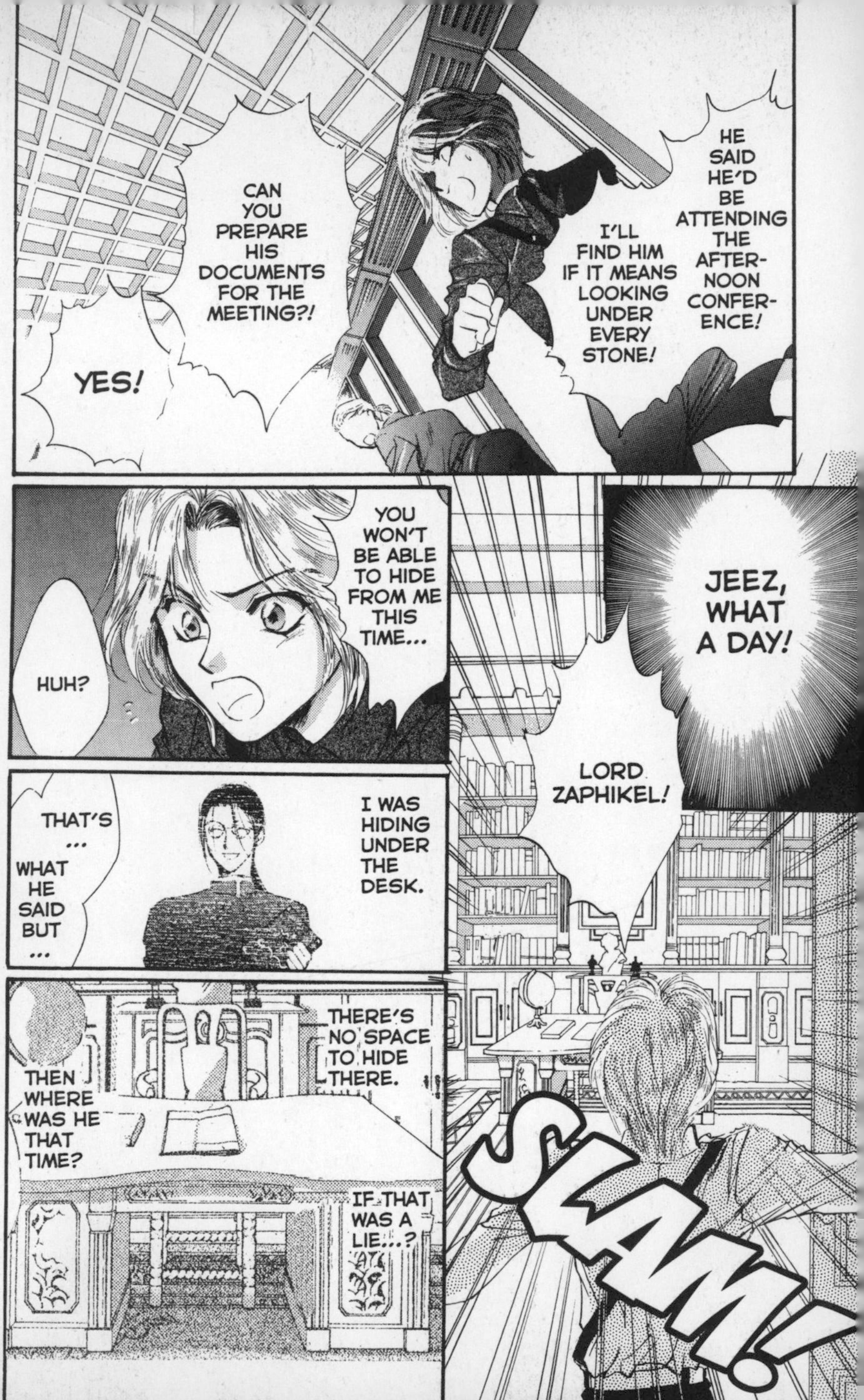
HE SAID HE'D BE ATTENDING THE AFTERNOON CONFERENCE!
I'LL FIND HIM IF IT MEANS LOOKING UNDER EVERY STONE!
CAN YOU PREPARE HIS DOCUMENTS FOR THE MEETING?!
YES!
JEEZ, WHAT A DAY!
LORD ZAPHIKEL!
SLAM!
YOU WON'T BE ABLE TO HIDE FROM ME THIS TIME...
HUH?
I WAS HIDING UNDER THE DESK.
THAT'S... WHAT HE SAID BUT...
THERE'S NO SPACE TO HIDE THERE.
THEN WHERE WAS HE THAT TIME?
IF THAT WAS A LIE...?

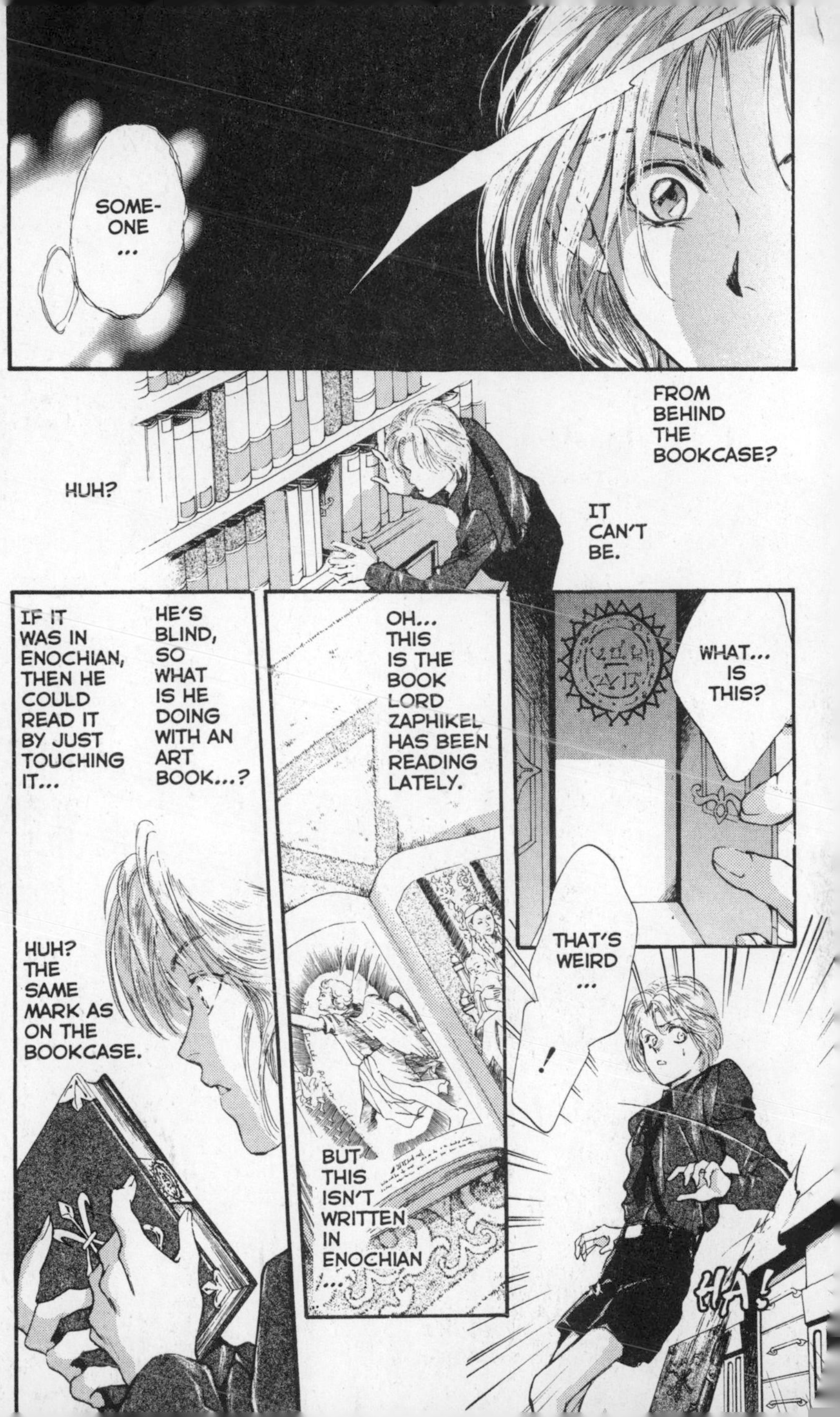
SOME-ONE ...
FROM BEHIND THE BOOKCASE?
IT CAN'T BE.
HUH?
WHAT... IS THIS?
THAT'S WEIRD ...
!
HA!
OH... THIS IS THE BOOK LORD ZAPHIKEL HAS BEEN READING LATELY.
BUT THIS ISN'T WRITTEN IN ENOCHIAN ...
HE'S BLIND, SO WHAT IS HE DOING WITH AN ART BOOK...?
IF IT WAS IN ENOCHIAN, THEN HE COULD READ IT BY JUST TOUCHING IT...
HUH? THE SAME MARK AS ON THE BOOKCASE.

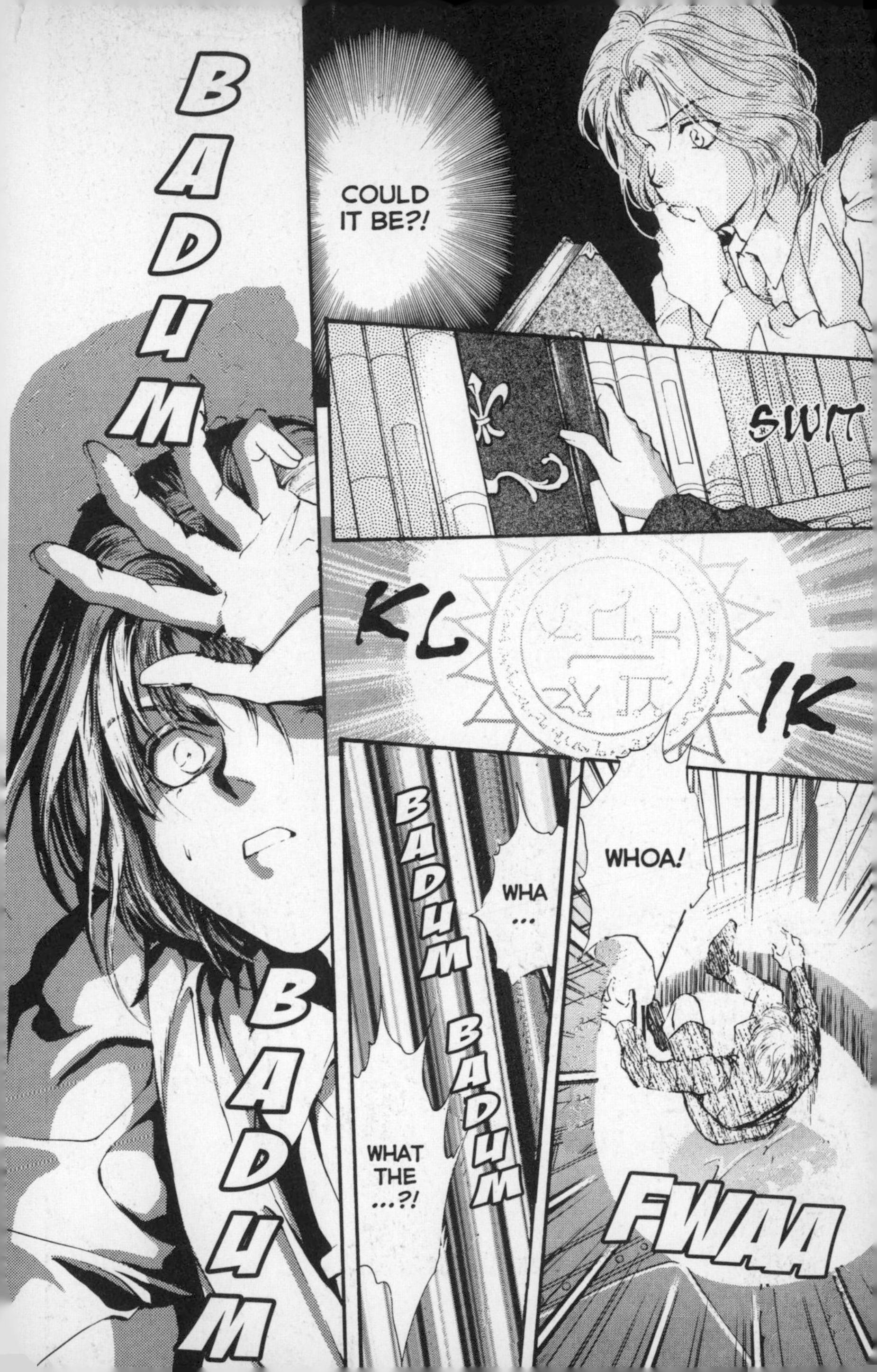
COULD IT BE?!
SWIT
KL IK
WHOA!
FWAA
WHA ...
BADUM BADUM
WHAT THE ...?!
BADUM
BADUM

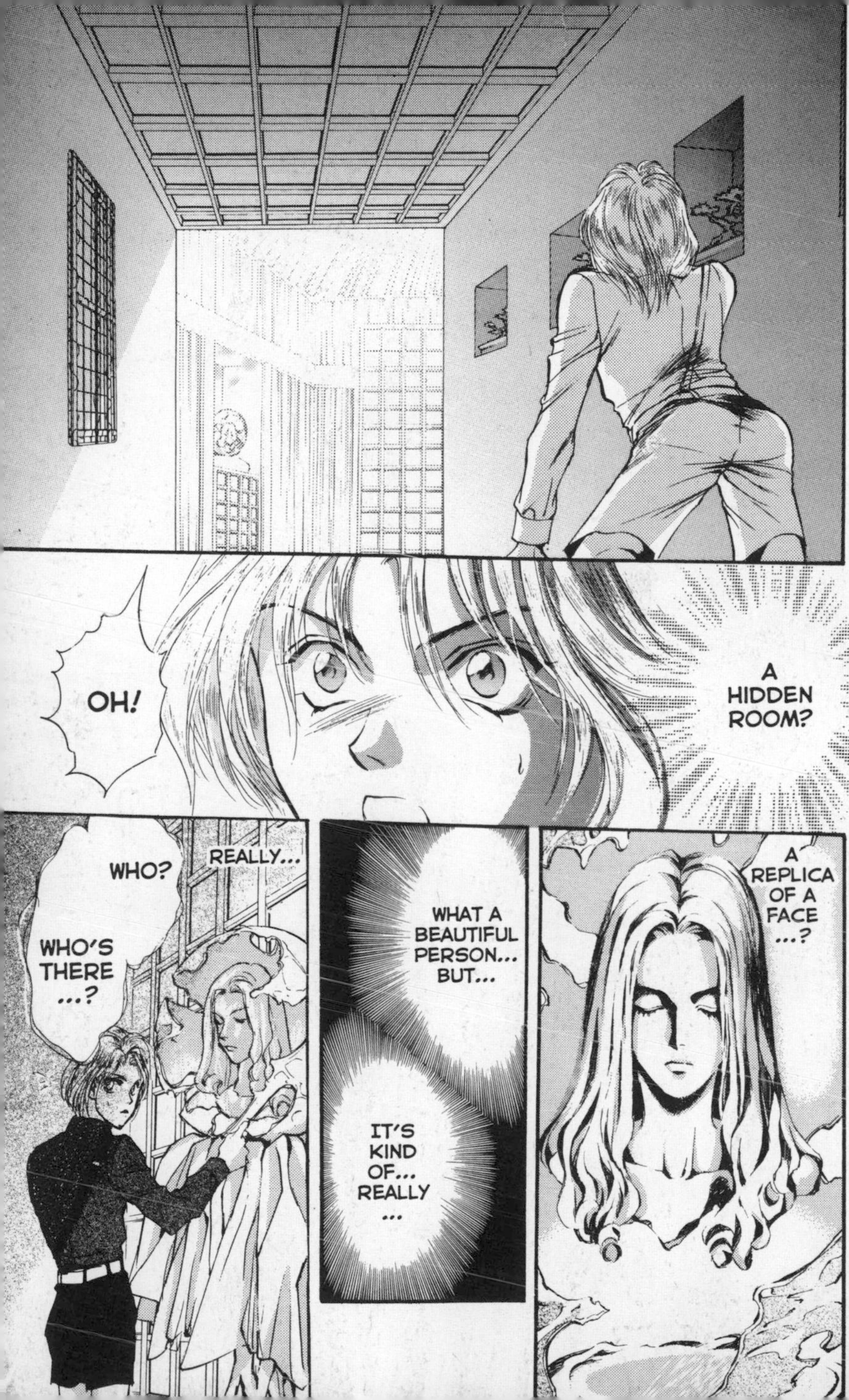
A HIDDEN ROOM?
OH!
A REPLICA OF A FACE ...?
WHAT A BEAUTIFUL PERSON... BUT...
IT'S KIND OF... REALLY ...
REALLY...
WHO?
WHO'S THERE ...?

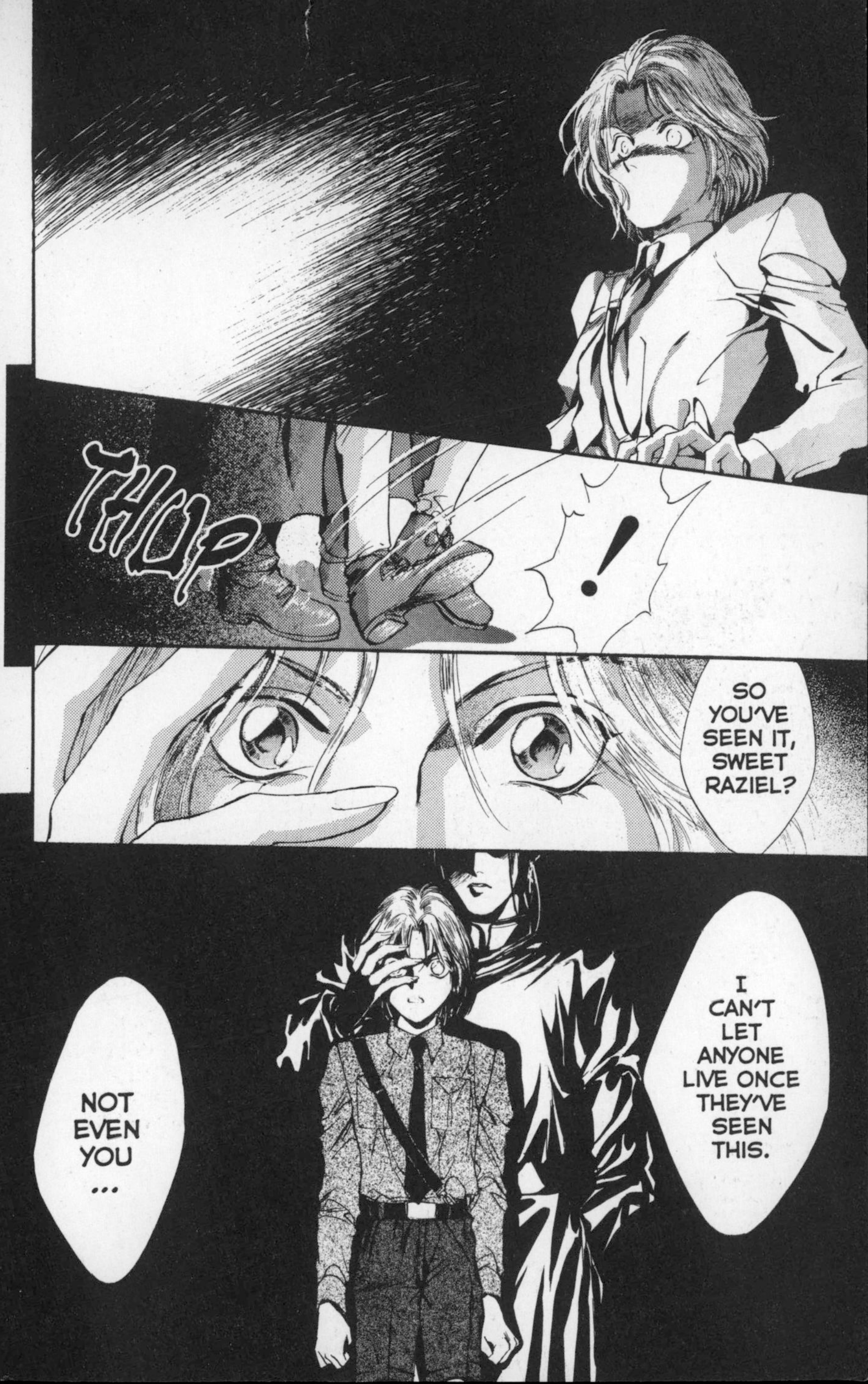
THUP
!
SO YOU'VE SEEN IT, SWEET RAZIEL?
I CAN'T LET ANYONE LIVE ONCE THEY'VE SEEN THIS.
NOT EVEN YOU ...

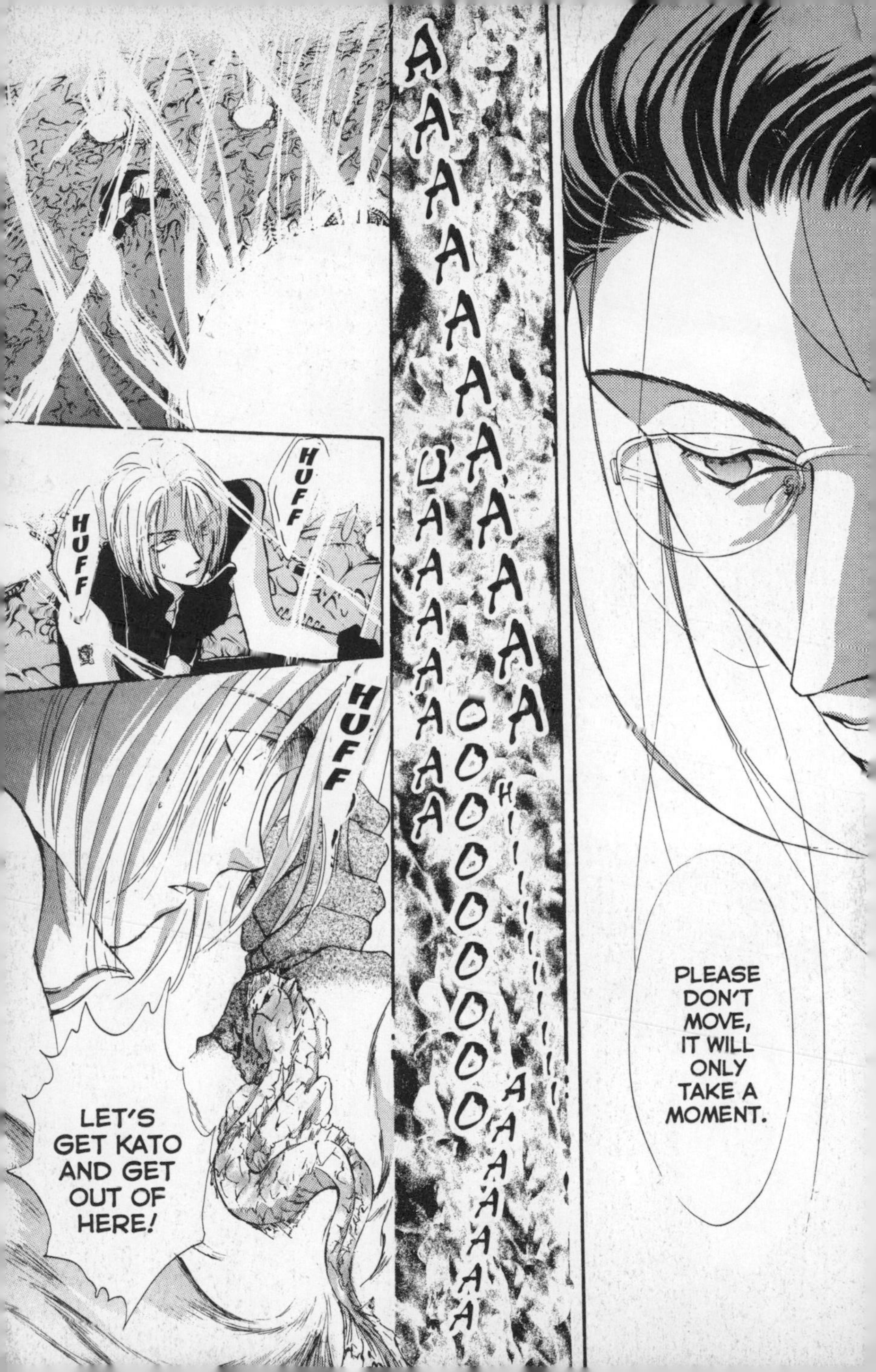
PLEASE DON'T MOVE, IT WILL ONLY TAKE A MOMENT.
AAAAAAAAAAAAAA
UAAAAAAAAOOOOOOOOOO
HI!!!!!!!
AAAAAAAA
HUFF
HUFF
HUFF
LET'S GET KATO AND GET OUT OF HERE!

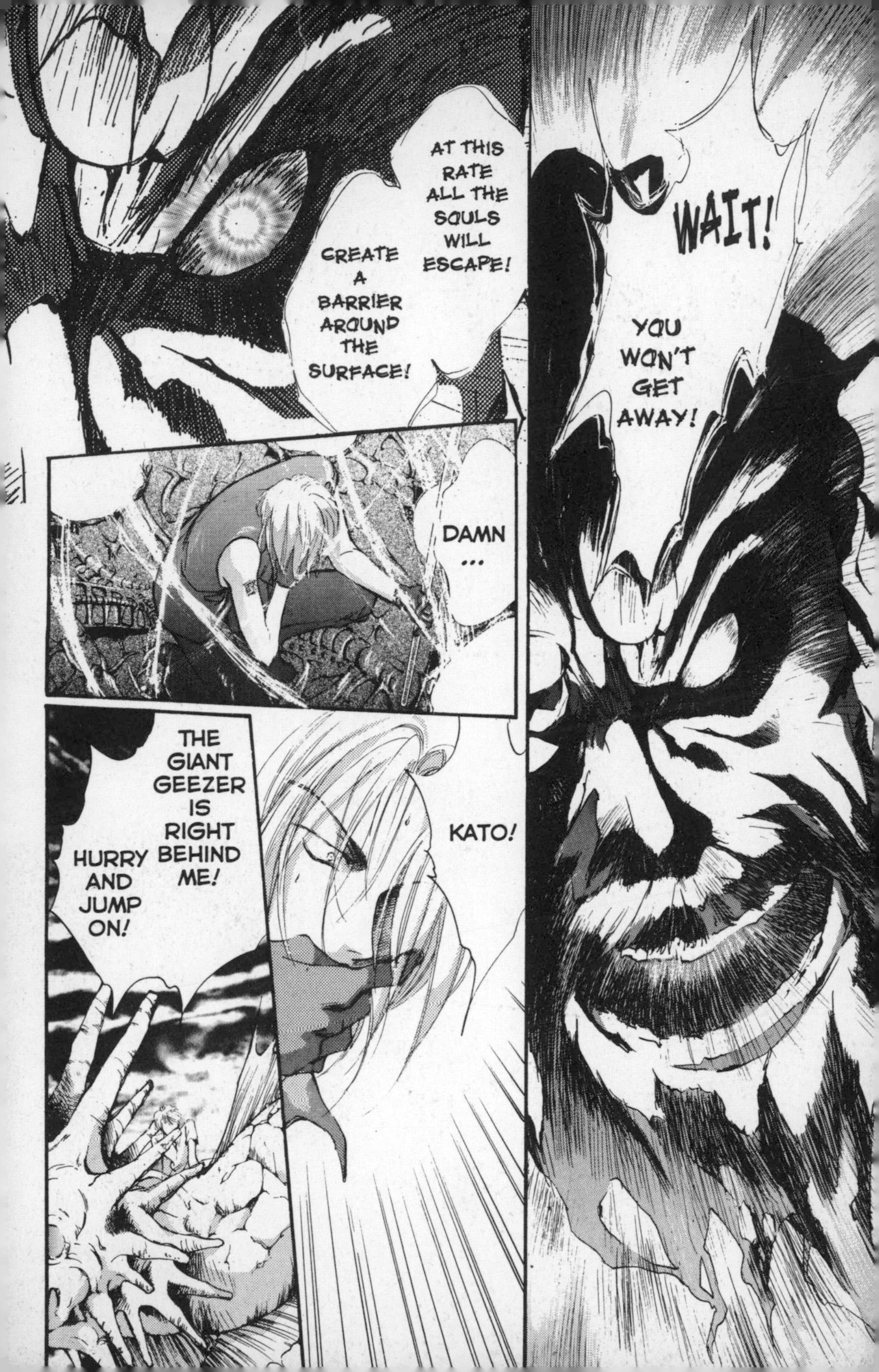
WAIT!
YOU WON'T GET AWAY!
AT THIS RATE ALL THE SOULS WILL ESCAPE!
CREATE A BARRIER AROUND THE SURFACE!
DAMN ...
KATO!
THE GIANT GEEZER IS RIGHT BEHIND ME!
HURRY AND JUMP ON!

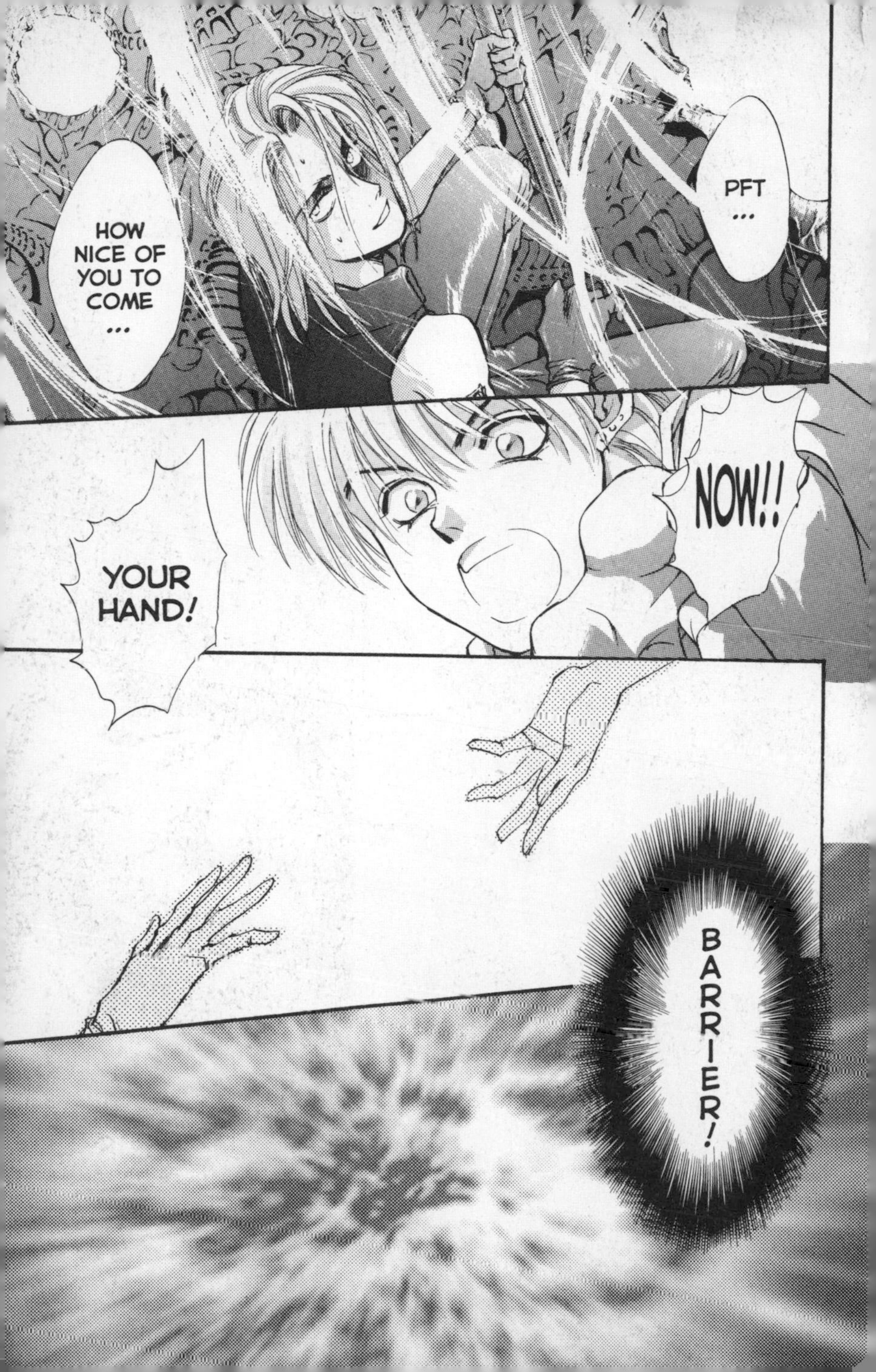
PFT ...
HOW NICE OF YOU TO COME ...
NOW!!
YOUR HAND!
BARRIER!

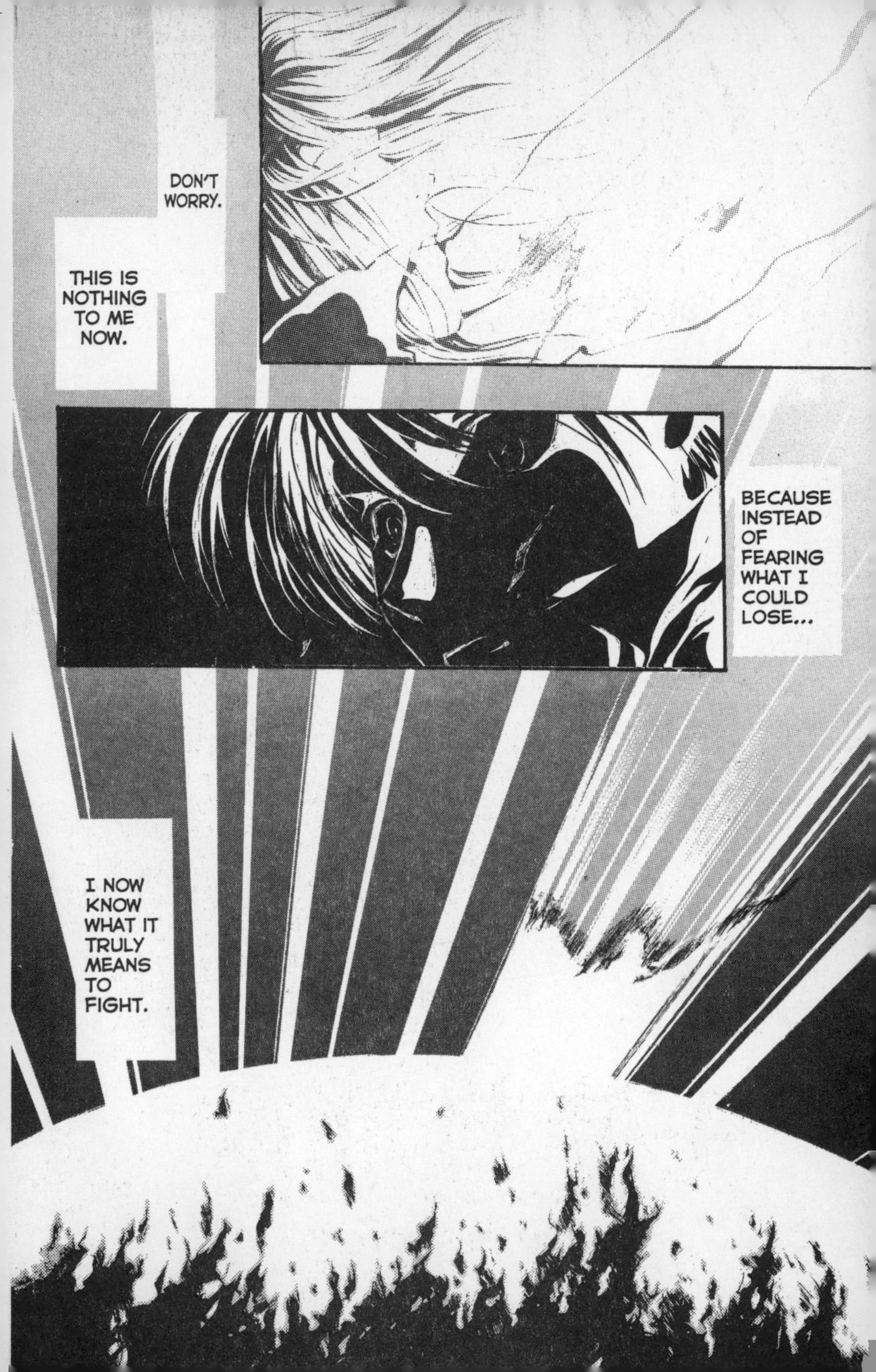
DON'T WORRY.
THIS IS NOTHING TO ME NOW.
BECAUSE INSTEAD OF FEARING WHAT I COULD LOSE...
I NOW KNOW WHAT IT TRULY MEANS TO FIGHT.

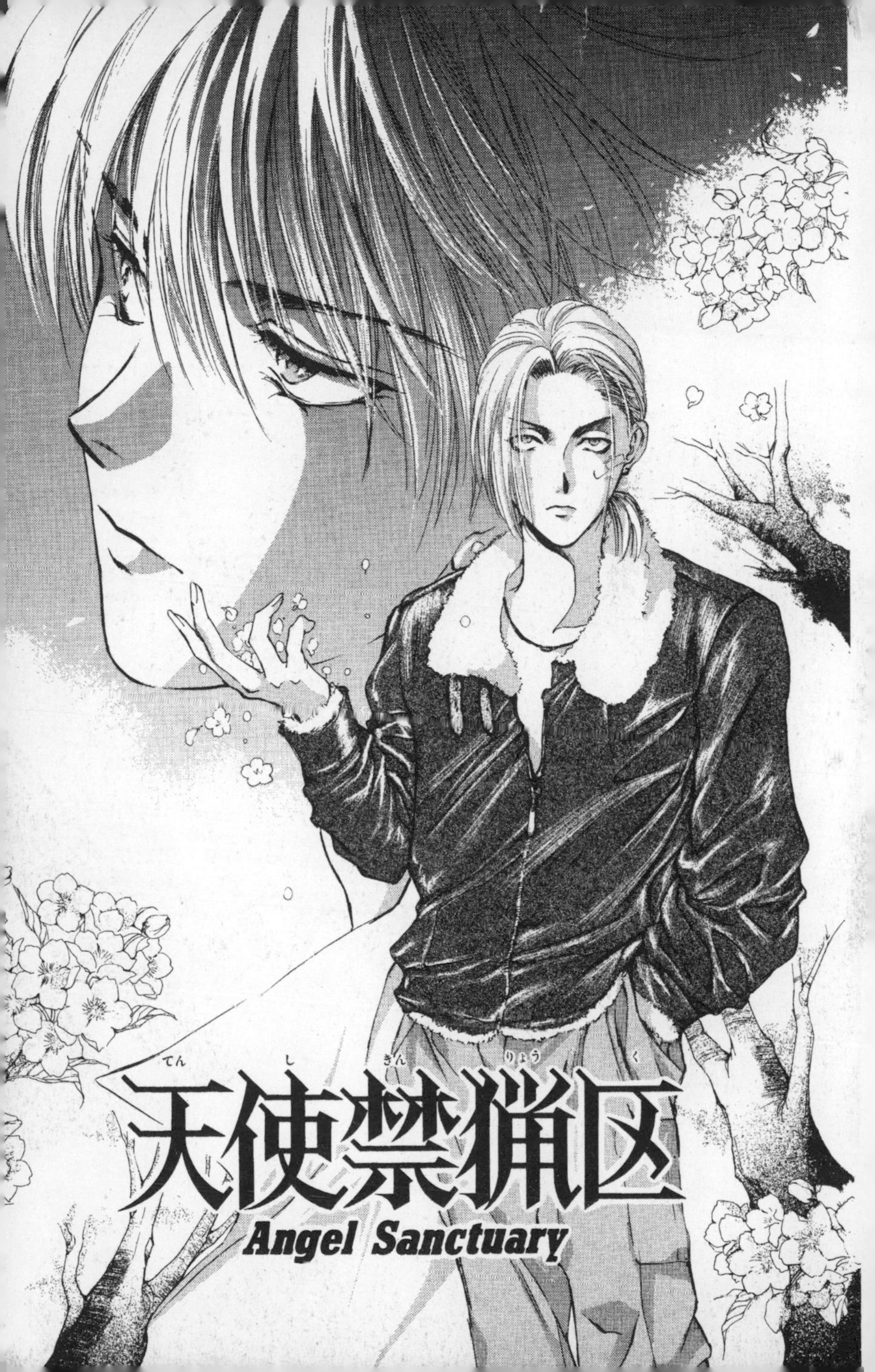
てん し きん りょう く
天使禁猟区
Angel Sanctuary

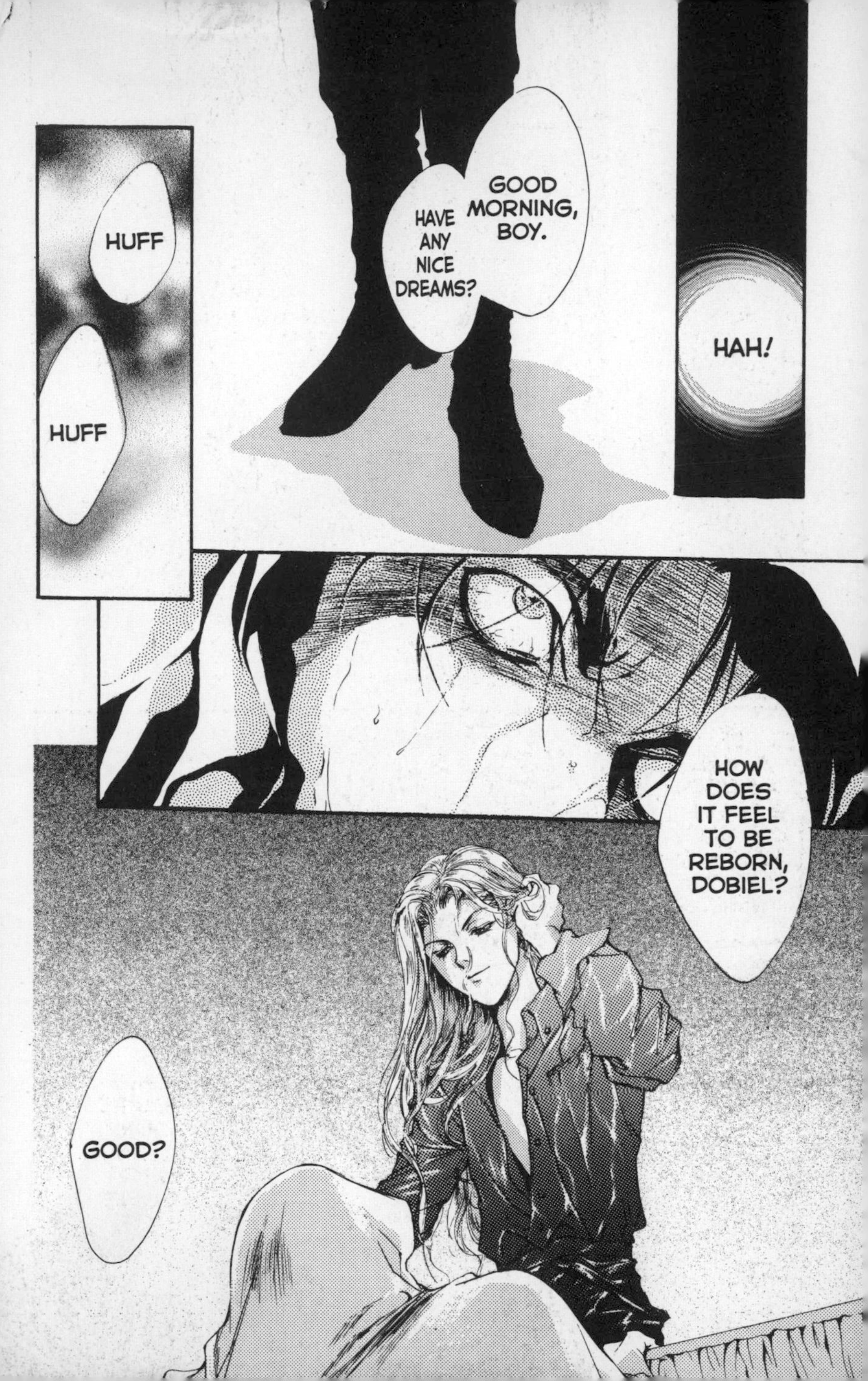
HAH!
GOOD MORNING, BOY.
HAVE ANY NICE DREAMS?
HUFF
HUFF
HOW DOES IT FEEL TO BE REBORN, DOBIEL?
GOOD?

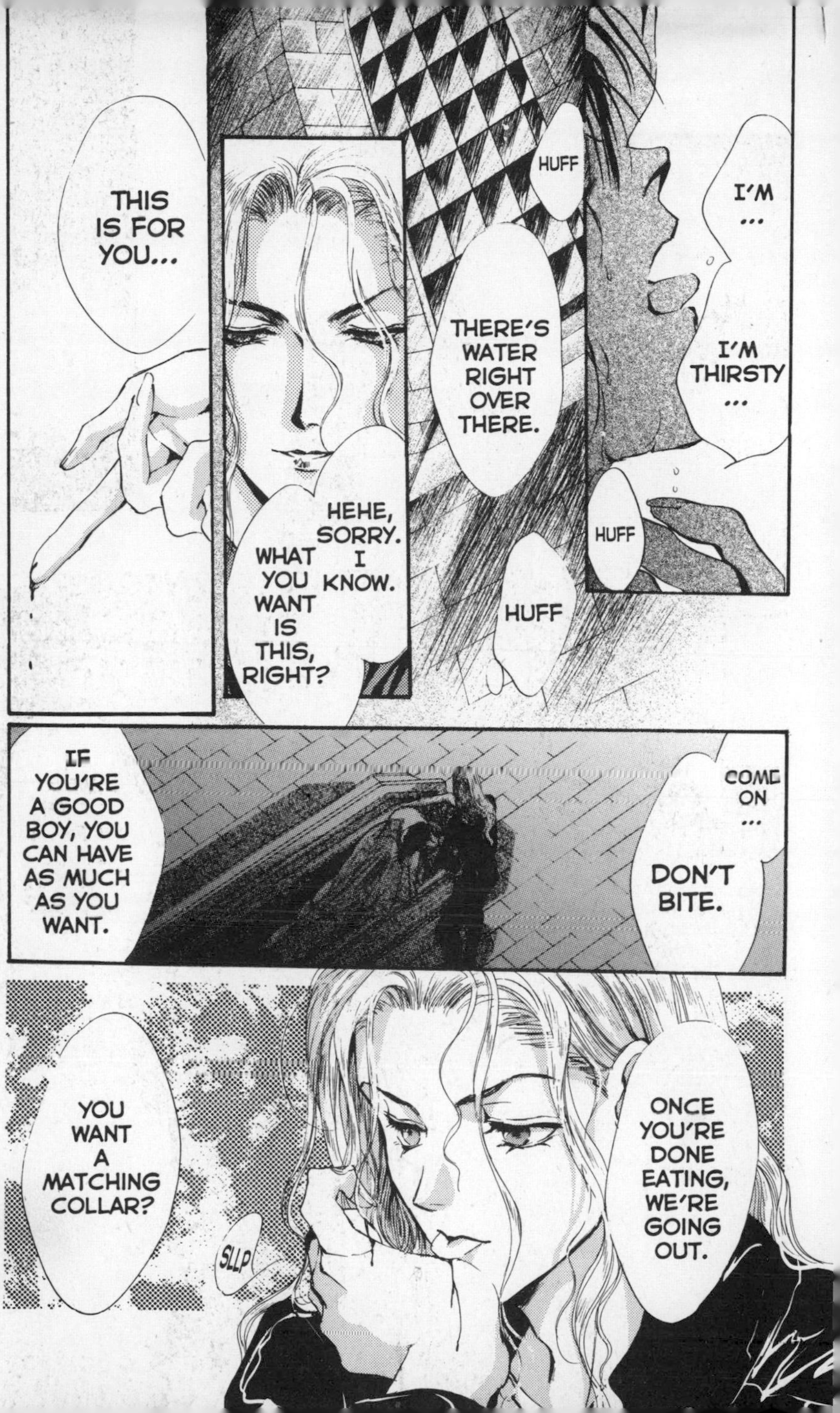
I'M ...
I'M THIRSTY ...
HUFF
HUFF
THERE'S WATER RIGHT OVER THERE.
HUFF
HEHE, SORRY. I KNOW.
WHAT YOU WANT IS THIS, RIGHT?
THIS IS FOR YOU...
COME ON ...
DON'T BITE.
IF YOU'RE A GOOD BOY, YOU CAN HAVE AS MUCH AS YOU WANT.
ONCE YOU'RE DONE EATING, WE'RE GOING OUT.
SLLP
YOU WANT A MATCHING COLLAR?

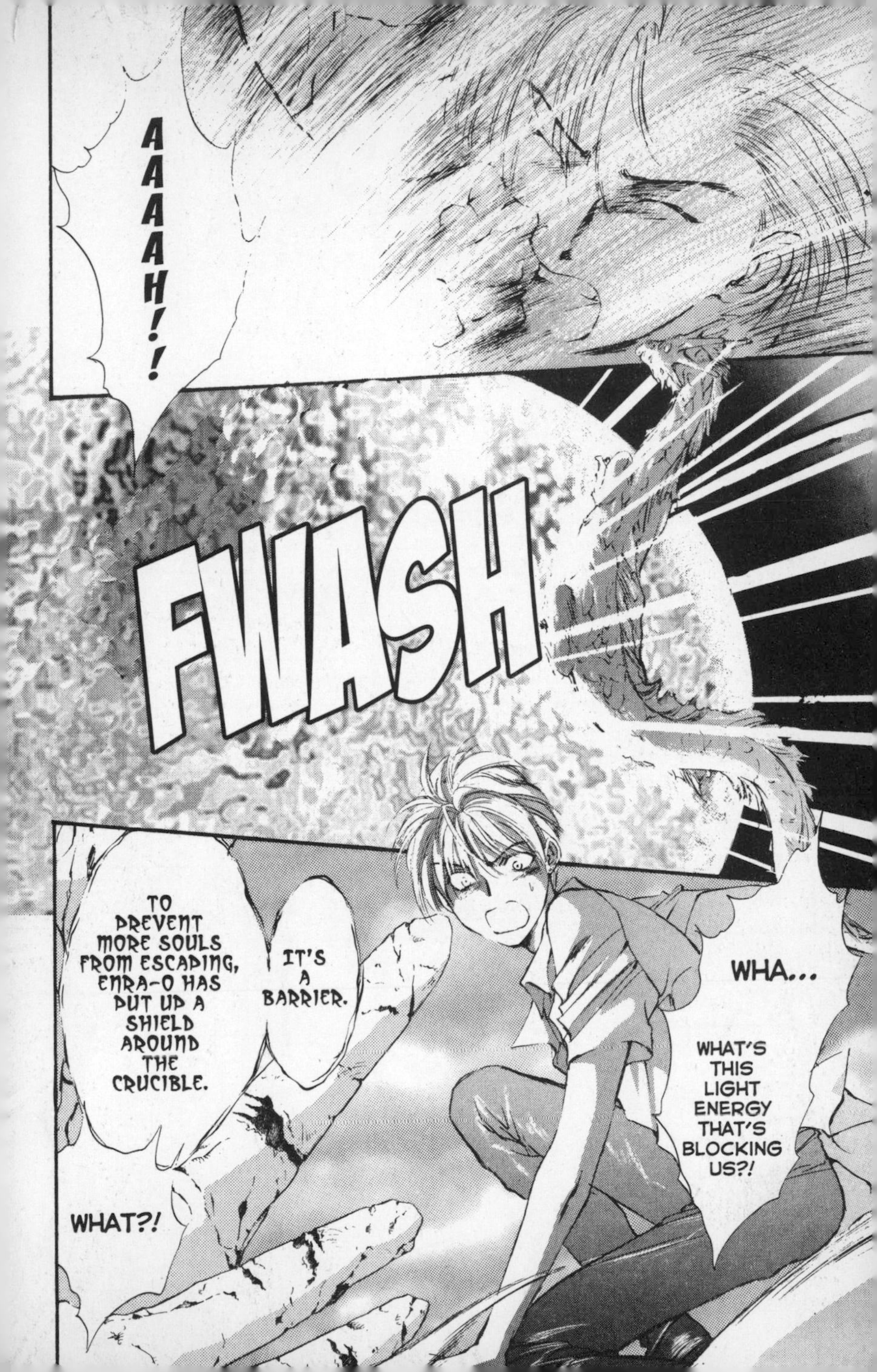
AAAAAH!!
FWASH
WHA...
WHAT'S THIS LIGHT ENERGY THAT'S BLOCKING US?!
IT'S A BARRIER.
TO PREVENT MORE SOULS FROM ESCAPING, ENRA-O HAS PUT UP A SHIELD AROUND THE CRUCIBLE.
WHAT?!

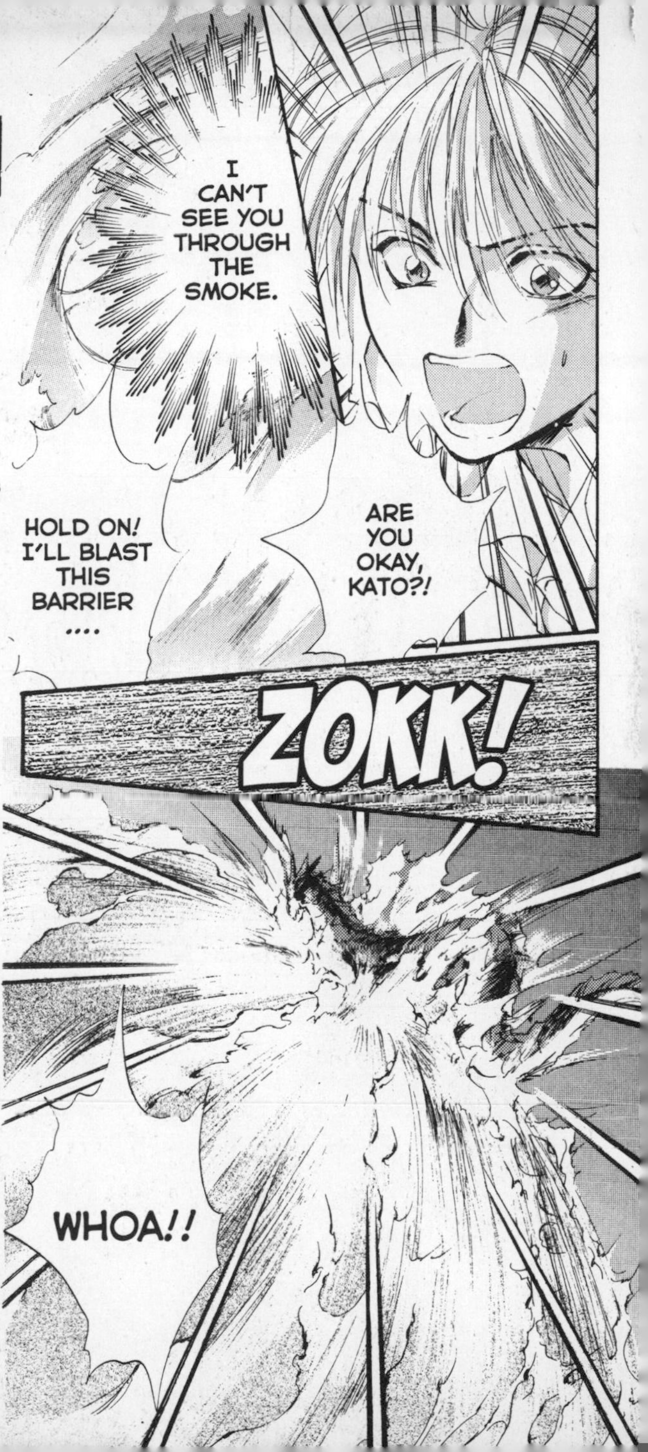
ARE YOU OKAY, KATO?!
I CAN'T SEE YOU THROUGH THE SMOKE.
HOLD ON! I'LL BLAST THIS BARRIER ....
ZOKK!
WHOA!!

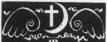

I didn't want to have to say it, but I was in a slump during this chapter. I couldn't draw well, I didn't like the rough draft, and I did it without any of my usual inspiration. The chapter cover has cherry blossoms, and this is the first time I've ever drawn them. (My assistant drew it though...) Cherry blossoms make me think of "departure" or "a beauty close to death" and so I put them behind Kato ... Aren't cherry blossoms pretty at night? So much so that it's scary. I sometimes just want to quietly stare at them by myself. As if I'd be happy if the night just sucked me in. They are pretty, but they feel like men to me. Am I the only one that feels like that? Cherry trees remind me of the "Tenka Densetsu" song. That was a song that killed with love, wasn't it...

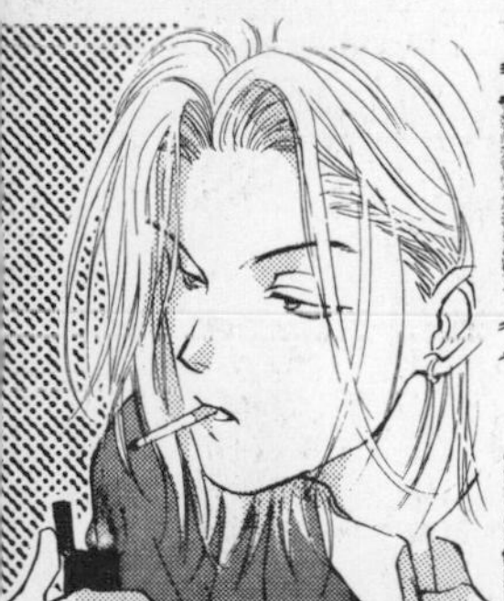

Kato looks like the guitarist from KonPure... no?

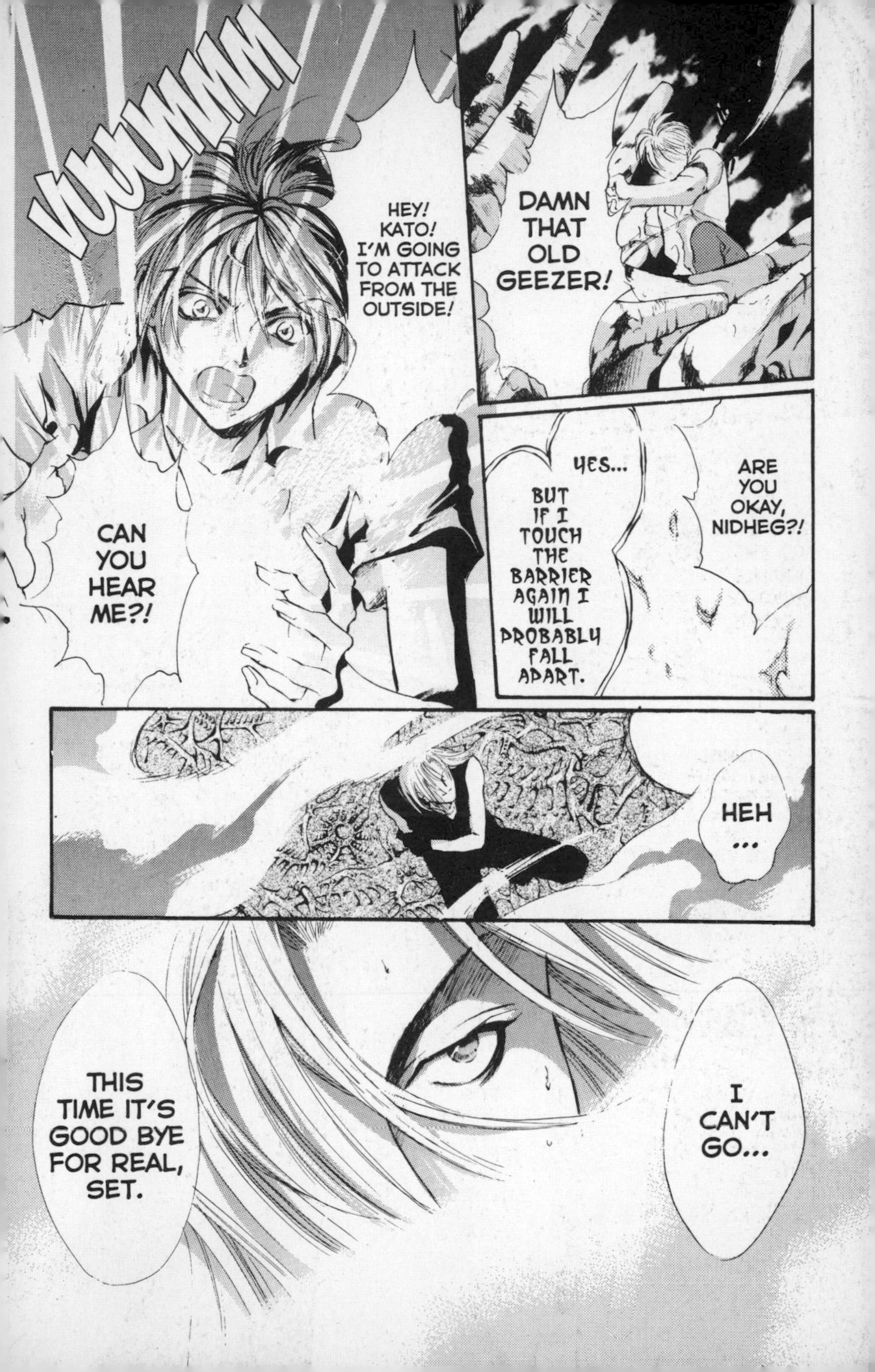
DAMN THAT OLD GEEZER!
ARE YOU OKAY, NIDHEG?!
YES...
BUT IF I TOUCH THE BARRIER AGAIN I WILL PROBABLY FALL APART.
VUUMMMM
HEY! KATO! I'M GOING TO ATTACK FROM THE OUTSIDE!
CAN YOU HEAR ME?!
HEH ...
I CAN'T GO...
THIS TIME IT'S GOOD BYE FOR REAL, SET.

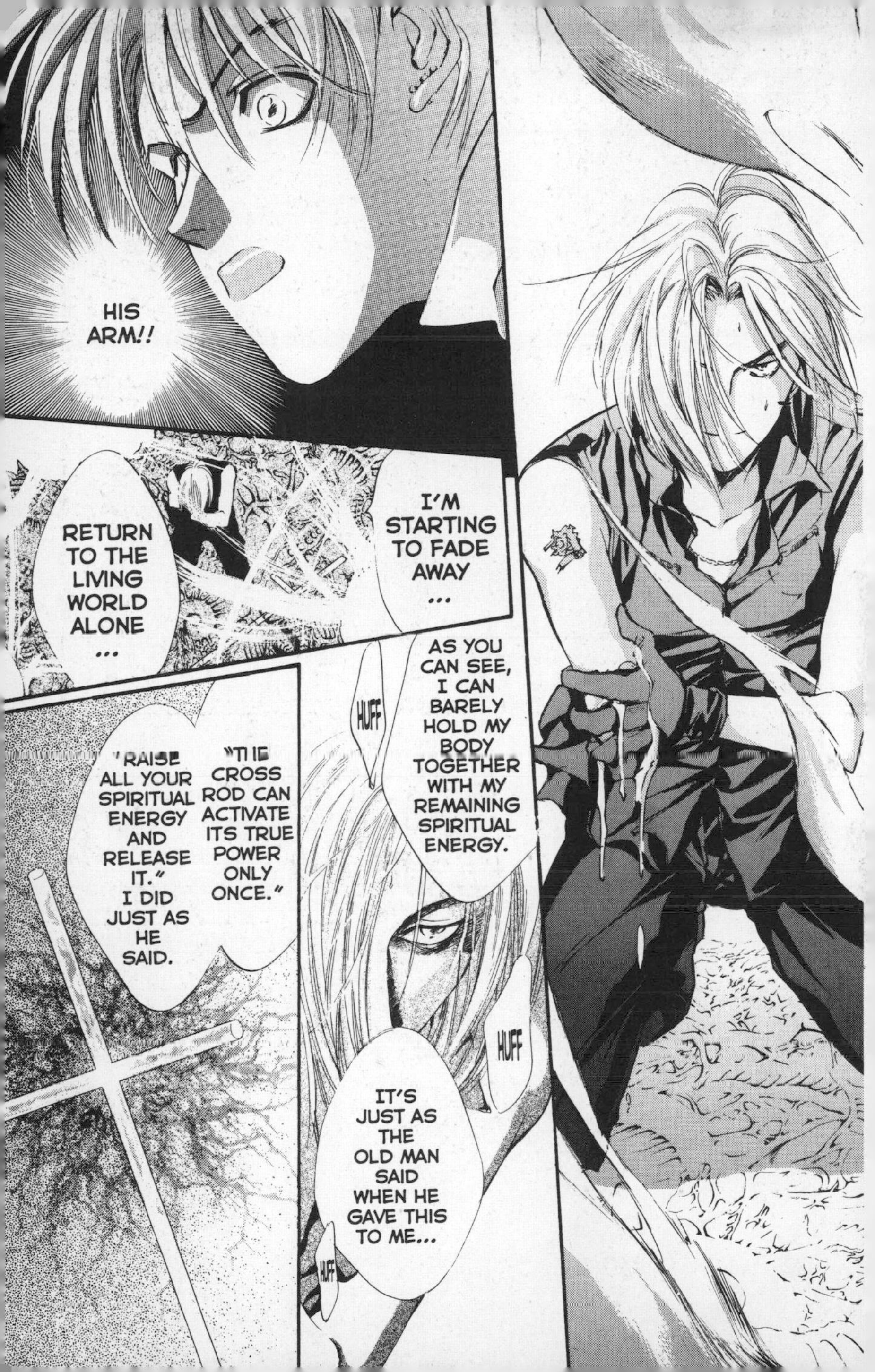
HUFF
AS YOU CAN SEE, I CAN BARELY HOLD MY BODY TOGETHER WITH MY REMAINING SPIRITUAL ENERGY.
HIS ARM!!
I'M STARTING TO FADE AWAY...
RETURN TO THE LIVING WORLD ALONE...
HUFF
IT'S JUST AS THE OLD MAN SAID WHEN HE GAVE THIS TO ME...
HUFF
"THE CROSS ROD CAN ACTIVATE ITS TRUE POWER ONLY ONCE."
"RAISE ALL YOUR SPIRITUAL ENERGY AND RELEASE IT." I DID JUST AS HE SAID.

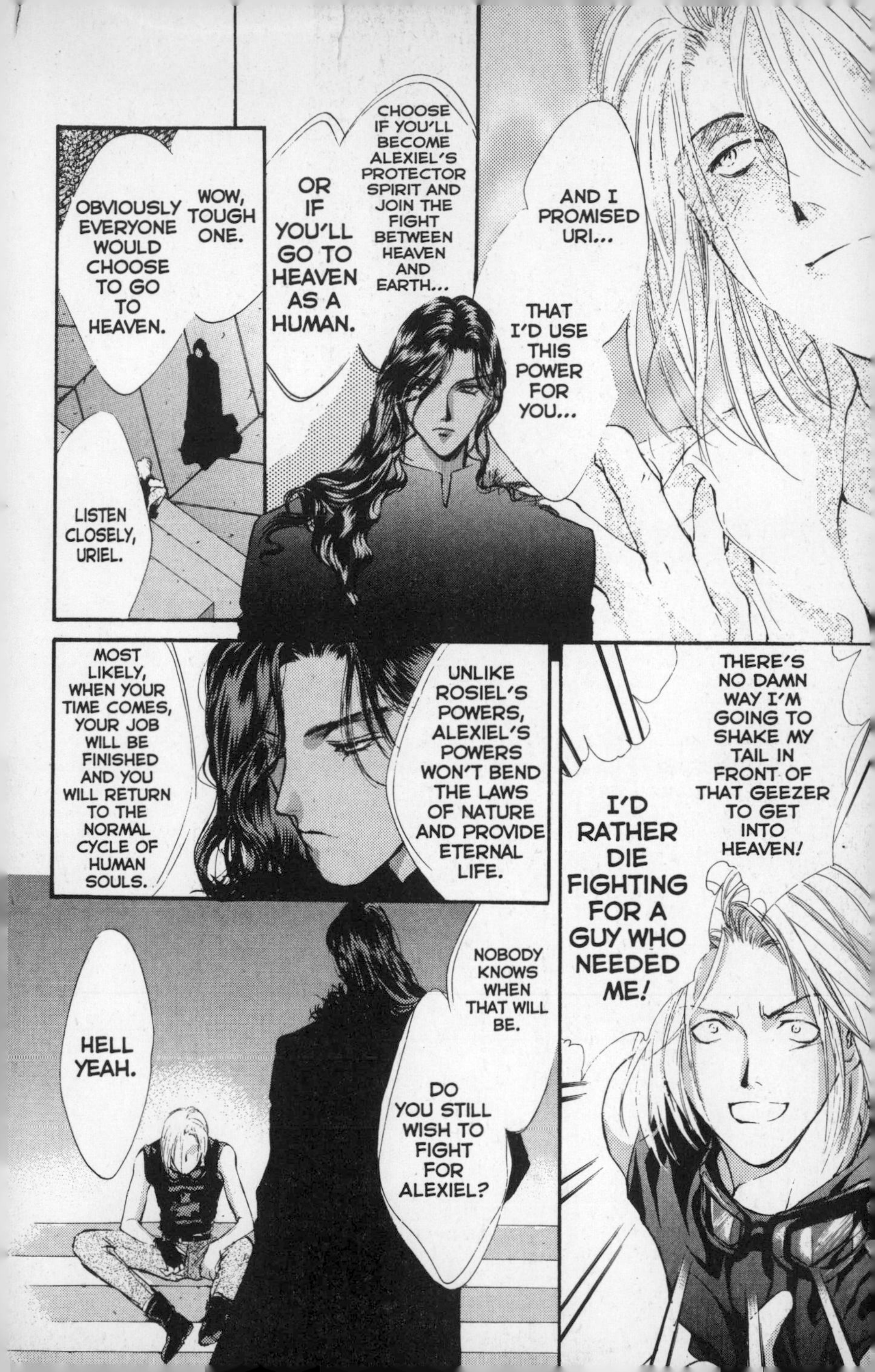

AND I PROMISED URI...
THAT I'D USE THIS POWER FOR YOU...
CHOOSE IF YOU'LL BECOME ALEXIEL'S PROTECTOR SPIRIT AND JOIN THE FIGHT BETWEEN HEAVEN AND EARTH...
OR IF YOU'LL GO TO HEAVEN AS A HUMAN.
WOW, TOUGH ONE.
OBVIOUSLY EVERYONE WOULD CHOOSE TO GO TO HEAVEN.
LISTEN CLOSELY, URIEL.
THERE'S NO DAMN WAY I'M GOING TO SHAKE MY TAIL IN FRONT OF THAT GEEZER TO GET INTO HEAVEN!
I'D RATHER DIE FIGHTING FOR A GUY WHO NEEDED ME!
UNLIKE ROSIEL'S POWERS, ALEXIEL'S POWERS WON'T BEND THE LAWS OF NATURE AND PROVIDE ETERNAL LIFE.
MOST LIKELY, WHEN YOUR TIME COMES, YOUR JOB WILL BE FINISHED AND YOU WILL RETURN TO THE NORMAL CYCLE OF HUMAN SOULS.
NOBODY KNOWS WHEN THAT WILL BE.
DO YOU STILL WISH TO FIGHT FOR ALEXIEL?
HELL YEAH.

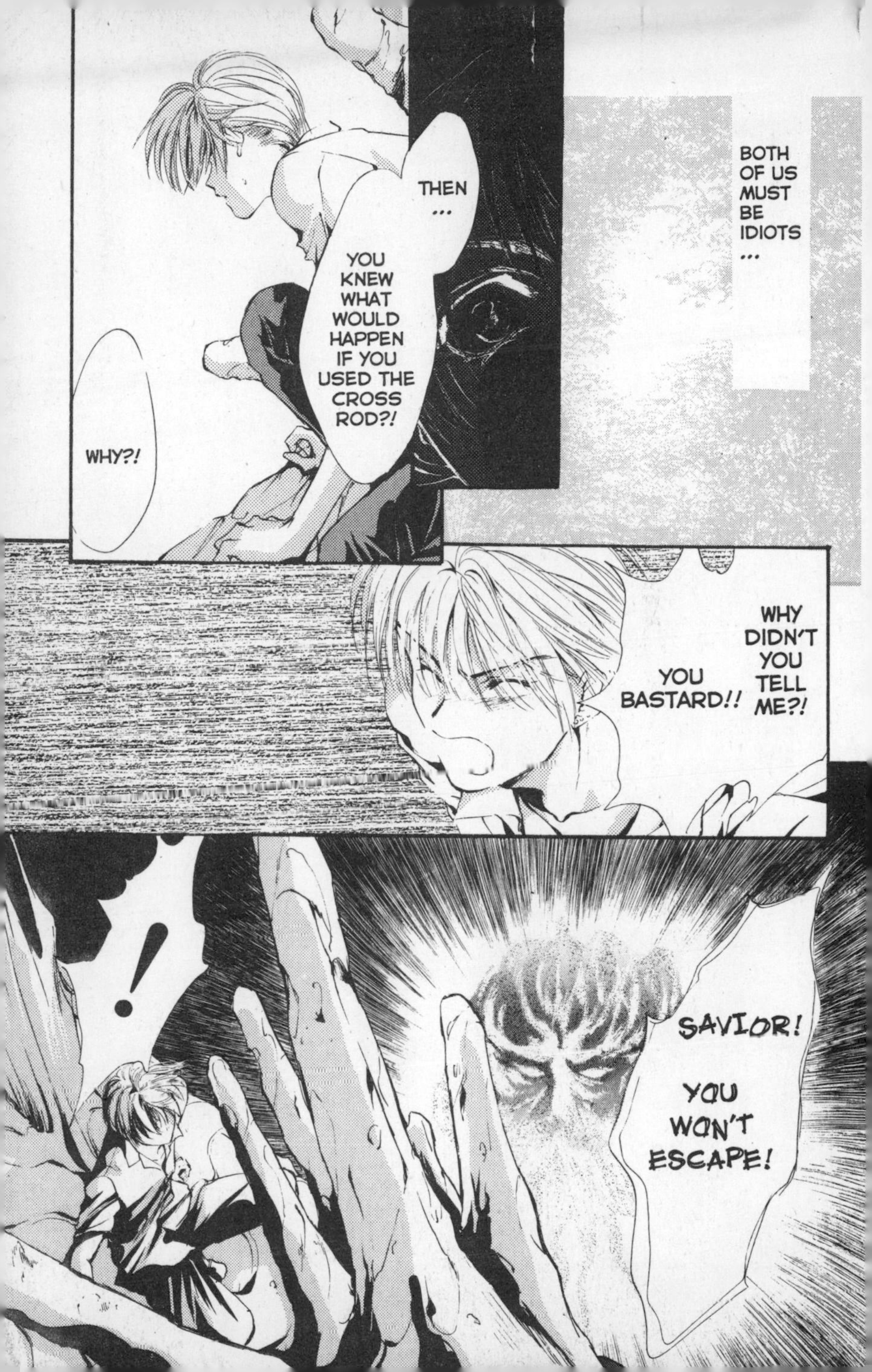
BOTH OF US MUST BE IDIOTS ...
THEN ... YOU KNEW WHAT WOULD HAPPEN IF YOU USED THE CROSS ROD?!
WHY?!
WHY DIDN'T YOU TELL ME?!
YOU BASTARD!!
SAVIOR! YOU WON'T ESCAPE!
!

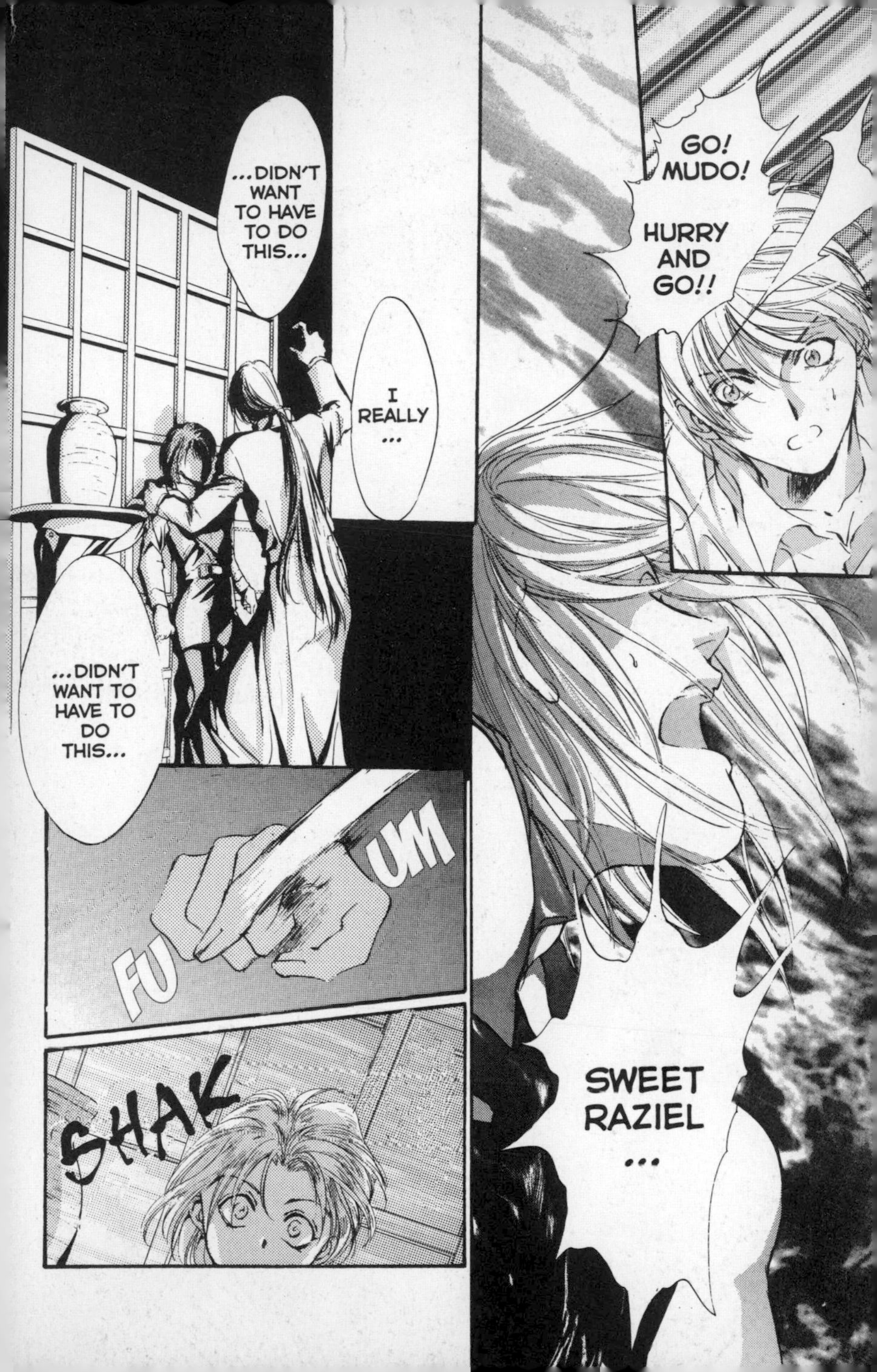
GO! MUDO!
HURRY AND GO!!
SWEET RAZIEL ...
I REALLY ...
...DIDN'T WANT TO HAVE TO DO THIS...
...DIDN'T WANT TO HAVE TO DO THIS...
FU UM
SHAK

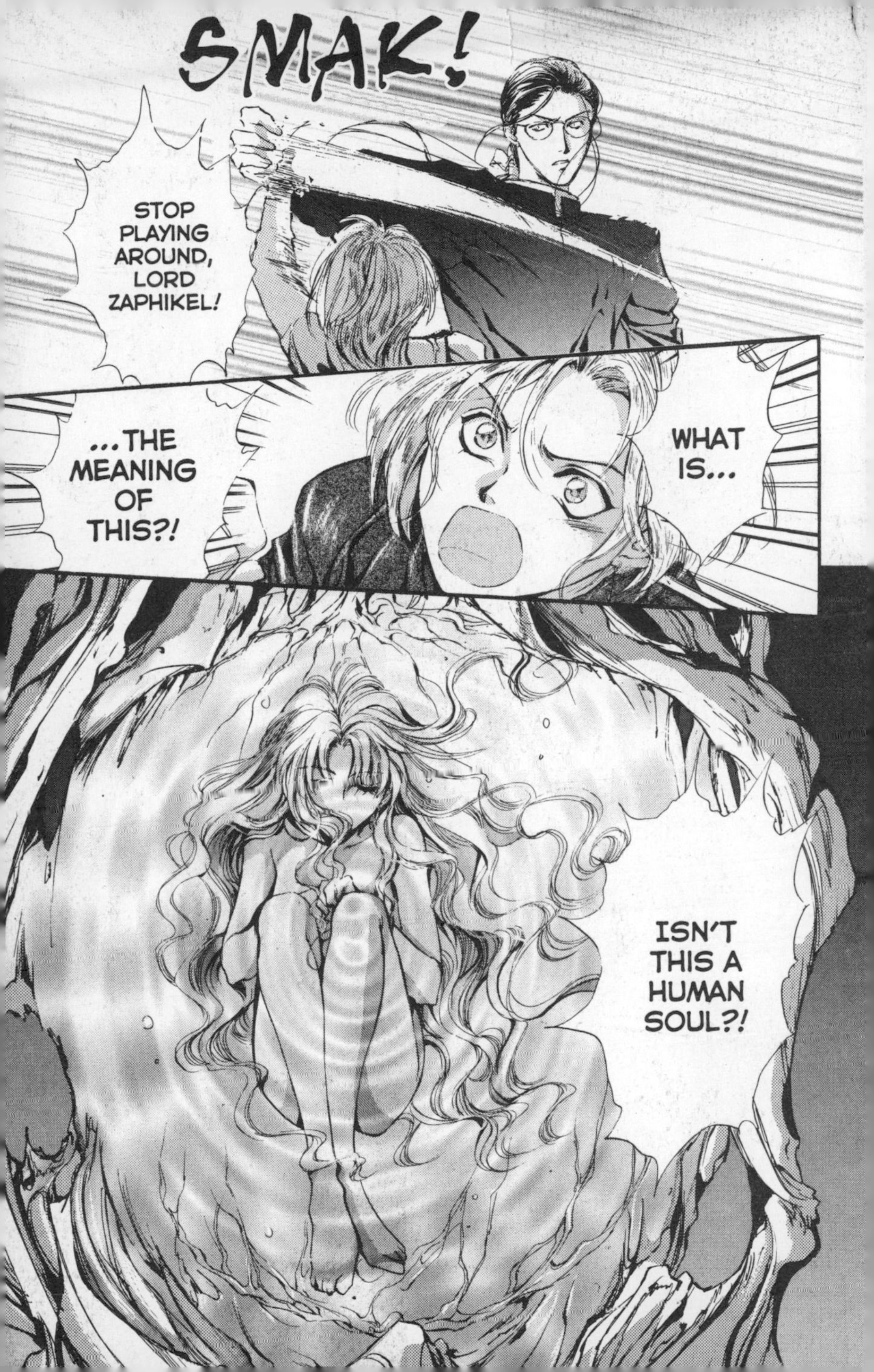
SMAK!
STOP PLAYING AROUND, LORD ZAPHIKEL!
WHAT IS...
...THE MEANING OF THIS?!
ISN'T THIS A HUMAN SOUL?!

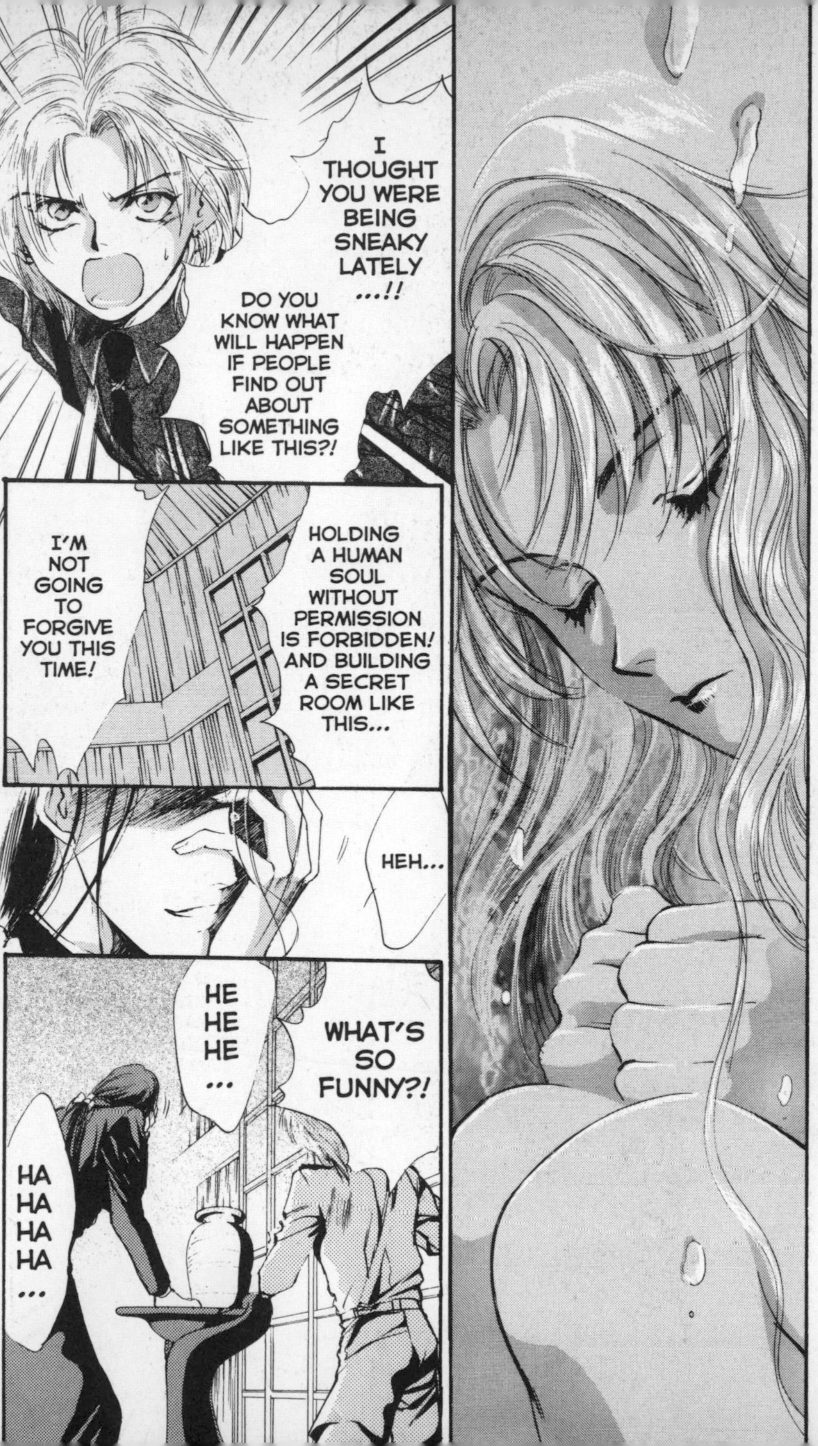
I THOUGHT YOU WERE BEING SNEAKY LATELY ...!!
DO YOU KNOW WHAT WILL HAPPEN IF PEOPLE FIND OUT ABOUT SOMETHING LIKE THIS?!
HOLDING A HUMAN SOUL WITHOUT PERMISSION IS FORBIDDEN! AND BUILDING A SECRET ROOM LIKE THIS...
I'M NOT GOING TO FORGIVE YOU THIS TIME!
HEH...
HE HE HE ...
WHAT'S SO FUNNY?!
HA HA HA HA ...

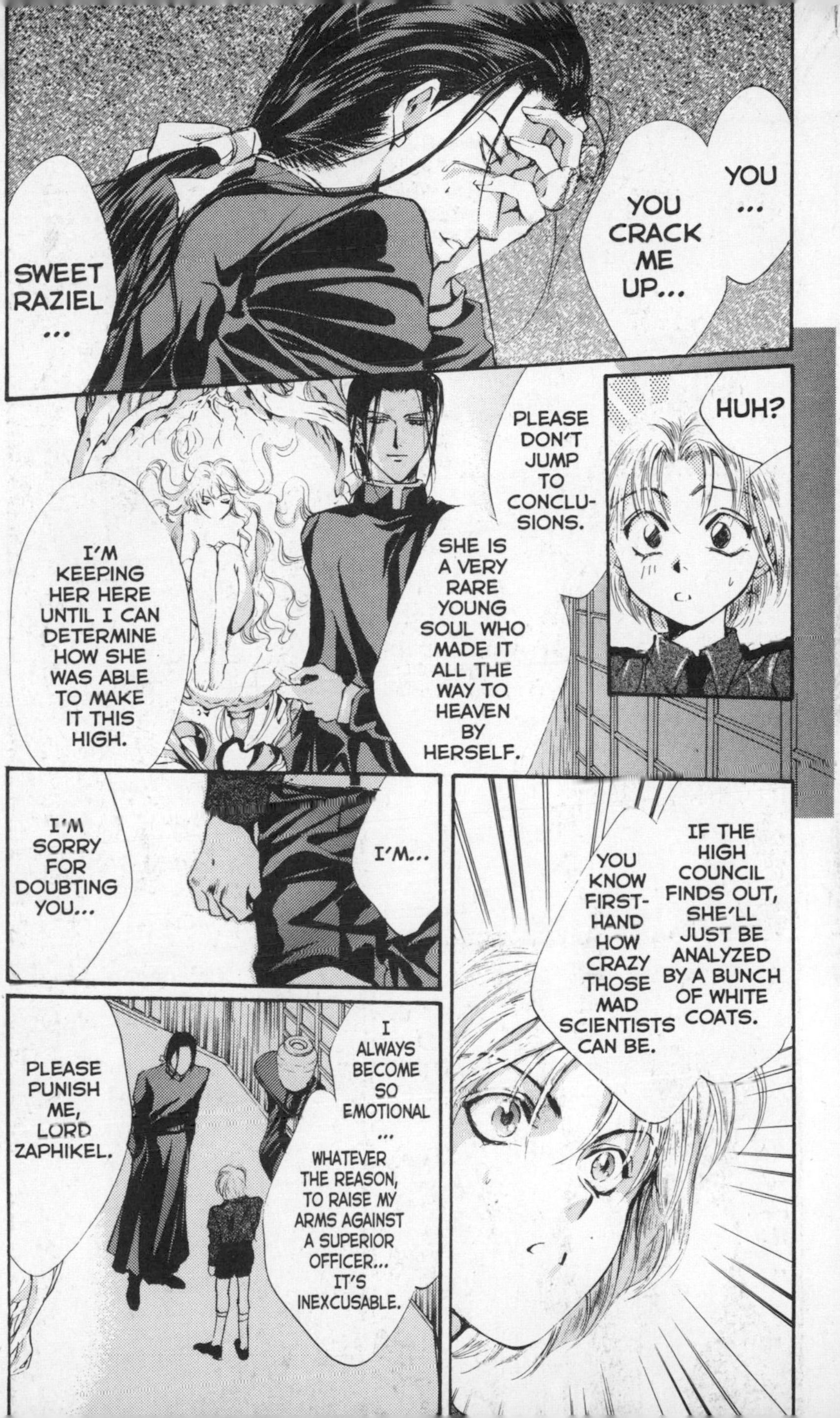
YOU ...
YOU CRACK ME UP...
SWEET RAZIEL ...
HUH?
PLEASE DON'T JUMP TO CONCLUSIONS.
SHE IS A VERY RARE YOUNG SOUL WHO MADE IT ALL THE WAY TO HEAVEN BY HERSELF.
I'M KEEPING HER HERE UNTIL I CAN DETERMINE HOW SHE WAS ABLE TO MAKE IT THIS HIGH.
IF THE HIGH COUNCIL FINDS OUT, SHE'LL JUST BE ANALYZED BY A BUNCH OF WHITE COATS.
YOU KNOW FIRST-HAND HOW CRAZY THOSE MAD SCIENTISTS CAN BE.
I'M...
I'M SORRY FOR DOUBTING YOU...
I ALWAYS BECOME SO EMOTIONAL ...
WHATEVER THE REASON, TO RAISE MY ARMS AGAINST A SUPERIOR OFFICER... IT'S INEXCUSABLE.
PLEASE PUNISH ME, LORD ZAPHIKEL.

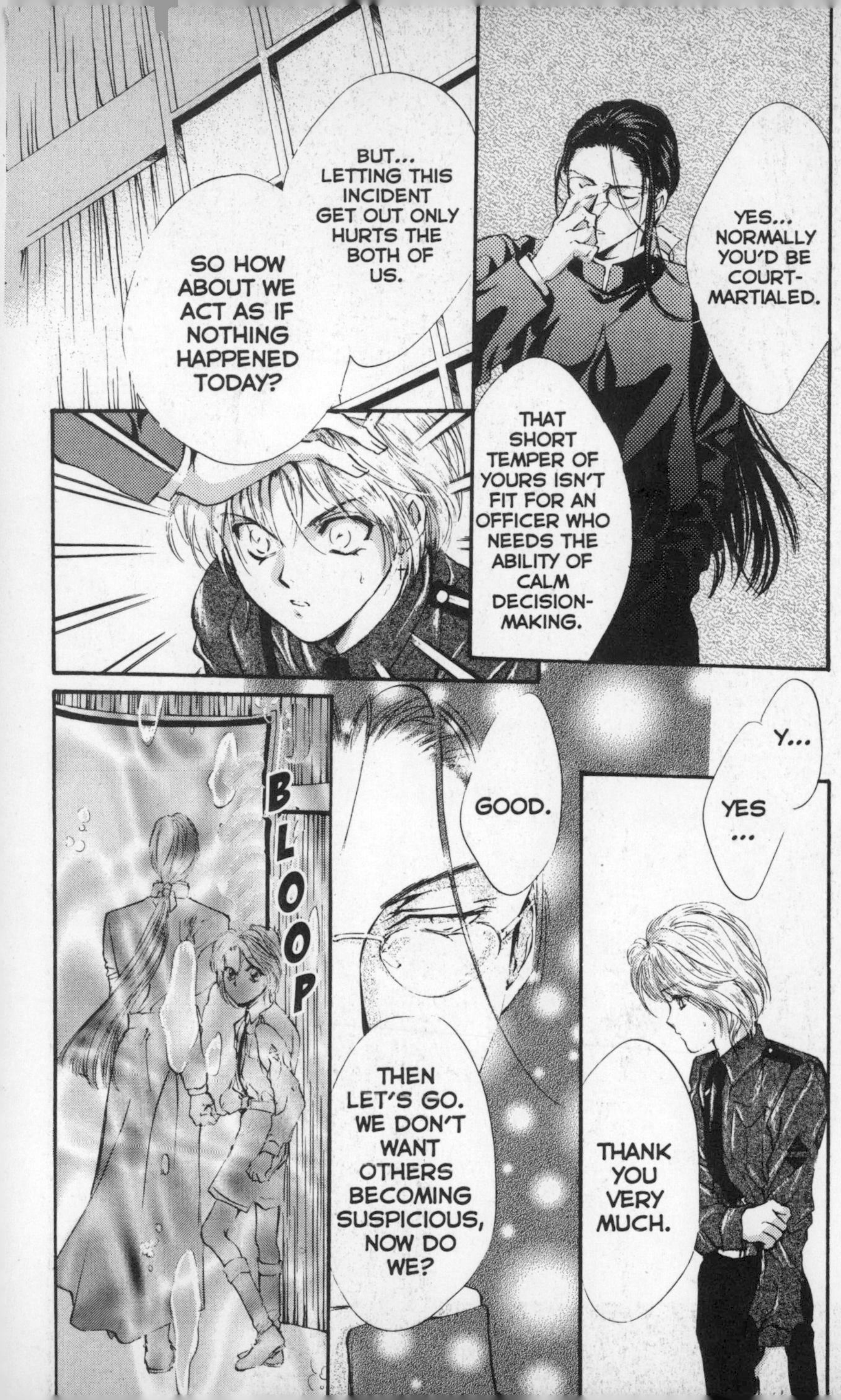
YES... NORMALLY YOU'D BE COURT-MARTIALED.
THAT SHORT TEMPER OF YOURS ISN'T FIT FOR AN OFFICER WHO NEEDS THE ABILITY OF CALM DECISION-MAKING.
BUT... LETTING THIS INCIDENT GET OUT ONLY HURTS THE BOTH OF US.
SO HOW ABOUT WE ACT AS IF NOTHING HAPPENED TODAY?
Y... YES ...
THANK YOU VERY MUCH.
GOOD.
THEN LET'S GO. WE DON'T WANT OTHERS BECOMING SUSPICIOUS, NOW DO WE?
BLOOP

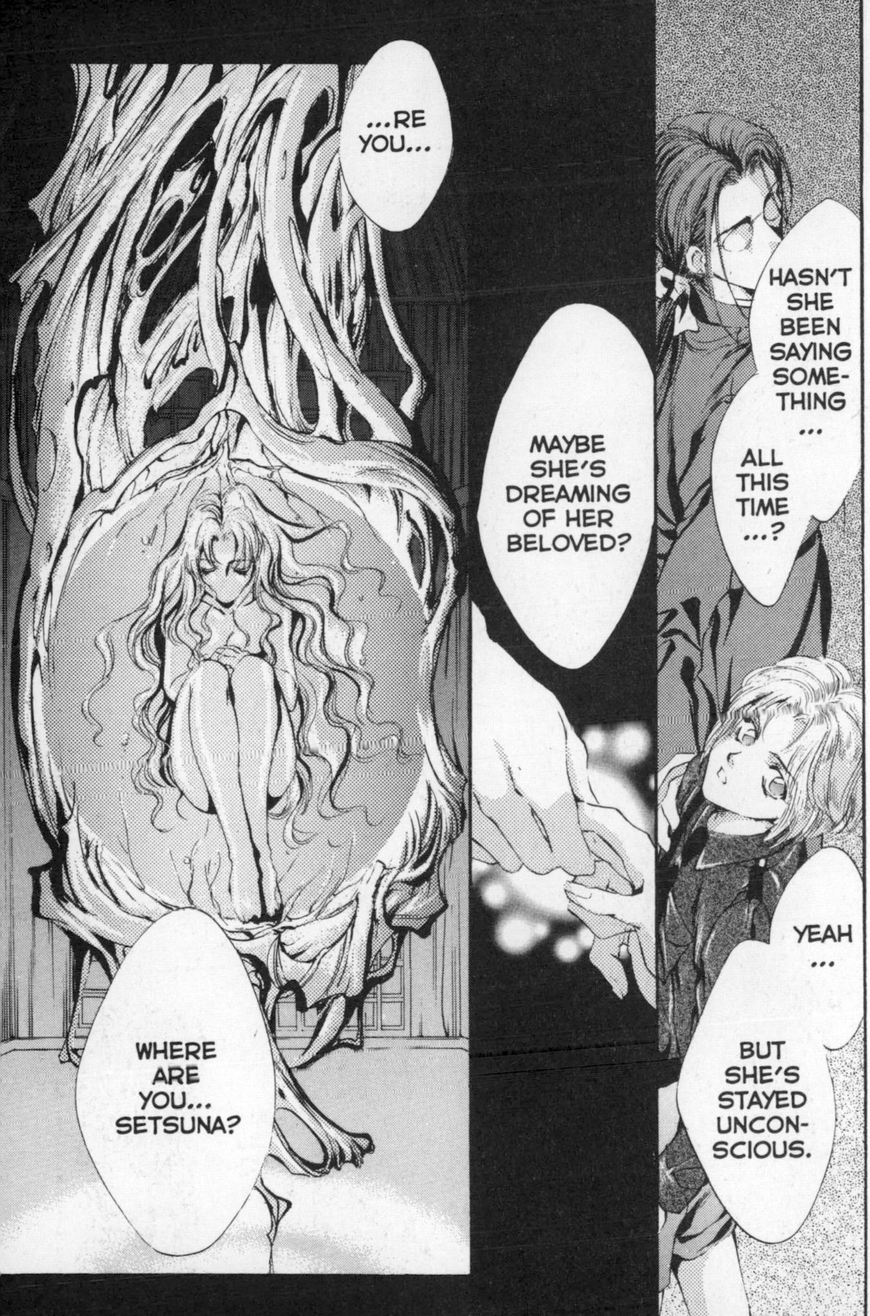
HASN'T SHE BEEN SAYING SOME-THING...
ALL THIS TIME...?
MAYBE SHE'S DREAMING OF HER BELOVED?
YEAH...
BUT SHE'S STAYED UNCON-SCIOUS.
...RE YOU...
WHERE ARE YOU... SETSUNA?

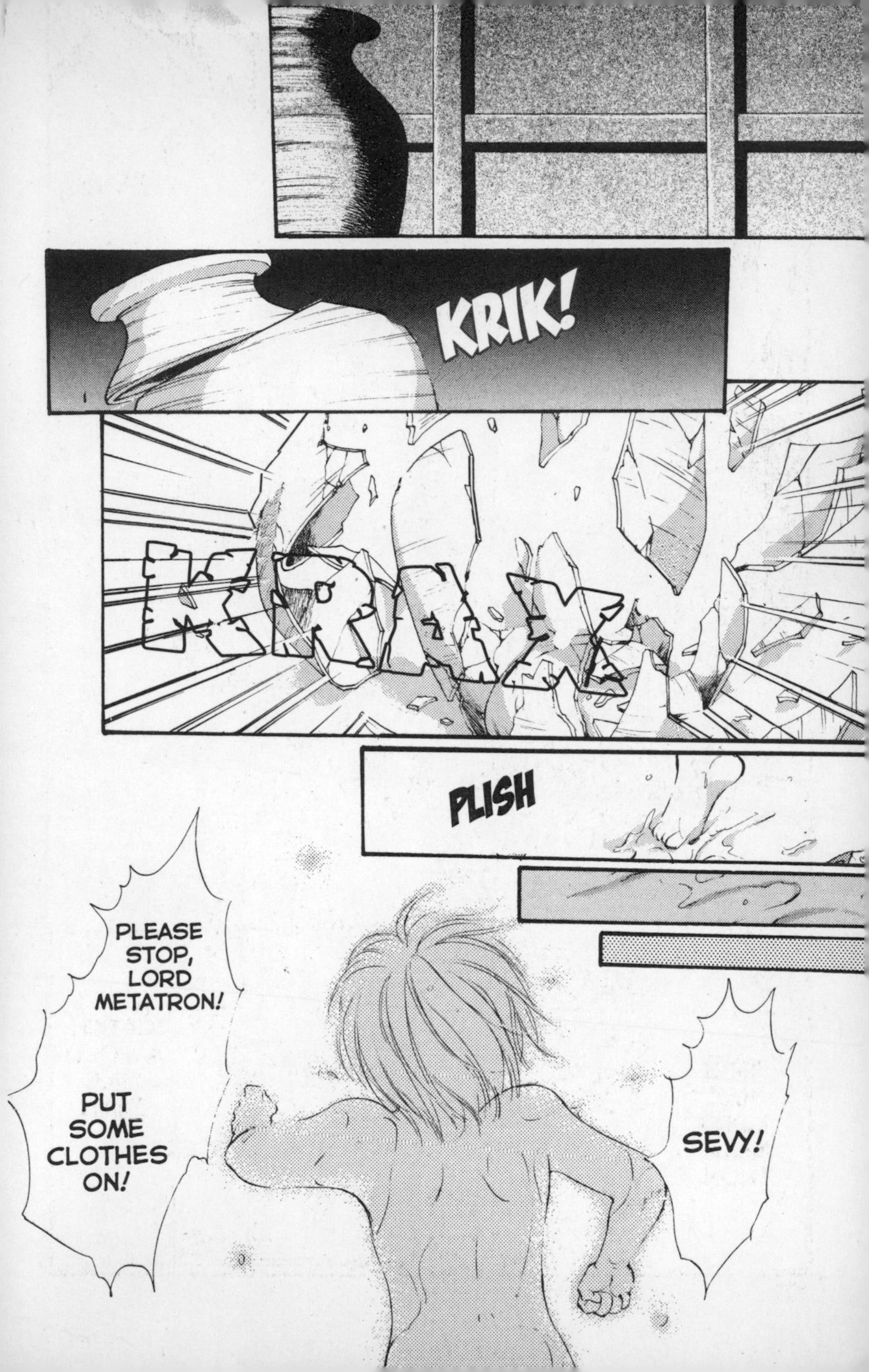
KRIK!
PLISH
SEVY!
PLEASE STOP, LORD METATRON!
PUT SOME CLOTHES ON!

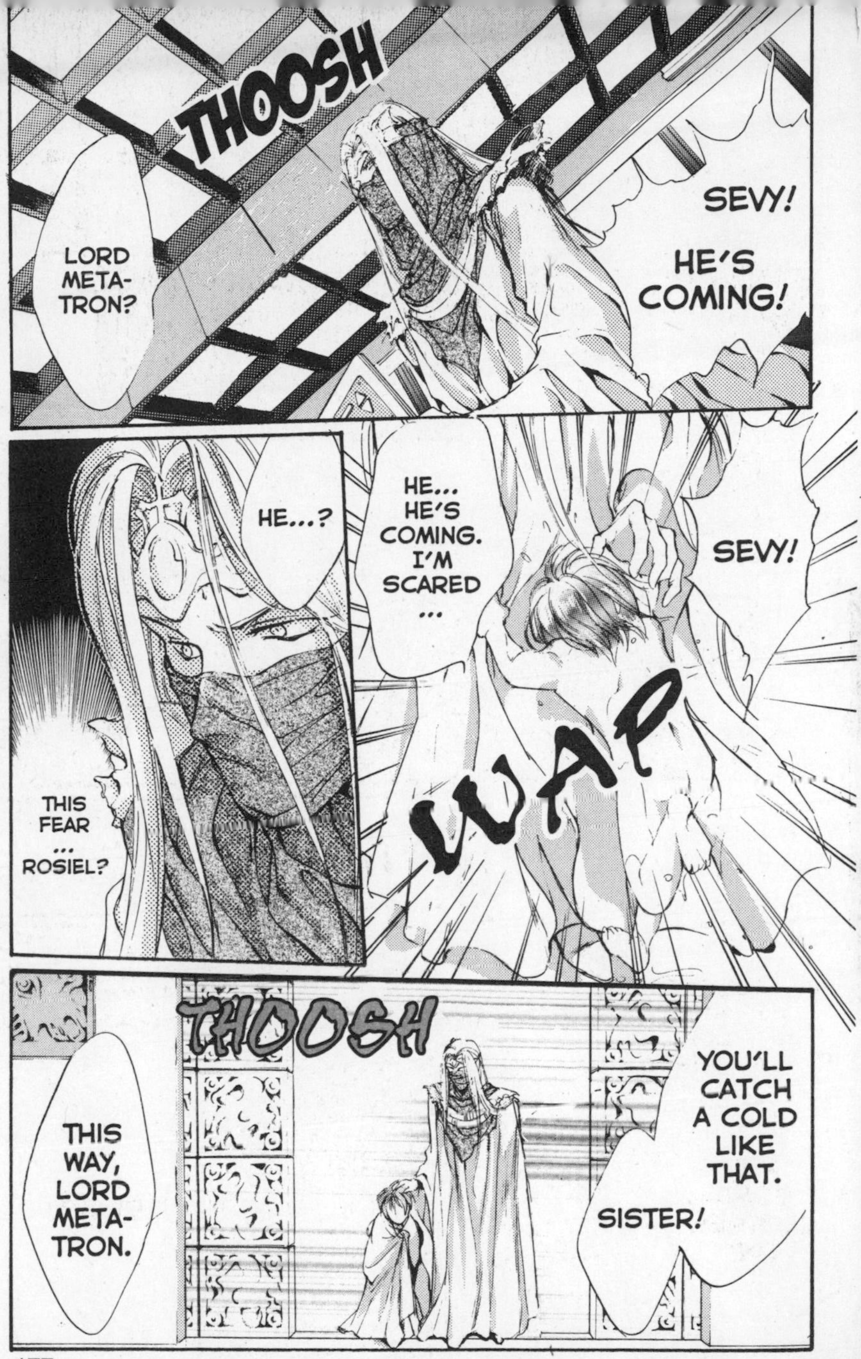
SEVY!
HE'S COMING!
THOOSH
LORD META-TRON?
SEVY!
HE... HE'S COMING. I'M SCARED ...
WAP
HE...?
THIS FEAR ... ROSIEL?
YOU'LL CATCH A COLD LIKE THAT.
SISTER!
THOOSH
THIS WAY, LORD META-TRON.

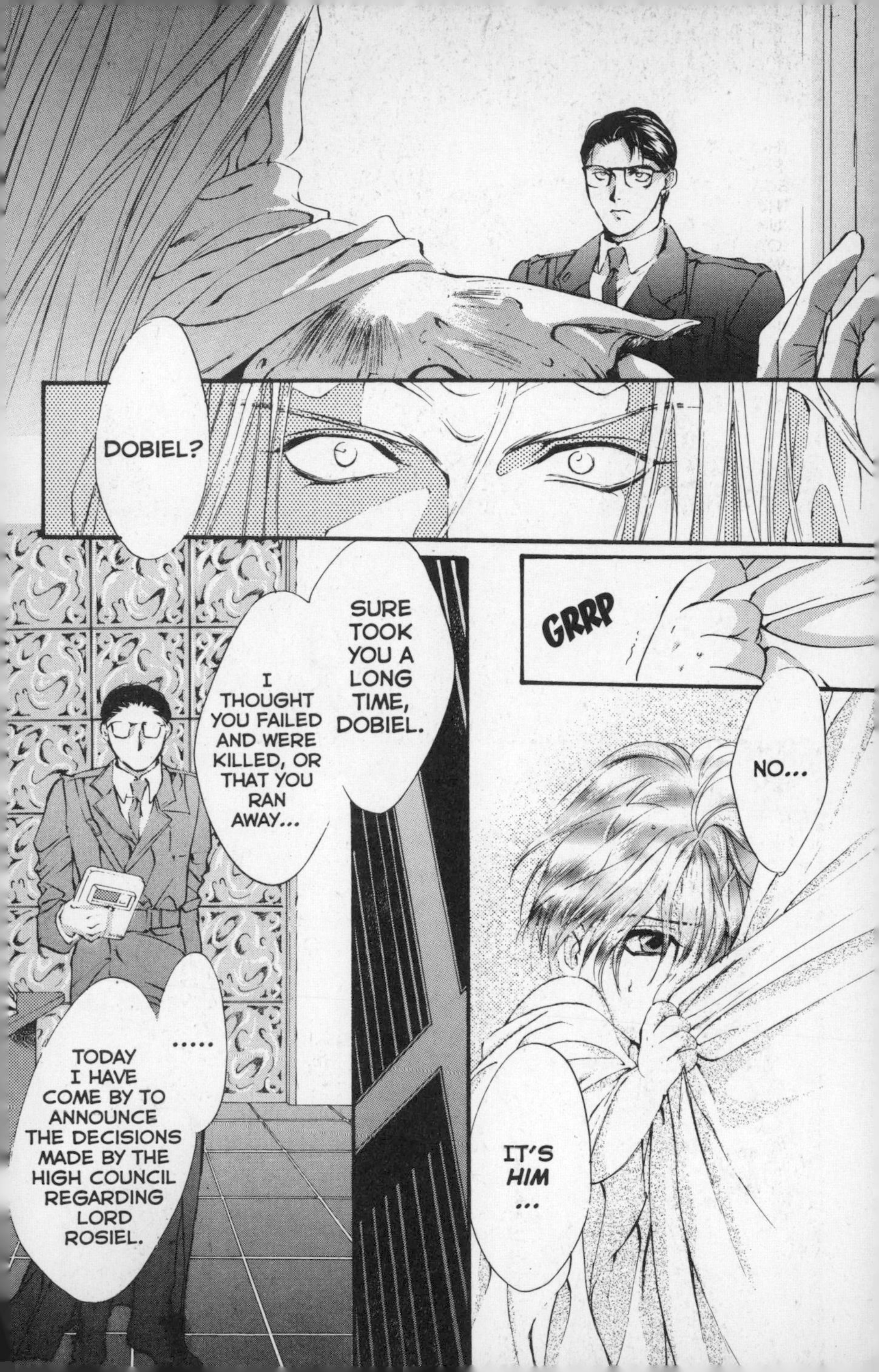
DOBIEL?
GRRP
NO...
IT'S *HIM* ...
SURE TOOK YOU A LONG TIME, DOBIEL.
I THOUGHT YOU FAILED AND WERE KILLED, OR THAT YOU RAN AWAY...
.....
TODAY I HAVE COME BY TO ANNOUNCE THE DECISIONS MADE BY THE HIGH COUNCIL REGARDING LORD ROSIEL.

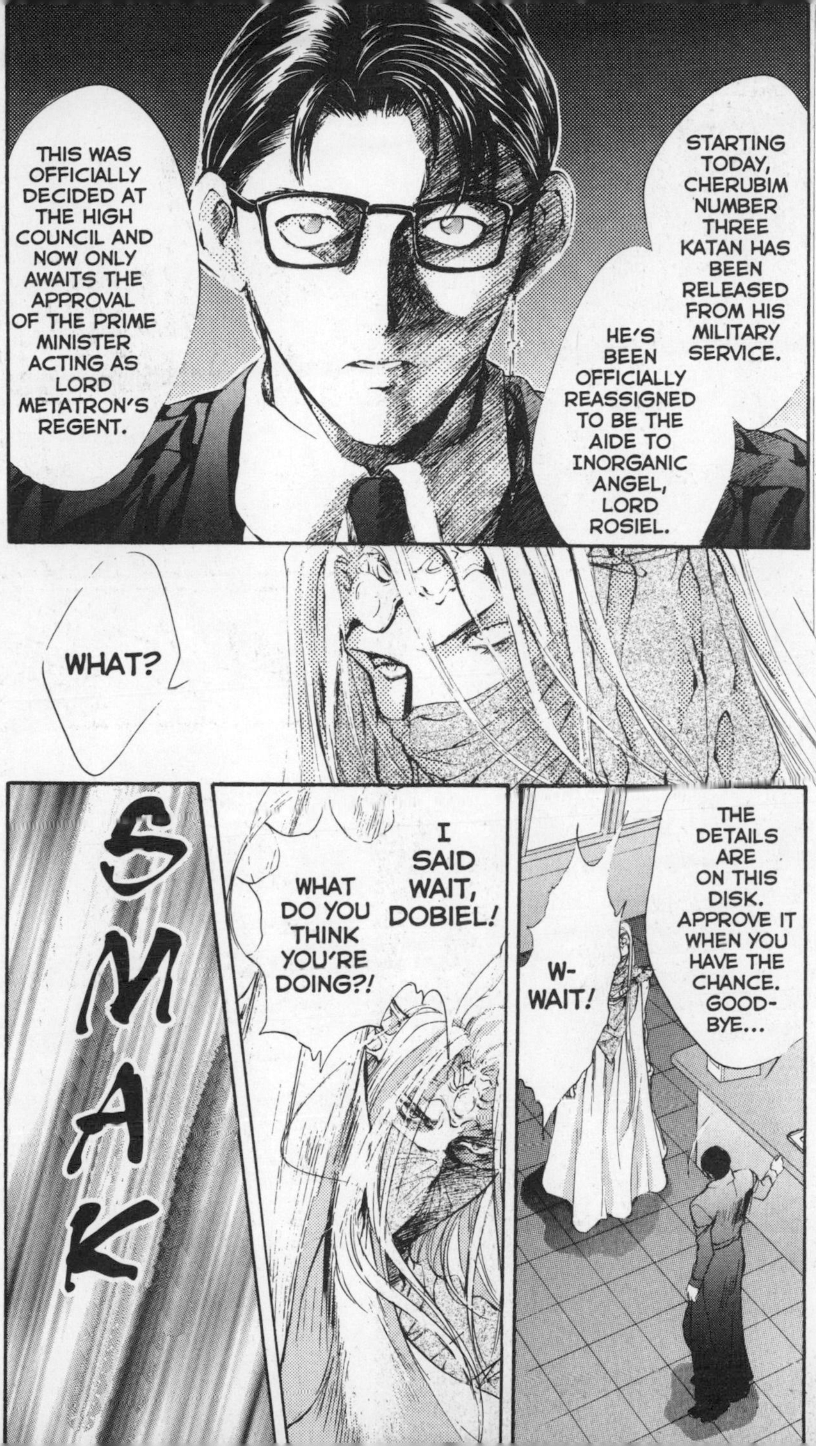
STARTING TODAY, CHERUBIM NUMBER THREE KATAN HAS BEEN RELEASED FROM HIS MILITARY SERVICE.
HE'S BEEN OFFICIALLY REASSIGNED TO BE THE AIDE TO INORGANIC ANGEL, LORD ROSIEL.
THIS WAS OFFICIALLY DECIDED AT THE HIGH COUNCIL AND NOW ONLY AWAITS THE APPROVAL OF THE PRIME MINISTER ACTING AS LORD METATRON'S REGENT.
WHAT?
THE DETAILS ARE ON THIS DISK. APPROVE IT WHEN YOU HAVE THE CHANCE. GOOD-BYE...
W-WAIT!
I SAID WAIT, DOBIEL!
WHAT DO YOU THINK YOU'RE DOING?!
SMAK

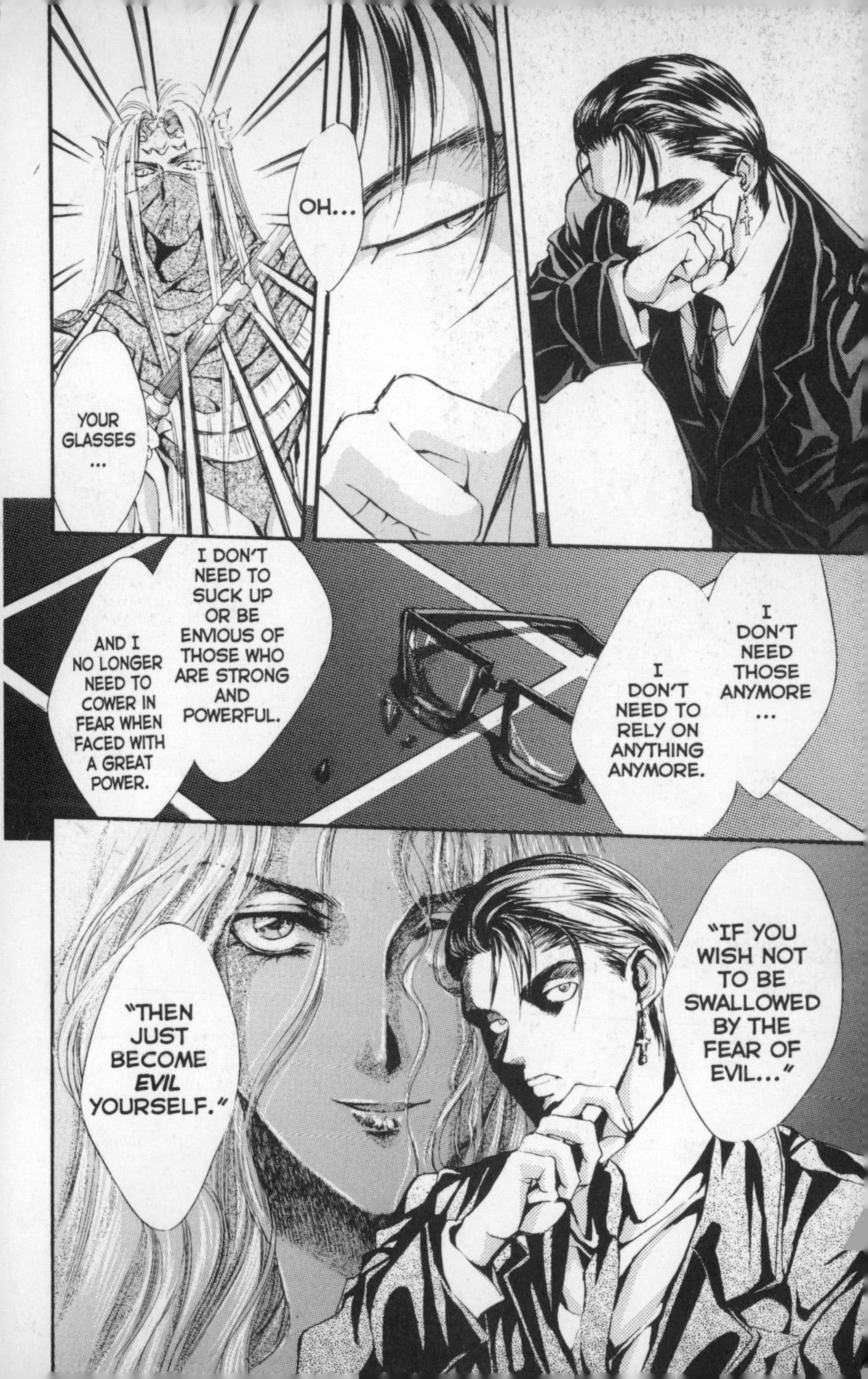
OH...
YOUR GLASSES ...
I DON'T NEED THOSE ANYMORE ...
I DON'T NEED TO RELY ON ANYTHING ANYMORE.
I DON'T NEED TO SUCK UP OR BE ENVIOUS OF THOSE WHO ARE STRONG AND POWERFUL.
AND I NO LONGER NEED TO COWER IN FEAR WHEN FACED WITH A GREAT POWER.
"IF YOU WISH NOT TO BE SWALLOWED BY THE FEAR OF EVIL..."
"THEN JUST BECOME *EVIL* YOURSELF."

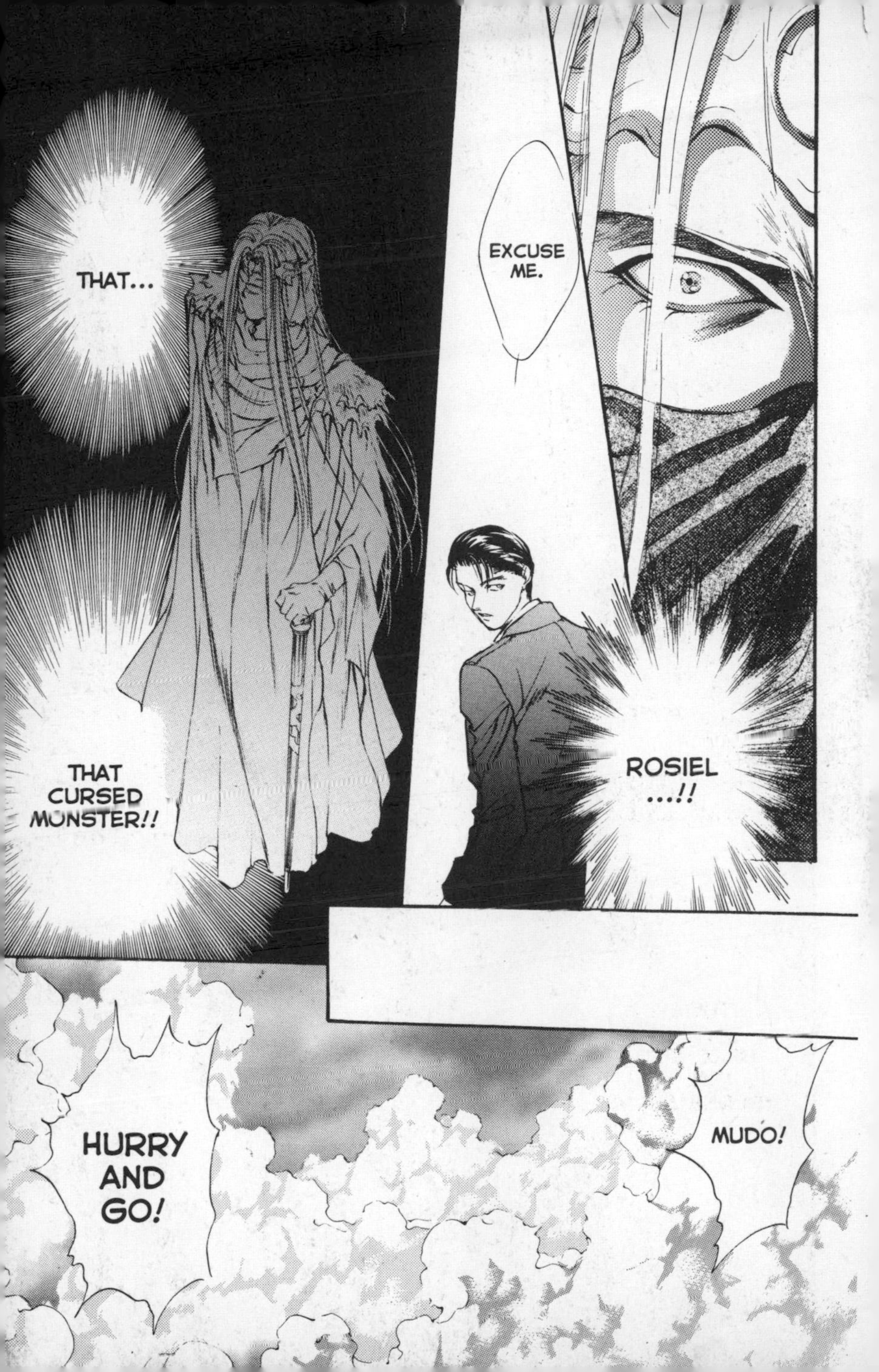
EXCUSE ME.
ROSIEL ...!!
THAT...
THAT CURSED MONSTER!!
MUDO!
HURRY AND GO!

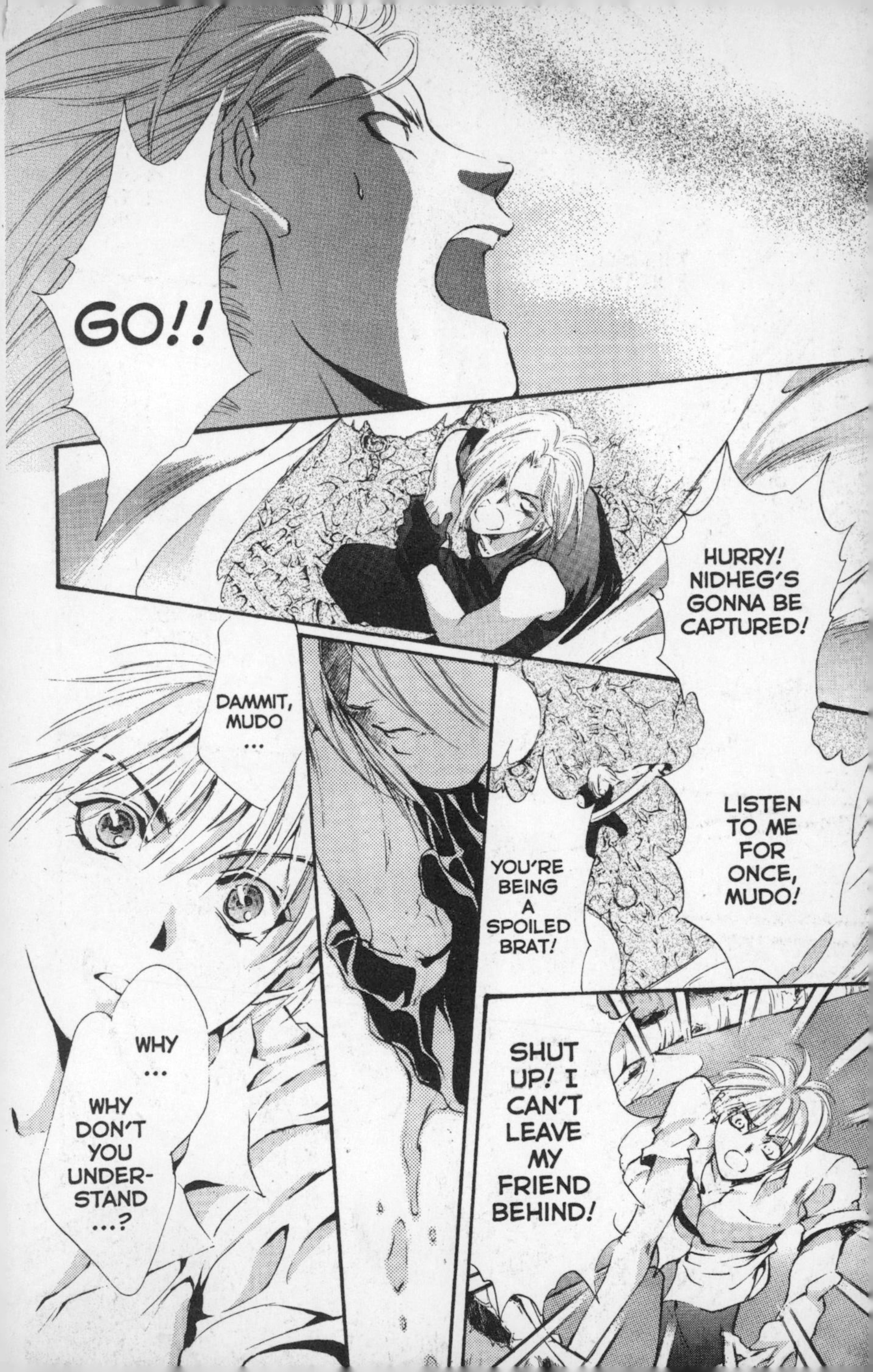
GO!!
HURRY! NIDHEG'S GONNA BE CAPTURED!
LISTEN TO ME FOR ONCE, MUDO!
YOU'RE BEING A SPOILED BRAT!
SHUT UP! I CAN'T LEAVE MY FRIEND BEHIND!
DAMMIT, MUDO ...
WHY ... WHY DON'T YOU UNDER-STAND ...?

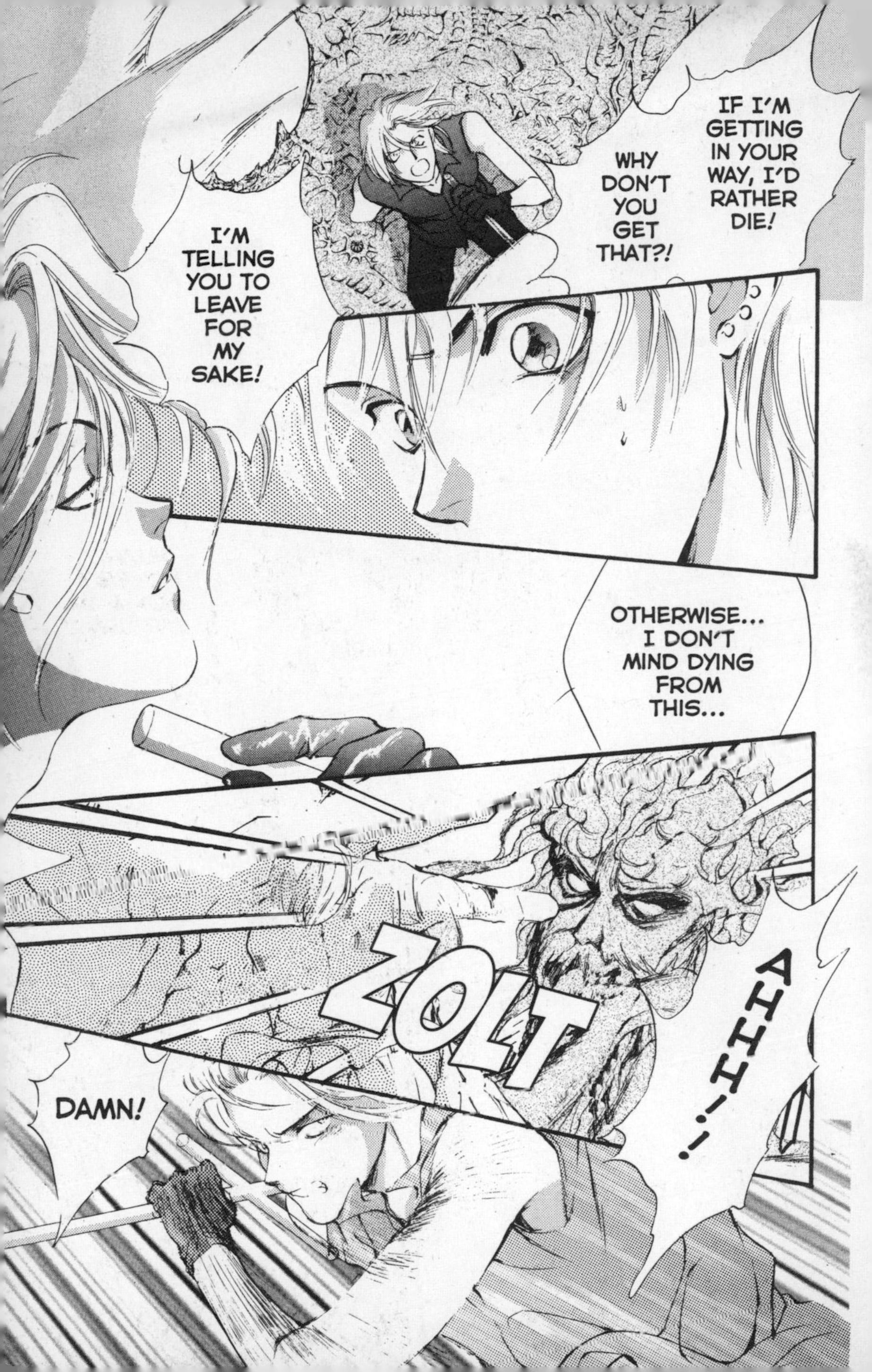
IF I'M GETTING IN YOUR WAY, I'D RATHER DIE!
WHY DON'T YOU GET THAT?!
I'M TELLING YOU TO LEAVE FOR MY SAKE!
OTHERWISE... I DON'T MIND DYING FROM THIS...
ZOLT
AHHH-!!
DAMN!

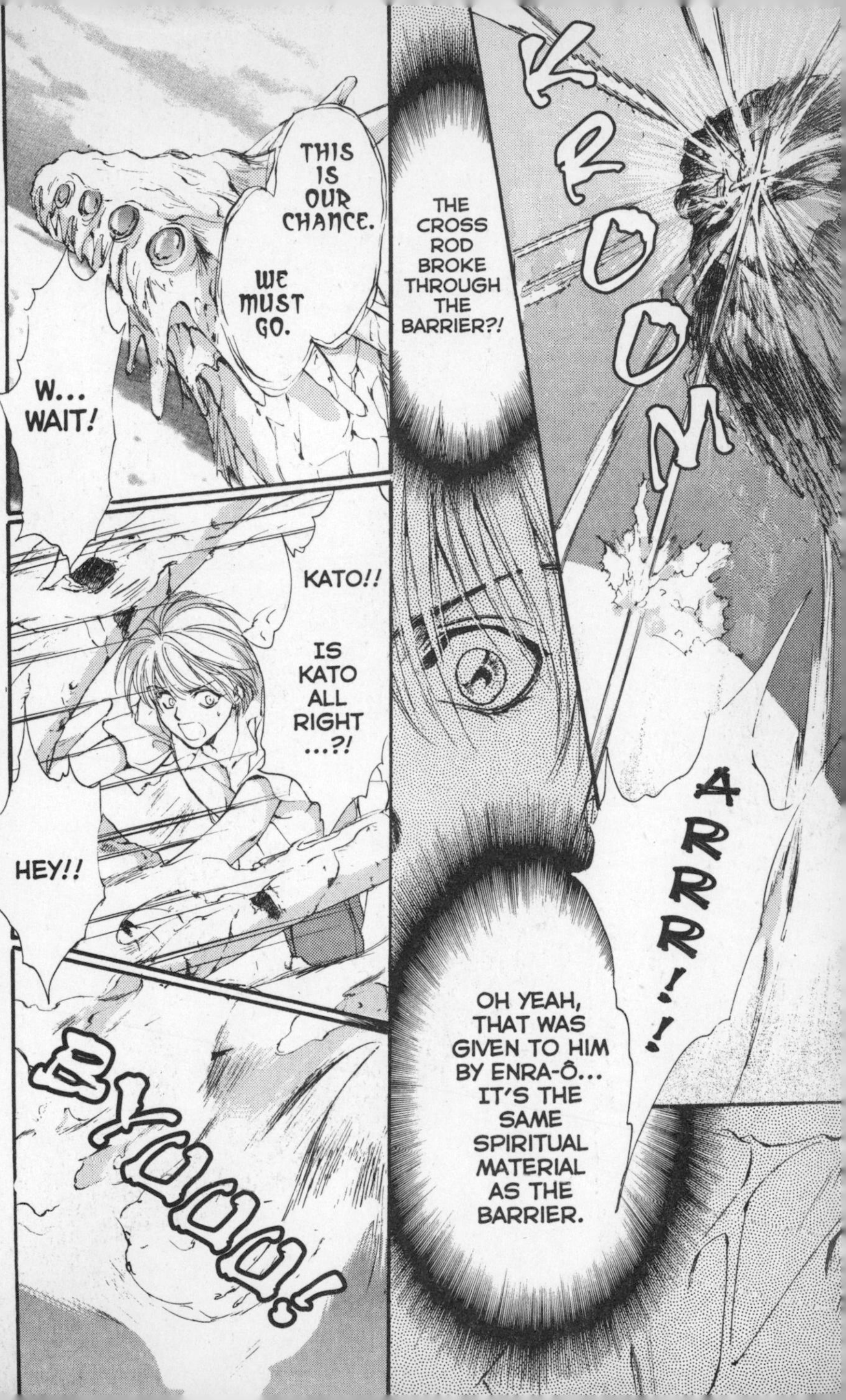
KROOM
THE CROSS ROD BROKE THROUGH THE BARRIER?!
ARRR!!
OH YEAH, THAT WAS GIVEN TO HIM BY ENRA-Ô... IT'S THE SAME SPIRITUAL MATERIAL AS THE BARRIER.
THIS IS OUR CHANCE.
WE MUST GO.
W... WAIT!
KATO!!
IS KATO ALL RIGHT ...?!
HEY!!
BYOOO!

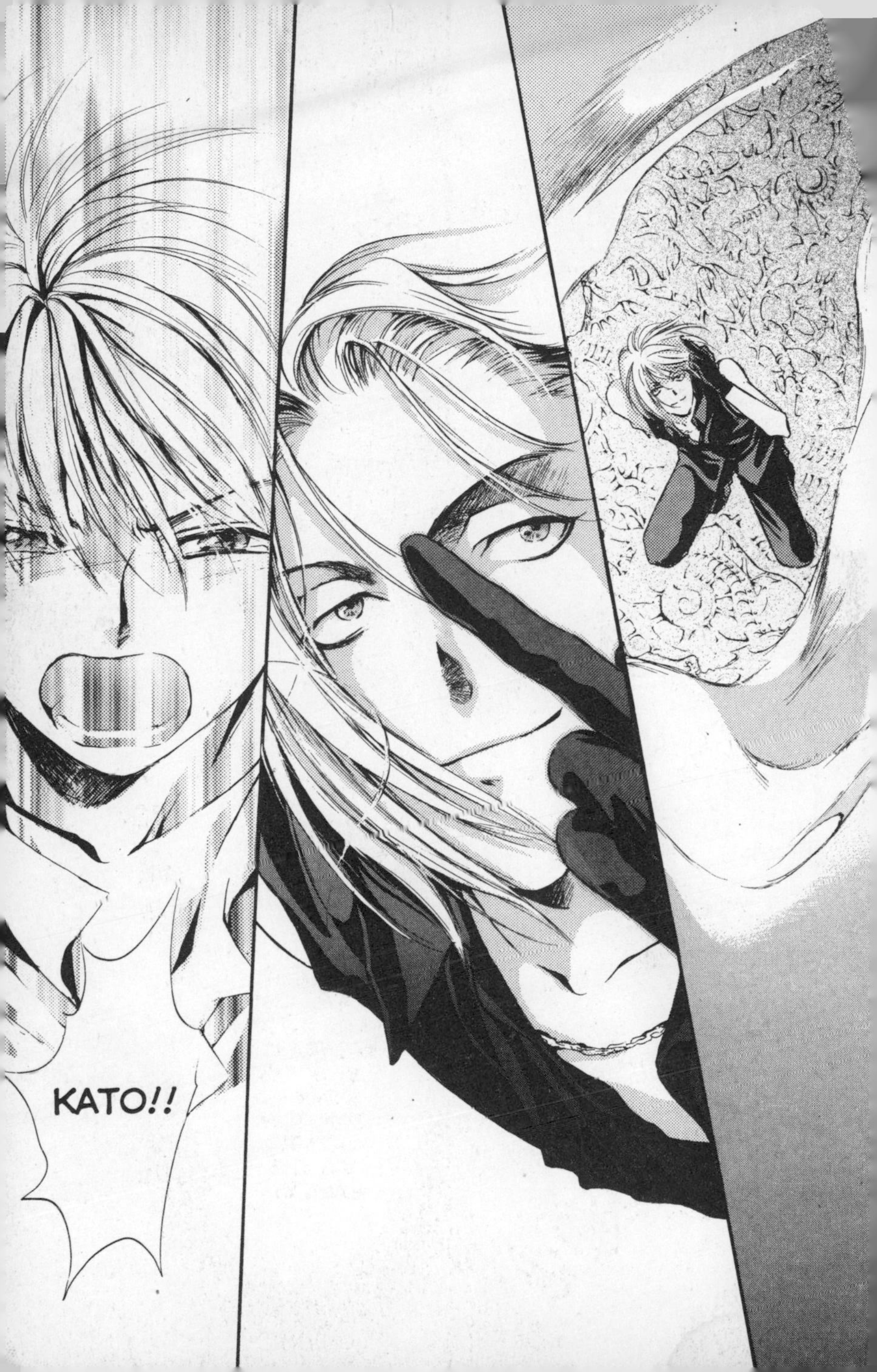
KATO!!

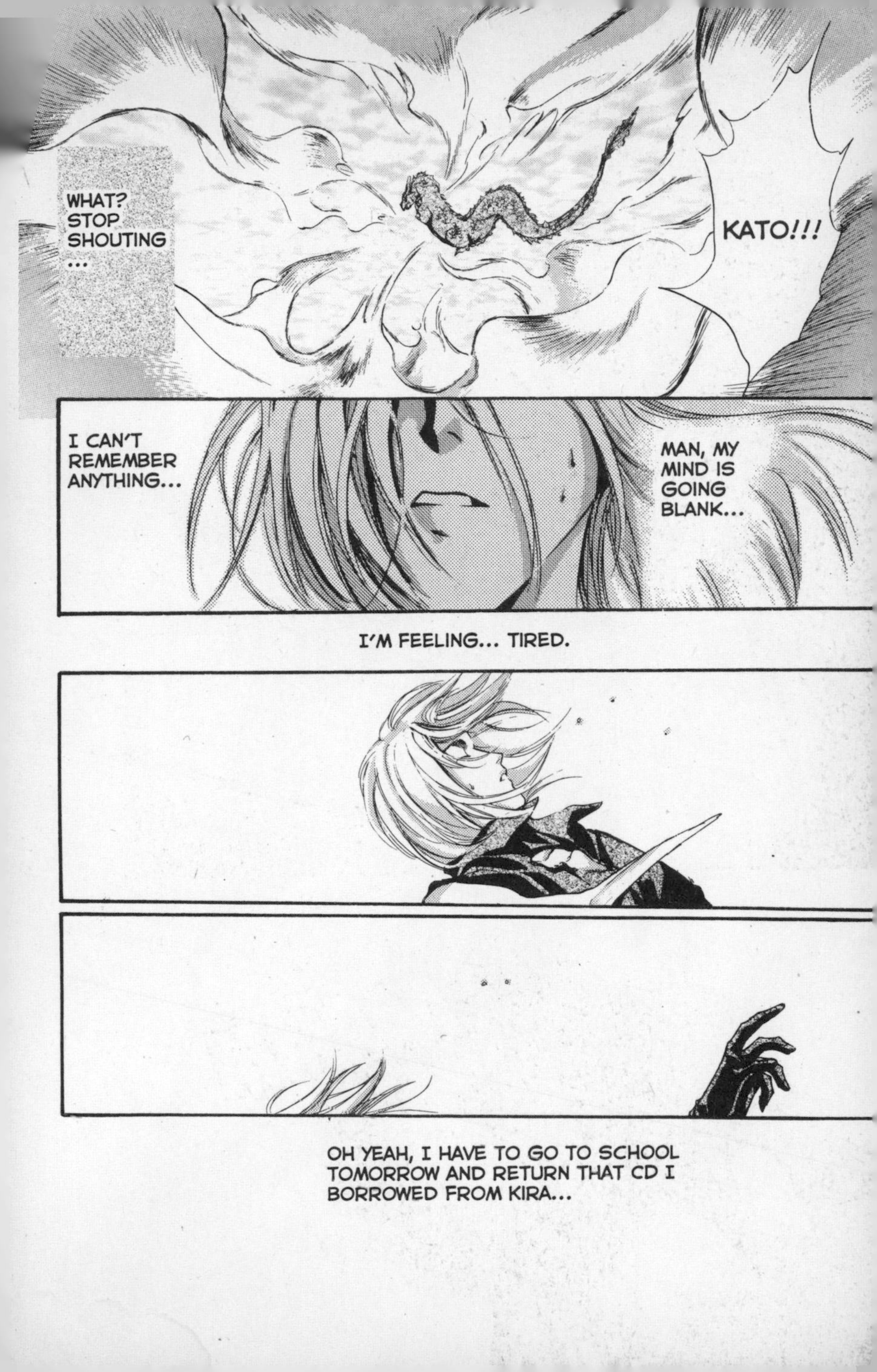
KATO!!!
WHAT? STOP SHOUTING ...
MAN, MY MIND IS GOING BLANK...
I CAN'T REMEMBER ANYTHING...
I'M FEELING... TIRED.
OH YEAH, I HAVE TO GO TO SCHOOL TOMORROW AND RETURN THAT CD I BORROWED FROM KIRA...

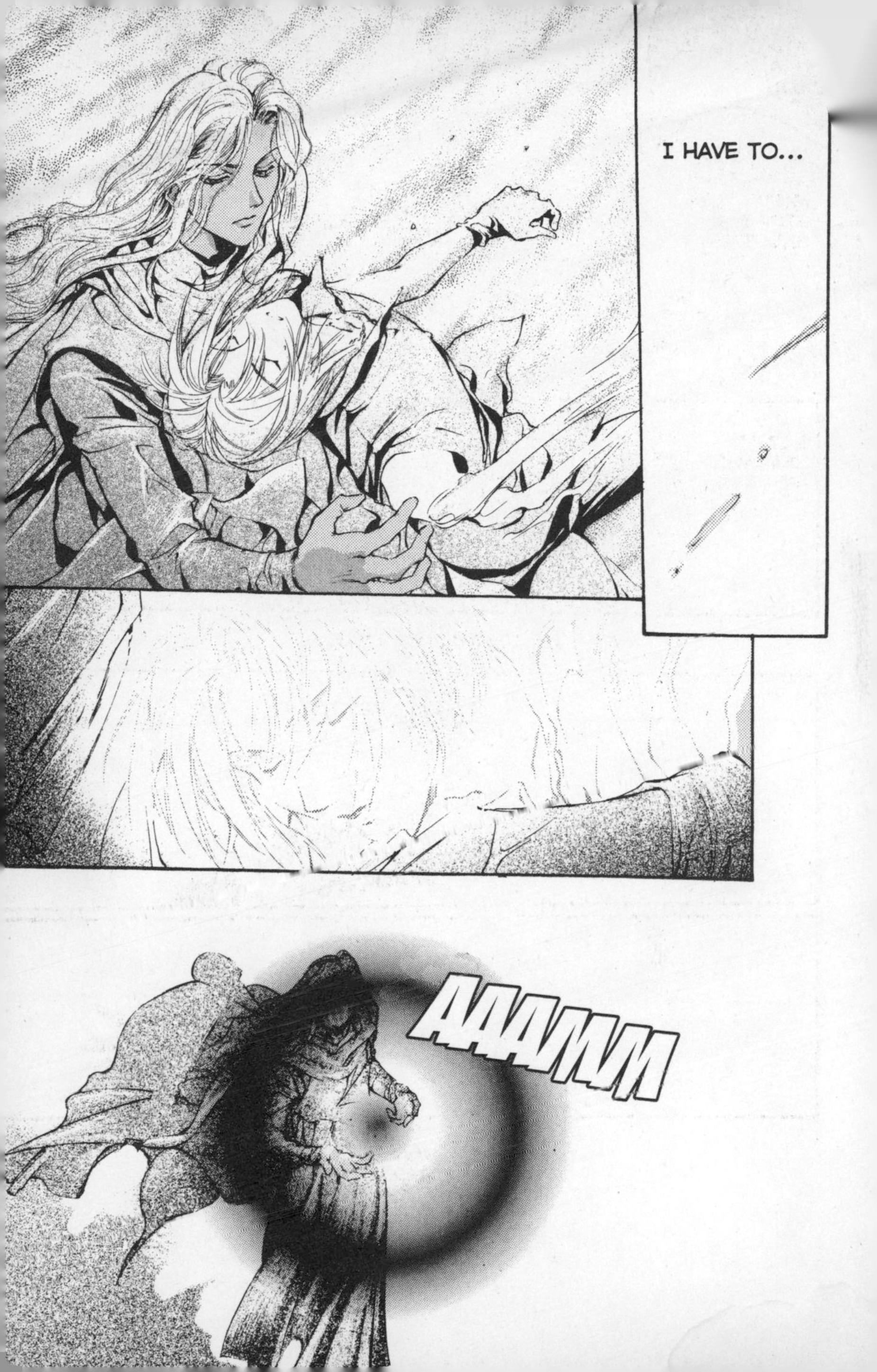
I HAVE TO...
AAAMM

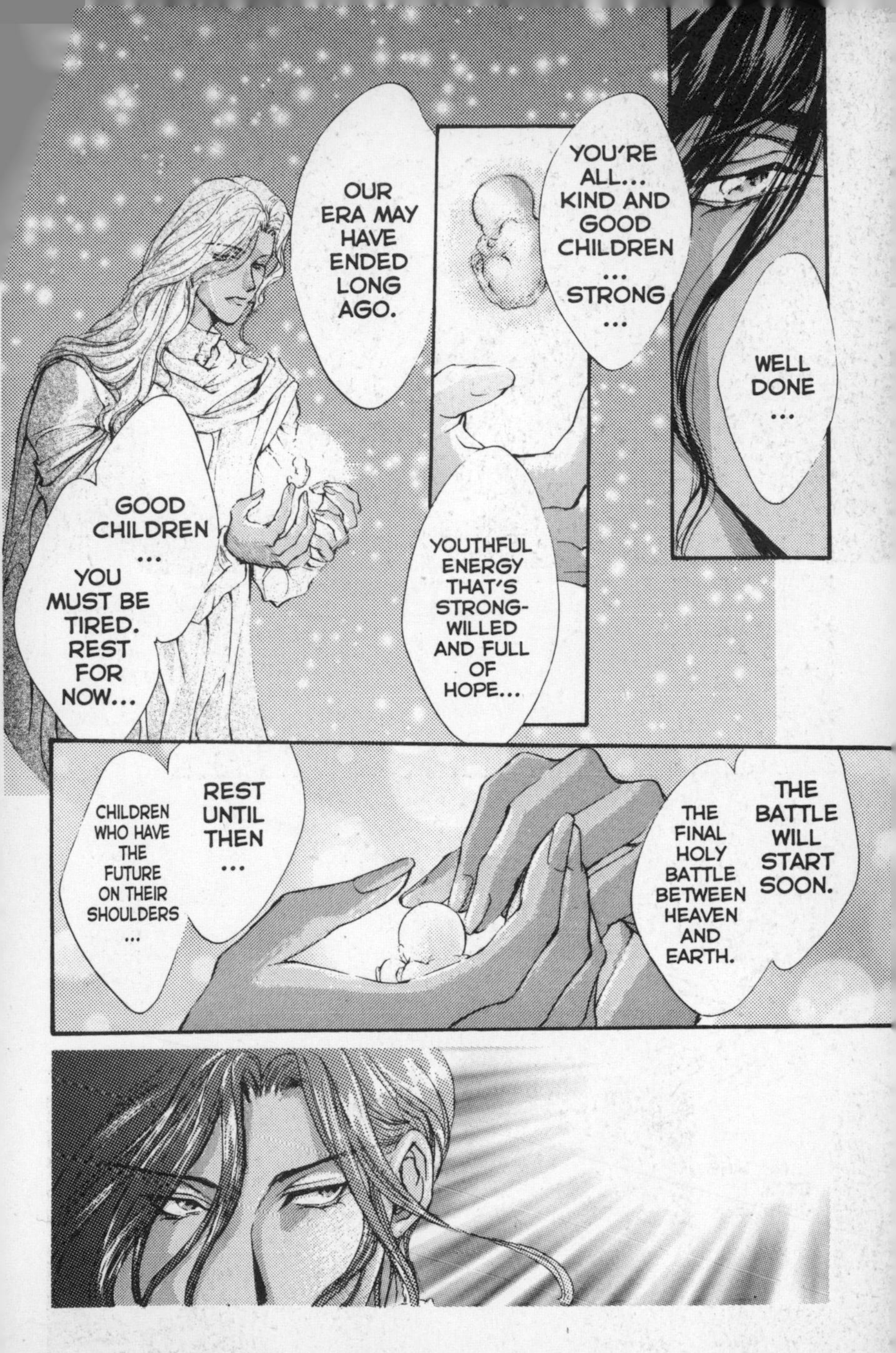
WELL DONE ...
YOU'RE ALL... KIND AND GOOD CHILDREN ... STRONG ...
YOUTHFUL ENERGY THAT'S STRONG-WILLED AND FULL OF HOPE...
OUR ERA MAY HAVE ENDED LONG AGO.
GOOD CHILDREN ... YOU MUST BE TIRED. REST FOR NOW...
THE BATTLE WILL START SOON.
THE FINAL HOLY BATTLE BETWEEN HEAVEN AND EARTH.
REST UNTIL THEN ...
CHILDREN WHO HAVE THE FUTURE ON THEIR SHOULDERS ...

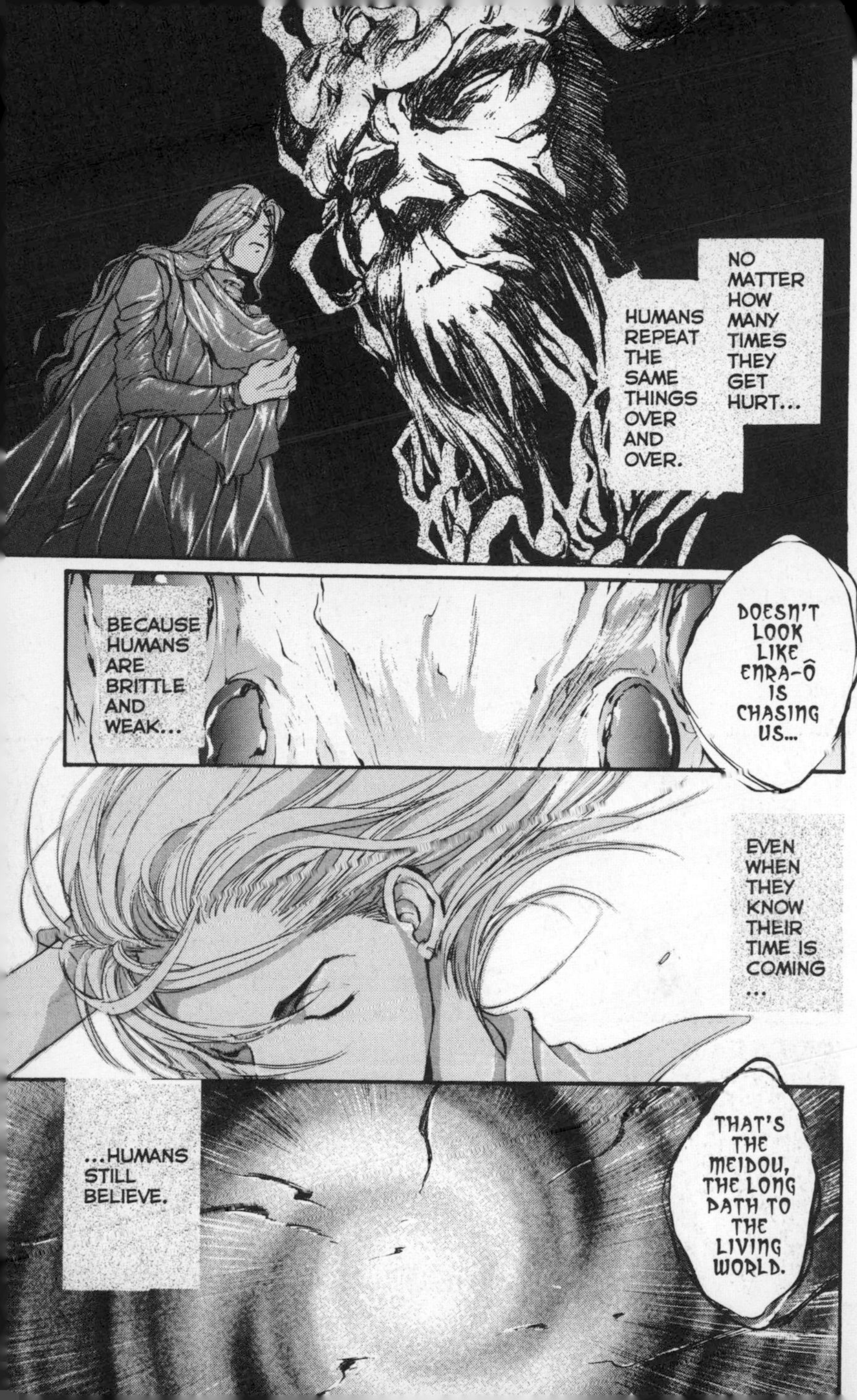
NO MATTER HOW MANY TIMES THEY GET HURT...
HUMANS REPEAT THE SAME THINGS OVER AND OVER.
DOESN'T LOOK LIKE ENRA-Ô IS CHASING US...
BECAUSE HUMANS ARE BRITTLE AND WEAK...
EVEN WHEN THEY KNOW THEIR TIME IS COMING ...
THAT'S THE MEIDOU, THE LONG PATH TO THE LIVING WORLD.
...HUMANS STILL BELIEVE.

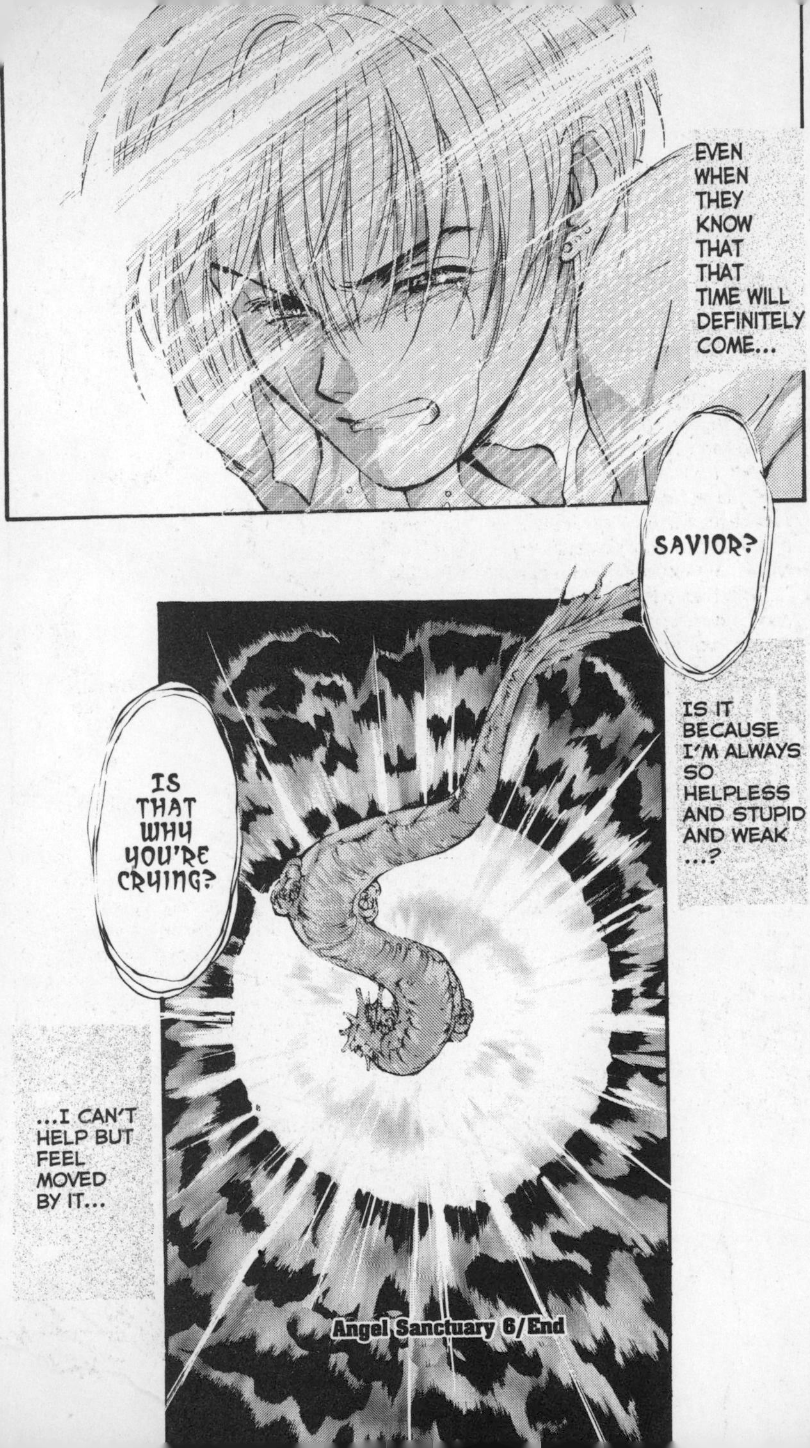
EVEN WHEN THEY KNOW THAT THAT TIME WILL DEFINITELY COME...
SAVIOR?
IS IT BECAUSE I'M ALWAYS SO HELPLESS AND STUPID AND WEAK ...?
IS THAT WHY YOU'RE CRYING?
...I CAN'T HELP BUT FEEL MOVED BY IT...
Angel Sanctuary 6/End

ANGEL'S SNITCHING DEVIL'S FLATTERY

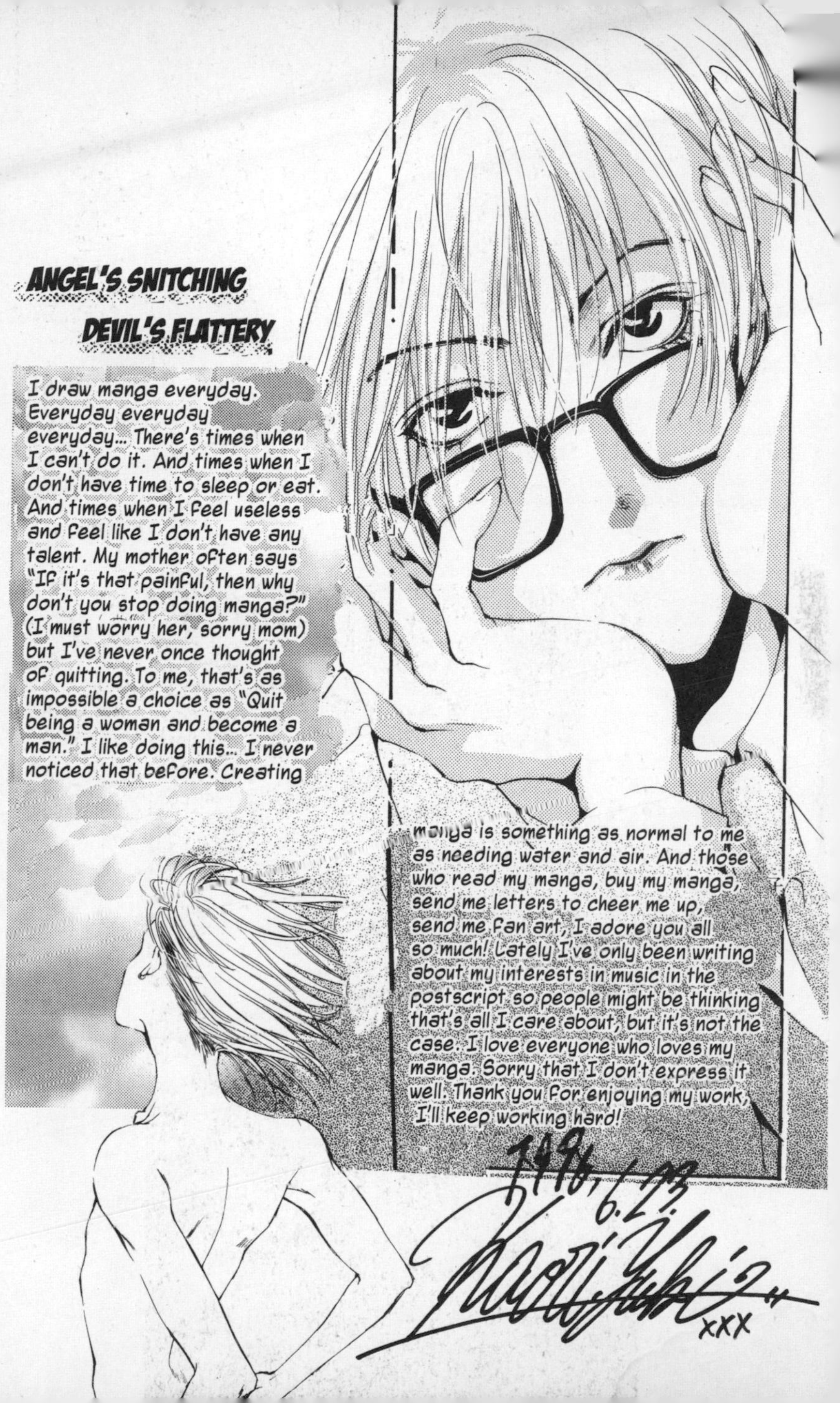

I draw manga everyday. Everyday everyday everyday... There's times when I can't do it. And times when I don't have time to sleep or eat. And times when I feel useless and feel like I don't have any talent. My mother often says "If it's that painful, then why don't you stop doing manga?" (I must worry her, sorry mom) but I've never once thought of quitting. To me, that's as impossible a choice as "Quit being a woman and become a man." I like doing this... I never noticed that before. Creating manga is something as normal to me as needing water and air. And those who read my manga, buy my manga, send me letters to cheer me up, send me fan art, I adore you all so much! Lately I've only been writing about my interests in music in the postscript so people might be thinking that's all I care about, but it's not the case. I love everyone who loves my manga. Sorry that I don't express it well. Thank you for enjoying my work, I'll keep working hard!

Well... Because my head is spinning right now...

RECOMMENDATIONS OF A DAY DREAM SLEEP WALKER

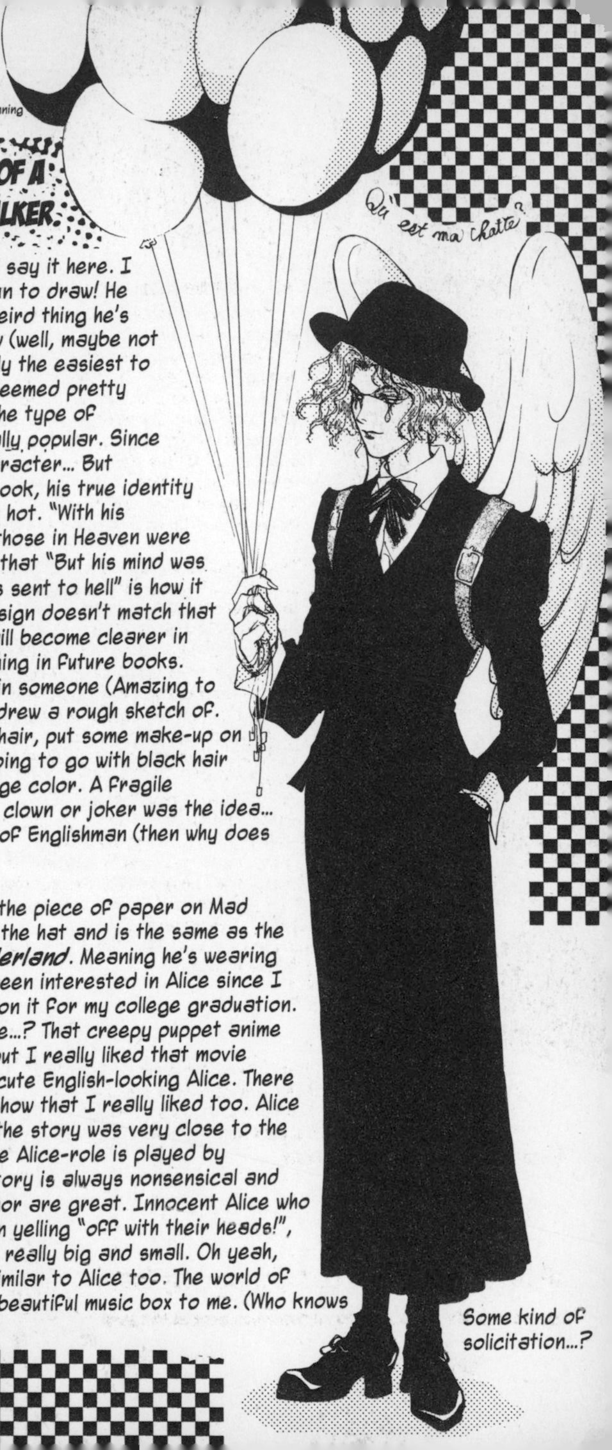
Qu'est ma chatte?

I haven't said this yet so I'll say it here. I love *Mad Hatter*, he's so fun to draw! He looks cool no matter what weird thing he's wearing. With Kato dead now (well, maybe not exactly) *Hatter* is most likely the easiest to draw. The reader reaction seemed pretty good, but I guess he's not the type of character that would be really popular. Since he's not a total *hottie!!* character... But according to my research book, his true identity is supposed to be amazingly hot. "With his elegance and grace, all of those in Heaven were overwhelmed." Though after that "But his mind was overcome by evil and he was sent to hell" is how it continues... Okay, so my design doesn't match that beauty... Well, these things will become clearer in the demon story that is coming in future books. He's modeled after a certain someone (Amazing to those who figured it out) I drew a rough sketch of. I then added in some wavy hair, put some make-up on and baam! At first I was going to go with black hair but I changed it to an orange color. A fragile asexual body, looking like a clown or joker was the idea... He's supposed to be a kind of Englishman (then why does he count in German...?).

Changing the subject a bit, the piece of paper on Mad Hatter's hat is the price of the hat and is the same as the Hatter from *Alice in Wonderland*. Meaning he's wearing a hat that's for sale. I've been interested in Alice since I created a calendar based on it for my college graduation. Who knew I would use it here...? That creepy puppet anime movie of *Alice* was good, but I really liked that movie "Dream Child" with a really cute English-looking Alice. There was also a BBC produced show that I really liked too. Alice was so small and cute and the story was very close to the book. I don't like it when the Alice-role is played by someone too old, but the story is always nonsensical and the craziness and dark humor are great. Innocent Alice who gets into trouble, the Queen yelling "off with their heads!", when only Alice's head gets really big and small. Oh yeah, the movie *Labyrinth* was similar to Alice too. The world of *Alice* is like a strange but beautiful music box to me. (Who knows what that means...?)

Some kind of solicitation...?

MUSIC AND THE MANGAKA

A lame but nice title!

All these music hobby stories full of blanks are just building up stress, so this time I'm not going to hide anything. Many may be looking forward to this corner while many might be angry and saying "Not again!!" (Those people might want to look away...) First off!! I got tons and tons of music tapes! Thank you so much! But... You really need to package tapes carefully or they will be damaged during shipping. That's a waste, so please write "Fragile: Breakable!" on the package. Some people sent me MDs but I can't listen to those unless I buy a player... Oh, and also because of what I was saying in the last corner, I got a lot of "Dune" tapes. (And indies info...) Those premium items are expensive eh...?

Thank you... Really! I listened to them all. Even the repeats. I was still happy. I got a lot of recommendations for L'arc en Ciel, Luna Sea, and Penicillin and GLAY and stuff like Sophia and Kuroyume ... And even Fanatic-Crisis and Ruage and Guniw tools. There were a lot that I already liked and was listening to and there was a lot more stuff but I can't list it all...Oh yeah, I only got about two or three songs from my favorite artist. (And one was sent by one of my assistants.) I can understand though, it doesn't match my manga at all. A totally different image... (none of their songs would match...) I couldn't concentrate on my work if I played it, so I don't play it very much while I draw. Oh yeah, I also received three videos, Thank you!! I didn't know that group was on TV! (well duh...) Because of those videos and other things, I barely made my deadline! As I write this right now things are tough because thanks to their new album, they are all over the TV and in tons of magazines. I have to go buy magazines instead of working... Well, still, I'm not as crazy as a lot of you fanatics. I don't wear those black outfits (though I do like black). Sometimes I don't feel like a real fan. Oh, I see I'm running out of space. Well, this was totally unfocused but that will do it for this volume.

Sorry, this isn't a musical group. They are some original designs I'd like to use sometime. But it's kind of a gay and perverted, dark story. There's so many things I want to draw. But I also want to keep doing AS!

A lot's going on but I'll do my best.

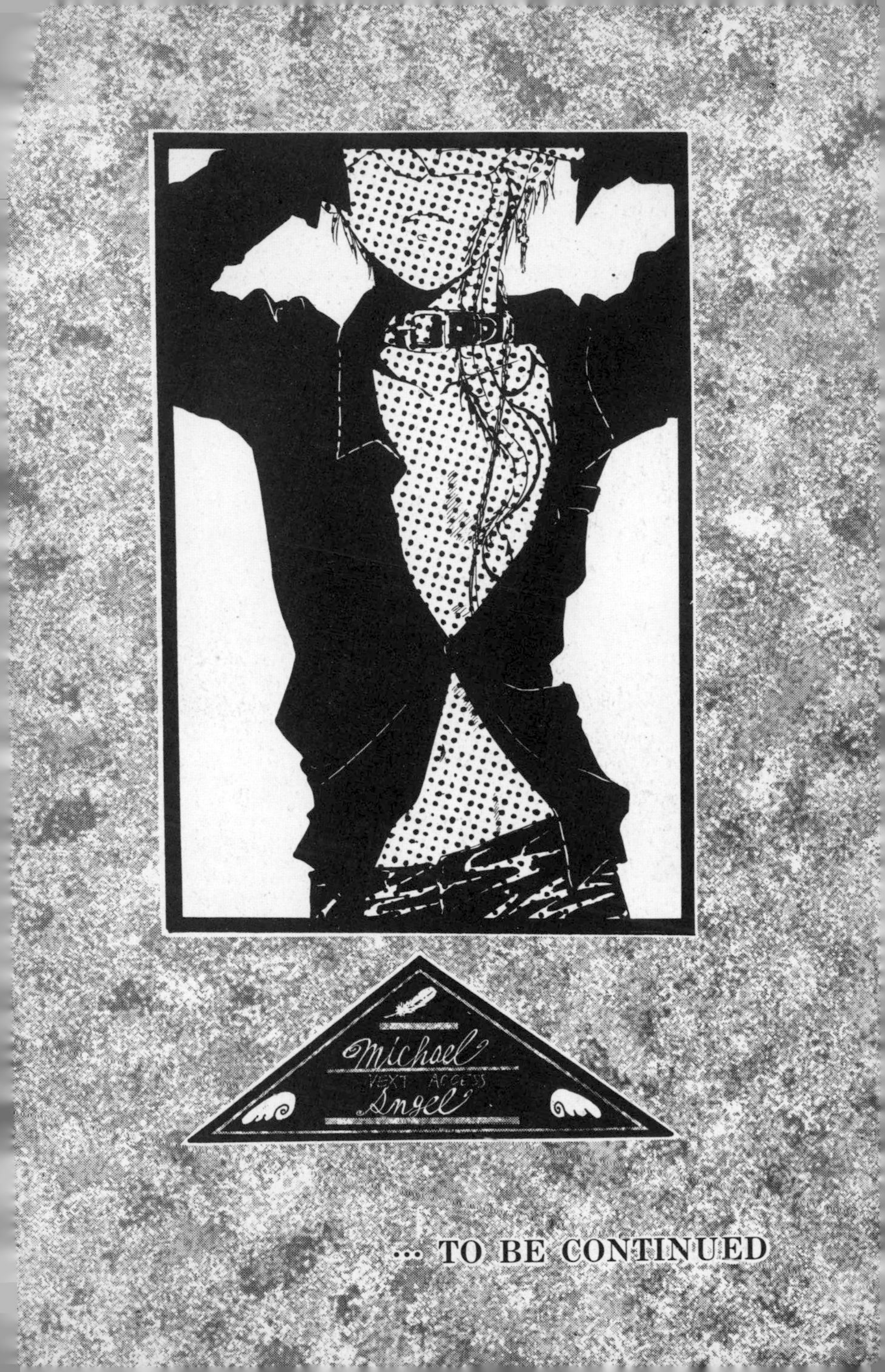
Michael
NEXT ACCESS
Angel

... TO BE CONTINUED

"Be Sworn My Love and I No Longer be a Girl?!"

Tomboyish Ito is chosen as Romeo in the school play. She doesn't want the male role, but more problematic is who'll play Juliet. Beautiful and vain Tsugumi wants the part, but has stiff competition from transfer student Makoto, whose secret may prove she's got the best acting skills in school!

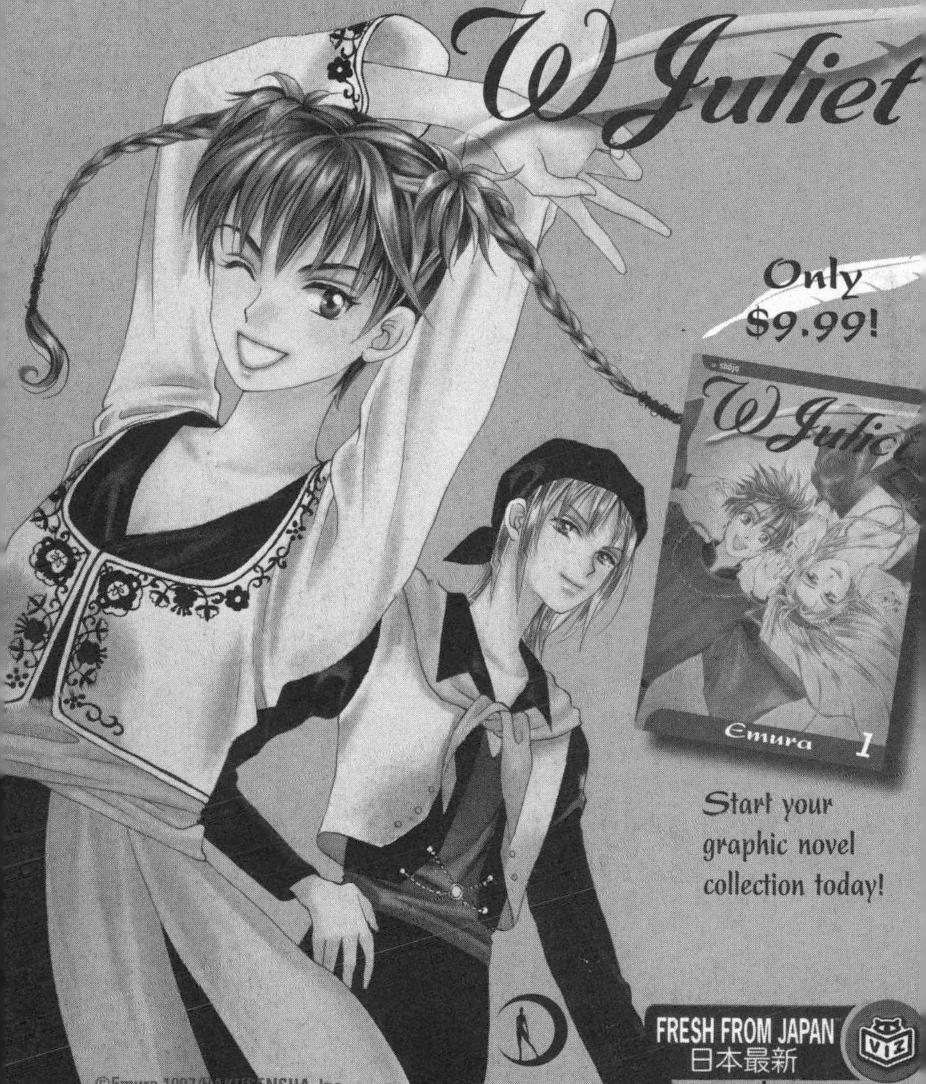

W Juliet

Only $9.99!

W Juliet
Emura 1

Start your graphic novel collection today!

©Emura 1997/HAKUSENSHA, Inc.

shôjo

FRESH FROM JAPAN
日本最新

VIZ

www.viz.com
store.viz.com

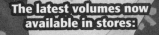

COMPLETE OUR SURVEY AND LET US KNOW WHAT YOU THINK!

☐ Please do NOT send me information about VIZ products, news and events, special offers, or other information.

☐ Please do NOT send me information from VIZ's trusted business partners.

Name: _____

Address: _____

City: _____ **State:** _____ **Zip:** _____

E-mail: _____

☐ Male ☐ Female **Date of Birth** (mm/dd/yyyy): ___/___/_____ (Under 13? Parental consent required)

What race/ethnicity do you consider yourself? (please check one)

☐ Asian/Pacific Islander ☐ Black/African American ☐ Hispanic/Latino

☐ Native American/Alaskan Native ☐ White/Caucasian ☐ Other: _____

What VIZ product did you purchase? (check all that apply and indicate title purchased)

☐ DVD/VHS _____

☐ Graphic Novel _____

☐ Magazines _____

☐ Merchandise _____

Reason for purchase: (check all that apply)

☐ Special offer ☐ Favorite title ☐ Gift

☐ Recommendation ☐ Other _____

Where did you make your purchase? (please check one)

☐ Comic store ☐ Bookstore ☐ Mass/Grocery Store

☐ Newsstand ☐ Video/Video Game Store ☐ Other: _____

☐ Online (site: _____)

What other VIZ properties have you purchased/own? _____

_____

How many anime and/or manga titles have you purchased in the last year? How many were VIZ titles? **(please check one from each column)**

ANIME	MANGA	VIZ
☐ None	☐ None	☐ None
☐ 1-4	☐ 1-4	☐ 1-4
☐ 5-10	☐ 5-10	☐ 5-10
☐ 11+	☐ 11+	☐ 11+

I find the pricing of VIZ products to be: **(please check one)**

☐ Cheap ☐ Reasonable ☐ Expensive

What genre of manga and anime would you like to see from VIZ? **(please check two)**

☐ Adventure ☐ Comic Strip ☐ Science Fiction ☐ Fighting

☐ Horror ☐ Romance ☐ Fantasy ☐ Sports

What do you think of VIZ's new look?

☐ Love It ☐ It's OK ☐ Hate It ☐ Didn't Notice ☐ No Opinion

Which do you prefer? **(please check one)**

☐ Reading right-to-left

☐ Reading left-to-right

Which do you prefer? **(please check one)**

☐ Sound effects in English

☐ Sound effects in Japanese with English captions

☐ Sound effects in Japanese only with a glossary at the back

THANK YOU! Please send the completed form to:

NJW Research
42 Catharine St.
Poughkeepsie, NY 12601

All information provided will be used for internal purposes only. We promise not to sell or otherwise divulge your information.